THE COMPLETE GREEK TRAGEDIES

VOLUME IV

EURIPIDES

1891-1991

A CENTENNIAL PUBLICATION OF

The University of Chicago Press

THE COMPLETE GREEK TRAGEDIES

CENTENNIAL EDITION

Edited by David Grene and Richmond Lattimore

VOLUME IV

EURIPIDES

THE UNIVERSITY OF CHICAGO PRESS

Chicago & London

The University of Chicago Press, Chicago 60637
The University of Chicago Press, Ltd., London
© 1958, 1959 by The University of Chicago
All rights reserved
Volume 4 published 1992
Printed in the United States of America

00 99 98 97 96 95 94 93 92   5 4 3 2 1

ISBN (4-vol. set) 0-226-30763-8
ISBN (vol. 4) 0-226-30767-0

Library of Congress Cataloging-in-Publication Data

The complete Greek tragedies / edited by David Grene and Richmond
    Lattimore.—Centennial ed.
        p.   cm.
        Contents: v. 1. Aeschylus—v. 2. Sophocles—v. 3–4. Euripides.
        1. Greek drama (Tragedy)—Translations into English.   I. Grene,
    David.   II. Lattimore, Richmond Alexander, 1906–   .
PA3626.A2G67   1992
882'.0108—dc20   91-45936
                                                                        CIP

CONTENTS

ION

Translated and with an Introduction by Ronald Frederick Willetts

INTRODUCTION TO *ION*

The *Ion* can be fairly certainly assigned, on stylistic and metrical grounds, to the decade 420–410 B.C. There is no conclusive evidence for a more exact date within this period.

Creusa was the daughter of Erechtheus, the autochthonous king of Athens. While still a girl, she was seduced by Apollo and gave birth to a son whom she exposed from fear of her parents. She naturally supposed that the child had died. But, unknown to her, Apollo sent Hermes to take the child to Delphi and leave him beside the temple. There he was found by the prophetess, who brought him up. He eventually became a steward in the temple. Knowing nothing of the circumstances of his birth, he lives a sheltered life and is happy in the service of the god. In the meantime his mother has married Xuthus. He, though a foreigner, won his bride as a reward for his services to Athens in war. Though long married, they are childless. They have therefore decided to come to Delphi to consult the god about their chances of having children.

Such is the situation at the opening of the play. It arose from an old wrong, the seduction of Creusa by Apollo. It lends itself to development in a number of different ways. The wrong can be righted and Athens glorified by accepting Ion's divine birth as a mark of favor to the Ionian tribes. Or the romantic can be rejected in favor of a more realistic approach. Euripides was sometimes romantic, more often realistic, in his treatment of myths. Here he chose to handle the theme realistically and was preoccupied with the human problem it presented. He weaves the strands of the Ion legend together to form the framework outlined above. He then tears from the story its mythological and supernatural pretensions—at least until Athene appears as *dea ex machina*. Here, at first sight, it seems that the playwright welcomes her with gratitude to supply a ready-made solution for his tangled plot.

The essence of the realist method in this play lies in the double-edged treatment of mythology. Euripides accepts Apollo as the divine lover of Creusa and then invests him with human attributes. In consequence, Apollo emerges in very poor light as a barbarian god whose ethics are shattered by the probings of a civilized and skeptical mind. This exposure is achieved not only by Creusa's intense denunciation of the god in a moment of high climax in the unfolding of the intricate plot. It is more subtly managed through the impact of the whole action upon the boy, Ion. Perhaps the chief merit of this well-designed play is the careful study of Ion's development, the revelation of the changes brought about by the abrupt contact of youthful, cloistered virtue with worldliness. At times we may suspect that the boy grows up too quickly—not so quickly, however, that he becomes a cynic: though he learns with rapidity, he also learns ingenuously. As he becomes more and more disturbed, and therefore more and more disturbing, to his initial charm are added self-confidence and strength of will.

As the plot is presented, Ion is foisted as a son upon Xuthus by the oracle. This leads to the attempt of the mother to kill her son. When this is foiled there follows the further attempt of the son to kill his mother. The rest of the play falls into two parts—the cleverly contrived recognition scene between mother and son and the appearance of Athene as *dea ex machina*.

To accept the resolution of the play at its face value is impossible if we are to believe that there is any serious purpose behind it. Until the end we have no doubts that Euripides is, in fact, dealing with an important theme in earnest. At the end we are likely to feel that our emotions have been cheated; for the explanations of the goddess seem paltry and inconsistent with the dramatic quality and the seriousness of all that has gone before. The contrast is so marked that the play cannot be easily accepted as a tragicomic fairy tale with a well-knit, tense plot and a happy ending, designed to extol the Apolline origin of the Athenian race. The poignant dramatic structure, we feel, must not be reduced to the level of a preface to a pamphlet, even if delivered by an Olympian.

In other words, there is a critical problem to be solved here. Now the "rationalizing" view of the play, associated particularly with A. W. Verrall, had the merit of recognizing that this problem exists.

Verrall agreed with the argument that the *Ion* is an attack upon
Delphi and must be interpreted in this way; that the oracle delivered
to Xuthus, like the recognition scene between Creusa and Ion, is a
Delphian fraud, the attribution of Ion to Apollo and Creusa being
due to a change of tactics following upon Creusa's confession and
denunciation of Apollo.

But this "rationalizing" solution ignores a most important point.
Creusa, even when Ion takes her aside in confidence and suggests the
possibility, will not admit that her lover was a mortal man. The
whole design of the play depends on the assumption that Apollo
seduced Creusa. Are the design and the assumption sustained
throughout? Let us examine the last two scenes with this query in
mind.

As Ion and the crowd advance threateningly toward Creusa, after
she has been discovered in refuge at the altar, the Pythian priestess
enters from the temple, carrying a cradle bound with fillets of wool
resembling those on the altar. She had kept the cradle in which she
had found Ion, together with his swaddling clothes and ornaments,
and now gives them to him in case he should find a clue to his
mother's identity in Athens or elsewhere. Ion examines the cradle
with great interest, marveling at the freshness of its fastenings. On
the "rationalist" view this would have been part of the fraud per-
petrated by the Delphians, since Euripides could not have intended
such magical hocus-pocus to be taken seriously: that would have
been inconsistent with his "rationalism." But Euripides is consist-
ently irrational in such respects in other plays; though inconsistency
is one of his strongest characteristics as a playwright.

When Ion unties the fillets, Creusa recognizes the cradle, is over-
whelmed for the moment and then rushes from the altar to embrace
him, prepared to risk death, and greets him as her child. He supposes
she is playing a trick on him, orders the guards to seize her, and then
decides on a better method. He will test her knowledge of the contents of the cradle. But Creusa answers all his questions. Ion is convinced she is his mother. In the joy of her discovery all thought of
Xuthus is obliterated. Her son has brought her her personal triumph.
As she had tried to murder him as a menace, so now she welcomes

him as the savior of her house. The stigma of childlessness is removed together with the memory of Xuthus as the partner of her unhappiness. He has no mention in her triumphant outburst.

Ion puts an end to this rapture by asking for his father to be there to share their happiness. Creusa is again obliged to describe the seduction by Apollo. Ion is guarded in his reception of the story, though his sympathy with his mother as she describes her suffering is spontaneously generous. He can credit the story—with reservations. This is clear when, after making some platitudinous remarks about the workings of providence, intended for the Chorus and others on the stage, he draws his mother aside and puts the question that is uppermost in his mind. Is Apollo being made into a convenient scapegoat?

This is a crucial passage where the "rationalist" explanation breaks down. Ion makes a natural assumption. It demands a truthful answer. There have been enough complications in the plot. Let us suppose that Creusa had agreed with his suggestion. She would presumably have made some confession of an intrigue in her youth. Ion would then have asked the reason for the oracle's deception in giving him to Xuthus as his son. The fraud which the "rationalizers" are anxious to prove would have been most obvious and the play would become more of an open attack upon Delphi than a criticism of Olympian morals. Creusa and Ion might then have agreed, for the sake of convenience, to leave Xuthus in blissful ignorance of the facts, the happy ending would be dramatically justified, the purpose of propaganda achieved, and Athene could have predicted Ion's future without having to make lame excuses for Apollo. The main objection to all this is that, since no one was aware of the birth and exposure of the child except the mother, there was no reason to put any blame upon Apollo. Yet Euripides purposely adopts that version of the story.

Instead, what happens? Creusa vehemently denies any suggestion of deceit. The play proceeds and still gains its effects from the assumption that Apollo was the father. The characters still continue to judge him by human standards. For Ion immediately asks why Apollo should give his own son to Xuthus, with the plain falsehood that he was the father. Creusa, now quite happy in the possession of her son, is content to let moral problems go by the board. Apollo, she says, practiced the deceit out of kindness to Ion. But Ion is not satisfied. He has already received some shocks to his beliefs. His only wish now is to decide finally whether Apollo is a sham:

> But, mother, does Apollo tell the truth,
> Or is the oracle false? With some good reason
> That question troubles me.

Creusa offers the same explanation again, but Ion's question "cannot be so lightly answered." He is about to enter the temple to ask the oracle if Apollo is his father when Athene appears. She begins by saying that Apollo did not care to come, since some criticism of his previous conduct might be expected. This answer to Creusa's earlier challenge is intentionally farcical. Apollo now becomes contemptible. Ion is saved the trouble of consulting the oracle. Athene assures him that Apollo is really his father. The legend is preserved to the end. But Ion's question is ignored. The answer is too obvious.

Athene's final remarks are all the more ironic because redundant. They are an appeal to faith, and Euripides has done his best to destroy the basis of faith. Even now Apollo can go merrily on from one deceit to another. Xuthus is not to know the truth, and Apollo makes Creusa and Ion partners in his falsehood. Only Athene, Hermes, and Creusa seem satisfied that Apollo "has managed all things well." Certainly no reader of the play can be. But Creusa, at least, may be pardoned for grasping her long-awaited reward without too much questioning.

Athene serves a double function. As in other plays of Euripides with a *deus ex machina*, she commemorates the foundation of a hero-cult and prophesies future Athenian history. At the same time, by uttering her divine commonplaces, she adds nothing to our knowledge but fits in with the dramatic purpose of the play. Before her appearance Apollo had still some chance to justify himself. After it, he retains no shred of dignity.

ION

CHARACTERS

Hermes

Ion

Chorus (Creusa's attendants)

Creusa

Xuthus

Old Man

A Servant

Pythian priestess

Athene

ION

Hermes

Atlas, who wears on back of bronze the ancient
Abode of gods in heaven, had a daughter
Whose name was Maia, born of a goddess:
She lay with Zeus and bore me, Hermes, servant
Of the immortals. I have come here to Delphi   5
Where Phoebus sits at earth's mid-center, gives
His prophecies to men, and passes judgment
On what is happening now and what will come.

   For in the famous city of the Greeks
Called after Pallas of the Golden Spear,
Phoebus compelled Erechtheus' daughter Creusa   10
To take him as her lover—in that place
Below Athene's hill whose northern scarp
The Attic lords have named the Long Rocks.
Her father, by the god's own wish, did not
Suspect her, and she carried her child in secret.   15
And when the time had come, her son was born,
Inside the palace. Then she took the child
To the same cave where she had lain with Phoebus,
And in a wicker cradle there exposed
Him to his death. She kept an ancient custom   20
Begun in Athens when Athene placed
By Erichthonius, son of Earth, two snakes
As guardians, when the daughters of Aglaurus
Were given charge of him.
               And so Creusa tied   25
To him whatever girlish ornaments
She had, before she left him to his death.
My brother Phoebus then made this request:

"You know Athene's city well," he said,
"Now will you journey to the earth-born people   30
  Of glorious Athens? There, inside a cave
  A newborn child is hidden. Take the child,
  His cradle, and his swaddling clothes and bring
  Them to my oracle at Delphi, where
  They must be left before the temple entrance.   35
  I will arrange the rest. The child is mine."
    I did as Loxias my brother wished,
  Took up the wicker cradle, brought it here,
  Setting it on the temple steps before
  I opened it, so that someone might see
  The child. Now when the sun began to ride   40
  In heaven, the prophetess was entering
  The holy shrine. Her eyes were drawn toward
  The helpless child. Astonished that a girl
  Of Delphi should dare to cast her secret child
  Before Apollo's temple, she would have taken it   45
  Outside the sacred precinct, but her pity
  Expelled the cruel impulse—and the god
  Designed to keep his son within his house.
  And so she took the child and reared him,
  Not knowing who his mother was, or that   50
  Apollo was his father; while the child
  Has never known his parents. His childhood home
  Has been about the altars where he played
  And wandered. But when he was fully grown,
  The Delphians appointed him their steward,   55
  The trusted guardian of Apollo's gold.
  And he has lived a holy life until
  This day, within the shrine.
                          Creusa, whose son
  He is, has married Xuthus. This is how
  The marriage occurred. A war was surging high
  Between Chalcidians of Euboea and Athens,   60
  Whose ally, Xuthus, helped to end the strife.

Though he was not a native, but Achaean,
Son of Aeolus, son of Zeus, the prize
He won was marriage to Creusa. But
In all these years no children have been born.   65
Desire for children is now bringing them
To Apollo's shrine. Apollo seems indifferent,
But he controls their fate and guides them here.
When Xuthus comes before the shrine, the god
Will give him his own son, declaring Xuthus   70
The father. Thus the boy shall be received
Into his mother's house, made known to her.
And while Apollo's intrigue is kept secret,
His son may have what is his due. Moreover,
Apollo will bestow on him the name
Of Ion, make that name renowned through Greece   75
As founder of ancient cities.
                Now, because
I wish to see this young boy's destiny
Complete, I shall conceal myself within
These laurel groves. This is Apollo's son,
Who comes here now, with branches of bay, to make
The portals bright before the temple. And I
Will be the first of all the gods to call   80
Him by his future name of—Ion.

(*The central doors of the temple open, and Ion comes out with
a group of Delphian servants. He is wearing a brightly colored
tunic and cloak, and on his head is a wreath of bay leaves.
He carries a bow and arrow, symbol of his service to
Apollo, which is to have a more practical purpose later
in the scene. The two peaks of Parnassus which
overlook the temple have caught the first rays of
the dawn, and Ion points to them as he
begins to speak.*)

Ion

Look, now the sun's burning chariot comes
Casting his light on the earth.

Banned by his flame, the stars flee
To the awful darkness of space.   85
The untrodden peaks of Parnassus,
Kindling to flame, receive for mankind
The disk of the day.

    The smoke of unwatered myrrh drifts
To the top of the temple.   90
The Delphian priestess sits on the
Sacred tripod chanting to the Greeks
Echoes of Apollo's voice.

    You Delphians, attendants of Phoebus,
Go down to Castalia's silvery eddies: 95
When you have bathed in its holy dews,
Return to the temple.
Let your lips utter no words
Of ill-omen, may your tongues
Be gracious and gentle to those who   100
Come to the oracle.

    As for myself, mine is the task
I have always done since my childhood.
With these branches of bay and these sacred
Garlands I will brighten Apollo's
Portals, cleanse the floor with   105
Sprinklings of water,
Put to flight with my arrows the birds
Who foul the offerings.
Since I have neither mother nor father,
I revere the temple of Phoebus   110
Where I have lived.

Come, fresh-blooming branch
Of lovely laurel,
With which I sweep clean
The precinct below the shrine,   115
Sprung from the eternal garden
Where the sacred spring sends
A welling, never failing stream

From the myrtle grove
To water the sacred leaves,   120
Leaves I brush over his fane,
Every day serving with my daily task
When the sun's swift wing appears.

O Healer! O Healer!   125
My blessing! My blessing!
O Leto's son!

Fair, fair is the labor,
O Phoebus, which
I am doing for you,
Honoring the prophetic place.   130
I have a glorious task:
To set my hands to serve
Not a man but the immortals.
I will never weary
Over my pious tasks.   135
I praise him who feeds me, Phoebus
My father—his love deserves the name,
Phoebus, lord of the temple.   140

O Healer! O Healer!
My blessing! My blessing!
O Leto's son!

Now I have finished my sweeping
With my broom of bay,   145
I will pour from golden bowls
Water risen from the earth,
Drawn from the spring
Of Castalia.
Myself holy and chaste, I can
Cast the lustral water.   150
Always thus may I serve Phoebus,
Service without end—
Or an end come with good issue.
    Look! Look!

Here come the birds already,
Leaving their nests on Parnassus.   155
Keep away from the cornices
And the gold-decked abode.
I will strike you again with my arrows,
You herald of Zeus,
Though your beak is strong,
Surpassing the other birds.   160
Here sails another to the temple steps,
A swan.—Take to another place
Your red shining feet.
You may have your music,
But Apollo's lyre will not save you
At all from my bow,   165
Turn your wings,
Speed on to the lake of Delos.
If you do not obey,
You will raise, and in blood,
That clear-toned song.
    Look! Look!   170
What is this other bird here on its way?
Is it going to build in the cornice
A nest of dry twigs for its young?
The twang of my bow will prevent it.
Go, I tell you and rear
Your young in the eddies of Alpheus   175
Or the Isthmian grove,
Without fouling the offerings
And Apollo's shrine.
Yet I scruple to kill you
Who announce to mankind
The will of the gods.   180
But I will bend to the labors
Of my devotion,
Never ceasing to honor him
Who gives me life.

*(Ion goes out. The Delphian servants enter in silence and per-
form a sacrifice on the altar in front of the temple. After the
sacrifice the Chorus, young girl servants of Creusa, enter.
They pass up and down, excitedly admiring the
temple buildings.)*

Chorus

Not only in holy Athens after all
Are there courts of the gods   185
With fair columns, and homage paid
To Apollo who protects the streets.
Here too on this temple
Of Leto's son shows
The bright-eyed beauty of twin façades.

Look, look at this: Zeus's son   190
Is killing the Lernaean Hydra
With a golden sickle,
Look there, my dear.

Yes—and near him another is raising
On high a flaming torch.   195
Can it be he whose story I hear
As I sit at my weaving,
Iolaus the shield-bearer,
Companion of Heracles,
Whom he helped to endure his labors?   200

And look at this one
On a horse with wings.
He is killing the mighty three-bodied
Fire-breathing monster.

My eyes dart everywhere.   205
See! The battle of the giants
On the marble walls.

Yes we are looking.

Can you see her, brandishing
Her Gorgon shield against Enceladus—?   210

I can see my goddess Pallas Athene.

Oh! The terrible thunderbolt
With fire at each end which Zeus holds
Ready to throw.

Yes I see. Raging Mimas
Is burnt up in the flames.   215

And Bacchus, the boisterous god,
With unwarlike wand of ivy is killing
Another of Earth's giant sons.

(Ion enters through the central doors of the temple.)

Chorus Leader
　　You there by the temple,
　　May we with naked feet   220
　　Pass into this sanctuary?

Ion
　　You may not, strangers.

Chorus Leader
　　Perhaps you would tell me—?

Ion
　　Tell me, what do you want?

Chorus Leader
　　Is it true that Apollo's temple
　　Really contains the world's center?

Ion
　　Yes, wreathed in garlands, flanked by Gorgons.

Chorus Leader
　　That is the story we have heard.   225

Ion
　　If you have offered sacrificial food
　　In front of the temple, and you have a question
　　For Apollo to answer, come to the altar steps.

But do not pass into the inner shrine
Unless you have slaughtered a sheep.

Chorus Leader
I understand.
We are not for transgressing Apollo's law.   230
The outside charms us enough.

Ion
Look where you please at what is lawful.

Chorus Leader
Our masters have allowed us
To look over this sanctuary of Apollo.

Ion
In whose house do you serve?

Chorus Leader
The dwelling place of Pallas   235
Is the house of our masters.
But the person you ask about is here.

                                    (*Enter Creusa.*)

Ion
Whoever you may be, you are a noble,
Your looks reveal your character: by looks
Nobility is often to be judged.   240
But?—You surprise me—why, your eyes are closed,
That noble face is wet with tears—and now!
When you have seen Apollo's holy temple.
What reason can there be for your distraction?
Where others are glad to see the sanctuary,   245
Your eyes are filled with tears.

Creusa
That you should be surprised about my tears
Is not ill-bred. But when I saw this temple,
I measured an old memory again,   250
My mind elsewhere, though I stand here.

(aside) Unhappy women! Where shall we appeal
For justice when the injustice of power
Is our destruction?

Ion

What is the cause of this strange melancholy?   255

Creusa

Nothing. Now I have loosed my shaft I shall
Be silent, and you will not think of it.

Ion

But tell me who you are, your family,
Your country. And what is you name?

Creusa

Creusa is my name, Erechtheus' daughter,   260
And Athens is my native land.

Ion

A famous city and a noble race!
How fortunate you are!

Creusa

Yes, fortunate in that—but nothing else.

Ion

There is a story told—can that be true?   265

Creusa

But tell me what you want to know.

Ion

Your father's ancestor sprang from the earth?

Creusa

Yes, Erichthonius—the glory is no help.

Ion

Athene really took him from the earth?

Creusa

Into her virgin arms, though not her son.   270

Ion

And then she gave him as we see in paintings—

Creusa

To Cecrops' daughters, who were to keep him hidden.

Ion

I have been told they opened the cradle.

Creusa

And died for it. The rocks were stained with blood.

Ion

Oh. (*pauses*)
The other story? Is that true or not?   275

Creusa

Which one is that?—I have time to answer.

Ion

Well, did your father sacrifice your sisters?

Creusa

He had the courage. They were killed for Athens.

Ion

How was it you were saved, the only one?

Creusa

I was a baby in my mother's arms.   280

Ion

And was your father buried in a chasm?

Creusa

The sea-god's trident blows destroyed him.

Ion

There is a place there which is called Long Rocks?

Creusa

Oh, why ask that?—You are reminding me.—

Ion

The lightning-fire of Phoebus honors it.   285

Creusa

Vain honor. I wish I had never seen it.

Ion

Why do you hate a place he dearly loves?

Creusa

No matter.—But I know its secret shame.—

Ion

And what Athenian became your husband?

Creusa

My husband is no citizen of Athens.   290

Ion

Who then? He must have been of noble birth.

Creusa

Xuthus, the son of Aeolus and Zeus.

Ion

A stranger. How then could he marry you?

Creusa

A neighboring land of Athens is Euboea—

Ion

Which has a sea for boundary they say.   295

Creusa

—Which Athens conquered with the help of Xuthus.

Ion

The ally came, and you were his reward?

Creusa

Dowry of war, the prize won with his spear.

Ion

And have you come alone or with your husband?

Creusa

With him. But he stayed at Trophonius' shrine.   300

Ion

To see it or consult the oracle?

Creusa
> To ask the same as he will ask of Phoebus.

Ion
> Is it about your country's crops—or children?

Creusa
> Though married long ago, we have no children.

Ion
> No children? You have never had a child?   305

Creusa
> Apollo knows my childlessness.

Ion
> Ah! That misfortune cancels all your blessings.

Creusa
> And who are you? Your mother must be happy!

Ion
> I am what I am called, Apollo's slave.

Creusa
> A city's votive gift or sold by someone?   310

Ion
> I only know that I am called Apollo's.

Creusa
> So now it is my turn to pity you!

Ion
> Because my parents are unknown to me.

Creusa
> You live inside the temple? Or at home?

Ion
> Apollo's home is mine, wherever I sleep.   315

Creusa
> And did you come here as a child?

Ion
> A child, they say who seem to know.

Creusa

What Delphian woman suckled you?

Ion

No breast fed me. But she who reared me.—

Creusa

Yes, who, poor child?

(*aside*) A sorrow like my own.   320

Ion

The prophetess, I think of her as mother.

Creusa

But what supported you as you grew up?

Ion

The altars and the visitors who came.

Creusa

And your unhappy mother! Who was she then?

Ion

My birth perhaps marked her betrayal.   325

Creusa

You are not poor? Your robes are fine enough.

Ion

These robes belong to him, the god I serve.

Creusa

But have you never tried to find your parents?

Ion

How can I when I have no clues to guide?

Creusa

Ah yes. (*pause*)

Another suffered as your mother did.   330

Ion

Who was she then? If she would help me in my grief!   331

Creusa

On her behalf I came before my husband.   332

Ion

    Why did you come? Tell me and I will help.   333

Creusa

    I have a friend—who says—she lay with Phoebus.   338

Ion

    Not Phoebus and a mortal woman. No!

Creusa

    And had a child unknown to her own father.   340

Ion

    She is ashamed to own some man's betrayal.

Creusa

    But she says not. Her life has been most wretched.

Ion

    Why, if her lover was a god?

Creusa

    She put from out the house the child she had.

Ion

    Where is the child? Is it alive?   345

Creusa

    I have come here to ask, for no one knows.

Ion

    If he is dead, how did he die?

Creusa

    Killed by wild beasts, she thinks.

Ion

    What reason could she have for thinking so?

Creusa

    She could not find him when she went again.   350

Ion

    But were there drops of blood upon the ground?

Creusa

    She says not, though her search was careful.

Ion

And how long is it since the child was killed?

Creusa

He would have been your age by now.

Ion

Apollo is unjust. She has my pity.   355

Creusa

For she has never had another child.

> (*Pause as Ion reflects. He is still unwilling*
> *to believe Apollo guilty.*)

Ion

Supposing Phoebus reared him in secret?

Creusa

To keep that pleasure for himself is wrong.

Ion (*sighs*)

Ah! This misfortune echoes my own grief.

Creusa

And some unhappy mother misses you.   360

Ion

Do not revive the grief I had forgotten.

Creusa

No.—Then you will see to my request?

Ion

But do you know where that request is faulty?

Creusa

What is not faulty for that wretched woman?

Ion

Will Phoebus tell the secret he wants to hide?   365

Creusa

If oracles are open to all Greeks.

Ion

Do not press him to reveal his shame.

Creusa

His shame means suffering to her!

Ion

No one will give this oracle to you.
Convicted of evil here inside his own temple,   370
Apollo would justly take vengeance on
His prophet. Think no more of it: avoid
A question which the god himself opposes.
This foolishness we should commit in trying
By any means to force reluctant answers,   375
Whether by slaying sheep before the altar
Or taking omens from the flight of birds.
The benefits we win by force against
Their will are never blessed. We only profit
By what the gods give with their blessing.   380

Chorus Leader

The woes assailing human life are many,
The forms of woe diverse. And happiness
Is rare and rarely comes to light on man.

Creusa

                    (*Raising her hands toward the temple.*)

Apollo! Then and now unjust to her,
The absent woman whose complaints are here.   385
You did not save the child you should have saved.
A prophet, you have no answer for its mother.
But now that hope must die, because the god   390
Prevents me learning what I wish to know.
But I can see my noble husband, Xuthus,
Arriving from Trophonius' cave. He is
Quite near; I beg you, stranger, tell him nothing
Of what we have been saying. Or I may   395
Be suspect, meddling in these secret matters,
And then this story will not have the end
We have designed. For trouble is very easy
When women deal with men. Since good and bad

Are not distinguished, all of us are hated.
To this misfortune we are born.   400

(Xuthus enters with servants and Delphians.)

Xuthus

My greeting first is to the god, and then
To you my wife.

(He sees she is upset.)

But has my long delay
Caused you alarm?

Creusa

No. Your arrival has prevented that.
What oracle did Trophonius give about   405
Our hopes of having children?

Xuthus

He was unwilling to anticipate
Apollo's answer. But he has told me this,
That neither you nor I shall go from here
Without a child.

Creusa

O holy mother of Apollo, may   410
Our journey here end well, our dealings with
Your son have a happier issue than before!

Xuthus

So it will be! But who speaks here for Phoebus?

Ion

Sir, that is my role outside the temple—
Inside are others, near the shrine, the nobles   415
Of Delphi, chosen by lot.

Xuthus

Ah! Good. I now know all I need to know,
And shall go in. They say the victim, which
Is offered on behalf of strangers, has
Already fallen before the altar. Omens   420
Today are good, and I would like to have

My answer from the oracle. Will you,
Creusa, with laurel branches in your hand,
Go round the altars praying to the gods
That I may bring an oracle with promise
Of children from Apollo's house.

> (*Xuthus enters the temple, Creusa watches him go and
> speaks with her hands raised toward the temple.*)

Creusa
So it will be! So it will be!

                    And now   425
If Phoebus at least amends his former wrongs,
Although his love can never be complete,
Because he is a god, I will accept
Whatever he bestows.

                                        (*Exit.*)

Ion
Why does this stranger always speak in riddles,
Reproach the god with covert blasphemy?   430
Is it through love of her on whose behalf
She comes before the oracle? Perhaps
She hides a secret which she cannot tell.
But what concern have I with Erechtheus' daughter?
No, that is not my business.—I will pour
The holy water out of golden pitchers   435
Into the lustral bowls. I must confront
Apollo with his wrongs. To force a girl
Against her will and afterward betray!
To leave a child to die which has been born
In secret! No! Do not act thus. But since
You have the power, seek the virtuous path.   440
All evil men are punished by the gods.
How then can it be just for you to stand
Accused of breaking laws you have yourselves
Laid down for men? But if—here I suppose
What could not be—you gave account on earth
For wrongs which you have done to women, you,   445

Apollo and Poseidon and Zeus who rules
In heaven, payment of your penalties
Would see your temples empty, since you are
Unjust to others in pursuing pleasure
Without forethought. And justice now demands
That we should not speak ill of men if they   450
But imitate what the gods approve, but those
Who teach men their examples.

                                                    (*Exit.*)

Chorus
                          STROPHE

O my Athene, born
Without birth pains,
Brought forth from the head of Zeus
By Prometheus, the Titan,   455
Blessed goddess of Victory,
Take flight from the golden halls
Of Olympus, come, I entreat you,
Here to the Pythian temple,   460
Where at earth's center Apollo's shrine
Proclaims unfailing prophecy,
At the tripod where they dance and sing.
Come with Artemis, Leto's daughter,   465
Virgin goddesses both,
Holy sisters of Phoebus.
Beseech him, O maidens,
That the ancient race of Erechtheus may
At last be sure by a clear response   470
Of the blessing of children.

                         ANTISTROPHE

Wherever gleams bright the flame
And strength of youth,
A promise to the house of growth,
There a man has a fund   475
Of joy overflowing;

From the fathers the children will gather
Hereditary wealth, and in turn
Pass it on to their own.   480
They are a defense in adversity,
In happiness a delight,
And in war their country's shield of safety.
For myself I would choose, rather than wealth   485
Or a palace of kings, to rear
And love my own children:
Shame to him who prefers
A childless life, hateful to me.
May I cling to the life of few possessions,   490
Enriched by children.

EPODE

O haunts of Pan,
The rock flanking
The caves of the Long Cliffs,
Where the daughters of Aglaurus   495
Dance, and their feet tread
The green levels before the shrines
Of Pallas, in time to the changing
Music of the pipes, when you play,   500
O Pan, in your sunless caves,
Where a girl in misery
Bore a child to Phoebus
And exposed it, a prey for birds,
Food for wild beasts to rend, shame
Of a cruel love.   505
Our legends, our tales at the loom,
Never tell of good fortune to children
Born of a god and a mortal.

(*Enter Ion from the central doors of the temple.*)

Ion

Serving women who are keeping watch here at the steps   510
Of the house of sacrifice, awaiting your master,

Tell me, has Xuthus already left the sacred tripod
And the oracle, or does he still remain within,
Seeking answer to his question?

Chorus Leader

He is still inside. He has not passed this threshold yet.
But the noise the door has made shows someone is now there.   515
Look, it is my master coming.

> (*Xuthus appears from the temple. As soon as he sees Ion, he
> shows great excitement, runs to him and tries to embrace
> him. Ion, much surprised by this behavior, resists.*)

Xuthus

Son, my blessing.—It is right to greet you in this way.

Ion

Sir, my thanks. We are both well—if you are not mad.

Xuthus

Let me kiss your hand, embrace you.

Ion

Are you sane? Or can the god have made you mad somehow?   520

Xuthus

Mad, when I have found my own and want to welcome him?

Ion

Stop.—Or if you touch it, you may break Apollo's crown.

Xuthus

I will touch you. And I am no robber. You are mine.

Ion

Must I shoot this arrow first, or will you loose me now?

Xuthus

Why must you avoid me just when you have found your nearest?   525

Ion

Mad and boorish strangers are no pleasure to instruct.

Xuthus

Kill me, and then bury me. For you will kill your father.

Ion

You my father! This is fool's talk.—How can that be? No!

Xuthus

Yes.—The story which I have to tell will make it clear.

Ion

What have you to say?

Xuthus

              I am your father. You are my son.   530

Ion

Who has told you this?

Xuthus

          Apollo, he who reared my son.

Ion

You are your own witness.

Xuthus

            But I know my oracle too.

Ion

You mistook a riddle.

Xuthus

         Then my hearing must have failed.

Ion

And what is Apollo's prophecy?

Xuthus

           That him I met—

Ion

Oh! A meeting? Where?

Xuthus

         As I came from the temple here.   535

Ion

Yes, and what would happen to him?

Xuthus

           He would be my son.

Ion

Your own son or just a gift?

Xuthus

A gift and my own son.

Ion

I was then the first you met?

Xuthus

Yes, no one else, my son.

Ion

But how strange this is!

Xuthus

I am just as amazed as you.

Ion

Well?—Who is my mother?

Xuthus

That I cannot say.   540

Ion

And Apollo?

Xuthus

Happy with this news, I did not ask.

Ion

Earth then was my mother!

Xuthus

Children do not spring up there.

Ion

How could I be yours?

Xuthus

Apollo, not I, has the answer.

Ion (*after a pause*)

Let us try another tack.

Xuthus

Yes, that will help us more.

Ion

Have you had a secret lover?

Xuthus

Yes, a youthful folly.   545

Ion

And before you were married?

Xuthus

Yes, but never afterward.

Ion

So that could be my origin?

Xuthus

Time at least agrees.

Ion

Then what am I doing here?

Xuthus

I cannot tell you that.

Ion

Here, so far away?

Xuthus

That is my puzzle too.

Ion

Have you been before to Delphi?

Xuthus

To the wine-god's torch feast.   550

Ion

You stayed with a temple steward?

Xuthus

He—there were girls of Delphi.   551

Ion

He introduced you to their rites?

Xuthus

Yes, they were Bacchanals.   552

Ion

You had drunk well?

Xuthus

I was reveling in the wine-god's feast.   553

Ion

Then that was the time.

Xuthus

         The girl perhaps exposed her child.   555

Ion (after a pause)
  I am not a slave then.

Xuthus

        And you can accept a father.   556

Ion
  Could I wish for better?

Xuthus

        That you might have seen before.   558

Ion
  Than descent from Zeus's son?

Xuthus

        This is indeed your birthright.   559

Ion
  Shall I touch my father then?

Xuthus

        Yes, have faith in the god.   560

Ion
  Father—

Xuthus

      How dear is the sound of the name you have spoken!

Ion
  We should both bless this day.

Xuthus

        It has brought me happiness.
                 (*They embrace.*)

Ion
  My dear mother! Shall I ever see your face as well?
  Now, whoever you may be, I long to see you even
  More. But she is dead perhaps, and I can have no hope.   565

Chorus Leader
  We also share this house's happiness.
  Yet I could wish my mistress too might have
  The joy of children, and Erechtheus' race.

Xuthus

My son, Apollo rightly prophesied
That I should find you, and united us.   570
You found a father whom you never knew.
Your natural desire I share myself
That you will find your mother, I, in her
The woman who gave me a son. And if
We leave all that to time, perhaps we shall   575
Succeed. But end your waif's life in the temple.
Let me persuade you, come with me to Athens,
For there your father's prosperous power awaits
You, and great wealth. Though now you suffer
In one respect, you shall not have the name
Of bastard and of beggar, but highborn   580
And well endowed with wealth. But why so silent?
Why do you hold your eyes downcast? Now you have changed
Your father's joy to fear.

Ion

Things have a different face as they appear   585
Before the eyes or far away. I bless
My fortune now that I have found a father.
But, father, listen to what is in my mind:
The earth-born people of glorious Athens are said
To be no alien race. I should intrude   590
There marked by two defects, a stranger's son,
Myself a bastard. And if I remain
Obscure, with this disgrace they will account
Me nothing, nobody's son. If I aspire
To the city's helm, ambitious for a name,   595
I shall be hated by the powerless.
Authority is never without hate.
And those who have ability for power
But wisely keep their silence, are not eager
For public life, will mock my folly, blindly   600
Deserting peace for Athens' crowded fears.
And then if I invade positions which

Are filled, I shall be countered by the moves
Of those with knowledge who control affairs.
For so it always happens, father: men
Who hold the cities and their dignities   605
Above all are opposed to rivalry.

    Then, coming to another's house, a stranger,
To live with one who has no children, who
Before had you to share the sorrow—now,
Abandoned to a private grief, she will   610
Have cause for bitterness and cause enough
To hate me when I take my place as heir:
Without a child herself, she will not kindly
Regard your own. Then you must either turn
To her, betraying me, or honor me   615
And bring confusion to your house: there is
No other way. How many wives have brought
Their men to death with poison or the knife!
Then, childless, growing old, she has my pity.
For this affliction does not suit her birth.   620

    The praise of royalty itself is false—
A fair façade to hide the pain within.
What happiness or blessing has the man
Who looks askance for violence, and fear
Draws out his days? I would prefer to live   625
A happy citizen than be a king,
Compelled to have the evil as his friends,
Who must abhor the good for fear of death.
You might reply that gold outweighs all this,
The joys of wealth—no joy for me to guard   630
A fortune, hear reproaches, suffer its pains.
Let me avoid distress, win moderation.

    But father, hear the good points of my life
In Delphi: leisure first of all, most dear
To any man, the friendly people, no one   635
To thrust me rudely from my path; to yield,
Give elbow room to those beneath us is

Intolerable. Then I was busy with
My prayers to gods or talk with men,
Serving the happy, not the discontented.
I was receiving guests or sending them   640
Away again, a fresh face always smiling
On fresh faces. I had what men should pray,
Even against their will, to have: duty
And inclination both contrived to make
Me righteous to god. When I compare the two,   645
Father, I think I am more happy here.
Let me live here. Delight in splendor is
No more than happiness with little: for both
Have their appeal.

Chorus (aside)
    Well have you spoken if indeed your words
    Mean happiness for her I love.

Xuthus
    No more of this! Learn to enjoy success.   650
    Let us inaugurate our life together
    By holding here, where I have found my son,
    A public banquet, and make the sacrifices
    Omitted at your birth. I will pretend
    To bring you to my house, a guest, and give
    A feast for you; and then take you along   655
    With me to Athens, not as my son but as
    A visitor. I do not want to hurt
    My childless wife with my own happiness.
    But when I think the time is ripe, I will
    Persuade my wife to give consent to your
    Assumption of my rule.   660
        Your name shall be Ion, a name to fit
    Your destiny; you were the first to meet
    Me coming from Apollo's shrine. But now
    Collect your friends together, say farewell
    With feast and sacrifice, before you leave   665

This town of Delphi. And, you women slaves,
I order you, say nothing of our plans.
To tell my wife will mean your death.

Ion

Yes, I will go. But one piece of good luck
Eludes me still: unless I find my mother,
My life is worthless. If I may do so, 670
I pray my mother is Athenian,
So that through her I may have rights of speech.
For when a stranger comes into a city
Of pure blood, though in name a citizen,
His mouth remains a slave: he has no right
Of speech. 675

(*Exeunt.*)

Chorus

STROPHE

I see tears and mourning
Triumphant, a sorrowful entrance,
When the queen hears of the son,
The blessing bestowed on her husband
Alone, still childless herself. 680
O Latona's prophetic son, what reply have you chanted?
From where came this child, reared
In your temple, and who is his mother?
This oracle does not please me.
There may be a fraud. 685
I fear the issue
Of this encounter.
For these are strange matters, 690
A strange command on my silence.
Treachery and chance combine
In this boy of an alien blood.
Who will deny it?

ANTISTROPHE

My friends, shall we clearly 695
Cry out in the ears of my mistress

Blame upon him who alone
Afforded her hope she could share?
Now she is maimed by his joy.
She is falling to gray age, he does not honor his love.   700
A stranger he came, wretch,
To the house, and betrays the fortune
Bestowed. He wronged her.—Die then!
    And may he not gain
      From god the prayer   705
      He sends with incense
Ablaze on bright altars.
He shall be sure of my feeling,
How much I love the queen.   710
The new father and son are now near
    To their new banquet.

EPODE

O the ridge of the rocks of Parnassus
Which hold in the skies the watchtower   715
Where Bacchus holds the two-flamed
Torch, leaping lightly with his
Nighttime wandering Bacchanals:
    Let the boy never see my city,
    Let him die and leave his new life.   720
    A city in trouble has reason
    To welcome the coming of strangers.
But Erechtheus, our ancient founder,
    United us long ago.

(Creusa enters with an Old Man, a slave and trusted servant
    of the family. They begin to climb the temple steps,
                Creusa supporting him.)

Creusa

Erechtheus, my father, long before he died   725
Made you the guardian of his children: (*pauses*)
Come up with me to Phoebus' oracle
To share my pleasure if his prophecy
Gives hope of children; since it is a joy

To share success with those we love; and if— 730
I pray that they may not—reverses come,
There is a balm in seeing friendly eyes.
And, though I am your mistress, I love you
As if you were my father, as you did
My own.

Old Man

My daughter, you preserve a noble spirit 735
And equal to your noble ancestors:
You have not shamed your fathers, sons of Earth.
Give me your help, and bring me to the temple.
The shrine is steep, you know. Support my limbs
And heal my weak old age. 740

Creusa

Come then. Be careful how you place your feet.

Old Man (as he stumbles)

You see. My mind is nimbler than my feet.

Creusa

Lean with your staff upon the path around.

Old Man

And that is blind now when my eyes are weak.

Creusa

Yes, true. But fight against your weariness. 745

Old Man

I do. But now I have no strength to summon.

(He turns slowly and with Creusa's help settles himself on the
temple steps, looking toward the audience. They
are now face to face with the Chorus.
Creusa addresses the Chorus.)

Creusa

You women, faithful servants of my loom
And shuttle, what hope of children did my husband
Receive before he left? We came for that.

Tell me; and if the news is good you will   750
Not find your mistress faithless or ungrateful.

Chorus
  An evil fate!

Old Man
  Your prelude is not one that suits good luck.

Chorus
  Unhappy lot!

Old Man
  But what is wrong about the oracle?   755

Chorus
  What can we do when death is set before us?

Creusa
  What strain is this? Why should you be afraid?

Chorus
  Are we to speak or not? What shall we do?

Creusa
  O speak! You know of some misfortune coming.

Chorus Leader
  You shall be told then, even if I die   760
  Twice over.—You will never have a child
  To hold, or take one to your breast.

          (Creusa sinks down to the steps beside the slave.)

Creusa
  I wish I were dead.

Old Man
  Daughter—

Creusa
          O this blow
      Is hard, this pain put upon me,
      I cannot endure it, my friends.

Old Man

  Hopeless now, my child.

Creusa

              Yes, ah! yes.   765
      This blow is fatal, a heart-thrust.
      The sorrow has pierced within.

Old Man

  Mourn no more—

Creusa

            I have reason enough.

Old Man

  Till we know—

Creusa

          Is there anything to know?   770

Old Man

  —If you alone have this misfortune, or
  Our master too must share the same.

Chorus Leader

  To him Apollo gave a son, but this
  Good luck is his alone, his wife has nothing.   775

Creusa

    One after the other you have cried out my griefs.
      This is the worst to deplore.

Old Man

  And did the oracle concern a living son,
  Or must some woman yet give birth to him?

Chorus Leader

  Phoebus gave him a son already born,   780
  A full-grown youth; and I myself was witness.

Creusa

    How can it be true? No! an incredible thing.
      It is surely fantastic.

Old Man

  Fantastic! Tell me how the oracle   785
  Is carried out, and who the son can be.

Chorus Leader

    He gave your husband for a son the one
    He should meet first as he came from the temple.

Creusa

      Then it is settled.
      Mine is the childless part,   790
      The solitary life in a desolate house.

Old Man

    Who then was chosen for Xuthus to meet?
    And tell me how and where he saw his child.

Chorus Leader

    There was a boy who swept the temple here.
    You know him? For he is the son.   795

Creusa

      Would that I might fly
      Through the gentle air far away
      From Greek earth to the evening stars.
        Such is my anguish, my friends.

Old Man

    What was the name his father gave to him?   800
    You know it? Or does that remain uncertain?

Chorus Leader

    He called him Ion, since he met him first.

Old Man

    Who is his mother?

Chorus Leader

            That I cannot say.
    But Xuthus, to tell you all I know, old man,
    Has gone away unknown to her, his wife,
    To offer in the consecrated tent   805
    A birthday sacrifice, to pledge the bond
    Of friendship in a banquet with his son.

Old Man

    My lady, we have been betrayed by your
    Own husband—for I share your grief; we are

Insulted by design, cast from the house 810
Of Erechtheus: this I say not out of hatred,
But rather since I love you more than him:
The foreigner who married you and came
Into the city and your house, received
Your heritage, and now is proved the father
Of children by another—secretly. 815
How secretly I will explain to you.
Aware that you would have no children,
He scorned to suffer equally with you
In this mischance, and had a secret child
By some slave woman, and sent him away
For someone in Delphi to rear. The boy 820
Was dedicated to Apollo's temple,
And there grew in concealment. While the father,
Now knowing that the boy was grown, pressed you
To travel here because you had no child.
And so Apollo did not lie, but he 825
Who has long reared the child. This is his web
Of deceit: discovered, he would lay the blame
Upon the god; if not, to guard against
The blows of time, his plan was to invest
Him with the city's rule. As time went on,
The new name Ion was invented, suiting 830
This trick of meeting him outside the temple.

Chorus Leader

I hate all evil men who plot injustice,
Then trick it out with subterfuge. I would
Prefer as friend a good man ignorant
Than one more clever who is evil too. 835

Old Man

Worst shame of all that he should bring into
Your house a cipher, motherless, the child
Of some slave woman. For the shame at least
Would have been open, if, with your consent,

Because you could not bear a child yourself,   840
He had an heir by one highborn. If this
Had been too much, he should have been content
To marry an Aeolian.

    And so you must now act a woman's part:
Kill them, your husband and his son, by sword,
By poison or some trick before death comes   845
To you from them. Unless you act your life
Is lost; for when two enemies have met
Together in a house, the one must be
Unlucky. Now I will help you kill the son: 850
Visit the place where he prepares the feast,
To pay the debt I owe my masters, thus,
To live or die. A slave bears only this
Disgrace: the name. In every other way   855
An honest slave is equal to the free.

Chorus Leader

I too, dear mistress, want to share your fate,
To die, or live with honor.

Creusa

                   (After a pause, then coming to the front.)
O my heart, how be silent?
Yet how can I speak of that secret   860
Love, strip myself of all shame?
Is one barrier left still to prevent me?
Whom have I now as my rival in virtue?
Has not my husband become my betrayer?
I am cheated of home, cheated of children,   865
Hopes are gone which I could not achieve,
The hopes of arranging things well
By hiding the facts,
By hiding the birth which brought sorrow.
No! No! But I swear by the starry abode   870
Of Zeus, by the goddess who reigns on our peaks
And by the sacred shore of the lake

Of Tritonis, I will no longer conceal it:
When I have put away the burden,
My heart will be easier.   875
Tears fall from my eyes, and my spirit is sick,
Evilly plotted against by men and by gods;
I will expose them,
Ungrateful betrayers of women.   880

O you who give the seven-toned lyre
A voice which rings out of the lifeless,
Rustic horn the lovely sound
Of the Muses' hymns,
On you, Latona's son, here   885
In daylight I will lay blame.
You came with hair flashing
Gold, as I gathered
Into my cloak flowers ablaze
With their golden light.   890
Clinging to my pale wrists
As I cried for my mother's help
You led me to bed in a cave,
A god and my lover,
With no shame,   895
Submitting to the Cyprian's will.
In misery I bore you
A son, whom in fear of my mother
I placed in that bed
Where you cruelly forced me.   900
Ah! He is lost now,
Snatched as food for birds,
My son and yours; O lost!
    But you play the lyre,   905
    Chanting your paeans.

O hear me, son of Latona,
Who assign your prophecies
From the golden throne

And the temple at earth's center,   910
I will proclaim my words in your ears:
You are an evil lover;
Though you owed no debt
To my husband, you have
Set a son in his house.   915
But my son, yes and yours, hard-hearted,
Is lost, carried away by birds,
The clothes his mother put on him abandoned.
   Delos hates you and the young
   Laurel which grows by the palm   920
   With its delicate leaves, where Latona
   Bore you, a holy child, fruit of Zeus.

(She breaks down, weeping, on the temple steps.
The Chorus gathers round her.)

Chorus Leader
   O what a store of miseries is now
   Disclosed; who could but weep at hearing them?

Old Man
   O child, your face has riveted my gaze,   925
   My reason is distracted. For just when
   I banished from my heart a wave of trouble,
   A second rose at the stern, caused by the words
   You spoke about your present woes, before
   You trod the evil path of other sorrows.   930
   What do you say? What child is this you claim
   To bear? Where in the city did you put
   This welcome corpse for beasts? Tell me again.

Creusa
   I will tell you, although I feel ashamed.

Old Man
   Yes, I know how to feel with friends in trouble.   935

Creusa
   Then listen. You know the cave which lies above
   The north of Cecrops' hill, its name Long Rocks?

Old Man

    I know. Pan's altars and his shrine are near.

Creusa

    It was there I endured a fearful trial.

Old Man

    Yes? My tears spring to meet your words.   940

Creusa

    Phoebus became my lover against my will.

Old Man

    My child, could that have been the thing I heard?

Creusa

    I shall acknowledge truth if you tell me.

Old Man

    When you were suffering from a secret illness?

Creusa

    That was the sorrow which I now reveal.   945

Old Man

    How did you hide this union with Apollo?

Creusa

    I had a child.—Please hear my story out.

Old Man

    But where, who helped you? Or were you alone?

Creusa

    Alone in that cave where I met Apollo.

Old Man

    Where is the child? You need not be childless.   950

Creusa

    Dead. He was left for beasts to prey upon.

Old Man

    Dead? Then Phoebus was false, gave you no help?

Creusa

    He did not help. The child grew up in Hades.

Old Man

But who exposed the child? Of course not you?

Creusa

I did: I wrapped him in my robes at night.   955

Old Man

And there was no accomplice in your deed?

Creusa

No, nothing but the silence and my grief.

Old Man

How could you leave your child there, in the cave?

Creusa

How, but with many tender words of pity?—

Old Man

Ah, you were harsh; Apollo harsher still.   960

Creusa

If you had seen the child stretch out his hands!

Old Man

To find your breast, lie in your arms?

Creusa

To find what I was cruelly refusing.

Old Man

But why did you decide to expose your child?

Creusa

Because I hoped the god would save his own.   965

Old Man

A storm embroils the fortunes of your house.

                                        (*A pause.*)

Creusa

Why do you hide your head, old man, why weep?

Old Man

I see your father and yourself so stricken.

Creusa

Such is man's life. All things must change.

(*A pause, as the Old Man leads Creusa to the front of the stage.*)

Old Man

My child, let us no longer cling to tears.   970

Creusa

What can I do? For pain has no resource.

Old Man

Avenge yourself on him who wronged you first.

Creusa

How can a mortal fight immortal power?

Old Man

Burn down Apollo's sacred oracle.

Creusa

I am afraid.—I have enough of sorrow.   975

Old Man

Then kill your husband. This is in your power.

Creusa

He was once loyal, and I honor that.

Old Man

The son then who has come to menace you.

Creusa

But how? If only I might! I would do that!

Old Man

By putting swords in your attendants' hands.   980

(*A pause.*)

Creusa

Let us begin. But where can it be done?

Old Man

The sacred tent, where he is feasting friends.

Creusa

Murder is flagrant; slaves are poor support.

Old Man (*despairingly*)
   You play the coward; come, give me your plan now.
                    (*A pause, as she prepares to explain her scheme; she goes
                          near to him, speaking softly and urgently, as if
                               to emphasize her own resolution.*)

Creusa
   Yes, I have something which is sure and subtle.   985

Old Man
   And I can help in both these ways.

Creusa
   Then listen. You know the war fought by Earth's sons?

Old Man
   When giants fought against the gods at Phlegra.

Creusa
   Earth there produced an awful monster, Gorgon.

Old Man
   To harass all the gods and help her children?   990

Creusa
   Yes, but destroyed by Zeus's daughter Pallas.

Old Man
   Is this the tale which I have heard before?

Creusa
   Yes, that she wears its skin upon her breast.   995

Old Man
   Athene's armor which they call her aegis?

Creusa
   So called from how she rushed into the battle.

Old Man
   What was the form of this barbaric thing?

Creusa
   A breastplate armed with serpent coils.

                              (*An impatient pause.*)

Old Man

But my child, what harm can this do to your foes?

Creusa

You know Erichthonius?—Of course you must.

Old Man

The founder of your house, the son of Earth.   1000

Creusa

A newborn child, Athene gave to him—

(She pauses.)

Old Man

Yes, what is this you hesitate to say?

Creusa (slowly)

Two drops of Gorgon's blood.

Old Man

And these have some effect on men?

Creusa

One is poisonous, the other cures disease.   1005

Old Man

But how did she attach them to the child?

Creusa

A golden chain which he gave to my father.

Old Man

And when he died it came to you?

Creusa

Yes, I always wear it on my wrist.

Old Man

How is the twofold gift compounded then?   1010

Creusa

The drop extracted from the hollow vein—

Old Man

How is it to be used? What power has it?

Creusa
It fosters life and keeps away disease.

Old Man
What action does the other of them have?

Creusa
It kills—a poison from the Gorgon's snakes.   1015

Old Man
You carry them apart or mixed together?

Creusa
Apart. For good and evil do not mingle.

Old Man
O my dear child, you have all that you want!

Creusa
By this the boy shall die, and you shall kill him.

Old Man
But when and how? Tell me, it shall be done.   1020

Creusa
In Athens when he comes into my house.

(A pause, as the slave considers.)

Old Man
No, I distrust this plan as you did mine.

Creusa
Why?—Can we both have seen the same weak point?

Old Man
They will accuse you, innocent or guilty.

Creusa
Since foster mothers must be jealous,   1025

Old Man
But kill him now and so deny the crime.

Creusa
And in that way I taste my joy the sooner.

Old Man
    And turn his own deceit upon your husband.

Creusa
    You know then what to do? Here, take
    This golden bracelet from my hand, Athene's   1030
    Old gift; go where my husband holds his feast
    In secret; when they end the meal, begin
    To pour the gods' libation, then drop this,
    Under cover of your robe, into
    The young man's cup—in his alone, no more.   1035
    Reserve the drink for him who would assume
    The mastery of my home. Once this is drained,
    He will be dead, stay here and never see
    Our glorious Athens.

Old Man
    Now go to our host's house, and I will do
    The task appointed for me.   1040
                                        (Pause.)

    Old foot, come now, take on a youthful strength
    For work, although the years deny it you.
    March with your masters upon the enemy,
    And help to kill and cast him from the house.
    Right that the fortunate should honor virtue,   1045
    But when we wish to harm our enemies
    There is no law which can prevent.

                                        (Exeunt.)
Chorus

                    STROPHE

    Demeter's daughter, guarding the roadway, ruling
    What wings through the paths of the night
    And the daytime, O guide the potion   1050
    Of the death-heavy cup
    To whom the queen sends it, brew
    Of the blood drops from the Gorgon's severed throat, 1055
    To him who lifts his presumptuous hand

Against the house of Erechtheus.
  Let no others ever have
  Sway in the city:
  Only the sons of Erechtheus.   1060

ANTISTROPHE

My mistress is planning a death, and if it should fail,
The occasion of action go past,
Now her sole anchor of hope,
She will sharpen a sword
Or fasten a noose to her neck,   1065
Ending sorrow by sorrows, pass down to the realm of change.
For she would never endure to see
Foreigners ruling the house,   1070
  Not while living her eyes
  Still have their clarity—
  She, born of a noble line.

STROPHE

O the shame to many-hymned Dionysus, if by the springs
Where lovely choruses are danced,   1075
Apollo's bastard son shall behold
Unsleeping, keeping the watch,
The torches burning on the festival night,
When the star-faced heavens join in the dance,   1080
With the moon and the fifty Nereids
Who dance in the depths of the sea,
In perennial river-springs,
Honoring the gold-crowned Maid   1085
And her mother, holy Demeter:
  There, where he hopes
  To rule, usurping
  What others have wrought.

ANTISTROPHE

All you poets who raise your unjust strains   1090
Singing the unsanctioned, unholy loves

Of women, see how much we surpass
In virtue the unrighteous race   1095
Of men. Let a song of different strain
Ring out against men, harshly indicting
Their love. For here is one
Of the offspring of Zeus who shows
His ingratitude, refusing   1100
To bring good luck to the house
With his and Creusa's child:
    But yielding to passion
    For another, has found
    A bastard son.   1105

          (*Enter a Servant of Creusa, greatly agitated.*)

Servant

Women, can you tell me where I may find
Erechtheus' noble daughter? I have searched
The city everywhere without success.

Chorus Leader

What is it, friend? Why are you hurrying?
What is the message you have brought?   1110

Servant

They are behind. The Delphian officers are looking
For her to stone to death.

Chorus Leader

What do you mean? Have they discovered then
The secret plot we made to kill the boy?

Servant

Correct—and you will not be the last to suffer.   1115

Chorus Leader

How was this scheme, unknown to them, discovered?

Servant

The god refused to be defiled, and so
Found means of combating the victory
Of justice over the unjust.

Chorus Leader

But how? I beg you tell me that: for if
I have to die, I shall die more content   1120
Because I know my fate.

(*The women press nearer to the Servant.*)

Servant

Creusa's husband came out from the shrine
Of Phoebus, and then took his new-found son
Away to join the feast and sacrifice
He was preparing for the gods. Xuthus
Himself was going to the place where   1125
The sacred Bacchanalian fires leap,
To sprinkle the twin crags of Dionysus
With victim's blood for having seen his son.
"My son," he said, "will you stay here and see
That workmen build a tent inclosed on all
Its sides. And if I should be long away,
While sacrificing to the gods of birth,   1130
Begin the banquet with such friends as come."
   He took the victims then and went away.
Ion had the framework built in ritual form
On upright poles without a wall, and paid
Attention to the sun, so that he might   1135
Avoid its midday and its dying rays
Of flame, and measuring a square, its sides
A hundred feet, so that he could invite
All Delphians to the feast. To shade the tent   1140
He took from store some sacred tapestries,
A wonder to behold. And first he cast
Above the roof a wing of cloth, spoil from
The Amazons, which Heracles, the son
Of Zeus, had dedicated to the god.   1145
And there were figures woven in design:
For Uranus was mustering the stars
In heaven's circle; and Helios drove his horses
Toward his dying flame and trailed the star

Which shines bright in the West. While black-robed Night,   1150
Drawn by a pair, urged on her chariot,
Beside the stars kept pace with her. The Pleiades
And Orion, his sword in hand, moved through
The sky's mid-path; and then, above, the Bear
Who turned his golden tail within the vault.
The round full moon threw up her rays, dividing   1155
The month; the Hyades, the guide most sure
For sailors; then light's herald, Dawn, routing
The stars. The sides he draped with tapestries
Also, but of barbarian design.
There were fine ships which fought with Greeks, and creatures,   1160
Half-man, half-beast, and horsemen chasing deer
Or lion hunts. And at the entrance, Cecrops,
His daughters near him, wreathed himself in coils
Of serpents—this a gift which had been given
By some Athenian. Then in the center   1165
He put the golden mixing bowls. A herald
Then went and announced that any Delphian
Who pleased was free to attend the feast. And when
The tent was full, they wreathed their heads with flowers
And ate the food spread in abundance till
Desire was satisfied. When they had done   1170
With eating, an old man came in and stood
Among the guests, and threw them into laughter
With his officious antics. He poured out water
From jars to wash their hands, or burned
The ooze of myrrh, and put himself in charge   1175
Of golden drinking cups. And when the flutes
Came in together with the bowl which all
Had now to drink, he said, "Enough of these
Small cups, we must have large; the company
Will then be all the sooner in good spirits."   1180
And now they busied themselves with passing gold
And silver cups; but he, as though he meant
To honor his new master, offered him

A chosen cup of wine, and put in this
A fatal poison which they say our mistress   1185
Had given, to have an end of this new son.
And no one knew. But when like all the rest
He held his cup, one of the slaves let fall
Some phrase of evil omen. He had been reared
Among good prophets in the temple, and knew   1190
The sign and ordered them to fill another.
The first libation of the god he emptied
On the ground and told the rest to pour
As he had done. A silence followed when
We filled the sacred bowls with Byblian wine   1195
And water. While this was being done, there came
Into the tent a riotous flight of doves—
They haunt Apollo's shrine and have no fear.
To slake their thirst, they dipped their beaks into
The wine the guests had poured and drew it down   1200
Their well-plumed throats; and all but one were not
Harmed by the god's libation. But she had perched
Where Ion poured his wine and tasted it.
At once her feathered body shook and quivered,
She screamed strange cries of anguish. All the band   1205
Of guests looked on amazed to see her struggles.
She died in her convulsions, her pink claws
And legs relaxed. The son the god foretold
Then stretched his uncloaked arms across the table,
And cried, "Who planned my death? Tell me, old man,   1210
Since you were so officious; you handed me
The drink." He held the old man by the arm
And searched him instantly, so that he might
Convict him in the act. His guilt was proved
And he revealed, compelled against his will,   1215
Creusa's plotting with the poisoned drink.

    The youth bestowed by Loxias collected
The guests, went from the tent without delay,
And took his stand before the Delphian nobles.

"O rulers of the sacred city," he said,   1220
"A foreign woman, daughter of Erechtheus,
   Has tried to poison me." The lords of Delphi
   By many votes decided that my mistress
   Be put to death, thrown from the rock, for planning
   The murder of a sacred person there
   Inside the temple. Now all the city looks   1225
   For her whom misery advanced on this
   Unhappy path. Desire for children caused
   Her visit here to Phoebus, but now her life
   Is lost, and with her life all hopes.

Chorus
   There is no escape, we are doomed,
   No escape from death.   1230
   It has been made clear,
   The libation of Dionysian grapes
   Mingled for murder with blood drops
   From the swift-working viper,
   Clear that in sacrifice to the gods below   1235
   Our lives are set for disaster.
   They will stone my mistress to death.
   What winged flight can I take,
   Down to what dark caverns of the earth
   Can I go to escape the stones of destruction?   1240
   By mounting a chariot
   Drawn by horses with speedy hooves,
   Or the prow of a ship?

   There is no concealment, unless a god wishes
   To withdraw men from sight.   1245
   O unhappy mistress, what sufferings
   Wait for your soul? Shall we not,
   For the will to do harm to our fellows,
   According to justice, suffer ourselves?

             (*Creusa rushes in, wildly agitated and despairing.*)

Creusa

They are in pursuit, my friends, they want to butcher me;　　　1250
By the judgment of the Pythian vote my life is forfeit.

Chorus Leader

Yes, we know in what distress you are, unhappy woman.

Creusa

Where can I find refuge then? For I have evaded them
By a trick, just left the house in time to save my life.

Chorus Leader

Where, but at the altar?

Creusa

　　　　　　　　　　What advantage will that give me?　　　1255

Chorus Leader

God defends the suppliant.

Creusa

　　　　　　　　Yes, but the law condemns me.

Chorus Leader

They must seize you first.

Creusa

　　　　　　　　And here my bitter rivals come,
Pressing on with sword in hand.

Chorus Leader

　　　　　　　　　　Sit at the altar now.
For if you die sitting there, your killers will be made
Guilty of your blood. Now destiny must be endured.　　　1260

　　　(*Creusa retires quickly to the altar at the back of the stage. She
　　　has hardly had time to sit there before Ion, sword in hand,
　　　comes in at the head of a group of armed men, closely
　　　followed by a crowd of Delphians. For some time
　　　he is not aware that Creusa is at the altar.*)

Ion

O Cephisus, her bull-shaped ancestor,
What viper or what serpent glancing out
A deadly flame of fire did you beget

In her, this woman who will balk at nothing,
Match for the Gorgon drops with which she tried   1265
To poison me! Take hold of her and let
Parnassus' top, when like a quoit she bounds
From rock to rock, comb out those perfect tresses.
    Luck favored me before I went to Athens
To fall a victim to a stepmother.   1270
For here, among my friends I learnt to measure
Your mind, your menace, and your enmity.
But if I had been trapped inside your house,
You would have sent me straight to death.

(He suddenly catches sight of Creusa cowering
at the altar. He strides up to her.)

    The altar will not save you, nor Apollo's   1275
House, since my greater pity is reserved
For myself and my mother. For although
She is not here, my thought of her is constant.

(He appeals to the people with him.)

You see her treachery—how she can twist
One scheme upon another! She has fled
To cower at the god's own altar, hoping   1280
Thus to avoid her penalty for wrong.

Creusa

I warn you not to kill me—and I speak
Not only for myself but for the god
Who guards this place.

Ion

What can you have in common with the god?

Creusa

My body is his to save, a sacred charge.   1285

Ion

You tried to poison me and I was his.

Creusa

No longer his; for you had found your father.

Ion

I belonged to Phoebus till my father came.

Creusa

But then no more. Now I belong to him.

Ion

Yes, but I had the piety you lack.   1290

Creusa

I tried to kill the enemy of my house.

Ion

I did not march upon your land with arms.

Creusa

You tried to set Erechtheus' house in flames!

Ion

What fiery flame, what torches did I carry?

Creusa

You hoped to force possession of my home.   1295

Ion

My father's gift—the land he gained himself.

Creusa

How can Aeolians share Athenian land?

Ion

Because he saved it, not with words, but arms.

Creusa

An ally need not own the land he helps!

Ion

You planned my death through fear of my intentions?   1300

Creusa

To save my life in case you ceased intending.

Ion

Childless yourself, you envied my father's child.

Creusa

So you will snatch those homes without an heir?

Ion

Had I no right to share my father's state?

Creusa

A shield and spear, these are your sole possessions.   1305

> (*Ion loses his temper.*)

Ion

Come, leave the altar and the shrine of god.

Creusa

> (*Her moral indignation yielding to spite.*)

Go, find your mother and give her advice.

Ion

While your attempted murder goes unpunished?

Creusa

Not if you wish to kill me in the shrine.

> (*She grasps the wreaths on the altar as if in supplication.*)

Ion

What pleasure can the god's wreaths give to death?   1310

Creusa

I shall thus injure one who injured me.

Ion

O this is monstrous! The laws of god for men
Are not well made, their judgment is unwise.
The unjust should not have the right of refuge
At altars, but be driven away. For gods   1315
Are soiled by the touch of wicked hands. The just—
The injured man, should have this sanctuary.
Instead both good and bad alike all come,
Receiving equal treatment from the gods.

> (*The Pythian Priestess now enters from the temple. She is old
> and very dignified, wearing long white robes fastened by
> a golden girdle at the waist; on her head is a wreath
> of bay leaves and the riband or fillet which is the
> sign of her office. She is carrying a cradle
> wrapped in bands of wool.*)

Priestess

O stop, my son. For I, the prophetess   1320
Of Phoebus, chosen by all the Delphians
To keep the tripod's ancient law, have left
The seat of prophecy to pass these bounds.

(*Ion greets her with great respect.*)

Ion

Dear mother, hail! Mother in all but name.

Priestess

Then let me be so called. It pleases me.   1325

Ion

You heard how she had planned to murder me?

Priestess

I heard—but your own cruelty is sinful.

Ion

Have I no right to kill a murderer?

Priestess

Wives are unkind to children not their own.

Ion

As we can be ill used by them.   1330

Priestess

No. When you leave the temple for your country—

Ion

What must I do? What is your advice?

Priestess

Go into Athens, with good omens.

Ion

All men are pure who kill their enemies.

Priestess

No more of that.—Hear what I have to say.   1335

Ion

Then speak. Your message could not be unfriendly.

Priestess

You see the basket I am carrying?

Ion

I see an ancient cradle bound with wool.

Priestess

I picked you up in this, a newborn child.

Ion

What do you say? This tale is new to me.   1340

Priestess

I kept it secret. Now I can reveal it.

Ion

How have you kept it from me all these years?

Priestess

The god desired to hold you as his servant.

Ion

And now he does not wish it? How can I know?

Priestess

Revealing your father, he bids you go from here.   1345

Ion

Why did you keep the cradle? Was that an order?

Priestess

Apollo put the thought into my mind.—

Ion

What thought? Tell me. I want to hear the end.

Priestess

To keep what I had found until this time.

Ion

And does it bring me any help?—or harm?   1350

Priestess

The swaddling clothes you wore are kept inside.

Ion

These clues you bring will help to find my mother.

Priestess

 Which now the god desires—though not before.

Ion

 This is indeed a day of happy signs!

        (*She offers him the cradle.*)

Priestess

 Take this with you—and now look for your mother.   1355

Ion

           (*Taking the cradle.*)

 Throughout all Asia, to Europe's boundaries!

Priestess

 That is your own affair. I reared you, child,
 For Phoebus' sake, and these restore to you,
 Which he wished me to take and keep, although
 Without express command. Why he so wished   1360
 I cannot say. There was no man who knew
 That I had these or where they were concealed.
 And now farewell. I kiss you as my son.

   (*She embraces him. She turns and takes a few steps toward the
       temple entrance. Then she faces him again, to prolong
         her farewell with a few last words of advice.*)

 As for the search, begin it as you ought:
 Your mother might have been a Delphian girl   1365
 Who left you at the temple; inquire here first,
 And then elsewhere in Greece. Now you have heard
 All that we have to say—Apollo, who had
 An interest in your fate, and I myself.

     (*She leaves the stage through the temple door.*)

Ion

       (*Putting his hands to his face.*)

 O how the tears well from my eyes whenever
 My mind goes back to the time when the woman   1370
 Who gave me birth, the child of secret love,
 Disposed of me by stealth, and kept me from

Her breast. Instead, unnamed, I had a life
Of service in Apollo's house; and fate
Was cruel, though the god was kind. I was
Deprived of my dear mother's love throughout
The time I might have lain content and happy,   1375
Held in her arms. My mother suffered too;
She lost the joy a child can bring.

                      And now
I will resign the cradle as a gift   1380
To god to ward away unpleasant news.
If by some chance my mother were a slave,
To find her would be worse than ignorance.
O Phoebus, to your shrine I dedicate—
    And yet, what does this mean? It is against   1385
The god's own wish; he has preserved for me
My mother's tokens. I must have the courage
To open it. I cannot shun my fate.
O sacred bands and ties which guard my precious
Tokens, what secret do you hide from me?   1390

            (*He unties the bands of wool from the cradle.*)
A miracle! See how the cradle's covering
Is still unworn; the wicker is not decayed,
Yet years have passed since they were put away.

            (*Creusa is trembling with excitement, her eyes
                        riveted upon the cradle.*)

Creusa
But what is this I see—beyond my hopes?   1395

Ion
Silence. You were my enemy before.

    (*Creusa controls her excitement with a great effort and gradually
           raises herself to a standing position by the altar. The
           crowd of Delphians, her own women, and Ion
           all gaze toward her in tense silence.*)

Creusa
This is no time for silence. Do not try
To check me. In that cradle I exposed

You then, my son, a newborn child,
Where the Long Rocks hang over Cecrops' cave.   1400
I will desert the altar even though
I have to die.

(She rushes away from the altar, runs up to Ion,
and throws her arms round his neck.)

Ion

Seize her! God's madness has made her leap away
From the altar's images. Now bind her arms.

Creusa

Go on and kill me. I will not lose you,
The cradle, or the tokens it contains.   1405

Ion

O hypocrite to cheat me with a trick!

Creusa

Oh no! You have found one who loves you.

Ion

What, you love me?—And try a secret murder?

Creusa

You are my son: a mother must love her son.

Ion

Stop spinning lies.—For I am sure to have you.   1410

(Decides to trick her.)

Creusa

O do so then! That is my aim, my son.

Ion

This cradle—has it anything inside?

Creusa

It has the things you wore when I exposed you.

Ion

And can you give their names before you see them?

Creusa

I can; and, if I fail, consent to die.   1415

Ion

Then speak. Your audacity is strange indeed.
(He opens the cradle, standing far enough away from Creusa
to prevent her seeing inside it.)

Creusa

Look for the weaving which I did in childhood.

Ion

Describe it; girls do many kinds of work.

Creusa

It is unfinished, a kind of trial piece.

Ion

And its design—You cannot cheat me there.   1420

Creusa

There is a Gorgon in the center part.

Ion (aside)

O Zeus! What fate is this to track us down!

Creusa

The stuff is fringed with serpents like an aegis.

Ion

And here it is—found like an oracle!

Creusa

The loomwork of a girl—so long ago.   1425

Ion

And anything else? Or will your luck fail now?

Creusa

Serpents, the custom of our golden race.

Ion

Athene's gift, who bids you wear them?

Creusa

Yes, in memory of Erichthonius.

Ion

What do they do with this gold ornament?   1430

Creusa

It is a necklace for a newborn child.

Ion

Yes, here they are.

> (*Shows them. He is now anxious for her success.*)
> I long to know the third.

Creusa

I put an olive wreath around you, from
The tree Athene first planted on the rock;
If that is there, it has not lost its green,   1435
But flourishes because the tree is holy.

> (*Ion, quite convinced, throws himself into his mother's arms.*)

Ion

O dearest mother, what happiness to see you,
To kiss you, and know that you are happy!

Creusa

O child! O light more welcome than the Sun.
—The god forgives me—I have you in my arms.   1440
I have found you against all my hopes,
Whom I thought underground in the world
Of Persephone's shades.

Ion

Dear mother, yes, you have me in your arms,
Who died and now have come to you alive.

Creusa

O radiant heaven's expanse,   1445
How can I speak or cry
My joy? How have I met
Unimagined delight, and why
Am I made happy?

Ion

There was no more unlikely chance than this,   1450
To find that I am, after all, your son.

Creusa

    I am trembling with fear.

Ion

    That I am lost, although you hold me now?

Creusa

    Yes, since I had cast all hope away.
    But tell me, priestess, from where
    Did you take the child to your arms?
    Whose hand brought him to Apollo's house?   1455

Ion

    It was the work of god. But as we have suffered
    Before, so now we must enjoy our fortune.

Creusa

    My child, you were born in tears,
    In sorrow torn from your mother.
    But now I can breathe on your cheek,   1460
    And am blessed with tender joy.

Ion

    I have no need to speak. You speak for both.

Creusa

    I am childless no longer,
    No longer without an heir.
    The hearth is restored to the home,
    The rulers return to the land,
    And Erechtheus is young once more;   1465
    Now the house is delivered from night
    And looks up to the rays of the sun.

Ion

    Mother, my father should be here with me
    To share the happiness I bring you both.

Creusa

    My child, my child—   1470
    How am I put to shame!

Ion

Yes?—Tell me.—

Creusa

You do not know your father.

Ion

So I was born before your marriage then?

Creusa

The marriage which gave you birth
Saw no torches or dancing, my son.   1475

Ion

A bastard son—My father? Tell me that.

Creusa

Athene who slew the Gorgon,
I call her to witness—

Ion

Why this beginning?

Creusa

By the rocks where the nightingales sing,   1480
Apollo—

Ion

Why name Apollo?

Creusa

Became my lover in secret—

Ion

Speak on; for what you say will make me happy.   1485

Creusa

When the time passed, I bore you,
The unknown child of Apollo.

Ion

How welcome this news is—if it is true.

Creusa

And these were your swaddling clothes;
In fear of my mother I wrapped you   1490

In them, the careless work of a girl
At her loom.
I gave you no milk,
You were not washed with my hands,
But in a deserted cave,
A prey for the beaks of birds,   1495
Delivered to death.

Ion

O mother, what horror you dared.

Creusa

Myself in the bondage of fear,
I was casting away your life,
But against my will.

Ion

And I attempted an impious murder.   1500

Creusa

Fate drove us hard in the past,
Just now oppressed us again.
There is no harbor of peace
From the changing waves of joy and despair.   1505
The wind's course veers.
Let it rest. We have endured
Sorrows enough. O my son,
Pray for a favoring breeze
Of rescue from trouble.

Chorus Leader

From what we have seen happen here, no man   1510
Should ever think that any chance is hopeless.

                           (*A pause. Ion is afflicted with doubt.*)

Ion

O Fortune, who has already changed the lives
Of countless men from misery to joy,
How near I was to killing my own mother,
How near myself to undeserved disaster.   1515

(Pause.)

But do the sun's bright rays in daily course
Illumine such events as this—all this?

(Pause, as he turns to his mother.)

It was so good at last to find you, mother,
And I can cast no blame upon my birth.
But there is something else I wish to say   1520
To you alone. Come here with me; my words
Are for your ear; your answer shall be hidden.

(He draws her aside.)

Now tell me, mother—are you not, deceived
As young girls are in love affairs kept secret,
Now laying blame upon the god, and say,   1525
Attempting to escape the shame I brought,
That Phoebus is my father, though in fact
He is no god at all?

Creusa

No, by Athene, Goddess of Victory,
Who in her chariot fought by Zeus's side
Against the Giant race, my son, your father
Was not a mortal, but the very god   1530
Who reared you, Loxias.

Ion

If this is true, why give his son to others,
Why does he say that Xuthus is my father?

Creusa

No, he does not; you are his son, a gift
Bestowed by him on Xuthus, just as a man   1535
Might give a friend his son to be his heir.

Ion

But, mother, does Apollo tell the truth,
Or is the oracle false? With some good reason
That question troubles me.

Creusa

   Then listen. This is what I think, my son:
   It is for your own good that Loxias   1540
   Is placing you within a noble house.
   Acknowledged as his son, you would have lost
   All hope of heritage or father's name.
   What chance had you when I concealed
   The truth, and even planned your death in secret?
   And so to help you he is giving you
   Another father.   1545

Ion

   My question cannot be so lightly answered;
   No, I will ask Apollo in his temple
   If I am his, or born of man.

            (As he steps toward the temple, he sees the goddess)
                      Athene appearing above it.)

   Ah!
   What goddess shows her face above the temple
   To look toward the sun? O mother, let us fly.   1550
   We should not see the gods unless the right
   Is given to us.

            (All on the stage bow their heads to the ground
                  and step backward from the temple.)

Athene

   No, stay. I am no enemy to flee,
   But well-disposed in Delphi as in Athens.
   I am Athene, whose name your city bears: 1555
   I have come here in haste, sent by Apollo,
   Who did not think it right to come himself
   Before you, lest he should be blamed for what
   Has happened in the past; he has sent me
   To give his message:
              This woman is your mother,   1560
   Your father is Apollo; the one you know
   Received you as a gift, and not because

You are his son; and this was done with purpose,
To find you an established place among
A noble house. But when this plan he made
Was open and laid bare, he was afraid
Your mother's scheme of murder would succeed,
Or she be killed by you, and found some means   1565
Of rescue; but for this he would have kept
The secret longer and in Athens revealed
Creusa as the mother and himself
The father of his child. But I must end
My task and tell the purpose of my journey.
Now hear Apollo's revelations.   1570
                    Creusa,
Go with your son to Cecrops' land, and then
Appoint him to the royal throne; for since
He is descended from Erechtheus, he has
The right to rule my land: and he shall be
Renowned through Greece. His sons, four branches from   1575
One stock, shall name the country and its peoples,
Divided in their tribes, who live about my rock.
The first shall be named Geleon, the tribe
Of Hopletes second, then Argades, and one   1580
Aegicores, the name from my own aegis.
At the appointed time, the children born
Of them shall colonize the Cyclades,
Possess the island cities and the coasts,
And thus give strength to my own land of Athens.
They shall live in the two broad plains of Asia
And Europe, which lie on either side the straits,   1585
Becoming famous under this boy's name,
Ionians. Moreover, you and Xuthus
Are promised children. First Dorus, whose name
Shall cause the Dorians to be hymned throughout   1590
The land of Pelops. Then Achaeus, king
Of that sea coast near Rhion, who shall mark
A people with his name.

Apollo then
Has managed all things well. He made your labor   1595
Easy, so that your parents should not know;
And when the child was born and you exposed
Him in his swaddling clothes, he ordered Hermes
To take him in his arms and bring him here,
And would not let him die, but reared him.   1600
But tell no one that Ion is your son,
And Xuthus will be happy in his belief,
While you may go away, Creusa, sure
Of your own blessings.—Now farewell;
You are delivered of your present evil,
The future holds good fortune.   1605

Ion (ironically)

O Athene, child of mighty Zeus, we have received
What you say on trust. And I believe myself Apollo's
And Creusa's son—though that was credible before.

(*To the end of the scene Ion stands in silence.*)

Creusa

Listen to my tribute. Though before I gave no praise,
Now I praise Apollo. For the son he had neglected   1610
Is restored to me; and now this oracle, these doors,
Wear a friendly look, though they were hateful in the past.
Joyfully I cling to them and bid farewell.

Athene

I approve this change, this praise of him. The gods perhaps
Move to action late, but in the end they show their strength.   1615

Creusa

Son, now let us go.

Athene

                         Yes, go, and I will follow you.

Creusa

Welcome guardian of our journey, one who loves the city.

Athene (*to Ion*)
   Mount the ancient throne.

                        (*Ion is silent. There is an embarrassing pause.*)
Creusa
                        That is a worthy prize for me.

                        (*The actors slowly move off the stage in procession.*
                                          Athene disappears.)
Chorus
                                          (*To the temple.*)
O Apollo, son of Zeus and Leto, now farewell.

                                          (*To the audience.*)
He whose house is pressed by trouble should respect the gods,   1620
So preserving courage. For at last good men are honored,
Evil men by their own nature cannot ever prosper.
                                          (*Exeunt.*)

RHESUS

Translated and with an Introduction by Richmond Lattimore

INTRODUCTION TO *RHESUS*

The ancient Argument, or Introduction, to *Rhesus* contains the following statement: "Some have suspected that this play is spurious, that is, not by Euripides. For it shows a character which is more like Sophocles. Nevertheless, it is recorded in the play-lists as a genuine play of Euripides; and the overelaborateness [? Greek *polypragmosyne*] with which elevation is striven for is in the manner of Euripides." Who these "some" were we do not know, but it seems plain that their suspicions were based on internal, not external, evidence. The play was officially credited to Euripides. Further, from the notes (*scholia*) on the text, line 529, we have the following: "Crates says that Euripides was ignorant of astronomy in this passage because he was still young when he presented *Rhesus*."

Thus we may say that, while *Rhesus* was firmly attested as a play by Euripides, there was a feeling that there was something peculiar about it, that it did not read, feel, sound like Euripides. Modern critics have generally shared the uneasiness which the writer of our Argument felt, though they have not shared, or even understood, his notion that it is "more like Sophocles." While in this brief unscientific introduction I can offer no full treatment,[1] the following characteristics may be noted.

1. The action is taken direct from the Tenth Book of the *Iliad*. Its chief events, the sortie of Dolon, the countermission of Odysseus and Diomedes, who kill Dolon, and the death of Rhesus, are all in Homer, though there are changes in emphasis, particularly in the importance of the part played by Athene, the importance of Rhesus for the Trojan cause, and the introduction of the Muse as Rhesus' mother. This is the only extant tragedy which takes its material straight out of the *Iliad*.[2] The regular practice of the tragic poets

---

[1] Those who are curious about the "Rhesus question" are referred to C. B. Sneller, *De Rheso Tragoedia* (Amsterdam: H. J. Paris, 1949). This is full and thorough. There is an excellent briefer discussion in G. M. A. Grube, *The Drama of Euripides* (London: Methuen & Co., 1941), pp. 439–47.

[2] The fragments of tragedy offer only one other certain case, the trilogy by Aeschylus which contained *The Myrmidons*, *The Nereids*, and *The Ransoming of Hector*. It is

when they dealt with the heroes and stories of the Trojan War was to choose episodes which fell outside the scope of the *Iliad*, before its opening or, more frequently, after its close.

2. This is the only extant tragedy whose action all takes place at night. But this is dictated by the facts of the situation in Homer.

3. Fate and divine mechanics are used more baldly than elsewhere in tragedy.

"If Rhesus survives this day or night [but he will not] all will be well." This is a minor motive in Sophocles' *Ajax* and serves better as such than as a major motive, which it is here.

"If Rhesus fights tomorrow, Achilles, Ajax, and all the rest of the Greeks cannot stop him." Why on earth should we believe this? He might, of course, be played in a costume, with built-up boots, that makes him tower, giant-like, over Hector himself. But belief in Rhesus is plainly enforced because a god guarantees him (Athene, ll. 600–605). Athene also tells Odysseus whom to kill, whom not to kill, because it is or is not authorized or "fated" (ll. 633–36).

"If a man is too confident, even if that confidence is justified, or if others speak too well of him, he is doomed to destruction" (see ll. 342–87, 447–53). The tragic poets may sometimes say that men are puppets in the hands of the gods, but they do not elsewhere make them so in action. This machinery is bare.

4. The iambics of *Rhesus* show resolution (three syllables for two) in 8.6 per cent of the lines, on my count.[3] It is well known that in the period of his extant plays Euripides indulged more and more freely in resolution as time went on. His earliest dated play, *Alcestis* (438 B.C.), shows resolution of 6.5 per cent. His latest, the posthumous *Bacchae* and *Iphigenia in Aulis*, have 37.5 per cent and 48 per cent respectively. The rate of increase is by no means constant, but we may

---

striking that here Aeschylus also departed from the usual convention in using the theme of homosexual love, which I have not found elsewhere in tragedy. If he repeated neither experiment, perhaps that means that this trilogy was not well received.

[3] Statistical counts will vary because the scholar has some latitude in deciding whether certain feet, apparently of three syllables, might actually be run together and read as two. I also think it fairer to count proper names. Some do not. One can make mistakes, too. But the variations will not be significant.

say flatly that *Rhesus* cannot be a play written by Euripides after 415 and that it is probably far earlier. There is, however, one complication. *Rhesus* has trochees; it should not. All but one of the latest plays, beginning with *The Trojan Women* (415; iambic resolution 22.5 per cent), contain trochees. The only earlier play which has them is *Heracles*, which, on metrical and material grounds, can probably be put about 422–420 B.C. Its resolution rate is 19 per cent. No extant play with a resolution rate below that of *Heracles* has trochees, except *Rhesus*. It is thus a metrical anomaly, and this is the strongest piece of internal evidence against Euripidean authorship. On the other hand, the fragments of Euripides' lost *Phoenix* do contain trochees, and *Phoenix* is securely dated before 425. The forty iambic lines preserved show a resolution rate of only 2.5 per cent. The conclusion must be that Euripides, while he made a habit of using trochees only in his late period, did use them occasionally long before.

The kind of scene which would call for trochees (the "meter of running") is precisely the kind of scene where we find trochees in *Rhesus:* a scene of activity, the scene where Odysseus and Diomedes are caught by the Chorus (ll. 683–91). In general, the characteristics of this play, material and metrical alike, its rapid, realistic action, its failure to find a central hero or a central dramatic problem, can plausibly be explained by the fact that its author did what the dramatic instinct of the fifth century said he should not: he made a book of the *Iliad* into a drama, but the story did better as an episode in epic than as a self-contained tragic action.

This author may not have been Euripides. If he was not, it by no means follows that the play belongs to the fourth century. Some minor poet of the late fifth is as good a guess.

Against the negative evidence, we should set the testimony of Crates that this is an early work by Euripides. This is evidence too, and it is supported by much that is in the play: the character of Odysseus, the messengers' speeches, the combined lament, explanation, and prediction of the Muse (why doesn't she have a name?),

and especially the way in which, while reproaching Athene for ingratitude, she contrives to glorify Athens. This is a regular bit of
Euripidean *sophia*.

Scholars will continue to doubt, and scholars who honestly doubt
must speak their minds. I now believe that *Rhesus* is the work of
Euripides and probably done before 440 B.C.

CHARACTERS

Chorus of Trojan guards

Hector

Aeneas

Dolon

Shepherd

Rhesus, king of the Thracians

Odysseus

Diomedes

Athene

Alexander (Paris)

Charioteer of Rhesus

Muse, mother of Rhesus

The manuscripts as usual do not distinguish between the lines spoken or sung by the Chorus as a group and those to be spoken by the Leader alone. In other translations I have followed the text without trying to discriminate. Here, however, the Leader seems to me to have a more definite actor's part then elsewhere in extant tragedy, especially at the beginning. Lines 7-10, for example, should be spoken by a single actor, not by a group; and the speaker must be the officer or non-com in charge of the detail, who is *also* the Leader heading the Chorus. I have therefore used my judgment in guessing where lines are to be given to the Leader and where they should be given to the Chorus.

RHESUS

SCENE: *The Trojan position on the plain between the city and the shore. It is late at night. Hector lies asleep on a pile of leaves with other Trojans asleep around him. Enter, in haste, the Chorus of sentries, headed by an officer or corporal of the guard (the Chorus Leader)*

Leader

Go find where Hector is sleeping. Ho there,
is any of the king's bodyguard awake,
or his armor-bearers?
There is a fresh report he must hear
from those who keep this quarter of the night's   5
guard duty for the entire army.

(Shaking Hector.)

Sit up, or lean your head on your arm;
unclose your lids. Open your keen eyes.
Rise now from the piled leaves of your bed,
Hector. A report. You must hear it.   10

Hector

Who speaks? Enemy or friend? What is
the word? But speak.
Who comes here out of the night to find
where I sleep? Declare.

Leader

Sentries of the army.

Hector

               What troubles you so?   15

Leader

Never fear.

Hector

      Not I.
What is it? A night raid?

Leader

No, not that.

Hector

Then why
have you left your post to come here and waken
the camp, unless we must form by night?
Do you realize that the Argive spears   20
are there, close by
where we sleep this night in our armor?

Leader

Arm, arm, Hector, and run to where
the allied forces lie sleeping.
Wake them, tell them to take their spears in their hands.   25

(*To various members of the Chorus.*)

You, send true men to run to your company.
You there, put the curb chains on your horses.
Someone go to Panthoüs' son
or Europa's, lord of the Lycian men. Who will?
Where are those who are in charge
of sacrifices?   30
Or the light-armed captains?
Where are the Phrygian archers?
Archers! Have your hornbows strung, quickly.

Hector

What you report seems partly alarm,
partly to be comfort. All is confusion.   35
What is this? Has the whiplash of Cronian Pan
struck you to shivering panic? Speak, say,
what *are* you reporting? You have talked a great deal
without telling me one thing clearly.   40

Leader

The Argive army has lit its fires,
Hector, all through the darkness.

The positions of their ships are clear in the firelight.
But all their army has gathered in darkness
by Agamemnon's shelter, noisily.   45
They must wish to consult, to take
counsel, since never before was this sea-borne army
so utterly routed. Therefore
I, to forestall anything that may happen,
came to report it, so that   50
you will not say I failed to do my duty.

Hector

Good. You are timely, though you come to us in alarm.
I see these people mean to row away by night,
quietly, when I cannot see them, and make good
their flight. I know exactly what their night fires mean.   55
O God, you robbed me, robbed the lion of his spoil.
All prospered, till you halted me before I swept
the Argive army to destruction with this spear.
For if the flaring lanterns of the sun had not
shut down against us, I would never have stayed my spear   60
in its fortune, until I had fired their ships, and made my way
through their camp, killing Achaeans with this murderous hand.
I myself was all ready to keep up the fight,
to use the darkness and the powerful hand of god.
But these diviners, these educated men who know   65
the mind of heaven, persuaded me to wait for day.
Thus no Achaean (they said) would be missed on land.
But will they wait to be carefully slaughtered? No,
not they. The runaway slave is a great man by night.
Come, then. We must pass the order to our men, at once.   70
Have them wake and put on the armor that lies by.
So the Achaean, even while he jumps for his ship,
shall be stabbed in the back and drench the ladderways
with blood. And the survivors can be caught, and tied,
and learn to work the wheat fields in our land of Troy.   75

Leader

> Too quick, Hector. You act before you understand.
> We are not certain yet that they are running away.

Hector

> For what cause did the Argives light their fires?

Leader

> I do not know. I am suspicious of the whole matter.

Hector

> If you fear this, you would be afraid of anything.   80

Leader

> The enemy never lit fires like this before.

Hector

> They never fled in such an awful rout before.

Leader

> Yes. It was your work. Now consider what comes next.

Hector

> There is only one order to give: arm and fight the enemy.

Leader

> Here comes Aeneas in great haste   85
> of foot, as one who has news for his friends to hear.

> > *(Enter Aeneas.)*

Aeneas

> Hector, why has the night-guard of the camp come here
> to where you were quartered? Is it panic? Here is talk
> going on at night, and all the army is disturbed.

Hector

> On with your armor quick, Aeneas.   90

Aeneas

Yes? What for?

Has someone come in to report the enemy
have made a surprise attack upon us in the dark?

Hector

No, no, they are withdrawing. They are boarding their ships.

Aeneas

And what good reason do you have to believe this?

Hector

Their watch fires are illuminating all the night,   95
and I believe they will not wait until the dawn
but burn them so that by their light they can escape
on their well benched ships, to leave this country and go home.

Aeneas

What will you do to stop them, then? Why are you armed?

Hector

To fall upon them as they flee and board their ships,   100
to charge with our spears against them, and hit hard.
It would be shame, and more than shame, sheer cowardice,
to let them, when they did us so much harm, escape
without a fight, when God has given them to our hands.

Aeneas

I wish you could make plans as well as you can fight.   105
But so it is: the same man cannot well be skilled
in everything; each has his special excellence,
and yours is fighting, and it is for others to make good plans,
not you. You heard how the Achaeans had lit their fires
and hope roused you to wish to lead the army on   110
across their deep moats in the time of night. Yet see,
suppose you do cross over the ditch, despite its depth,

and meet an enemy not withdrawing from our coast
as you think, but standing with spears faced to your attack,
you will have no free way to escape if they defeat you.   115
How will a beaten army cross the palisades?
How will your charioteers drive over the embankments
without smashing the axles of their chariots?
Then, even if you win, they have Achilles in reserve.
He will not sit by while you fire their ships, he will   120
not let you prey on the Achaeans, as you hope.
The man is hot, and he has massive strength of hand.
No, better, let us hold our army out of the way
of hard strokes; let them sleep at peace upon their shields;
but send one volunteer to scout the enemy.   125
So I think best. Then, if they really are in flight,
we can advance in force upon the Argive host.
But if this burning of their fires leads to some trick,
our scout will inform us what they are doing.
Then take our measures. This, my lord, is what I urge.   130

Chorus

This is what I think best. Change your mind and accept it.
I do not like it when the general uses power that is
unsure. What could be better
than that a swift-paced man should go to spy on their ships,
from close, and see what it means   135
when our enemies have fires burning where their prows are
    beached?

Hector

Have your way, then, since this is approved by all. Go, you,
and quiet our allies, let them sleep, since the whole army
might well be restless, hearing how we consult at night.
I will send a man to spy upon the enemy,   140
and if we find out that there is some stratagem,
you shall hear all, Aeneas, and be called to plan
with us; but if it is flight and they are casting off,

be ready for action when you hear the trumpet speak;
because I will not wait for you, I shall be there   145
among the Argives and their cables, now, tonight.

Aeneas

Send him with all speed. Now your plan is sound. And if
the need comes for it, I will be as bold as you

                                                        (Exit.)

Hector

Is there a Trojan, then, present at this council,
who volunteers to spy upon the Argive ships?   150
Who is there who would have his country in his debt?
Who speaks? I cannot, by myself, do everything
that must be done to help our city and our friends.

Dolon

I will do it. I willingly undertake this cast
of hazard. I will go and scout the Argive ships   155
and listen to everything they plan to do and bring
word back. On such conditions I accept the task.

Hector

You are well named, my crafty Dolon, and you love
your city well. Your father's house was bright in name
before. Now you have made it twice as bright.   160

Dolon

It is good to work and fight, but when I do, it also
is good to be rewarded. For in every work
a reward added makes the pleasure twice as great.

Hector

True. I will not deny that what you say is fair.
Name your price. Anything except my royal power.   165

Dolon

I do not want your royal power, nor to rule a city.

Hector

Marry a daughter of Priam. Be my brother-in-law.

Dolon

I think it best not to marry above my station.

Hector

I have gold to give, if that is what you will be asking.

Dolon

We have it at home. We do not lack for anything.   170

Hector

What would you have out of the treasures of Ilium?

Dolon

Nothing. Catch the Achaeans, and then grant my gift.

Hector

I shall. But do not ask for the leaders of their fleet.

Dolon

Kill them. I will not ask for Menelaus' life.

Hector

It is not the son of Oïleus you are asking me for?   175

Dolon

Those well-bred hands would never work well in the fields.

Hector

Is there any Achaean you would have alive, for ransom?

Dolon

I told you before. We have gold aplenty in our house.

Hector

Well, you shall come and take your own pick from the spoils.

Dolon

Take them, and nail them on the houses of the gods.   180

Hector

What prize greater than such things can you ask me for?

Dolon

The horses of Achilles.
                    Since I risk my life
on dice the gods throw, it must be for a high stake.

Hector

Ah. You are my rival, for I want those horses too.
They are immortal, born of an immortal strain,   185
who bear the fighting son of Peleus. The king
of the sea, Poseidon, broke them once and tamed them and gave
them to Peleus, so the story goes. Yet I have raised
your hopes, and I will not be false. I give you them:
Achilles' horses, a great possession for your house.   190

Dolon

I thank you. Thus my courage shall have a reward
that will outshine all others in the land of Troy.
But you should not be jealous. There is much besides
for you, our best and greatest, to take glory in.

(Hector retires to the rear of the stage and rests.)

Chorus

High is the venture, high are the honors you hope to capture.   195
Blessed will your name be called if you win. For here
is glorious work to be done.
It would have been bold to marry into the house of our kings.
May the gods grant that Right's eyes be on you,
as men now grant that all you deserve shall be yours.   200

Dolon

I am ready, once I have gone inside my house
and put upon my body the necessary gear.
From there, I shall take my way against the Argive ships.

Chorus

What costume will you wear in place of what you have on?

Dolon

One suited to my venture and my stealthy way.   205

Chorus

Some cleverness is to be learned from the clever man.
Tell me then, how do you mean to have your body arrayed?

Dolon

I shall put a wolfskin upon my back, fitted
so that the grinning jaws of the beast are on my head,
then, with the forepaws on my hands and the hind feet   210
upon my legs, shall imitate the four-foot tread
of the wolf, to puzzle the enemy who track me there
beside the ditch and by the bows of the beached ships.
Then when I reach the lonely stretch where no one is
I shall go upright. Thus my strategy is planned.   215

Chorus

May Hermes, son of Maia, bring you there and bring
you back, since Hermes is the friend of slippery men.
You know your business. All you need now is good luck.

Dolon

I shall come safely back, but kill Odysseus first
and bring his head to you, to give you solid grounds   220
for saying Dolon won through to the Argive ships.
Or maybe Diomedes—but my hand will not
be bloodless when, before the day breaks, I come home.

                                                              (*Exit.*)

Chorus

Lord of Thymbraeum, lord of Delos, who stand
upright in the Lycian shrine,   225
Apollo, O shining presence, come with your bow
armed, come in the night,
lead, preserve, and guide on his way this man
of battles, lend your strength to Dardanus' children,   230
O power complete, who long ago
founded the walls of Troy.

Grant that he reach their shipsteads and come to spy
on the spread army of Greece
and turn and make his way back to the house of his father
and the sacred hearth, in Troy;   235
and grant, some day, he may mount the Phthian horse-chariot,
after our chief has smashed the war strength of Achaea,
and win the gift the sea god gave   240
once to Peleus, son of Aeacus.

Yes, for he alone dared go down to spy on their ships
for our land and people. I admire
his courage; for indeed few   245
are found brave when the city
is a ship riding a hard
storm on the open
water. There is still manhood alive in Phrygia   250
and valor left still in her spears.
What Mysian is there who holds
scorn that I fight beside him?

What shall that man of Achaea be whom our stalking killer
will spear among the shelters as he goes   255
on fours in the pace of a lurking
beast? Might it be Menelaus!
Or might he kill Agamemnon
and bring the head back

as a gloomy gift for the arms of his evil sister   260
by marriage, Helen. For he
it was led the thousand ships
and the army here against Troy.

(Enter hastily a shepherd. As he speaks, Hector
rises and comes forward.)

Shepherd

My lord, I hope I can always bring my masters news
as good as what I bring you now, for you to hear.   265

Hector

What crude creatures these yokels are. They have no sense.
You think it fitting to report about the flocks
to the armed nobility? You have no business here.
Do you not know where my house is, or my father's throne?
Go there for your announcement that the sheep are well.   270

Shepherd

We herdsmen are crude creatures, I will not say no.
Nevertheless, I am the bringer of good news.

Hector

Will you stop trying to tell me about what goes on
in the farmyard? We have spears and fighting on our hands.

Shepherd

But it is just such matters I report to you.   275
There is a man, with strength of thousands at his back,
who comes to fight for our country at your side.

Hector

Where are the native plains that he has emptied of men?

Shepherd

Thrace; and his father is called Strymon.

« 98 »

Hector

                                         Do you mean
that Rhesus has set foot on Trojan soil?   280

Shepherd

You have it. So saved me half of what I had to say.

Hector

How did he lose the carriage road on the broad plains
to wander through the herds on Ida's mountainside?

Shepherd

I do not know exactly. I can guess at it.
It is no small thing to bring an army through the night   285
when you know the plain is full of enemies in arms.
We countrymen, who live where Ida runs to rock,
and plant our hearth on the bare ground, took alarm, as he
came through the oak wood with its animals in the night.
Because this army of the Thracians streamed along   290
with great clamor, and we, terror-stricken, ran away
to the high pastures, fearing some Argives had come
on a plundering expedition and to rob your folds.
But then our ears made out their language; it was not
anything Greek, and now we were no more afraid.   295
I went and stood before the pathway of their king,
hailed him, and questioned him aloud in Thracian speech:
"Who rides as general here, and of what father called
comes he in arms to fight by Priam's citadel?"
Then, having heard answers to all I wished to know,   300
I stood and watched. There I saw Rhesus like a god
upright behind his horses in the Thracian car.
The golden balance of a yoke inclosed the necks
of his young horses, and these were whiter than snow.
The buckler on his shoulders glowed with beaten plates   305
of gold, and as upon a goddess' aegis, the bronze
face of a gorgon on the horses' frontlet shields

glared, and with bells beat out a clashing sound of fear.
I could not reckon on an abacus the count
of all their army, so innumerable did it seem,   310
horsemen in numbers, numerous squads of buckler men,
many archers with unfeathered arrows, and, besides,
the light troops, in their Thracian costume, followed with them.
Such is the man who comes to fight for Troy. Neither
by flight, nor yet by standing to him with the spear,   315
will Peleus' son Achilles find escape from death.

Leader

When the gods change and stand behind the citizens,
our depressed fortune climbs uphill, and wins success.

Hector

Now that my spear is fortunate, and Zeus is on
our side, we shall be finding that we have many friends.   320
We can do without them. We want none who did not fight
our perils, past now, when the driving God of War
blew big upon our city's ship and wrecked our sails.
Rhesus has shown what kind of friend he is to Troy.
He is here for the feasting, but he was not there   325
with spear in hand to help the huntsmen catch the game.

Leader

Your grievance and complaint of friends is just. And yet,
accept those who, of their free will, will fight for us.

Hector

We have saved Ilium this long time. We are enough.

Leader

Are you so sure you have the enemy beaten now?   330

Hector

I am so sure. God's daylight, which is near, will show.

Leader

Look to the future. God often reverses fortunes.

Hector

I hate it in friends when they come too late to help.   333
As for this man, since he is here, let him be here   336
as a stranger guest at our table, but as no fighting man.   337
He has lost all the kind feelings of the sons of Troy.   338

Leader

Spurn allies, lord, and you gain peril and lose love.   334

Shepherd

If the enemy only saw him they would be afraid.   335

Hector
                                                    (To Chorus.)
You urge me faithfully.
                                                    (To Shepherd.)
                    You have given a timely report.   339
So, for the sake of what the messenger has said,   340
let golden-armored Rhesus come as our ally.

Chorus

Adrasteia: Necessity: Zeus'
daughter! Keep bad luck from my mouth.
For I will speak what is in my heart.
All I wish shall be spoken.   345
You are here, child of the River,
here, at long last now in the court of Friendship,
and welcome, since it was long, before
the Muse your mother and the grand-channeled
River-God sent you to help us.   350

This was Strymon, who with the Muse
melodious, in the clear shining
and watery swirl of their embrace

begot your youth and glory.
You come, a Zeus resplendent   355
for show, driving behind your dappled horses.
Now, O my country, my Phrygia,
now, with gods' will, we can claim the aid
of Zeus himself, Liberator.

Will it ever happen again that our ancient Troy   360
will know the day-long revelries,
the love pledge and companionship,
the strumming on the lyres and the wine cups circling,
passed to the right, in sweet contention,
while on the open water the sons
of Atreus make for Sparta,   365
gone from the shores of Ilium.
O friend, could it only be
that with hand and spear you could do
this before you leave us.

O come, appear, lift and flourish your golden buckler,   370
slant it across the eyes
of Peleus' son, over
the split chariot-rail, feint with your feet, then
cast the twin javelins. None
who stands against you shall dance   375
ever again on the level lands
of Argive Hera. He shall die
here, by a Thracian death, a welcome
weight on this land, which will take him.

Great King, he comes, O great King.

                    (*Rhesus enters, with some of his following.*)

Gallant, O Thrace,   380
is this youngling you bred, a monarch to behold.
See the great force on his gold-armored body,
hear the brave noise of his clashing bells

that jangle on the shield rim.
A god, O Troy, a god, a real Ares   385
is this stallion sired by the singing muse
and Strymon, who comes to inspire you.

Rhesus

Great son of a great father, despot of this land,
O Hector, hail. On this late day I greet you,
and greet the good success that finds you so advanced   390
against the enemy's fortress. I am here to help
you knock their walls to rubble and to burn their ships.

Hector

O son of a melodious mother, one of the Nine,
and Strymon, the River of Thrace: it is my way
always to speak the truth. I have no diplomacy.   395
Long, long ago you should have come to help our struggle.
For all you have done, Troy could have fallen to Greek arms.
This should not be.
You will not say it was because your friends never called you
that you did not come, and did not help, and paid no heed.   400
What herald or what aged representatives
did not reach you, to entreat you to our city's help?
What honorable gifts did we not send? For all
you did, you might as well have thrown us to the Greeks,
though you and we are non-Greek, one Barbarian blood.   405
Yet it was I who with this hand made you so great
and lord of Thrace, though you were but a small baron
before I swept Pangaeum and Paeonia,
fought with the Thracian bravest face to face, and broke
their lines of bucklers, made slaves of their people, turned 410
them over to you. You owe us much. You have spurned it
and to your friends in distress come with late relief.
Yet here are others, who are not our kin by blood,
who came long ago, and some of them have fallen and lie
buried in their mounds, who greatly kept faith with our city, 415

while others, in their armor, by their chariot teams,
have stood whatever cold winds or thirsty heat the god
sends, and still do endure it, without
sleeping, as you did, snug beneath the covers.
There, you may know that Hector speaks his mind.   420
I have my grievance, and I tell you to your face.

Rhesus

I am another such as you. I have a path
straight through arguments. I too have no diplomacy.
But I have been hurt more at the heart than you, more vexed
and shamed, not to be here in your country.   425
But see. There is a land neighbor to mine, its people
are Scythian, and as I was about to keep appointment
at Ilium, these attacked me. I had reached the shores
of the Euxine Sea, to put my Thracian army across,
and there the ground was sopped with Scythian blood, and
    Thracian   430
too, as the spearwork made commingled slaughter.
Such were the accidents that kept me from my march
to Troy's plain and my arrival as your ally.
Once I had beaten them, made hostages of their children,
and set a yearly tribute to be brought to us,   435
I crossed the sea gate with my ships, went on by land
over the intervening country, and so am here;
not, as you claim, because I stayed in comfort, not
because I slept at leisure in my golden house.
For I know well, I have endured them, those stiff winds   440
of ice that sweep Paeonia and the Thracian Sea.
Sleepless, and in this armor, I have come through these
and come to you behind my time, but timely still,
for here is the tenth summer of your years of war,
and *you* have made no progress, but day after day   445
you throw your dice against the hazard of Argive arms;
one single day of sunlight is enough for *me*
to storm their walls and burst upon their mooring-steads

and kill the Achaeans. On the next day after that
I am off for home, having disposed of your whole war.   450
Not one of your people needs to lift a single shield.
I will deal with these vaunted Achaeans and their spears,
and destroy them, even though I came behind my time.

Chorus

Hail, hail,
welcome your cry, welcome, you come from Zeus, only I pray   455
that Zeus keep away
the invincible Spirit of Envy from cursing your words.
For what man from Argos
did the sea-armament bring, before   460
or now, stronger than you? Say how
could even Achilles endure your spear?
How could Ajax endure it?
If I could only see, my lord, only see that day
when your spear hand   465
is bloody with retribution.

Rhesus

Now for my too-long absence I will make amends
thus (but may Adrasteia not resent my words):
when we have liberated this city of yours and when
you have chosen first spoils and devoted them to the gods,   470
I am willing to sail with you against the Argives, storm
and ravage the whole land of Hellas with our spears.
So let them learn what it is like to be attacked.

Hector

If I could only get rid of my present troubles
and rule a peaceful city as I did before   475
I would be very grateful to the gods.
As for the Argive country and the Greek domain,
they are not so easy to devastate as you seem to think.

Rhesus

Do they not say the greatest of the Greeks are here?

Hector

They are great enough for me. I want no more.   480

Rhesus

Then, once we have killed these, have we not done everything?

Hector

Do not plan for ventures before finishing what's at hand.

Rhesus

You seem content to be acted on, not to act.

Hector

I have my own kingdom here, and it is large.
Now, whether you want the left wing, or the right,   485
or to be among the central allies, take your choice,
and plant your shields, station your army where you wish.

Rhesus

My wish, Hector, is to fight the enemy alone;
but if you think it shame to take no hand in burning
their beached ships, an end for which you fought so long,   490
set me face to face with Achilles and his men.

Hector

It is not possible to set your eager spears
against him.

Rhesus

          The story was he sailed to Troy.

Hector

He sailed. He is here. But angry
with their generals, and takes no part in the fighting.   495

Rhesus

Who is most famous in their army after him?

Hector

Ajax, I think, is just as good, and Tydeus' son
Diomedes. Then there is that talker, that big mouth,
Odysseus, but his heart is brave enough, who has done
more damage to our country than any single man.   500
He it was who crept in the night to Athene's shrine
and stole her image and took it to the Argive ships.
There was a time the Argives sent him to scout us,
and in a beggarman's miserable outfit, disguised,
he got inside our walls and did us great mischief.   505
For he killed the sentries and the gate guards and got free
away. Constantly he is observed, under cover
by the Thymbraean altar, near the city, watching
his chance. A wicked planner, always on our hands.

Rhesus

Why, no true man of spirit deigns to kill his man   510
by stealth. One should go forward and attack direct.
This man you speak of, crouching in thievish ambuscades
and scheming stratagems, this man I will seize alive,
impale him through the back where the road goes out the gates,
and leave him there to feed the vultures.   515
That is the kind of death that such a man should die
for being a simple brigand and a temple robber.

Hector

Well, it is night now, and time for you to bivouac.
I will show you your place, apart from where the rest
of the army is stationed. There your men can spend the night.   520
Should you want anything, the watchword is "Phoebus."
Learn it. Remember. Tell it to your Thracian force.

(To the Chorus.)

Now, you must go out in advance of our position,
keep a sharp watch, and be on the lookout for Dolon
who scouted the ships, for, if he is still alive,   525
he must be almost back now to the Trojan camp.

*(Exeunt all principals. The Chorus have the stage to themselves.
There is some business of waking men who lie asleep on the
ground or calling to imaginary persons off stage.)*

Leader

Whose is the watch now? Who relieves
mine? The early constellations
are setting. The Pleiades' sevenfold course
rides high, and the Eagle soars in the center of heaven.   530
Wake. What keeps you? Wake
from your sleep, to your watch.
Do you not see how the moon shines?
Dawn is near, dawn   535
is breaking now, here is the star
that runs before it.

Who was announced for the first watch?

First Soldier

Coroebus, they say, Mygdon's son.

Leader

Who was after that?

First Soldier

                              The Paeonian force   540
relieved the Cilicians. Mysians relieved us.

Leader

Then is it not time to go wake the Lycians
and relieve, take the fifth
watch, in our turn, as allotted?   545

Second Soldier

I hear. But perched above Simois
the nightingale,
the own-child-slayer in vociferous chant
sings her murderous marriage, sings her song and her sorrow.　　550

Third Soldier

The flocks are pasturing on Ida
now. I can hear the night-murmuring
call of the shepherd's pipe.

Fourth Soldier

Sleep is a magic on my eyes.
It comes sweetest　　　　　　　　　　555
to the lids about dawn.

Fifth Soldier

Why is the scout not here, that one
Hector sent to spy on their ships?

Sixth Soldier

I fear for him. He is long gone.

Fifth Soldier

Might he have stumbled into an ambush　　560
and been killed?

Sixth Soldier

He might. It is to be feared.

Leader

My orders are to go wake the Lycians
and relieve, take the fifth
watch, in our turn, as allotted.

*(The Chorus file out, leaving the stage empty. Then
enter, furtively, Odysseus and Diomedes.)*

Odysseus

    Diomedes, did you hear? Or was it a noise without   565
    meaning that falls on my ears? Some clash of armor?

Diomedes

    It was nothing, the jangle of iron on the harness
    against the chariot rails. But I was frightened too,
    at first, when I heard the clanking of the harness.

Odysseus

    Be careful. You might run into their sentries in the dark.   570

Diomedes

    I will watch how I step despite the darkness.

Odysseus

    If you do wake anyone, do you know what their watchword is?

Diomedes

    I know it. It's "Phoebus." Dolon told me.

Odysseus

    Look!
    Here are some bivouacs of the enemy. But empty.

Diomedes

    Dolon spoke of this too. He said Hector should be sleeping   575
    here. And it is for Hector that this sword is drawn.

Odysseus

    What can it mean? Is there an ambush set up somewhere?

Diomedes

    He may have gone to work some stratagem against us.

Odysseus

    Hector is bold, very bold, now that he is winning.

Diomedes

What shall we do now, Odysseus? We hoped to find   580
our man asleep, but we've failed.

Odysseus

We must go back to our mooring-place as quick as we can.
Whatever god it is who grants him his success
is watching over him now. We must not force Fortune.

Diomedes

But should we not look for Aeneas? Or for that Phrygian   585
we hate worst of all, Paris? Cut his head off?

Odysseus

How, without deadly peril, can you find these men
in the dark, and here among our enemies?

Diomedes

But it is shameful to go back to the Argive ships
without doing our enemies the least damage.   590

Odysseus

How can you say you have done no damage? Did we not kill
Dolon, who scouted our ships? Do we not carry his armor
here, our spoils? Do you think you can rout their whole army?

Diomedes

You are right. Let us go back. May we only succeed!

> (*The voice of Athene is heard, but, though visible to the
> audience, she is not visible to the characters.*)

Athene

Where are you going? Why do you leave the Trojan camp   595
biting your very hearts for disappointed spite
because the god will not allow you to kill their Hector
or their Paris? Have you not heard of the ally,

Rhesus, who has come to Troy in no mean circumstance?
For if he survives this night and is alive tomorrow,   600
not even Achilles, and not Ajax with his spear,
can keep him from destroying all the Argive fleet,
smashing, demolishing your walls and storming in
to fight with level spears.
Kill him, and all is won. Let Hector bivouac   605
in peace, nor try to murder him.
His death shall come, but it shall come from another hand.

Odysseus

Athene, mistress, for I recognized your voice
and way of speaking that I know so well, and know
how you are always with me and watch over me,   610
tell me, where is this man sleeping whom you bid us
attack? Where is his station in the Trojan camp?

Athene

He is camped right here and has not joined the main army.
Hector gave him this place to sleep, outside the lines,
until this night passes and day comes, and by him   615
are picketed the horses from the Thracian
chariots, so white that you can see them through the dark
gleaming, as if they were the wings of swans on water.
Kill their master and bring these home to your camp,
spoils of surpassing splendor, for no place on earth   620
contains a team of chariot horses such as these.

Odysseus

Diomedes, yours be the work of killing Thracians—
or let me do it, and you look after the horses.

Diomedes

I will do the killing, you manage the horses.
You are the experienced one, the quick improviser.   625
One ought to place a man where he can do most good.

Athene

> Alexander is here, I see him, coming our way
> in haste. He must have heard from some of the guards
> confused rumors about the presence of enemies.

Diomedes

> Does he have others with him or is he by himself?   630

Athene

> He's alone. He seems to be making for where Hector sleeps,
> so he can report to him the presence of spies in the camp.

Diomedes

> Well, should he not be killed and his account settled?

Athene

> No. You must not go beyond what has been destined for you.
> There is no authority for you to kill this man.   635
> You came here, bringing their destined death to certain others.
> Do it. Dispatch. Now to this man I shall pretend
> I am his Cyprian ally, standing beside him
> in all perils. I'll hold him here with rotten lies.
> This I have said. But though my victim stands close by   640
> he's heard and knows nothing of what's in store for him.

> *(Diomedes and Odysseus vanish as Alexander [Paris] appears.)*

Paris

> Hector, my general, my brother, Hector I say,
> are you sleeping? How can you sleep? Waken, will you?
> Here is some enemy got close inside our lines;
> someone has come to rob us, or to spy on us.   645

Athene

> Fear not. Here is your faithful Aphrodite
> watching over you. Your war is my war. I do not forget
> your favor and your kindness to me. I am grateful,

and now, to your Trojan army in its high success
I come, bringing a friend and mighty man of war,   650
the Thracian, child of that divine maker of melodies,
the Muse herself; the River Strymon is named his father.

Paris

Always you are in truth the good friend of my city
and me. I think the best thing I ever did
in my life was to judge you first and win you to my city.   655
What brings me here—there are wild rumors flying about
among the sentries, nothing clear. Achaean spies
said to be among us. One man reports but has not seen them;
another saw them coming but knows nothing else
about it. This is why I came to Hector's quarters.   660

Athene

Never fear. There's nothing wrong in the camp.
Hector is gone to give the Thracians a place to sleep.

Paris

I trust you. I always believe what you say. I'll go
and keep my station, free of this anxiety.

Athene

Go, for your interests are always on my mind,   665
and all my purpose is to see my friends succeed.
Oh, you will learn soon how I shall take care of you.

(*Paris goes. Athene calls inward to Odysseus and Diomedes.*)

You two, in there. You are too bold. You, I am calling
you, son of Laertes, put your sharp sword away.
Our Thracian captain's down.   670
We have his horses, but the enemy are aware
and coming at you. Now is the time for speed, speed,
to run for where the ships are moored. What keeps you?
The enemy are upon you. Save your lives.

(From one side Odysseus and Diomedes, from the other the
Chorus of Trojan sentries, come cautiously on,
and run into each other, to their mutual
surprise, as Athene vanishes.)

First Soldier

There they go, there!

Second Soldier

Shoot, shoot.   675

Third Soldier

Spear them.

Fourth Soldier

Who is it? Look! That's the man I mean.

Fifth Soldier

They have come to rob us in the night, and they have roused the
camp.

Leader

This way all.   680

Sixth Soldier

Here they are. We have them fast.

Leader

What's your regiment? Where do you come from? Who are you?

Odysseus

Nothing for you to know. You have done an evil day's work.
You shall die.

Leader

Tell me the watchword, will you, before you get this spear stuck
through your chest.

Odysseus

Stop. There's no danger.

Leader

Bring him here. Now, everyone, strike him.   685

Odysseus

Was it you killed Rhesus?

Leader

No. You tried to kill him. We'll kill *you!*

Odysseus

Hold hard everyone.

Leader

We will not.

Odysseus

Hold. You must not kill a friend.

Leader

What's the watchword?

Odysseus

Phoebus.

Leader

I acknowledge it. Down spears all.
Do you know where the men have got to?

Odysseus

Yes, I saw them go this way.

> (*He points. As the Leader and his men start in
> that direction, Odysseus and Diomedes
> slip out on the opposite side.*)

Leader

On their trail, then, everyone.

Seventh Soldier

                  Should we raise a general alarm?   690

Leader

No. It would be bad to disturb our friends with an alarm in the
night.

> *(All go off, but almost immediately begin to
> return, singing the following ode as
> they re-enter severally.)*

Chorus

Who was the man who was here?
Who is it so hardy that he shall boast
that he escaped my hand?
Where shall I find him now?   695
What shall I think he can be,
that man who came on fearless foot through the dark
across the stations of our ranks and our guards?
Some Thessalian
or some dweller in a seaside Locrian city?   700
One whose living is made on the scattered islands?
Who was it? Where did he come from? What country?
Which god does he acknowledge as god supreme?

First Soldier

Was this the work of Odysseus after all? Or whose?

Second Soldier

If we are to judge by past deeds, who else?   705

First Soldier

You think so?

Second Soldier

            I must do.

First Soldier

He has been bold against us?

Third Soldier

    Bold? Who? Whom are you praising?

First Soldier

                  Odysseus.

Third Soldier

    Never praise him, that thief, that treacherous fighter.

Chorus

    He came once before   710
    into our citadel, bleary eyed
    and huddled in a disguise
    of rags, his sword hand
    hidden under his clothes,
    begging his bread he crept in, a wretched vagrant,   715
    dirty, unkempt, foul.
    and much evil he spoke
    against the royal house of the sons of Atreus
    as if he had hated all the lords of their host.
    I wish he had died, died as he deserved   720
    before he ever set foot on the Phrygian shore.

Leader

    Whether it was Odysseus or not, I am afraid.
    We are the picket, and Hector will hold us to blame.

First Soldier

    With what charge?

Leader

    With curses.

First Soldier

    For doing what? What do you fear?   725

Leader

    Because they got through us.

First Soldier
Who did?

Leader

Those men who got into the Phrygian camp tonight.

Thracian Charioteer (within)

Oh god. Disaster.

Leader

Listen!
Silence. Keep your places all. Perhaps someone is in our nets.   730

Charioteer

Halloo, help!
Disaster and ruin of the Thracians.

Leader
This is one of our allies

in pain or terror.

Charioteer (entering)

Halloo!
I am hurt, I am done. And you, lord of the Thracians,
how hateful that day you saw Troy,
what an end to your life.   735

Leader

You must be one of our allies, but who? My eyes
fail me in the dark. I cannot clearly make you out.

Charioteer

Where can I find some chief of the Trojans?
Where is Hector himself?
Drowsing somewhere, sleeping under arms?   740
Is there none in command to whom I can report
what happened to us, what someone has done

and got clean away, vanished, leaving plain to see
the hurt he inflicted on the Thracians?

Leader

Some mishap has come to the Thracian force, it seems   745
from what this man says.

Charioteer

The army is shattered, the king is killed
by a traitor's stroke,
and oh, my own wound hurts   750
deep and bleeds. Shall I die? Must both
Rhesus and I be basely killed
in Troy, which we came to help?

Leader

There is no mystery in ill news he reports
now; it is plain that some of our allies are killed.   755

Charioteer

There has been wickedness done here. More than wickedness;
shame too, which makes the evil double its own bulk.
To die with glory, if one has to die at all,
is still, I think, pain for the dier, surely so,
but grandeur left for his survivors, honor for his house.   760
But death to us came senseless and inglorious.
When Hector with his own hand led us to our quarters
and gave us the watchword, we lay down to sleep, worn out
with the fatigue of our long march. No one kept watch
in our contingent for that night, nor were our arms   765
stacked out in order, nor were the goads in place beside
the yokes of the horses, since our king had been assured
that you were masters of the field and your pickets threatened
their anchorage; so we dropped in our tracks, and grossly slept.
Yet my own heart was restless, and I woke again   770
to give some fodder to the horses, thinking we must

harness them for the dawn's fighting, so I heaped their food
lavishly. Now I see two fellows stealing through our camp
in the dim dark, but when I started in their direction
they dodged away and made off.   775
I called out and warned them to stay away from the camp.
I thought some of the allies had gone out to steal
from us.
        No reply.
                I did not give it another thought.
I went back to where I had been, and slept again.
But now there came an apparition to my sleep.   780
Those horses, that I trained and drove as charioteer
at Rhesus' side, I saw them, as one sees in a dream,
but wolves had got astride their backs and rode them now,
and stabbed and gored their backs and rumps with goads, and
    the mares
went wild with terror, bucking and fighting, snorting   785
from flared nostrils.
I started up to drive those savage beasts away
from the mares, for the dream's terror had awakened me.
As I raised my head I heard a moan such as men make
when they die, and a jet of hot fresh blood splashed me. It came 790
from my master, who had been murdered, and died hard.
I leapt upright, but there was no spear in my hand,
and as I looked about and fumbled for a weapon
somebody coming close up slashed me hard in the side
with a sword. I took and felt a cut from the blade   795
that ripped me deep.
I fell on my face. He and the other man seized the team
and car, mounted, galloped away, and escaped.
Ah.
I am faint from my wound, I cannot stand.
I know what happened, for I saw it, but do not   800
understand in what way these men could have been killed
nor what hand killed them. I can guess.
My guess is that our friends were the ones who hurt us.

Leader

    O charioteer of that unfortunate Thracian king,

    do not be angry with us. The enemy did this.   805

    And here is Hector in person, who has heard the news

    and comes, I think, in sympathy for your misfortune.

                                    (Hector enters hastily.)

Hector (to the Chorus)

    You are responsible for a disaster. How did it happen

    that these marauders sent out by the enemy

    got past you and made havoc in our camp? Disgraceful!   810

    Why did you neither head them off as they came in

    nor catch them as they went out? Someone will pay for this,

    and who but you? I hold you responsible. You had the watch.

    Now they are gone, untouched, and much amused, no doubt,

    with the feebleness of the Trojans, and of me, their leader.   815

    I tell you now—father Zeus be witness to my oath—

    death by flogging or by the headsman's ax awaits you

    for your part in this. Else, say Hector is a weakling.

    Say he is nothing.

Chorus

    No, no!   820

    We came to you, lord, defender of the city, we did,

    we came (it must have been these),

    we told you their fires were burning beside the ships.

    Since then, all through the night's vigil   825

    our eyes have not deadened, they have not slept,

    by the springs of Simois we swear it. O my lord,

    do not be angry with us. None of all this

    that has happened is our fault.

    If again, in the course of time, you prove we have said or done   830

    anything wrong, then bury us

    alive in the ground. We will not protest.

Charioteer (to Hector)

You are Barbarian, so are we. Why do you parry
my charge by threatening these men? Why make a Greek
lawyer's speech here?
You did this.
               We Thracians,   835
the wounded and the dead, will not be satisfied
with anyone else. It would take you a long and artful speech
to convince me that you have not been killing your friends.
You coveted those horses. For their sake, you murdered
your own allies, whose coming you had begged so hard.   840
They did come. They are dead. When Paris shamed hospitality
he was better than you—you murderer of your friends and
    helpers.
Never tell me it was one of the Argives
got through to destroy us. Who could slip through the Trojan
    lines
without detection and reach us?   845
You and the whole of the Phrygian army lay between.
Who of your own particular allies is dead,
or wounded, by those enemies you speak of? We
who lay beyond are wounded, some, while others fared worse
and do not look any longer on the light of the sun.   850
I tell you plain. I do not think this was any Achaean.
Who could pick a path through the enemy in the dark
and find where Rhesus lay—unless they were directed
by a god? They would not even know
of his arrival. Your defense is artificial.   855

Hector

We have had the help of our allies through all the time
that the Achaean army has been on our shores,
and not one word of complaint has come from any of them
of ill treatment. You would be our first. I hope
no greed for horses ever makes me kill my friends   860
to get them. This is more of Odysseus. What man else

among the Argives could have planned and done it?
I fear him. The thought, too, racks my mind,
he might have chanced to meet Dolon and killed him. Dolon
has been gone for a long time, and there's no sign of him.   865

Charioteer

I don't know what "Odysseuses" you're talking about.
I do know we're hurt, and it was no enemy did it.

Hector

Since you cannot think otherwise, you must think this.

Charioteer

O land of my fathers, how can I reach you, and there die?

Hector

No dying. Too many have died already.   870

Charioteer

I have lost my masters. Where shall I turn me?

Hector

My own house will take you in and make you well.

Charioteer

How shall the hands of his murderers take care of me?

Hector

This man keeps saying the same thing. He will not stop.

Charioteer

Perish the murderer. I do not mean you,   875
you need not protest. The Spirit of Justice knows who did it.

Hector

Take him up. Help him into my house,
then look after him carefully, so that he will not
be complaining any more.

        You go to the forces on the wall,
to Priam and the elders. Tell them it is time   880
to bury these dead beside the highway where it leaves
our city.

        (Some soldiers [not the Chorus] lift the Thracian
        charioteer and carry him out, while others
        leave to deliver the last message.)

Chorus

After our high success, does the god
now change Troy's luck, bring us back, to suffer
new losses? What does he plan?

        (The Muse appears above, holding in her
        arms the body of Rhesus.)

But see, see,   885
my King, over your head, what goddess
hovers, carrying aloft in her arms
the man lately slain?
A pitiful sight. It fills me with fear.

The Muse

Behold me, Trojans, and fear not. I am the Muse,   890
one of the Nine and prized among the poets, who stand
before you. I have seen the death of my dear son
so sadly slain by the enemy. His killer, treacherous
Odysseus, some day shall be punished as he deserves.

With my own song of mourning   895
I mourn you, my child. Oh, you hurt
your mother when you went
that day to Troy,
a cursed, wretched way.
I would not have had you go, but you went.   900
Your father restrained you, but you broke away.
I mourn you, my child, dear,
dearest head, I mourn you.

Chorus

I, too, as much as ever one can grieve
who has no kinship with the dead, grieve for your son.   905

The Muse

Perish the scion of Oeneus.
Perish the son of Laertes.
He made me childless, who had
the best child in the world.
Perish the woman who forsook   910
her Greek home for a Phrygian bed.
She, dearest son, she is your true destroyer,
she, who made the unnumbered cities
empty of the brave.
Philammon's son, who live and die your many lives   915
and deaths, you have struck back and wounded me deep,
O Thamyris.
Rude violence did all. It brought you down. The quarrel
of the Muses, too, made me bear this unhappy son;
for as I waded through the waters of the Strymon,
the River-God was on me, I was in his arms   920
and conceived. It was when we Muses, all arrayed
with instruments, went to the gold-soiled mountain-mass
of Pangaeus, and the high contest of melody
with that great Thracian singer, and we blinded him,
Thamyris, who had vilified our craft of song.   925
When you were born, in shame over my maidenhood
and before my sisters, I flung you into the great waters
of your father, and Strymon gave you into the care
of no mortals, but the maiden nymphs of his own springs
who nursed you to perfection and then sent you forth,   930
child, to be king of Thrace and first of mortal men.
There in the bloody valors of your land's defense
I never feared your death.
Only to Troy I warned you you must never go
knowing what waited you there, but Hector's embassies   935

and the repeated conclaves of the men of state
persuaded you to move to the defense of friends.

Athene! You alone are guilty of this death.
Odysseus and the son of Tydeus were your agents,
they could have done nothing. Never think I do not know.   940
And yet I and my sister Muses make your Athens
great in our art, and by our presence in the land;
and it was Orpheus, own blood cousin to this man
you have slain, who first instructed your people in the rites
of mystery and secrets revealed; last, it was we   945
the sisters who with Phoebus educated
Musaeus, your great and respected citizen,
so he surpassed our other pupils.
Here is your gratitude. I hold my son in my arms
and mourn him.
        I need no advocate, Athene.

Chorus

Hector, that Thracian charioteer with his mad charge   950
that we plotted Rhesus' murder is proved wrong.

Hector

I knew that well. It took no divination
to see the hand of Odysseus in this warrior's death.
And as for my part, when I saw the Greek army camped
on our shores, what should I do but send my heralds out   955
to our allies and ask them to come and help?
I sent heralds. This man was in my debt. He came to help.
But do not think I am unmoved by his death.
I am even ready to make him a great funeral mound
and burn the glory of innumerable robes.   960
He was my friend. He came to help. His loss is mourned.

The Muse

Rhesus will not go to the black meadow in the earth.
So much at least I claim from the infernal bride,

the daughter of Demeter, goddess of the fields,
that she remit his life. She is in debt to me   965
for her ordaining of the Orphics' revelations.
For me he will be as one dead, with no more light
in his eyes, for the rest of time. He will not come again
to where he looks upon his mother any more.
Hidden deep in the caves among the silver mines   970
he shall live on, a human Spirit underground,
where Bacchus' medium under the Pangaean horn
is housed, a holy god to the initiate.
The load of grief that I must bear is lighter
than that of the sea goddess. Her son too must die.   975
I with my sisters first shall dirge your death, my son,
then mourn Achilles, on Thetis' day of sorrow.
Pallas, who killed you, cannot save him.
Apollo's quiver holds the shaft which means his death.

O making of children, hapless work, sorrow of mankind,   980
the man who reasons well
will live his life through childless and not risk the children
whom some day he must bury.

(*The Muse disappears.*)

Leader

Rhesus is in his mother's hands, and she will mourn him.
Hector, your work lies now before you. It is dawn.   985
It is time. What would you have us do?

Hector

About your business. Tell the allies to arm with speed,
and yoke their horses to the chariots,
then, when full armed, await the call of the Tyrrhenian
trumpet. For I am confident we can overrun
the camp and walls of the Achaeans, fire their ships,   990
and that this sunlight that begins to climb
brings us of Troy our day of liberty.

Leader

Obey the King. Let us march, well armed,
in good order, give the word
to the allies. Who knows? The god who is on our side   995
might grant us the victory.

THE SUPPLIANT WOMEN

Translated and with an Introduction by Frank William Jones

INTRODUCTION TO
THE SUPPLIANT WOMEN

Tʜɪs play, which may be dated between 420 and 415 B.C., deals
with the aftermath of the war stirred up against Eteocles, a son of
Oedipus, by his brother Polynices, who had quarreled with him over
the kingship of Thebes after their father's death. Aeschylus, in *Seven
against Thebes;* Sophocles, in *Antigone* and *Oedipus at Colonus;* and
Euripides, in *The Phoenician Women*, present other aspects of this
story of rival brothers. Euripides here concerns himself not with the
rights and wrongs of the dispute, but with the sufferings war brings
to civilians. The play is best understood as a plea against inhumanity,
especially in wartime. It is similar, in this respect, to Euripides' *The
Trojan Women*, with the addition of a scene or two in favor of de-
mocracy, suggesting that the basic decencies of life have a better
chance of being observed under popular than under autocratic gov-
ernment. And yet eloquent praises of peace (ll. 476–93) are put into
the mouth of an antidemocratic person. Historically, this may reflect
the war-weariness of the time; artistically, it shows that Euripides,
like Shaw, lets all his parties have their say and say it well.

The action of the play is primarily ethical and political. Individual
feelings take a minor role. Aethra, as her son points out (l. 292), has
nothing to gain or lose by supporting the plea of the mothers of the
seven warriors who fell in the attempt on the Theban throne. Theseus, at first reluctant to do anything for the pathetic Adrastus, overcomes his dislike of that ineffective person to the extent of defending
his cause by force. It is evident that Euripides is holding Theseus up
as an example of civic virtue, which he sees as flexible but not pliant
—ready to change, for the better, under the influence of moral and
religious arguments.

With Aethra and Theseus, models of principled moderation,
Adrastus and Evadne provide an effective contrast. Both of them are
capable of being carried away by feeling: Adrastus by guilt and
shame, Evadne by love and grief. And both of them shock and repel

better-balanced people: Adrastus irritates Theseus, Evadne horrifies her father and even the chorus, who interrupt their grief over their fallen sons to express amazement at Evadne's suicide (ll. 1072, 1076). Here Euripides' pity for humanity finds noble expression. He sees how war, and other extreme situations, bring out the essence of every individual: self-reproach in Adrastus, fanatical loyalty in Evadne, filial devotion in the sons of the Seven. And he also feels deeply the futility and cruelty of war, which keeps breeding new wars from old (ll. 1142–49), kills the noblest men, and lets Adrastus survive. With the morbid timidity of this king's actions and attitudes—for example, in lines 765–69—we may contrast the excellences he sees in his fallen companions (ll. 856–917). Yet even Adrastus redeems himself, somewhat, in the course of the action: his utterances become less hysterical and self-pitying, and he speaks out as an advocate of peace (ll. 949–54). He represents, in his fashion, the type of tragic hero who learns by suffering.

The intervention of Athene, at the end of the play, may seem pointless to modern readers. The passage possibly refers to an alliance of Athens with Argos, about 420 B.C. At any rate, Euripides here leaves the territory of philanthropic principle and talks hard political sense. Or perhaps he is suggesting that one is not much use without the other.

Lines 176–83 present some difficulty. It is likely that the poet is here defending himself against charges that he broke the decorum of tragedy by presenting paupers and slaves as serious personages. In lines 180–83, he is perhaps implying that sad scenes in a man's plays do not mean that he leads a sad life. The passage as a whole has little to do with what Adrastus is saying. Perhaps it was interpolated from another play, or lines linking it with Adrastus' main point have been lost. The opening of Theseus' answer (ll. 195–200) does not refer directly to anything Adrastus has said. It may be aimed at pessimistic implications of lines 176–79, which present life as perpetual conflict between wealth and poverty. These implications were perhaps more clearly worked out in the correct text. Whatever Adrastus said, Theseus thought he was questioning the motives or the very existence of the gods, on the ground that human life has more bad than good in it.

Lines 1026–30 are obscure in the original. Evadne seems to be inveighing against marriage, perhaps to fortify her resolve to die with the man she loves; but her picture of a happy home life belies her embittered intent. Either Euripides is being very subtle here or the text is corrupt.

The translation follows Gilbert Murray's text as edited by T. Nicklin (Oxford, 1936). At line 763 there is a lacuna, which I have ventured to fill with a question from Adrastus, as Nicklin suggests. But lines 844–45 of the Oxford text appear as lines 858–59 in this translation. If Theseus said (as he does in the text) "I saw the deeds . . . by which they hoped to take the city," it would mean that he had witnessed the attack of the Seven against Thebes. This is unlikely, and since the words would come much more properly from Adrastus at this point, I have transferred them to him. For similar reasons, line 162, spoken by Adrastus in the Oxford text, has been transferred to Theseus, as Valckenaer recommends.

THE SUPPLIANT WOMEN

CHARACTERS

Aethra, mother of Theseus

Theseus, king of Athens

Adrastus, king of Argos, and leader of the Theban adventure

A Herald from Thebes

A Messenger from Thebes

Evadne, widow of Capaneus, who fell in the Theban adventure

Iphis, her father

Athene

Chorus: Mothers of the Seven against Thebes

A group of sons of the fallen fighters

THE SUPPLIANT WOMEN

SCENE: *The temple of Demeter, at Eleusis, near Athens.*

Aethra

Demeter, enshrined in this land Eleusis,
And you who tend the goddess' temple,
Bless me and bless Theseus my son
And the city of Athens, and Pittheus' land,
Where in prosperous halls my father reared me,   5
Aethra, and wed me to Pandion's son
Aegeus, as Loxias' oracle bade him.

So I pray as I look upon these women
Burdened with years, who left their homes in Argos
To fall with suppliant branches at my feet   10
In dreadful loss: their seven noble sons
Are dead at Cadmus' gates, and they are childless.
Adrastus, lord of Argos, led the men
To claim for his son-in-law, exiled Polynices,
A share of Oedipus' inheritance.   15
They perished in the struggle, and their mothers
Desire to bury them; but those in power
Spurn what the gods hold lawful and refuse
Even to grant removal of the bodies.
The burden of these women's need for me   20
Adrastus also bears: look where he lies,
With tearful face mourning the grievous doom
That met the army he despatched from home.
Through me he seeks a champion in my son
Who shall prevail by words or force of arms   25
To take the dead and give them burial.
Only this he asks of my child and Athens.

My visit was for sacrifice
That the land be fruitful; I left my house

For this sanctuary, where soonest   30
The corn-ear bristles above the ground.
And still I stay by the holy hearth
Wearing a bondless bond of leaves,
In pity for these gray, childless mothers   35
And reverence for their sacred wreaths.
I have sent a herald to town, to summon
Theseus, that either he drive from the land
These people and the distress they bring,
Or free them from their suppliant needs—
A pious action for the gods.   40
It is proper for women, if they are wise,
Always to get things done by men.

Chorus

I appeal to you
From aged mouth:
Old, I fall at your knee.
Free my children—   45
Left by lawless men
To body-slackening death,
Food for mountain beasts!
See the piteous
Tears at my eyelids
And wrinkled tearings of hands   50
At hoary flesh
Because I could not lay out
My dead sons in my house
Or see their tombs of earth!

Gracious lady, you too have borne a son,
In blessing of the bed   55
For your husband: now to me
Grant a part of your loving-kindness,
In recompense for grievous pain

From the death of those I bore:
Prevail, we beg, upon your son   60
That he go to Ismenus and bring to my hands
The bodies of youthful dead that long for the tomb.

Not for holy rites but in need I came
To fall and pray at the goddesses'
Fire-receiving altars;
Justice is ours, and you have power—   65
For you are happy in your child—
To take away my trouble.
My plight is pitiful: I beseech
Your son to bring to these poor hands
The corpse, my son's sad limbs, for my embrace.   70

(The temple attendants begin to chant.)

And now the strife of wailing, wailing!
Cry against cry, clashing of priestesses' hands!
Let blows resound together!
Moan in the strain
Of the dance that Hades loves!   75
Bloody the white fingernail
Along the cheek, and stain the skin!
To mourn the dead
Brings honor to those who live.

Insatiable delight of wailing,
Abounding in labor, carries me away,
As from a towering rock   80
Cool water flows
Unceasing ever: I wail,
For to bear the death of children brings
A labor of lament to women.   85
Would that in death
I might forget these griefs!

(Enter Theseus, attended.)

Theseus

>What were those wails I heard, and breast-beating,
>And dirges for the dead? Here, from the temple,
>The echoes came. Alarm takes hold of me:
>My mother has been long away from home;   90
>I come to find her; has she met with trouble?
>
>Aha! What's there? I see strange things to talk of!
>My aged mother sitting by the altar,
>And foreign women with her, all awry
>In shapes of woe: from age-dimmed eyes they shed   95
>Piteous tears to earth; their hair is shorn,
>The robes they wear are not for festivals.
>Mother, what does this mean? Yours to reveal,
>And mine to listen. I expect some ill.

Aethra

>These women, child, are mothers of the sons—   100
>Seven commanders—who died at Cadmus' gates;
>And now with suppliant boughs they watch and wait,
>Circled around me, as you see, my son.

Theseus

>And that one, groaning bitterly at the door?

Aethra

>They say he is Adrastus, lord of Argos.   105

Theseus

>And the boys beside him? Children of the women?

Aethra

>No, they are sons of the warriors who fell.

Theseus

>Why do they stretch out suppliant hands to us?

Aethra

I know; but let them have the word, my son.

Theseus

I call on you, hidden beneath your cloak!　　　　　110
Leave off your wailing, bare your head and speak:
Nothing goes far that does not pass the tongue.

Adrastus

O glorious victor king
Of the land of the men of Athens,
Theseus: I come as suppliant
To you and to your city.

Theseus

What do you seek, and what is your need?　　　　　115

Adrastus

You know of my ruinous campaign.

Theseus

Your passage through Greece was hardly silent.

Adrastus

In it I lost the chiefs of Argos.

Theseus

Such are the doings of wretched war.

Adrastus

I went to the city to find the dead.　　　　　120

Theseus

For burial, by the laws of war?

Adrastus

And now the slayers will not let me.

Theseus

What are their grounds? Your wish is sacred.

Adrastus

They have no grounds. They are bad winners.

Theseus

So you come to me for advice—or what?   125

Adrastus

I want you to bring back Argos' sons.

Theseus

And where stands Argos? Are her boasts vain?

Adrastus

Defeated, finished. We come to you.

Theseus

By your design or that of all the city?

Adrastus

We, the Danaids, beg you to bury our dead.   130

Theseus

Why did you go with seven bands to Thebes?

Adrastus

To please the men who married my two daughters.

Theseus

To which of the Argives did you give your children?

Adrastus

The bond I formed was not among my kind.

Theseus

To strangers, then, you wedded Argive girls?   135

Adrastus

Yes: Tydeus, and Polynices, of Theban stock.

Theseus

How did you come to want them for your kin?

Adrastus

Puzzling riddles of Phoebus lured me on.

Theseus

What words of Apollo meant marriage for the maidens?

Adrastus

That I give my daughters to a boar and a lion.   140

Theseus

And how did you unravel the god's pronouncement?

Adrastus

The pair of exiles came to my door at night—

Theseus

What pair? You speak of two at once: explain.

Adrastus

Tydeus and Polynices—and fought each other.

Theseus

They were the beasts? You gave your girls to them?   145

Adrastus

Yes, they looked like two wild creatures fighting.

Theseus

Why had they left the borders of their countries?

Adrastus

Tydeus in guilt of shedding kindred blood.

Theseus

And what brought Oedipus' son away from Thebes?

Adrastus

A father's curse: that he should kill his brother.   150

Theseus

Then voluntary flight was wise of him.

Adrastus

True; but those remaining wronged the absent.

Theseus

You mean his brother robbed him of his goods?

Adrastus

That is the case I went to judge; and lost.

Theseus

You asked the seers, and watched their victims burn?   155

Adrastus

Ah! You pursue me to my weakest point.

Theseus

The gods, it seems, did not approve your mission.

Adrastus

It also flouted Amphiaraus' will.

Theseus

So lightly you ignored divinity?

Adrastus

Unruliness of youthful men confused me.   160

Theseus

You followed strength of heart, not strength of mind—
A course that ruins many generals.

Adrastus

O Lord of Athens! Crown of power in Hellas!
I am ashamed—a gray-haired man who once
Was king, and fortunate—that now I fall
To earth and clasp your knee; and yet I must   165
Submit to my disaster. Save my dead!
Have pity on my woes, and on these mothers
Of fallen sons! Struck childless in old age   170
With feeble limbs they come to a strange land—
Not to attend Demeter's mysteries,
But seeking burial of the dead whose hands,
In manly duty, should have buried *them*.   175
The sight of poverty is wise for wealth;
The poor should gaze with envy on the rich,
To learn the love of goods; untroubled men
Are well advised to look at wretchedness.
The poet bringing songs into the world   180
Should work in joy. If this is not his mood,
He cannot—being inwardly distressed—
Give pleasure outwardly. That stands to reason.
You may well ask: "Why pass by Pelops' land,
And seek to lay this task of yours on Athens?"   185
In fairness, I would make this answer. Sparta
Is fierce; her ways are artful; and the others
Are small and weak. Yours is the only city
With strength enough to undertake the task:
She sees what misery is and has for leader,   190
In you, a good and youthful shepherd; ruin
Has come to many states for lack of such command.

Chorus

Theseus! I join my prayer to his:
Pity my wretchedness.

Theseus

I have heard such arguments before, from others,   195
And fought them hard. It has been said that life
Holds more of worse conditions than of better;
But I oppose that doctrine. I believe
The good outweighs the bad in human life.
If it did not, the light would not be ours.   200
I praise the god who set our life in order,
Lifting it out of savagery and confusion.
First he put wits in us, and then gave language,
Envoy of words, to understand the voice;
And fruits of earth to eat, and for this food   205
Watery drops from heaven, to quench our thirst
And nourish the yield of the land; providing also
The fortress winter, against the sun-god's fire,
And commerce over sea, that by exchange
A country may obtain the goods it lacks.   210
Things without mark, not clearly visible,
Are brought to light by seers who study fire,
The folds of entrails, and the flight of birds.
Now, if all this is not enough for us—
So well equipped for living, by God's gift—   215
Are we not pettish? But intelligence
Wants more than heavenly power; our minds grow proud,
Until we think we are wiser than the gods.
That is the brand of folly you have shown.
First, bowing to Phoebus' words, like one who thinks   220
The gods exist, you gave your girls to strangers:
A mating of fair with foul, to hurt your house!
Wrongdoers' bodies should not be joined to the just;
A wise man will ally his family
With well-regarded people. Sickness spreads: 225
A man may do no wrong; yet, if he suffers
From the same ill as one marked out for ruin,
God fells them both at once.

                              Then, when you took
All Argos with you on that expedition,
The seers spoke omens but you slighted them,   230
Flouted the gods, and laid your city low.
You were led astray by glory-loving youngsters,
Promoters of unjust wars, who spoil the townsmen.
One of them wants to be a general;
Another to seize power and riot in it;   235
A third is set on gain. They never think
What harm this brings for the majority.
The classes of citizens are three. The rich
Are useless, always lusting after more.
Those who have not, and live in want, are a menace,   240
Ridden with envy and fooled by demagogues;
Their malice stings the owners. Of the three,
The middle part saves cities: it guards the order   245
A community establishes.
                              And so
I am to be your ally? What fine words
Will make my citizens favor that? Farewell!
You planned your actions poorly. Take what comes:
Wrestle with fate alone, and let me be.

Chorus

  He blundered. That is natural in the young,   250
  And should be pardoned in him. We have come
  To you, my lord, as healer of these ills.

Adrastus

  In choosing you, my lord, I did not think
  That you would sit in judgment on my woes,
  Or estimate and punish any act   255
  I may have lacked the skill to carry out;
  I only wanted help. If you refuse,
  I have no choice; I must obey.

Now, aged dames, go forth. Lay on that spot
The verdant twigs, and turn the leaves face down,
Calling to witness heaven and earth and sun   260
And Queen Demeter, bearer of the torch,
That prayers to the gods availed us nothing.

Chorus

O King, you are of Pelops' line, and we are from his country:
The same ancestral blood is ours. How can it be
That *you* forsake this cause, and drive out of your land   265
Old women who have gained nothing that is owed them?
We pray you not to do this. Beasts have rocks for refuge;
Slaves, the altars of the gods; city huddles with city
When storms come. Nothing mortal prospers to the end.   270

—Woman of sorrows! Leave Persephone's sacred ground;
Go up to him and put your hands about his knees;
Beg him to bring my sons' dead bodies—Oh, the grief!
The young men whom I lost beneath Cadmean walls.

—Alas! these poor old hands: take them, guide them, support   275
them.

—Friend! Honor and glory of Hellas! I touch your beard;
Here at your knees I fall and seek your hand in my woe.

—If you would shelter a wanderer, pity me—   280
Suppliant for my children, piteously lamenting.

—Child! I appeal to you: do not leave boys your age
Unburied in Cadmus' land, to gladden the wild beasts!

—I fall and clasp your knees: see the tears at my eyelids!
I beg you, bring to fulfilment the burial of my children!   285

Theseus

Mother: you hold your fine-spun cloak to your eyes.
Why do you weep? Is it because you hear

The lamentations uttered by these women?
Somehow, they pierce me too. Raise your white head:
No more tears, at Demeter's sacred hearth!   290

Aethra

  Alas!

Theseus

      Their troubles should not make you moan.

Aethra

  Poor women!

Theseus

          You do not belong to them.

Aethra

  Child! May I speak, for the city's good and yours?

Theseus

  Many wise things are said even by women.

Aethra

  I shrink from showing what I have in mind.   295

Theseus

  It is shameful to hold back words that might help your kin.

Aethra

  I would not now be still, and afterward
  Blame myself for a silence wrongly kept;
  Or fear that women's well-meant words are wasted,
  And in that dread let my good will be lost.   300
  My child: I bid you: first, look to the gods;
  For if you slight them you will fall. Intentions
  Good in themselves are wrecked by that one fault.
  If you were asked to launch an enterprise
  That would not right a wrong, then certainly   305

I would be silent. But you must be told
How greatly it would honor you (so much
That I am not afraid to urge it, child!)
If cruel men, who would deny the dead
The rights of burial and their funerals,
Were forced to grant this, by your hand, and stopped   310
From violating what all Greece holds lawful.
The power that keeps cities of men together
Is noble preservation of the laws.
It will be said that, lacking manly strength,
You stood aside in fear and lost a chance   315
To win a crown of glory for the city.
They will say you hunted boars, a mean pursuit,
And proved a coward at the call of action,
The time for spear and helmet. Child of mine,
This must not be! Remember your descent!   320
Do you see your country's Gorgon stare when taunted
With lack of resolution? Athens thrives
On strenuous action; but the states that work
In stealth and darkness wear a somber look   325
To match their caution. Child, will you not help
The dead, and these poor women in their need?
Your setting forth is just; I do not dread it.
The sons of Cadmus now have won the throw,
But soon the dice will fall another way.   330
I hold this certain. God reverses all.

Chorus

O best-loved lady! Nobly have you spoken,
For him and me, giving a double joy.

Theseus

Mother, what I have said about this man
I still consider right. I spoke my mind   335
On the designs that led him to his ruin.
But I also see the truth of what you tell me:

That it is not in keeping with my ways
To run from risk. By many noble deeds
I have made myself a byword to the Greeks: 340
They count on me to punish wickedness.
I am unable to refuse a task.
What then will hostile persons say of me
If you, my parent, you who fear for me,
Must urge me first to undertake this labor?   345
Forward, then; I shall go and free the dead.
Persuasion first: if that does not succeed,
Then force of arms will gain my end. The gods
Will not be jealous. I desire the city
With all its voices to approve this plan.
It will approve because I want it to: 350
But if I state my reasons, I shall have
More favor from the people, whom I made
Sole rulers when I set their city free
And gave them equal votes. So I shall take
Adrastus to support my argument
And go to all the citizens assembled,   355
Convince them that this must be done, pick out
A group of young Athenians, and return.
Then, resting on my weapons, I shall send
To ask the bodies of the dead from Creon.
Matrons: take off my mother's ritual garlands.
I must conduct her to the house of Aegeus,   360
Clasping her loving hand. I think it wrong
That a child should not return his parents' care.
Noblest of gifts! by granting it, he earns
From his own children what he gives his elders.

Chorus

Argos, my fatherland, pasture of horses: 365
You heard him speak, you heard from the king
Words that respect the gods,
Words that mean greatness for Greece and Argos.

May he go to the end of my woes, and beyond;
May he bear the mother's murdered idol   370
Away, and then make friendship
Firm with the land of Inachus.

A work of piety brings honor and glory to cities
And earns thanks that last forever.
What dare I hope from the city? Will it truly gain   375
A pledge of friendship, and graves for my sons?

City of Pallas! A mother begs you to prevent
The desecration of human law.
You revere right, despise crime, and are ready
Always to help ill-fated men.   380

Theseus (*to an Athenian herald*)
   The skill you have as bearer of proclamations
   Has given constant service to me and the city.
   Now you must cross the streams Asopus and Ismenus
   And tell the haughty ruler of the Cadmeans this:
   "Theseus asks you, by your grace, to bury the dead. His country   385
   Neighbors yours, and he believes the request is worth the
       granting.
   Do this and you will have all of Erechtheus' folk for friends."
   If they consent, commend them and hasten back.
   If they refuse, deliver a second message:
   "Welcome my band of revelers, men who carry shields!"   390
   A ready task-force waits, under review,
   Here and now at the sacred Fount of the Dance.
   The city, when it saw I willed this effort,
   Was ready to accept it, even glad.

   But who comes here, to interrupt my words?   395
   I cannot tell for sure; he seems to be
   A Theban herald. Stay a while. His coming
   Might change my plans, and you would be released.

(Enter a Herald from Thebes.)

Herald

What man is master in this land? To whom
Must I give the word I bring from Creon, ruler　　　400
In Cadmus' country since Eteocles
Fell at his brother Polynices' hand
Beside the seven-mouthed gates?

Theseus

　　　　　　　　　　One moment, stranger.
Your start was wrong, seeking a master here.
This city is free, and ruled by no one man.　　　405
The people reign, in annual succession.
They do not yield the power to the rich;
The poor man has an equal share in it.

Herald

That one point gives the better of the game
To me. The town I come from is controlled　　　410
By one man, not a mob. And there is no one
To puff it up with words, for private gain,
Swaying it this way, that way. Such a man
First flatters it with wealth of favors; then
He does it harm, but covers up his blunders　　　415
By blaming other men, and goes scot-free.
The people is no right judge of arguments;
Then how can it give right guidance to a city?
A poor man, working hard, could not attend　　　420
To public matters, even if ignorance
Were not his birthright. When a wretch, a nothing,
Obtains respect and power from the people
By talk, his betters sicken at the sight.　　　425

Theseus

What bombast from a herald! Waster of words,
If it is argument you want—and you yourself

« 153 »

Have set the contest going—listen. Nothing
Is worse for a city than an absolute ruler.
In earliest days, before the laws are common,   430
One man has power and makes the law his own:
Equality is not yet. With written laws,
People of small resources and the rich
Both have the same recourse to justice. Now
A man of means, if badly spoken of,
Will have no better standing than the weak;   435
And if the little man is right, he wins
Against the great. This is the call of freedom:
"What man has good advice to give the city,
And wishes to make it known?" He who responds   440
Gains glory; the reluctant hold their peace.
For the city, what can be more fair than that?
Again, when the people is master in the land,
It welcomes youthful townsmen as its subjects;
But when one man is king, he finds this hateful,
And if he thinks that any of the nobles   445
Are wise, he fears for his despotic power
And kills them. How can a city become strong
If someone takes away, cuts off new ventures
Like ears of corn in a spring field? What use
To build a fortune, if your work promotes   450
The despot's welfare, not your family's?
Why bring up girls as gentlewomen, fit
For marriage, if tyrants may take them for their joy—
A grief to parents? I would rather die
Than see my children forced to such a union.   455
   These are the darts I shoot at what you say.
What have you come to ask of this, our country?
You talk too much; you would regret your visit
Had not a city sent you. Messengers
Should state their mission promptly, then return.   460
I hope that henceforth, to my city, Creon
Sends a less wordy messenger than you.

Chorus

When fortune aids the wicked, how they revel!
They act as if their luck would last forever.

Herald

Now I shall speak. On what has been debated,   465
You may hold your views; I the opposite.
    I and the whole Cadmean people say
Adrastus must not pass into this land.
If he has entered it, you must strip off
His sacred ritual wreaths and drive him out   470
Before the sun-god's flame is down. His dead
Must not be removed by force; the Argives' city
Is no concern of yours. Do what I say
And you will steer your city's course in calm.
If you refuse, there will be much rough water
For us, for you, and for our allies: war.   475
Think now: do not let anger at my words
Goad you to puffed-up answers. You are free;
That does not make you powerful. Hope has driven
Many cities against each other; she stirs
An overreaching heart; she is not to be trusted.   480
When the people vote on war, nobody reckons
On his own death; it is too soon; he thinks
Some other man will meet that wretched fate.
But if death faced him when he cast his vote,
Hellas would never perish from battle-madness.   485
And yet we men all know which of two words
Is better, and can weigh the good and bad
They bring: how much better is peace than war!
First and foremost, the Muses love her best;
And the goddess of vengeance hates her. She delights   490
In healthy children, and she glories in wealth.
But evilly we throw all this away
To start our wars and make the losers slaves—
Man binding man and city chaining city.

And you would help our enemies in death,
Taking away for burial men who fell   495
By their own pride? Do you not think it right
That thunderbolts made smoke of Capaneus,
The one who thrust the ladders at the gates
And swore to sack the city whether God
Willed it or not? The bird-interpreter,
Was he not swallowed by a gulf that opened   500
Around his four-horse chariot? There they lie,
The other squadron-leaders, by the gates;
Rocks have crushed the framework of their bones.
Now boast a greater mind than Zeus, or grant
That the bad are justly punished by the gods.   505
Wise men should cherish children first, then parents,
Then fatherland—and that they ought to strengthen,
Not enervate. A bold leader or sailor
Brings peril; the man who knows when not to act
Is wise. To my mind, bravery is forethought.   510

Chorus

Zeus the punisher was enough. No need
For you to gloat like this over their doom.

Adrastus

You miserable wretch—

Theseus

                   Silence, Adrastus!
Restrain yourself. Do not give precedence
To your words over mine. This challenge comes   515
To me, not you; and I must answer it.

                             (To the herald.)

I have not heard that Creon is my master,
Or even more powerful than I. How then
Can he compel Athens to do his bidding?
If we serve him, the world runs backward! I   520

Did not begin this war: I was not with them
When they went to Thebes; I only think it just
To bury their dead. I mean no harm to the city,
No man-destroying struggles: I uphold 525
The law of all the Greeks. Is that unfair?
Yes, certainly the Argives did you wrong,
But they are dead. You fought them off with honor,
To their disgrace; and now the case is closed. 530
Come! Let the dead be covered by the ground,
And let each part regain the element
From which it came to light: the spirit, air;
The body, earth. The flesh is only ours
To dwell in while life lasts; and afterward 535
The giver of its strength must take it back.
Do you think to hurt Argos by leaving her dead unburied?
You miss your mark. All Hellas is concerned
When anyone tries to strip the dead of their due
And keep them from the tomb. If that were law, 540
Brave men would turn cowards. And yet you come
To threaten me with frightful words. Do you dread
The corpses? If they are hidden in earth, what then?
Will they overthrow your country from the grave,
Or beget children in the womb of earth 545
Who will avenge them some day? Fears like these
Are base and vain, a waste of breath to speak.
Fools! Be instructed in the ills of man.
Struggles make up our life. Good fortune comes 550
Swiftly to some, to some hereafter; others
Enjoy it now. Its god luxuriates.
Not only is he honored by the hapless
In hope of better days, but lucky ones
Exalt him too, fearing to lose the wind.
Aware of this, you should not take it hard 555
When moderately wronged, or do a wrong
So great that it will hurt your city. Therefore
You ought to grant the bodies of the fallen

To us, who wish to do them reverence.
If you choose otherwise, my course is clear: 560
I shall compel their burial. Never the Greeks
Shall have this news to tell: that ancient law,
Established by the gods, appealed to me
And Pandion's city, only to be shattered.

Chorus

Courage! Keep alive the light of justice,
And much that men say in blame will pass you by.   565

Herald

May I make a speech that is short and plain?

Theseus

Say what you like: you are no mute.

Herald

You will never take Argos' sons from my country.

Theseus

Now hear me, if you will, in turn.

Herald

I listen; I must grant your due.   570

Theseus

I shall bury the dead away from Thebes.

Herald

First you must risk a clash of shields.

Theseus

I have come through many other trials.

Herald

Did your father make you a match for all?

Theseus

Offenders, yes; I do not crush virtue.   575

Herald

You and your city have busy habits.

Theseus

Endeavor brings prosperity.

Herald

Go, and be caught by a Sown Man's spear!

Theseus

What martial fury can come from a dragon?

Herald

Feel it and know it. You are still young.   580

Theseus

You cannot rouse my mind to wrath
By boasting. Take the foolish words
You brought, and leave the country. Talk
Will gain us nothing.

(*The Theban Herald goes out.*)

Forward, every man   585
Who fights on foot or from a chariot!
Let cheek-pieces rattle, flecking the horses' mouths
With foam as they gallop toward the Theban land!
I march on Cadmus' seven gates; I bear
Sharp iron in my hand and act as herald   590
In my behalf. Adrastus, I command you,
Stay here; do not attach your fate to me.
I shall lead the army, guided by my god,
As a new campaigner with a new intent.
Only one thing I need: to have with me
The gods who honor justice. That support   595

Gives victory. Human excellence means nothing
Unless it works with the consent of God.

(*Exeunt Theseus and attendants; Aethra.*)

Chorus

Pitiful mothers of lost commanders!
Yellow fear sits on my heart.

—What new word is this you bring?   600

—How will the mission of Pallas stand the test?

—By fighting, did you say, or exchange of words?

—I pray that good will come of it!
But what if it ends in slayings by Ares,
Battles, din of beaten breasts throughout the city?   605
Then, alas! What could I find to say,
I, who caused it all?

—The man who glories in his luck
May be overthrown by destiny;
In that hope I rest secure.

—Then you believe in gods who stand for justice.   610

—Of course; what other beings make things happen?

—I see much else in the way they treat us.

—That is because you are crushed by fear
From the past. But justice has called for justice, blood for blood;
The gods, who hold in their hands the end of all,
Now give men rest from pain.   615

—How might we leave the sacred fount of the goddess
And reach the plains with the beautiful towers?

—If one of the gods would give you wings,   620

—On the way to the two-rivered city.

—You would know, then you would know how our friends are
faring.

—What destiny, what turn of fate, I wonder,
Is waiting for this country's mighty lord?   625

—Again we call on gods invoked already:
Here is the foremost hope of the frightened.

—O Zeus, who fathered a child for the heifer
Of Inachus, mother of old,
Favor this my city and help its cause.   630
Your image, the city's mainstay, has been outraged;
And I would make it ready for the pyre.

                    (Enter a Messenger from Thebes.)
Messenger
Women, I bring much news that you will welcome.
I have come through to safety after capture   635
In the battle which the seven companies
Of fallen masters fought by Dirce's stream.
I am here to tell of Theseus' victory.
To spare you long inquiry: I was a servant
Of Capaneus, whom Zeus's flaming bolt   640
Riddled to ashes.

Chorus
                    Oh, with joy we greet
Your news of coming home, and hear the word
You bring of Theseus! If Athens' army too
Is safe, then all you have to tell is welcome.

Messenger
Safe; and it did what should have been achieved
By Adrastus with the Argives whom he marched   645
From Inachus against the Cadmean city.

Chorus

How did the son of Aegeus and his comrades
Gain victory? Tell us now. You saw it happen;
You can give joy to those who were not there.

Messenger

A brilliant shaft of sunlight, straight and clear,   650
Lit up the field as I stood at Electra gate,
Where a tower gave a sweeping view. I saw
Three forces marshalled. Infantry with armor
Extended toward high ground: the Ismenian hill,   655
I heard it called. The famous son of Aegeus,
With men from old Cecropia held the right;
The left wing, spear-armed Coast men, took positions
Beside the spring of Ares. Cavalry massed   660
At each wing's end, in equal groups; and chariots
Stood at the foot of Amphion's sacred mound.   665
Cadmus' men, posted before the walls, had put
The bodies, cause of conflict, at their rear.
Horsemen faced horsemen; chariots stood ready,
Equipped to battle four-horse chariots.
Then Theseus' herald spoke these words to all:
Silence, my men; silence, Cadmean troops.
Hear me: we come to take the dead. We wish   670
To bury them, and so uphold the law
Of all the Greeks. It is not our desire
To shed more blood." Creon gave no command
To answer this, but stood in silence, ready.
Then the charioteers began the combat.   675
Driving their chariots toward and past each other,
They set their fighters down, in line of battle.
While these crossed swords, the drivers turned their horses
Back to support their men. When Phorbas, captain   680
Of Athens' horsemen, and the overseers
Of Theban cavalry saw the chariots clustered,
They threw their forces into the tide of war.

As witness, not from hearsay—I was close
To the battleground of chariots and riders—   685
I know the many horrors there, but not
Where to begin. With the dust that rose toward heaven?
How thick it was! Or men tossed up and down,
Caught in the horses' reins? Or streams of blood   690
From men who fell, or were flung head first to earth
When cars were shattered, leaving life beside
Wreckage of chariots? When Creon saw
Our mounted forces winning, he took his shield   695
And moved to keep his allies from despair.
Then all the middle of the field was spattered
As men slew and were slain; and the word passed,   700
Shouted aloud among them: "Strike! Thrust back
The spear at Erechtheus' sons!" But Theseus' fortunes
Were not to fall by terror. Snatching up
His shining arms, he charged at once. Fiercely
The host that grew to men from dragon's teeth
Opposed us, pushing our left wing back; but theirs   705
Lost to our right and fled. The scales of war
Stood even. Then our general earned praise;
Not seeking only to follow up advantage,
He hurried to his forces' breaking-point,
Shouting so loud that he made the earth resound: 710
"Hold, lads, against these dragon men's stiff spears,
Or else farewell to Athens!" That stirred courage
Throughout the Cranaid army. Then he seized
His Epidaurian weapon, a ghastly club,
And swung it right and left, dealing his blows   715
On heads and necks together; the wooden blade
Mowed off and snapped their helmets; turning to flee,
They could hardly move their feet. I shrieked and danced
And clapped my hands. The Thebans made for the gates.   720
Then there were cries and groans throughout the city
From young and old; frightened, they thronged the temples.
Now Theseus might have gone inside the walls;

But he held back, declaring that his purpose
Was not to sack the town but claim the dead.   725
  That is the kind of general to elect:
One who puts forth his strength in time of trouble,
And hates the greedy mob that tries to climb
To the top of the ladder even when times are good,
And wrecks the happiness it might enjoy.   730

Chorus

  Now, having seen this day, surpassing hope,
  I believe in gods. The lesser share of evil
  Seems to be mine now; Thebes has paid the price.

Adrastus

  Zeus! Who dares call us hapless mortals wise?
  You dangle us; whatever you want, we do.   735
  Argos, we thought, was irresistible:
  We were so many, young, and strong of arm!
  Eteocles would have come to terms; his claims
  Were fair; but we refused, and lost.   740
  The winner then, malignant folk of Cadmus,
  Ran riot like a pauper newly rich;
  But now their rioting brings them down, in turn.
  O you who try to shoot beyond the mark!
  O witless mortals! Richly you deserve   745
  Your many woes; you listen not to friends,
  But to your interests. Cities! You might use
  Reason to end your troubles; but with blood,
  Not words, you ruin your affairs.—Enough!   750

                                    (To the messenger.)

  I would like to know how you reached safety;
  Then I will ask my other questions.

Messenger

  When the city shook in turmoil of war,
  I went through the gates where the troops came in.

Adrastus

Do you bring the dead for whom they fought?

Messenger

Yes, the heads of the seven great houses.   755

Adrastus

But the mass of the fallen—where are they?

Messenger

Buried near Cithaeron's folds.

Adrastus

This side, or that? By whom were they buried?

Messenger

At Eleutherae's shady ridge. By Theseus.

Adrastus

Those he did not bury—where have you left them?   760

Messenger

Close by. Speed makes all roads short.

Adrastus

Did it pain the servants to bring them out of the carnage?

Messenger

No one who was a slave had charge of that.

Adrastus

Did Theseus welcome the task?

Messenger

                              You would have said so
If you had seen his loving salute to the dead.

Adrastus

And did he wash the victims' stains himself?   765

Messenger

He even spread the couches and covered the bodies.

Adrastus

That was a dreadful burden, bringing shame.

Messenger

How can our common ills be shameful to us?

Adrastus

Oh, how much rather had I died with them!

Messenger

Your laments are vain, and make these women weep.   770

Adrastus

Yes. It was they who taught me. Now I cease.
Let me lift up my hand when I meet the dead,
And speak, in long and tearful chants of Hades,
To friends by whom I am left to mourn alone.
If you lose money you can get it back, but no one   775
Recovers this expense: a human life.

(*The Messenger goes out.*)

Chorus

Part well, part ill—this turn of fate.
For city and soldiers who went to war,   780
Glory and honor redoubled;
For me, to look upon my children's bodies—
A bitter, lovely sight, if ever I see it
And the day despaired of,
Greatest pain of all.   785
Would that old Time, father of days,
Had left me unwed all my life.
What need had I of children?
Once, I thought, I could not bear the sorrow   790

Of being barred from wedlock. Now—
In loss of dearest children—
Its evil is plain to see.

(*Attendants enter, bearing the corpses
of the fallen chiefs.*)

The woeful sight has come: my fallen children's bodies!   795
Oh, to join them in death and go down to Hades together!

Adrastus

Mothers! Wail for the dead who lie on the ground!
Wail in answer when you hear my moans!   800

Chorus

Children! I bid you now in death
A bitter farewell for loving mothers.

Adrastus

O grief, O grief!

Chorus

For my own woes I cry.   805

Adrastus

We have borne

Chorus

the most tormenting evils.

Adrastus

O Argive city! Do your folk not see my downfall?

Chorus

They see me too in my wretched state, barren of children.   810

Adrastus

Bring on the bloodstained bodies of the doomed—
Champions in war, laid low by lesser men.

Chorus

Give me my children to take in my arms;   815
My hands are ready for that embrace.

Adrastus

You have and hold

Chorus

                    burden enough of woes.

Adrastus

Alas!

Chorus

    No word for the parents?

Adrastus

Hear me.

Chorus

            You groan with your pain and mine.   820

Adrastus

I wish the Theban columns had struck me down in the dust.

Chorus

Would that my body had never been yoked to a husband's bed.

Adrastus

O wretched mothers of children!   825
Behold, a sea of troubles.

Chorus

Our nails cut furrows down our cheeks;
We have poured dust over our heads.

Adrastus

Oh, Oh, alas, alas!
Swallow me, earth!

Hurricane, tear me apart!　　　　　　　　　　　830
Blaze of Zeus's fire, swoop down upon me!

Chorus

Bitter the wedding you saw,
Bitter the word of Phoebus;
A Fury, bringer of grief,
Has abandoned Oedipus' house and come to yours.　　835

(Enter Theseus and Athenian soldiers.)

Theseus

(To an Argive captain.)

During your long lament before the army
I would have asked you this, but I refrained
From speaking then, and now I let it pass;　　　840
Here is Adrastus.

(To Adrastus.)

　　　　These are men whose spirit
Has brought them fame. What is their lineage?
Speak, from your greater knowledge, to the young
Among our citizens; you have understanding.　　845
One thing I ask not, or you'd laugh at me;
Beside whom every warrior stood in battle,
Or from what foe he took a spear-wound. Vain
To tell or hear such tales—as if a man　　　850
In the thick of combat, with a storm of spears
Before his eyes, ever brought back sure news
On who was hero. I can neither ask
Such questions nor believe those who make bold
To answer them. When you stand against the foe,　855
It is hard enough to see what must be seen.

Adrastus

Hear, then. By granting me the privilege
Of praising friends, you meet my own desire
To speak of them with justice and with truth.

« 169 »

I saw the deeds—bolder than words can tell—
By which they hoped to take the city. Look:
The handsome one is Capaneus. Through him   860
The lightning went. A man of means, he never
Flaunted his wealth but kept an attitude
No prouder than a poor man's. He avoided
People who live beyond their needs and load
Their tables to excess. He used to say
That good does not consist in belly-food,   865
And satisfaction comes from moderation.
He was true in friendship to present and absent friends;
Not many men are so. His character
Was never false; his ways were courteous;
His word, in house or city, was his bond.   870
Second I name Eteoclus. He practiced
Another kind of virtue. Lacking means,
This youth held many offices in Argos.
Often his friends would make him gifts of gold,   875
But he never took them into his house. He wanted
No slavish way of life, haltered by money.
He kept his hate for sinners, not the city;
A town is not to blame if a bad pilot
Makes men speak ill of it. Hippomedon,   880
Third of the heroes, showed his nature thus:
While yet a boy he had the strength of will
Not to take up the pleasures of the Muses
That soften life; he went to live in the country,
Giving himself hard tasks to do, rejoicing   885
In manly growth. He hunted, delighted in horses,
And stretched the bow with his hands, to make his body
Useful to the city. There lies the son
Of huntress Atalanta, Parthenopaeus,
Supreme in beauty. He was Arcadian,
But came to Inachus' banks and was reared in Argos.   890
After his upbringing there, he showed himself,

As resident foreigners should, not troublesome
Or spiteful to the city, or disputatious,
Which would have made him hard to tolerate   895
As citizen and guest. He joined the army
Like a born Argive, fought the country's wars,
Was glad when the city prospered, took it hard
If bad times came. Although he had many lovers,
And women flocked to him, still he was careful   900
To cause them no offense. In praise of Tydeus
I shall say much in little. He was ambitious,
Greatly gifted, and wise in deeds, not words.
From what I have told you, Theseus, you should not wonder
That these men dared to die before the towers.   910
To be well brought up develops self-respect:
Anyone who has practiced what is good
Is ashamed to turn out badly. Manliness
Is teachable. Even a child is taught
To say and hear what he does not understand;   915
Things understood are kept in mind till age.
So, in like manner, train your children well.

Chorus

O my child, to an evil fate I bred you!
I carried you in my womb
And felt the pangs of birth;   920
Now, alas! Hades holds my burden,
And I have none to cherish me in age,
Though I bore a child, to my sorrow.

Theseus

And what of Oicles' noble son? His praises   925
Are uttered by the gods, who bore him off
Alive, with his chariot, into the depths of earth.
I too, in all sincerity, might honor
Oedipus' son: I speak of Polynices.
After leaving Cadmus' town, he stayed with me   930

Till he chose Argos for his place of exile.
Now, do you know what I wish to do with the fallen?

Adrastus

This only I know—to obey your orders.

Theseus

Capaneus, struck by Zeus's fire—

Adrastus

You will bury apart, as a sacred corpse?   935

Theseus

Yes. One pyre for all the others.

Adrastus

Where will you set his single memorial?

Theseus

Beside this shrine I will build the tomb.

Adrastus

The slaves may look to that labor now.

Theseus

And I to the rest. Bearers, move on.   940

(*The attendants take up the biers.*)

Adrastus

Sorrowful mothers! Draw near your children!

Theseus

Adrastus! That was not well said.

Adrastus

Why? Must the parents not touch their children?

Theseus

To see their state would be mortal pain.

Adrastus

Yes; corpse-wounds and blood are a bitter sight.   945

Theseus

Then why would you increase the women's woe?

Adrastus

I yield.

(To the women.)

You must be brave, and stay where you are.
Theseus is right. When we put them to the fire,
You will take home their bones. O wretched mortals,
Why do you slaughter each other with your spears?   950
Leave off those struggles; let your towns take shelter
In gentleness. Life is a short affair;
We should try to make it smooth, and free from strife.

Chorus

Blest no more with children, blest no more with sons,   955
I have no share in happiness
Among the boy-bearing women of Argos.
And Artemis, who watches over birth,
Would have no word for childless women.
Life is a time of woe;   960
I am like a wandering cloud
Sent hurtling by fierce winds.
Seven mothers, we gave birth to seven sons
Who gained the heights of fame in Argos;   965
But that has brought us suffering.
And now, without a son, without a child,
Most miserably I grow old,
Neither a living creature
Nor one of the dead, my fate
Somehow apart from both.   970

Tears are left to me; sad
Memorials of my son are in my house:

Locks of his hair, and wreaths for mine, in mourning,
Libations for the vanished dead, and songs   975
Unwelcome to golden-haired Apollo.
At every dawn I shall wake to weep
And drench the folds of my dress at the breast with tears.

Already I can see the vaults   980
Of the sacred tomb of Capaneus,
And Theseus' memorials to the dead, outside the temple.
And close at hand I see Evadne,
Famous wife of him who died by lightning,   985
Daughter of Iphis the king.
Why has she climbed that path
To stand on a lofty rock
That towers above this shrine?

                                        (*Enter Evadne.*)
Evadne

Over what blaze, what gleam did sun and moon   990
Drive their chariots through the air
Where the light-bringers ride,
On that dark day when Argos' city   995
Built towers of song and greetings
For my wedding and the bridegroom,
Bronze-armored Capaneus? Alas!
To you I come, wildly running from home!   1000
I shall enter the glow of the pyre and share your grave,
Making Hades my release
From the weary weight of life
And the pain of being.   1005
This is the sweetest death: to die with loved ones dying,
If God should so decree.

Chorus

You see the pyre; you stand above and near it;
It is a treasure-house of Zeus. There lies   1010
Your husband, victim of the lightning-flash.

Evadne

From here I see how I shall end.
May fortune guide the leap of my feet to glory.   1015
From this rock I will dive
Into the flames. My body will mingle
In fiery glow with my husband,   1020
His loved flesh close to mine.
So shall I come to Persephone's halls,
Resolved never to cheat your death by living
Upon this earth. Daylight, wedlock, farewell!   1025
Away with Argive marriages
Shown to be true by children!
Out of my sight,
Devoted man of the house, drawn to your noble wife
By steady winds of love!   1030

Chorus

Your father, aged Iphis, comes upon
Strange words, unheard-of, that will hurt to hear.

                                                  (*Enter Iphis.*)

Iphis

O women of sorrows! To my sorrowful age
My family has brought a double grief.   1035
I have come to take my dead son home by ship—
Eteoclus, who fell to the Theban spear—
And to seek my daughter, wife of Capaneus,
Who sped from my house in longing to die with her husband.
In former days, she was watched at home; beset   1040
By present troubles, I dismissed the guards;
And she has gone. I think she must be here;
If you have seen her, tell me.

Evadne

                        Why ask them?   1045
I am here on a rock above his pyre, my father—
Lightly poised, like a bird, for a flight of doom.

Iphis

My child, what wind has blown you here? What errand?
Why did you slip from home and come to this land?

Evadne

You would be angry if I told my plans;   1050
I do not wish you to hear about them, Father.

Iphis

What? Is it not right that your father should know?

Evadne

You would not be an able judge of my intent.

Iphis

For whom have you put on this finery?

Evadne

My dress has glory in its meaning, Father.   1055

Iphis

You are not like one in mourning for her husband.

Evadne

No, I have made myself ready for something new.

Iphis

And yet you appear beside a tomb and a pyre!

Evadne

I come to celebrate a victory.

Iphis

I beg you, tell me over whom you won it.   1060

Evadne

Over all women on whom the sun looks down.

Iphis

In Athena's skills, or in the ways of prudence?

Evadne

In valor: I shall lie with my husband in death.

Iphis

You speak in sickly riddles. What is this?

Evadne

I rush to the pyre of fallen Capaneus.   1065

Iphis

My daughter! Do not speak that word to many.

Evadne

I want it known by everyone in Argos.

Iphis

I shall not suffer you to do this thing.

Evadne

No matter; I am beyond the reach of your hand.
My body falls! a flight not dear to you   1070
But to me and the husband who will burn with me.

(She leaps into the pyre.)

Chorus

Woman! Terrible the deed you brought to pass!

Iphis

Daughters of Argos! I am ruined, doomed.

Chorus

Having borne this heavy woe,
Alas! you will grieve to see   1075
Her wildly daring deed.

Iphis

The world holds no more miserable man.

Chorus

What suffering is yours! A part of Oedipus' doom
Has befallen you, old sire, and me and my poor city.

Iphis

In grief I ask: Why cannot mortals be   1080
Twice young, then reach old age a second time?
If anything goes wrong at home, we right it
By afterthoughts; but not so with a life.
If youth and age came twice, a double life   1085
Would be our lot, and we could set things right
No matter what mistakes were made. When I saw others
With families, I became an adorer of children
And sorely longed for some to call my own.
If I had come to this experience
With children, and known what it is for a father to lose them,   1090
Never would I have reached the point of woe
Where now I stand: to have started into life
A noble youth, and then be robbed of him.
And now, in my wretchedness, what shall I do?
Return to my house, to see the emptiness   1095
Of many rooms, and a hopeless round of living?
Or shall I go where Capaneus once dwelt?
What a delight that was, when I had this child!
But now she is no more—she who would draw   1100
My cheek to her lips and clasp my head in her hands.
To an old father, nothing is more sweet
Than a daughter. Boys are more spirited, but their ways
Are not so tender. Quickly, take me home
And give me to the dark, to starve until   1105
My aged frame is wasted and I rot.
What will I gain by touching my child's bones?
O harsh old age! How loathsome is your reign!

How I hate those who want to stretch life out,
Counting on meats and drinks and magic spells   1110
To turn the stream aside and stave off death.
When useless to the world, they ought to die:
Away with them! Let them leave it to the young.

(The ashes of the fallen chiefs are brought in.)

Chorus

Look, look! Alas! They are bringing
The bones of my children who perished.
Attendants, take them from a weak old woman.   1115
Grief for my children has robbed me of my strength.
I have been alive for many lengths of time
And many woes have made me melt in tears.
What greater pain can mortals feel than this: 1120
To see their children dead before their eyes?

Boys

Sorrowful mothers! Out of the fire
I bring, I bring my father's limbs;
A weight not weightless, so great is my grief   1125
As I gather my all in a little space.

Chorus

Alas, alas! Why do you bring
Tears for the mother whom the fallen loved?
A little heap of dust instead of bodies   1130
Once glorious in Mycenae?

Boys

You are childless! childless! and I,
Having lost my unhappy father, will dwell
An orphan in a house of loss,
Cut off from the man who gave me life.

Chorus

Alas, alas! Where is the labor   1135
Spent on my children? Where, the reward of childbirth,

A mother's care, sleepless devotion of eyes,
The loving kiss on the face?

Boys

They have gone, they are no more. Alas, my father!
They have gone.   1140

Chorus

                    The air holds them now,
Crumbled to dust in the fire;
They have winged their way to Hades.

Boys

Father, I beg you, hear your children's cries!
Shall I ever set my shield against your foes,
Making your murder engender death? May that day come!   1145
If God is willing, justice will be done
For our fathers.

Chorus

                    This evil sleeps not yet.
It grieves me. I have had enough
Ill chance, enough of woe.

Boys

Some day Asopus' gleam will welcome me   1150
As I march in the bronze armor of Danaus' sons
On a campaign to demand revenge for my fallen father.
Still I seem to see you, father, before my eyes—

Chorus

Planting your kiss, so loved, upon my cheek.

Boys

But your encouraging words   1155
Are borne away on the air.

Chorus

> He left woe to us both: your mother,
> And you, whom grief for your father will never leave.

Boys

> I bear so great a burden that it has destroyed me.

Chorus

> Come, let me lay the dear dust close to my breast.   1160

Boys

> Oh, piteous words! I weep
> To hear them; they pierce my heart.

Chorus

> Child, you have gone: never again
> Shall I see you, idol of your beloved mother.

Theseus

> Adrastus! Women of the race of Argos!   1165
> You see these youths, holding in their hands
> The bodies of their fathers, noble men
> Whom I took up for burial. To them
> I and the city now present the ashes.
> You, who behold what you have gained from me,   1170
> Must keep this act in grateful recollection,
> And tell your children constantly to honor
> This city, handing down from son to son
> The memory of answered prayers. Zeus
> And the gods in heaven know the kindnesses   1175
> Of which we thought you worthy. Go in peace.

Adrastus

> Theseus, we are aware of all the good
> You have done the land of Argos, in its need

Of benefactors, and our gratitude
Will never fade. We have been nobly treated
By you, and owe you action in return.

Theseus

How can I be of further service to you?   1180

Adrastus

By faring well, as you and your city deserve.

Theseus

We shall; and may you have the same good fortune.

                        (*Athene appears*, ex machina.)

Athene

Theseus, hear what I, Athene, tell you.
There is a duty that you must perform
To help the city now. Do not intrust   1185
These bones to the boys, to take to the land of Argos,
Releasing them so lightly. First exact
An oath, in compensation for the efforts
You and the city have made. Adrastus here
Must swear—he has authority, as king,
To take an oath on behalf of all the land   1190
Of Danaus' sons. And this shall be the oath:
"Argos will never move against this country
In hostile panoply. If others try
To invade it, she will hinder them by arms."
If they forsake the oath and come, then pray
That the Argive land may fall again to ruin.   1195
Now hear me name the vessel for the blood
From the rite you must perform. You have
Inside your house a tripod with feet of bronze.
After destroying Ilium's foundations
Long years ago, Heracles, going forth
On another labor, bade you set that vessel   1200

On the altar of Apollo. Over it
You must cut the throats of three sheep, and inscribe
The oath on the hollow of the tripod; then
Present it to the god who has charge of Delphi,
To be preserved in memory of the oath
And as witness to it in the eyes of Hellas.
The sharp-edged knife, with which you will perform   1205
The sacrifice and deal the death-wound, you must bury
Deep in the earth, here, beside the seven
Pyres of the fallen. Then, if the Argives ever
Move on the city, the knife, revealed, will work
Fear in their hearts, and an evil journey home.
When this is done, you must send the dead from the land,   1210
And dedicate a shrine of the Isthmian goddess
Beside the triple crossroads, where the bodies
Were purified by fire. These are my words
To you. To the sons of the Argives, I proclaim:
When you are men you will sack Ismenus' city,
Avenging the murder of your fallen fathers.   1215
You, Aigialeus, will take your father's place
As a young campaigner, and you, the son of Tydeus
From Aetolia, named Diomedes by your father.
No sooner shall you get your beards than march
A mighty force of bronze-clad Danaids   1220
Against the Thebans' seven-mouthed walls. Your coming
Will bring them sorrow—lion-cubs you are,
True-bred sackers of cities! This shall befall:
Hellas will know you as the Sons of Sons,
A theme of future song. So great will be   1225
Your expedition, favored by the gods.

Theseus

I shall obey your orders, Queen Athene!
You have corrected me; I err no more.
Now I shall bind this man to me by oath.
Only, I pray you, set me in the right path;   1230

So long as you mean kindly to the city,
Our life will be secure to the end of time.

Chorus

Now let us go, Adrastus, and give our word
To this man and his town, whose deeds for us
Deserve the highest honors we can give.

ORESTES

Translated and with an Introduction by William Arrowsmith

INTRODUCTION TO *ORESTES*

Tragic in tone, melodramatic in incident and technique, by sudden wrenching turns savage, tender, grotesque, and even comic, combining sheer theatrical virtuosity with puzzling structural violence and a swamping bitterness of spirit, the *Orestes* has long been an unpopular and neglected play, almost an unread one. Undeservedly so, I think; but like so many Euripidean plays, *Orestes* has had to pay the price for affronting the pat handbook theories of the well-constructed Greek play, and its very "queerness" and bravura of bitterness have seemed to violate both the idea of tragedy and tragic dignity itself. Actually, like Shakespeare's *Troilus and Cressida*, the *Orestes* is that rare thing, a work which fits no category or ready-made genre but whose real power and odd brilliance demand a place and indict the theories which oust it from serious consideration. But so long as the standard image of the Greek play remains that of the tense and archaic ordered calm and balanced harmony of Sophoclean folklore, a play of "howling spiritual lunacy" like the *Orestes* must appear an unwelcome and unsettling freak.

What we get in the *Orestes* is, in fact, very much like what we get in *Troilus and Cressida:* tragedy utterly without affirmation, an image of heroic action seen as botched, disfigured, and sick, carried along by the machinery and slogans of heroic action in a steady crescendo of biting irony and the rage of exposure. It is neither a satire on heroic tragedy, however, nor a mere melodramatic perversion, but a kind of negative tragedy of total turbulence, deriving its real power from the exposure of the aching disparity between the ideal and the real, dooming all possibility of order and admitting dignity only as the agonizing absence by which the degree of depravity is to be judged. If, in the end, nothing but the sense of bitterness and alienation survives the corrosive effect of the action, the intensity of that experience in a world of impending disaster is in itself the bedrock of the tragic. Out of balance perhaps, distorted by a bitterness so pervasive that it seems at times almost gratuitous, it is nevertheless the anguished, despairing portrayal of a society taken in the act of self-betrayal and the defeat of political commitment.

In its material, the *Orestes* is almost entirely free invention, an imaginative rendering of the events which follow the murder of Clytemnestra by her children. Dramatically, the unifying motif of the play is the gradual exposure of the real criminal depravity of Orestes and his accomplices, an exposure made possible by a typical and deliberate piece of Euripidean anachronizing. In play after play, that is, Euripides uproots a myth from the cultural context of a remote and different time and intrudes it forcibly into a contemporary world, thereby altering its motives, its characters, and its meaning. By so doing, he effectively contrasts the ideal with the operative values of his own society. The *Orestes*, though freely invented, observes the same technique. Whereas, for instance, in the *Oresteia* of Aeschylus, Orestes' murder of his mother is the source from which the institution of civil justice flows, in the Euripidean play Orestes' matricide is set in a context where civil justice already exists. The consequence of this anachronism is to throw the whole burden of the cultural disparity upon the character of Orestes, a burden which makes him either suspect or criminal. He murders his mother, that is, in the everyday world of the audience, and the audience is therefore compelled to judge him as a man who murdered when he might have had recourse to the courts. True, he may have obeyed the command of Apollo, but, by virtue of the same anachronizing process, Apollo is here transformed from a cool and infallible Olympian into the interested and suspect god of contemporary Delphian politics, neither impartial nor infallible nor even godlike. But once shorn of his legendary aura of heroism and his justifying necessity, Orestes is revealed in action as sick, brutal, cowardly, and weak, redeemed only by his tenderness for the stronger sister and friend who dominate him and push him on to murder.

In itself the exposure of Orestes' criminal nature is both gradual and dramatic. Indeed, through the first half of the play, Euripides allows Orestes to profit from his reputed heroism and necessity, and, with the exception of several savage lapses which prepare the way for the exposure to come, he is presented as a more or less sympathetic figure. Thus everybody pities him as the suffering victim of a callous god; all blame Apollo as the true culprit, and even the trenchant remarks of Tyndareus and Menelaus are half elided because Tyndareus is made vindictive and Menelaus opportunistic. Orestes himself disarms condemnation by cleanly admitting his guilt at one point (by a forceful irony he is most sane when apparently most mad, and maddest when he is at his most lucid); and his own sickness and desperation in the face of Menelaus' abandonment of him operate insensibly to palliate or excuse his conduct. But suddenly with the decision to murder Helen and take Hermione as hostage, his true criminal nature is revealed: murder, we see now, was always in his heart, for these actions are commanded by no god but are born of desperation, spite, and hatred. And then, point for point, the depravity and cowardice which move him are exposed. Thus the man who could taunt his mother with cowardice for not having killed herself when taken in adultery willingly contemplates two more murders to save his own life, while, in pointed reversal and parody of his own cowardly lust to live and his sneers at Menelaus' cowardice, he brutally plays cat-and-mouse with a cowering, defenseless Trojan slave. And so by the end of the play, along with Electra and Pylades, he stands nakedly exposed as the degenerate heir of a great house, willing to bring down his accomplices, his innocent victim, and his house in his own ruin.

But everywhere, in the situations, in the characters, the bitterness is unrelieved, the quality of nightmare pervasive. Thus with the single exception of Hermione, a mere pawn whose compassion is typically exploited by the brutal Electra, there is not a good character in the play. Helen herself, vain of her beauty still, is shallow, selfish, and tactless and, like Orestes, shirks responsibility by blaming the gods for her conduct. Pylades (whom an insane scholiast referred to as the only good character of the play) is a monster of perverted loyalty, the exact foil to Menelaus, a man who is not even permitted the luxury of a struggle between duty and greed but is presented as a straightforward demagogue, treacherous and corrupt. Tyndareus, it is true, is permitted the only valid insight into the murder of Clytemnestra and its alternative, but his vindictiveness

and harshness (he deserves comparison to Pheres in the *Alcestis*) obscure his own insight, and finally he betrays even his devotion to
precedent and law in his conduct at Orestes' trial. Except for her
loyalty and devotion to her brother, Electra is a piece of complete
viciousness, stubborn in spite and malice with the bitterness born of
envy and resentful virginity. The foolish messenger who reports the
trial is, of course, *parti pris* and warped by the disease of demented
loyalty that pervades the play, while the pathetic and ridiculous
Phrygian slave is no more than a comic messenger designed, in his
whirling helplessness and terror, to stress Orestes' brutality and perhaps to satirize contemporary Persia. The same warping that extends to all the characters extends also to all the situations, moral and
political, of the play. Thus even the possibility of justice is precluded
in the messenger's portrayal of the Argive assembly, dominated by
demagogues and crossed by political motives that have nothing to
do with justice. And so too all the parties to the action are defined
either by inhuman devotion to sound principle, by patent treachery,
or by nightmare loyalty of complicity or stupidity, and slowly, in-
exorably, all moral terms are either inverted or emptied of their
meaning.

With great vividness the final tableau crowns the nightmare. On
the roof of his own palace in the lurid light of smoking torches
Orestes with Pylades beside him holds a drawn sword at Hermione's throat; farther back stands Electra with blazing torches, on
the point of firing the roof, while below, in petrified horror, stand
Menelaus and his men watching. The impasse is complete; in any
natural world the whole cumulative experience of the play points
unmistakably to disaster. But then, suddenly, incredibly, Apollo appears, halts the violence, and methodically hands out their known
mythical futures to all the characters. In no other extant Greek play
does a part of a play stand in more glaring contrast to the whole than
it does here; in no other play are the futures of the characters made to
clash so violently with their portrayal and development in the play.
Thus, says Apollo, Orestes will marry Hermione (and we must imagine an insane *pas de deux* as Orestes drops his sword and embraces his
victim); Pylades will marry Electra and live in happiness (but how

could this marriage be happy, one wonders); and finally, and most incredible of all, Helen—the same shallow, tactless, empty-headed Helen of the play—is exhibited by Apollo as nothing less than a goddess, "enthroned forever, a star for sailors."

How is this strange epiphany to be understood? The stressed contradictions between it and the play proper rule out any ordinary *deus ex machina* intervening to save an impossible situation, as they equally rule out the common notion that Euripides has introduced Apollo to salvage a botched play. And while it is certainly true that Apollo's arrangements show a degree of stupidity rare even in a Euripidean god and operate to arraign the god who announces them, this hardly seems enough. What we have here, I think, is a transparent tour de force, an apparent resolution which in fact resolves nothing, the illusion of a *deus ex machina* intervening to stop the terrible momentum of the play by means of a solution so inadequate and so unreal by contrast with the created reality of the play that it is doomed into insignificance. The resolution, that is, is so designed as to be merely an apparent resolution: if the experience of the play is a real one, what remains after Apollo leaves is not the taste of the happy ending but the image of total disaster: the burning palace, the dead girl, the screaming mob, and the degenerate heirs dying in the arson of their own hatred. Or so I see it. As so often, Euripides has here juxtaposed two conflicting realities—one, the harsh irrefutable reality of experience the play makes, the other, the storied reality of myth and "things as they are said to be"—and left them there, without bridge, without explanation, without resolution. But here the violence of contrast is without parallel, almost as though Euripides had deliberately inverted the *deus ex machina* to show precisely that *no* solution was possible; not even a god could halt the momentum of these forces in their sweep toward inevitable disaster. The magician waves his wand, but the nightmare survives the magic; the discord outlasts both the coda and the concert. As a previous translator shrewdly remarks, "Apollo speaks with the voice of a cracked phonograph-record."

The *Orestes* can be accurately dated to the year 408 B.C., that is, just a year or so before Euripides, old, embittered, and disillusioned with Athens, withdrew in voluntary exile to Macedon, where he died a few years later. The political climate of the play itself graphically represents the state of affairs in Athens, and, presumptuous or not, I am tempted to see in the play Euripides' prophetic image of the final destruction of Athens and Hellas, or that Hellas to which a civilized man could still give his full commitment. It is a simple and a common symbolism: the great old house, cursed by a long history of fratricidal blood and war, brought down in destruction by its degenerate heirs. The final tableau is the direct prophecy of disaster, complete, awful, and inevitable, while Apollo intervenes only as an impossible wish, a futile hope, or a simple change of scene from a vision that cannot be brooked or seen for long because it is the direct vision of despair, the hopeless future.

CHARACTERS

Electra

Helen

Hermione, daughter of Menelaus and Helen

Chorus of women of Argos

Orestes

Menelaus

Tyndareus, father of Helen and Clytemnestra

Pylades

Messenger

Phrygian slave

Apollo

For N. O. Brown

*Apes enim ego divinas bestias puto, quae mel vomunt,
etiam si dicuntor illud a Iove afferre; ideo autem pungunt, quia
ubicunque dulce est, ibi et acidum invenies.*

ORESTES

SCENE: *Before the palace of Agamemnon in Argos, six days after the murder of Clytemnestra. Near the door, huddled under blankets on a
pallet, lies Orestes asleep. Electra, an embittered and exhausted
woman, rises from the bedside to speak the prologue.*

Electra

    There is no form of anguish with a name—
no suffering, no fate, no fall
inflicted by heaven, however terrible—
whose tortures human nature could not bear
or might not have to bear.
                  I think of Tantalus,   5
born—or so they say—the son of Zeus himself
and blessed by birth and luck as few men are:
happy Tantalus. . . .
             I do not mock his fall,
and yet that same Tantalus now writhes and trembles
in terror of the rock that overhangs his head,
though even as a man he sat as honored equal
at the table of the gods, but could not hold his tongue,   10
being sick with pride.
             Or so the legend goes.
I do not know.
           The son of Tantalus was Pelops,
father of Atreus for whom the weaving Fates
wove the threads of war, a war with his own brother,
Thyestes—
           But why should I linger on the horrors
of my house?
           Atreus feasted him on his murdered sons.   15
I pass over, in the interests of decorum,
the succeeding years.

By Aërope, however,
Atreus became the father of two sons,
Menelaus and famous Agamemnon—
if what he had was fame.
     The wife of Menelaus
was Helen, whom the gods in heaven themselves   20
despise, while Agamemnon married Clytemnestra
in a marriage that became the scandal of Hellas.
By her he had three daughters—myself
and my two sisters, Chrysothemis and Iphigenia—
and one son, Orestes there. All of us his children
by that one wife—I cannot call her mother—
who snared her husband in the meshes of a net   25
and murdered him.
     I leave it to the world
to guess her motive. It is no topic for a virgin
like myself.
    And why repeat the old charges
against Apollo?
     The world knows all too well
how he pushed Orestes on to murder the mother
who gave him birth, that act of matricide   30
which wins, it seems, something less than approval
in men's eyes. But persuaded by the god, he killed,
and I did all a woman could to help him,
while Pylades, our friend, shared the crime
with us.
    After the murder Orestes collapsed   35
to bed. There he lies, wasted by raging fever
and whirled on to madness by his mother's blood—
I dare not breathe the name of those Eumenides
who pursue him now, hounding him with terror.
 Six days now since our mother's murder;
six days since we sent her body to the fire.   40
And all that time he has not tasted food
or wet his lips or bathed, but lies there

huddled in the blankets. When the fever lifts,
he turns lucid and cries; then suddenly, madly,
bolts from the bed like an untamed colt   45
bucking the bridle.
     Meanwhile the people of Argos
have passed a decree, declaring us matricides
and outlaws, forbidding anyone to speak to us
or give us shelter.
     But this day decides our fate.
On this day the city of Argos assembles
to vote whether we shall live or die,
and, if we die, then the manner of our death—   50
by stoning or the sword.
      One single hope is left.
Our uncle Menelaus has just come home
from Troy. His fleet fills the harbor at Nauplia,
riding at anchor just offshore after all those years
out of Troy and lost at sea.
      Helen, however—   55
who now styles herself "the queen of sorrows"—
was so terrified that she might be seen
and stoned by the fathers of those who died at Troy,
that Menelaus sent her on ahead last night
under cover of darkness.
     She is here now,   60
inside the house, weeping over her sister's death
and the ruin of our house.
     She has, I might add,
some consolation—her daughter, Hermione,
whom Menelaus, before he sailed for Troy,
brought from Sparta and intrusted to my mother's care.   65
So *she*, at least, has some comfort left;
she can afford to forget.
     But we cannot.
I stand here now, watching the road in the hope
of seeing Menelaus on his way.

Unless he helps us now, unless he rescues us,
then we must die. Nothing is so weak
and helpless as a fallen house.   70

> (*Enter Helen from the palace. She is middle-aged but still hand-*
> *some and still vain of her beauty. She carries a pitcher for*
> *libations and several small clippings of her own hair.*)

Helen

                  There you are.
Oh, dear Electra, Clytemnestra's daughter....
But you poor girl, still not married!
And how are you, dear?

                And how is poor Orestes?
How you must suffer!

                I can't believe it.
To murder your own mother! How horrible!
But there, dear, I know. You were not to blame.   75
The real culprit was Apollo. And for my part,
I can see no reason on earth for shunning you,
none at all.

          And yet, poor Clytemnestra—
my only sister!

            And to think I sailed for Troy
on that tragic voyage without even seeing her!
Some god must have driven me mad.

                And now she is gone,
and I am the only one left to mourn for her....   80

Electra

Why tell you, Helen, what you can see for yourself?
There lies the wreck of Agamemnon's son,
while I sit here at my sleepless post
beside his corpse. But for a little breath,
a corpse is what he is.

             I do not complain   85
on his account.

But *you*, you and your husband,
with your reek of triumph, your smug success,
you come to us in our utter misery—

Helen

When did he collapse?

Electra

The day he spilt
his mother's blood.

Helen

One day and two deaths,   90
a mother and her son.

Electra

Yes, he killed himself
when he killed her.

Helen

I wanted to ask, niece,
could you do me a favor?

Electra

I have a moment free.
He is sleeping now and does not need my care.

Helen

Would you go for me to my sister's grave?   95

Electra

What!
You want *me* to go to my mother's grave?
But why?

Helen

To pour libations on her grave
and leave this little clipping of my hair.

Electra

But she was *your* sister. You should go yourself.

Helen

I am afraid, ashamed to show my face
in Argos.

Electra

        This repentance comes a little late.
Where was your shame when you ran away from home
and left your husband?

Helen

               Spoken with more truth than kindness   100
to your aunt.

Electra

        Then why are you ashamed?

Helen

The fathers of those who died fighting at Troy—
they frighten me.

Electra

        Well they might. You are a byword
here in Argos.

Helen

        Please go. Save me.

Electra

               No.
I could not bear the sight of my mother's grave.   105

Helen

But it wouldn't do to send a servant there.

Electra

Then send Hermione.

Helen

                    Send an unmarried girl
on an errand in public?

Electra

                  It is her duty.
She owes it to my mother for bringing her up.

Helen

Quite right, my dear.
                   An excellent suggestion.   110
I'll call her out.

                        (Helen calls into the palace.)
            Hermione, dear,
come outside.

           (Hermione, a young girl, emerges from the palace.)

           Now do exactly what I say.
Take this libation and these clippings of hair
and go to Clytemnestra's grave. Stand there
and pour this mixture of honey, milk, and wine   115
over the grave and, as you pour, repeat
these words:
           "Your loving sister Helen,
prevented by fear of the Argives from coming
to your grave in person, sends you these gifts."
Then implore her to be gracious to us all,
to my husband and me and these poor children   120
whom Apollo has destroyed. Promise her besides
that I will labor to perform, like a good sister,
all the dues and rites of the gods below.
Now go, dear. Hurry there, make your offering
and then come back as quickly as you can.   125

     (Exit Hermione with offerings. Helen retires into the palace.)

Electra

Oh, what a vileness human beauty is,
corroding, corrupting everything it touches!

What a curse, and yet the glory of the good. . . .
Did you see how she clipped the merest tips of her curls,
so stingy with her loveliness?

      The same old Helen.
O gods, how can you help loathing this woman,   130
this monster who has ruined my brother and me
and all Hellas?

    (*Slowly and silently the Chorus of Argive women
       begins to file into the orchestra.*)

    But here they come again,
those loving friends who keep their watch with me
and mourn.

    But if they wake him from his sleep,
if I must see my brother going mad   135
once more, I shall cry out my eyes with grief.

        (*To Chorus.*)

Walk softly, friends. Gently. . . .
       Hush.
Quiet, quiet. Not a step or sound,
not a whisper.

    Your kindness is well meant,
but if you wake him now, I shall die. . . .

Chorus

 Hush.

    Not a sound. Tiptoe softly.   140
 Barely, barely touch the ground.

Electra

 Back, back from the bed!

Chorus

 Back we go.

Electra

    Your music, friends—
 keep it down, flute it low,   145

as soft as gentle breath may go
down the stem of your reed.

Chorus

There. Hear it, so soft,
so low—

Electra

No. Lower still.
Now tiptoe to me, softly, so—
and tell me why you come   150
now that he sleeps at last,
he sleeps. . . .

Chorus

How now? How?
Will he live? Will he die?

Electra

He breathes, he breathes—
his breath comes slow.   155

Chorus

O gods,
help him to live!

Electra

If his eyes
so much as move, you kill him. . . .
O gods, he sleeps, he sleeps
at last.

Chorus

Condemned to suffer   160
for a god's command!
How terribly he suffers—

Electra

Evil the act, evil the god,
that evil day Apollo on his throne

commanded my mother's death,   165
murder for murder!

Chorus
                    Look, look!
In the bed—his body stirring!

Electra
    Hush.
            In god's name, be still!
Look, your cries have wakened him,
have broken his sleep—

Chorus
                    No, no.
He sleeps, he sleeps....

Electra
                    Back,
    back from the bed.   170
                    Not a sound,
    not a cry.
                For god's sake, go!
Chorus
    Now he sleeps.

Electra
                Then let him sleep.
Chorus
    O night, mother of mercy,
    blessed night,
    who gives to human anguish   175
    the lovely gift of sleep,
    rise,
        rise from your abyss
    and soar to Agamemnon's house,
    where all is ruin,
                all is loss!   180

Electra
                    Hush.
                        No more.

In the name of god, be still,
be still! No more mourning,
or you rob him of his peace,
this gracious peace of sleep—   185

Chorus

Where, where will it end?

Electra

Death, death.
                    What is left
but death? He refuses food.

Chorus

Then death must come.   190

Electra
                        Yes,
and I must die with him.
Apollo killed us both,
vengeance for our mother
when our father's ghost cried out
against our mother, *blood, blood!*

Chorus

Just the act, crime unjust.
Right and wrong confounded
in a single act.

Electra

            O Mother,
mother who gave me birth,
who killed and was killed,   195
you slew your husband,
you killed your children too.

By your death we died.
We are the living dead.   200
You are dust and ashes,
while I, a living ghost,
dead to this sunlit world,
stalk with withered life,
childless, unmarried,   205
crying my sorrow, lost,
alone in the endless night.

Coryphaeus

Electra! Look and see if your brother has died
while we were mourning. He lies so still now—   210
I do not like it.

> (*Orestes suddenly stirs and wakes.*)

Orestes

       O sweet wizard sleep,
savior of the sick, dear loveliness
that came to me in my worst need of you!
O goddess sleep, goddess of forgetting,
to whom the unhappy make their prayers,
how skilled, how wise....
         But what happened?
Who put me here?
         I somehow—can't remember....   215

Electra

How happy it made me to see you fall asleep
at last.
      Should I raise your head, dear?

Orestes

Yes, please. Help me up.
         Now wipe away
this crust of froth around my mouth and eyes.   220

Electra

This service is sweet, and I do it gladly,
nursing my brother with a sister's love.

Orestes

Sit here
beside me. Now brush this matted hair
from my eyes so I can see.

Electra

Oh, that poor head!
And look at your hair, so snarled and dirty.... 225
And those tangled curls!

Orestes

(*Suddenly slumping back.*)
Let me lie back down.
That's better. After these attacks of fever,
my arms and legs seem somehow limp....

Electra

Lie down
and don't move. Sick men must stay in bed.
Frustrating, I know, but it can't be helped. 230

Orestes

Prop me up again. Now turn me around.
What a nuisance I am in my helplessness.

Electra

Would you like to try walking a step or two?
The change may do you good.

Orestes

With all my heart.
Right now even the suggestion of health, 235
however false, would be welcome.

Electra
                              Listen, Orestes,
I have something to say. But you must listen now
while your mind is clear and the Furies leave you free.

Orestes

If your news is good news, by all means tell me.
If not, I have troubles enough.   240

Electra
                              Listen then.
Our uncle Menelaus is *here*, in Argos.
His fleet lies at anchor at Nauplia.

Orestes
                              What?
Is it true? Then this darkness has a dawn!
Our uncle here? The man for whom our father
did so much?

Electra
                    Here in person. And the proof   245
is Helen. He has brought her home from Troy.

Orestes

I would envy him more if he'd left her there.
If Helen is here, he has brought his trouble home.

Electra

Poor Tyndareus.
                    What daughters he fathered!
Helen and our mother, Clytemnestra!
And both disgraced him in the eyes of Hellas.   250

Orestes

Take care that you act differently: *you* can.
I mean chastity of heart as well as word.

                    (*Orestes suddenly starts wildly up, then cowers
                              back, his eyes wild with terror.*)

Electra

 Orestes!

   O gods, his eyes are whirling!

 Oh no! *No!*

    Help! He is going mad!

Orestes

 No, Mother!

   For god's sake, Mother,   255
keep them away, those bitches with bloodshot eyes,
those writhing snakes!

    Help! They're coming,
they're leaping at me—

   (*Electra seizes him by the arm and leads him to his bed.*)

Electra

    Please, go back to bed.
There is nothing there, nothing at all.
These are only phantoms in your mind.

Orestes

 Apollo, save me!

    They want to kill me,   260
those bitches with gorgon eyes, those goddesses
of hell!

Electra

   No, stop! I won't let you go.
You must not go. I'll hold you by the waist
and keep you here by force!

      (*She grasps Orestes around his waist and
      holds him down on the bed.*)

Orestes

    Let me go!
I know *you.* You're one of my Furies too!
You're holding me down to hurl me into hell!   265

   (*He breaks loose, shoves her aside, and springs up.*)

Electra

What can I do?

How can I help him now?
Nothing human can save him now. No,
heaven hates us both.

Orestes

Get me my horn-tipped bow,
the bow Apollo gave me to scare these bitches off   270
if they threatened me with madness.

> *(Electra hands him the bow and quiver. Orestes
> notches an arrow and draws the bow.)*

Vanish, demons!
Goddesses you may be, but unless you go,
this human hand shall draw your blood.

Damn it, go!
Ignore me, do you?

Do you see this bow
already drawn, this arrow notched and ready?
What? Still here?

Vanish, spread your wings!   275
Skim the air, will you! Go hound Apollo,
accuse his oracle. But go! Go!

> *(He suddenly stumbles, dropping his bow, and sanity returns.)*

What was I saying?

And why am I panting so?
What am I doing here, out of bed?

But wait—
I remember now—a great storm, the waves crashing—
but now this calm—this peace. . . .

> *(He catches sight of Electra, her face hidden in
> her robes, sobbing softly by the bed.)*

Why are you crying?   280
Why do you hide your face?

Oh, my poor sister,
how wrong it is that what I have to suffer,
this sickness, this madness, should hurt you too
and cause you shame.

Please, please don't cry,
not on my account.

Let me bear the shame.
I know, you consented to the murder too,
but I killed, not you.

No—
I accuse Apollo. The god is the guilty one.   285
It was he who drove me to this dreadful crime,
he and his words, egging me, encouraging me,
all words, no action.

I think now
if I had asked my dead father at the time
if I should kill her, he would have begged me,
gone down on his knees before me, and pleaded,   290
implored me not to take my mother's life.
What had we to gain by murdering her?
Her death could never bring him back to life
and I, by killing her, would have to suffer
as I suffer now.

It seems so hopeless, dear,
I know.

But lift your head; do not cry.   295
And sometimes when you see me morbid and depressed,
comfort me and calm me, and I in turn,
when you despair, will comfort you with love.
For love is all we have, the only way
that each can help the other.

Now go inside.   300
Bathe and eat and give those tired eyes
their needed sleep. If you should leave me now,
if you fall ill yourself from nursing me,
then I am dead. You are all my help;   305
you are my hope.

Electra

I could never leave you.
Live or die, I live or die with you, Orestes.
For you are my hope too, as I am yours.
What am I without you?

A woman,
brotherless, fatherless, friendless, alone
and helpless.

But since you think it best, dear,   310
I'll go inside.

But you go back to bed
and rest. Above all else, try to stay calm
and master your terror, if you can. Remember:
no getting out of bed.

Your sickness may be real
or something in your mind, but in either case,
brooding on it will not make you well.   315

(*Electra enters the palace. Orestes lies down on the bed.*)

Chorus

Goddesses of terror,
runners on the wind,
revelers of sorrow
whose rites are tears!   320
Women of darkness,
Eumenides whose wings
shiver the taut air,
demanding blood,
avengers of murder,
we implore you—
release this boy,
Agamemnon's son,   325
from madness of murder,
the blood that whirls him on!
Pity, pity we cry,
pity for the crime,

murder that came on,
drove from Apollo's throne,
the god's command to kill
breaking the hushed, the holy air,
with the word of blood—
blood drenching the shrine   330
of Delphi—
        Delphi,
holiest of holies
and navel of the world!

O Zeus, what mercy?
What mercy for this boy
on whom the fiend descends,   335
the spirit of vengeance
for his mother's blood,
savage spirit, driving on his house
in gust on gust of grief,
blood and the madness of blood,
madness born of murder?
We mourn for this boy;
we grieve for this house.

Happiness is brief.
It will not stay.   340
God batters at its sails,
the tossing seas are wild;
anguish like a wind
whips down,
sorrow strikes,
swamps the scudding ship
and happiness goes down
and glory sinks.
        And yet
what other house, what name   345
more deserves our praise

than this line of glory,
born of Tantalus and Zeus?

And now behold the king—
royal Menelaus
whose magnificence declares   350
the blood of Tantalus!

(Enter Menelaus, with great magnificence and pomp,
followed by a large retinue.)

All hail, the king!
Hail to the king who led
a thousand ships to Troy,
and did with heaven's help
all he vowed to do!   355
Hail him! Glory and success
go beside the king!

Menelaus

Home from Troy at last.
                        How happy I am
to see this house once more—
                        but also sad,
for never have I seen a house more hedged about
by suffering than this.
                        I was putting in to shore
near Cape Malea when I first heard the news   360
of Agamemnon's murder at the hands of his wife.
For Glaucus, the god of sailors and a prophet
who does not lie, suddenly rose from the sea
in clear view of the ships and cried:
                        "Menelaus,   365
your brother lies dying in his bath,
the last bath his wife will ever give him."
My crew and I alike burst into tears
at this dreadful news.

Well, so we reached Nauplia.
My wife Helen came on ahead at night,   370
and I was looking forward to seeing Orestes and his mother,
thinking, of course, that they at least were well,
when some sailor told me of the shocking murder
of Clytemnestra.

        Can you tell me, women,   375
where I might find my nephew Orestes?
He was still a baby in his mother's arms
when I left for Troy, so I would not know him
if I saw him.

Orestes

        Here I am, Menelaus:
Orestes in person, and only too willing   380
to tell you the story of my sufferings.
But first I fall before you on my knees
and beg you, implore you, to rescue me from death.
You come in the nick of time.

Menelaus

        Gods in heaven,   385
is this some corpse I see?

Orestes

        More dead than living,
I admit. Still alive, but dead of my despair.

Menelaus

And that wild, matted hair—how horrible you look!

Orestes

It is my crimes, not my looks, that torture me.

Menelaus

That awful stare—and those dry, cold eyes. . . .

Orestes

My body is dead. I am the name it had.   390

Menelaus

But I did not expect this—alteration.

Orestes

I am a murderer. I murdered my mother.

Menelaus

So I have heard. Kindly spare me your horrors.

Orestes

I spare you—although no god spared me.

Menelaus

What is your sickness?

Orestes

      I call it conscience.   395
The certain knowledge of wrong, the conviction of crime.

Menelaus

You speak somewhat obscurely. What do you mean?

Orestes

I mean remorse. I am sick with remorse.

Menelaus

A harsh goddess, I know. But there are cures.

Orestes

And madness too. The vengeance of my mother's blood.   400

Menelaus

When did this madness start?

Orestes

      The very day
we built her tomb. My poor mother's tomb. . . .

Menelaus

What were you doing when the madness struck?
Were you inside or at the pyre?

Orestes

It was night.
I was standing by the pyre to gather her ashes.

Menelaus

Was there anyone there who could help you?   405

Orestes

Pylades. My accomplice in the murder.

Menelaus

But these phantoms. Can you describe them?

Orestes

I seemed to see three women, black as night—

Menelaus

Say no more. I know the spirits you mean.
I refuse to speak their name.

Orestes

You are wise.   410
They are awful.

Menelaus

And these women, you say,
hound you with madness for killing your mother?

Orestes

If you knew the torture, knew how they hounded me!

Menelaus

That criminals should suffer is hardly strange.

Orestes

There is one recourse left.

Menelaus

Suicide, you mean?

Most unwise.

415

Orestes

No, not that. I mean Apollo.

It was he who commanded my mother's murder.

Menelaus

A callous, unjust, and immoral order.

Orestes

We obey the gods—whoever the gods may be.

Menelaus

Apollo, despite all this, refuses to help?

Orestes

Oh, he will. In his own good time, of course. 420
Gods are slow by nature.

Menelaus

How long has it been

since your mother's death?

Orestes

Six days now.

Her pyre is still warm.

Menelaus

Only six days?

Gods, you say, are slow, but how quickly
your mother's avengers came!

Orestes

Menelaus,

I lack your clever wit. But I was—and am—
loyal to those I love.

Menelaus
               What of your father?   425
Is there any help from him?

Orestes
                  Nothing yet.
And nothing yet means nothing ever.

Menelaus
How do you stand with the city?

Orestes
                      So hated
and despised that not one person in Argos
will speak to me.

Menelaus
            Have your hands been cleansed
of the blood you shed?

Orestes
                They shut their doors in my face.   430

Menelaus
Who is your worst enemy in Argos?

Orestes
                        Oeax,
Palamedes' brother. He hated my father
because of what happened at Troy.

Menelaus
                I see.
He wants your death in revenge for his brother.

Orestes
Whom I never hurt. And yet his death kills me.

Menelaus
Any others? Aegisthus' men, I suppose?   435

Orestes

Yes, they all hate me, and the city gives them
a hearing now.

Menelaus

But will they let you keep
your father's scepter?

Orestes

Let me keep the scepter
when they won't let me live?

Menelaus

What are their plans?

Orestes

The city is voting on our sentence today.   440

Menelaus

What is the verdict? Banishment or death?

Orestes

Death by stoning.

Menelaus

Then why not try to escape?

Orestes

We are surrounded by a ring of solid steel.

Menelaus

Are they Argive soldiers? Or mercenaries
hired by your enemies?

Orestes

It comes to this: 445
everyone in Argos wants me dead.
They are unanimous.

Menelaus

In that case, my boy,
your chances look very slim.

Orestes

                              And that is why
I turn to you.
                    You are now our only hope.
Menelaus, we are desperate. You, in contrast,
arrive in Argos at the moment of success,   450
flushed with triumph, prosperous and happy.
I implore you: share that happiness with us;
do not hoard your power and success.
Help us.
            Repay my father's services to you
by saving us. Share, if only for an hour,
our dangers and disgrace.
                              Friends show their love
in times of trouble, not in happiness.   455

Coryphaeus

Look, Menelaus:
                    Tyndareus of Sparta
on his way here, his hair shorn close
and dressed in black mourning for his daughter.

Orestes

O gods, this is the end.
                    What can I do?
Menelaus, of all the men on earth I dread to meet,   460
this is the one I dread the most, the one man
in whose presence I feel the wrenching shame
of what I did.
                    My grandfather, Tyndareus—
the man who cared for me when I was small,
who held me in his arms so tenderly—
Agamemnon's baby boy—who loved me,
he and Leda both, no less than their own sons,   465
Castor and Polydeuces.
                    They loved me,
and how have I returned their tenderness and love?

O gods, this worthlessness I am!
Where can I run?
                    Where can I hide
from that old man's eye?

(Enter Tyndareus, a spare, gaunt figure of great age, dressed in
                    mourning black. His speech is harsh, spoken with the
                    crabbed authority of Spartan style and
                    the bitterness of old age. He is
                    followed by attendants.)

Tyndareus
                    Where can I find   470
my son-in-law Menelaus, women?
I was pouring libations on my daughter's grave
when I heard the news of his arrival home
at Nauplia after those long years abroad.
Helen is also here, I understand.
Can you show me the way?
                    I am most eager
to see him again after his long absence.   475

Menelaus
    Tyndareus!

Tyndareus
        Menelaus, my son!

        (He stops short as he suddenly catches sight of Orestes.)
Is he here?
        If I had known that he was here,
I never would have come.
                    Look at him,
Menelaus: the man who murdered his mother,
coiled like a snake at the door, those sick eyes
glowing like coals—
                    What a loathsome sight!   480
How can you bear to speak to a thing like this?

Menelaus

Why not? I loved my brother. This is his son.

Tyndareus

This, Agamemnon's son? This *thing?*

Menelaus

Yes.

His son, in trouble, and I honor him.

Tyndareus

Your foreigners, I see, have taught you their ways.   485

Menelaus

It is a Greek custom, I think, to honor your kin.

Tyndareus

But not to put yourself above the laws.

Menelaus

Necessity is legislator here.
Under compulsion, no man on earth is free—
or so I hold.

Tyndareus

That is your theory then.
It is not mine and I want none of it.

Menelaus

Your age—and anger—cripple your understanding.   490

Tyndareus

Understanding, you say?
                              What in the name of god
does understanding have to do with *him?*
Is there some *moral* question here in dispute
between us?
                    If moral facts are clear to all,

if right and wrong are plain as black and white,
what man ever acted more blindly,
more stupidly, with smaller understanding
of right and wrong than this man?
                                    Not once,
mind you, did he weigh the justice of his cause
or avail himself of the law and our courts for murder!   495
What should he have done?
                                    When his father died—
killed, I admit, by my own daughter's hand,
an atrocious crime which I do not condone
and never shall—he should have haled his mother
into court, charged her formally with murder,   500
and made her pay the penalty prescribed,
expulsion from his house.
                                    Legal action,
not murder. That was the course to take.
Under the circumstances, a hard choice,
true, but the course of self-control
and due respect for law, and the better choice
of two evils.
                                    But as things stand now,
what difference is there between him and his mother?
No, vicious as she was, if anything,
the evil he has done by killing her   505
has far surpassed her crime.
                                    Think again,
Menelaus.
                                    Suppose a wife murders her husband.
Her son then follows suit by killing her,
and his son then must have his murder too
and so on.
                                    Where, I want to know, can this chain   510
of murder end? Can it ever end, in fact,
since the last to kill is doomed to stand
under permanent sentence of death by revenge?

No, our ancestors handled these matters well
by banning their murderers from public sight,
forbidding them to meet or speak to anyone.
But the point is this: they purged their guilt   515
by banishment, not death. And by so doing,
they stopped that endless vicious cycle
of murder and revenge.
                              Do not mistake me.
I despise adultery and unfaithful wives,
and my daughter Clytemnestra, an adulteress
and murderess to boot, most of all.
As for your wife Helen, I loathe her too   520
and never wish to speak to her again.
Nor, I might add, do I envy you
your trip to Troy to bring your whore back home.
No sir, not my daughters, but the law:
that is my concern. There I take my stand,
defending it with all my heart and strength
against the brutal and inhuman spirit of murder
that corrupts our cities and destroys this country.   525

                    (*He turns on Orestes in fury.*)
Yes, you heard me, monster!
                              Inhuman spirit,
I said.
          Where was your pity, your humanity,
when your mother bared her breast and begged you
for her life?
               I did not see that pitiful sight,
but the very thought of it makes the tears come
to these eyes.
               One thing I know for certain: 530
heaven loathes you. These fits of madness
are the price you pay for murder; heaven itself
has made you mad. No further proof is needed.
So be warned, Menelaus.

If you help this man,   535
if you so much as lift a finger in his defense,
you challenge the express will of heaven.
So let him be. Let them stone him to death
or—I give you warning, sir—never set foot
in Sparta again.
              My own daughter is dead,
and she deserved to die, but it was wrong
that he should kill her.
                    Except for my daughters,   540
I might have lived a happy man and died in peace.
But there my fortunes failed.

Coryphaeus

                    Lucky that man
whose children make his happiness in life
and not his grief, the anguished disappointment
of his hopes.

Orestes

              Sir, I shrink from speaking,
knowing almost anything I say will displease you   545
or offend you.
              My murder of my mother was,
I admit, a crime. But in another sense,
since, by killing her, I avenged my father,
there was no crime at all.

                    (*Tyndareus starts to walk away in disgust.*)

                    Wait. Listen.
Let me speak. This respect I feel for your age
cripples me, shames me. If you only knew
how that white hair of yours harrows me   550
with shame.

                    (*Tyndareus stops and listens.*)

              What else *could* I have done?
I had two duties, two clear choices,
both of them conflicting.

My father begot me,
my mother gave me birth. She was the furrow
in which his seed was sown. But without the father,
there is no birth. That being so, I thought,   555
I ought to stand by him, the true agent
of my birth and being, rather than with her
who merely brought me up.

          And then your daughter—
I blush with shame to call that woman my mother—
in a mock marriage, in the private rites of lust,
took a lover in her bed. And I hurt myself
as much as I hurt her by that admission.
But I admit it: what does it matter now?   560
Yes, Aegisthus was her lover; he was the husband
hidden in the house. And so I killed them both,
two murders, both committed for the single motive
of avenging my father.

          For this you threaten me
with stoning. But, in fact, I did a service,   565
a patriotic service.

          Tell me, what would happen
if our women decided to adopt my mother's example,
killed their husbands and then came rushing home
to their children, exposing their breasts for pity?
Why, they could murder a man for any trifle,
on any pretext. But my "crime," as you call it,   570
has stopped that practice for good or kept it
from spreading.

          I had every right to kill her.
I hated her, and I had every reason in the world
to hate.

          Gods, my poor father away from home,
a soldier fighting in war in his country's service,
and what did she do? She took a lover   575
and betrayed his bed!

          And when she was caught,

did she do the proper thing and put herself
to death?

        Not my mother. No, she murdered him
to save herself.

          I should not invoke the gods
when defending myself on a charge of murder,
but *in god's name, in the name of heaven,*
what was I supposed to do?

              Shout hurrah   580
by keeping still?

          And what would *he* have done?
Hounded me with the Furies of a father's hatred!
Or are there Furies on my mother's side,
but none to help him in his deeper hurt?
It was *you: you* destroyed me, Tyndareus.
You were the father of that woman who killed   585
my father and made a murderer of me.
And what of this?

        Odysseus had a son,
but was Telemachus compelled to kill *his* mother?
No. And why? She refused to take a lover.   590
She was loyal to Odysseus.

          And what of this?
Or have you forgotten Apollo, the god of Delphi,
navel and center of the world? The one god
whose every oracle and word mankind obeys
blindly? He *commanded* my mother's murder.
Accuse *him* of murder, then. Put *him* to death.   595
He is the culprit, not I.

         What could *I* do?
Or was he competent to command a murder,
but now incompetent to purge the guilt?
Then where *can* I go, what *can* I do,
if the god who ordered me to kill my mother
cannot, or will not, save me?

          One more thing.

Let no man say that what we did was wrong, 600
but that doing what we did, we did it
to our great cost and misery.
                              As in action,
so in marriage too. Marry, and with luck
it may go well. But when a marriage fails,
then those who marry live at home in hell.

Coryphaeus

Women by nature, it seems, were born to be 605
a great impediment and bitterness
in the lives of men.

Tyndareus

                              Since bluster is your answer,
since you insist on brazening it out
and every word you speak is said in spite,
I am even more impatient than before
to see you die.
                              My purpose in coming here
was to lay some flowers on your mother's grave. 610
But now, by god, I have a deeper motive—
your death!
                              I will go to the Argives myself.
They may resent it, but, by heaven, I'll hound them
until they stone your sister and you to death!
Yes, your sister too!
                              She deserves it, 615
by god, even more than you!
                              It was *she*,
that girl, who incited you against your mother,
stuffing your ears day in and day out
with her malice and venom, telling you her dreams
of Agamemnon's ghost and what he said,
tattling to you of your mother's adultery—
which I dearly hope offends the gods below 620

as much as it disgusted us on earth!
That was her effort. Yes, she worked on you
until she set this whole house on fire
with the arson of her malice.

                    One thing more,
Menelaus.

            I warn you, if my love or hate
matter to you at all, do not oppose the gods
by rescuing this man.

                  No, let them stone him,   625
or—mark my words—never set foot in Sparta
again.

         I warn you, do not make the mistake
of siding with outlaws and criminals like this
against god-fearing and law-abiding men.
Servants, lead me away.

               (Exit Tyndareus, escorted by attendants. Menelaus
                     begins to pace anxiously up and down.)

Orestes

              Good. Go.   630
Let Menelaus hear the rest of my appeal
uninterrupted. Spare us the nuisance
of respecting your old age.

            —But, Menelaus,
why that troubled look? And why are you pacing
up and down that way?

Menelaus

             Let me think.
I am trying to decide on the wisest course.   635
And, frankly, I am puzzled.

Orestes

            Then postpone decision
for a while. Hear what I have to say
and then decide at leisure.

Menelaus

                    Fair enough.
There are times for keeping still and times
for speaking out. This is the time to speak.
Go ahead.

Orestes

                    Forgive me if I speak at length.   640
But the more comprehensive I can be,
the better.
                    Let me be honest, Menelaus.
It is not your money that I need. What I want
from you is what my father gave you once—
by which I do not mean money. I mean life.
Give me life and you give me something more precious   645
than money.
                    I committed a crime, and I admit it.
But right or wrong, it is only right
that you should do some wrong to help me now.
When my father mustered an army for the siege
of Troy, he also did a wrong—and yet
that wrong was generous. He did that wrong for you,
to right the wrong that your wife Helen did.   650
And wrong for wrong, you owe me that wrong now,
Menelaus.
                    Good brother that he was,
my father volunteered his life for you,
fighting as a soldier at your side
for ten long years of war. And why?
For this alone: to help you win your wife
and bring her home.
                    What you had of him,   655
I now exact of you. Fight on my behalf,
not ten long years, but one brief day.
Again, my sister Iphigenia died at Aulis
on your account. But any claim I have on you

for my sister's death, I freely waive.
Hermione may live. For as things stand now,   660
I cannot press my claim, and I forgive you
your advantage.

                But repay my father's loan;
settle your score with him by saving us.
Think: if I die, I leave my father's house
heirless, orphaned of life.

                    Impossible,   665
you say?

            But surely this is just the point,
Menelaus.

             If you love us, *this* is the time
to help, *now*, when everything we have
is lost.

          Who wants help when the gods are good
and all is well? No, the man whom heaven helps
has friends enough. But now we need your help.
    All Hellas knows how much you love your wife.
I am not trying to flatter you or wheedle you,   670
but in Helen's name, I beg you—

                      (*Menelaus turns away.*)

                It is no use.
He will not help.

            But let me make one last attempt.

                (*He falls at Menelaus' feet.*)

In the name of all our house, our family,
O Uncle, my father's brother, save us now!
Imagine that my dead father in his grave   675
listens to me now, that his spirit is hovering
over you, that he himself is speaking, pleading
through my lips!

                You have seen our sufferings
and our despair, and I have begged you for my life—
life, the one hope of every man on earth,
not mine alone.

Coryphaeus

                I am only a woman,   680
but I implore you: help them, save them.
It lies in your power.

Menelaus

               Believe me, Orestes,
I sympathize from the bottom of my heart.
And nothing in this world would please me more
than to honor that touching appeal for help.
We are joined, besides, by a common bond of blood,
and I am honor bound to come to your defense   685
against your enemies, even at the cost
of my life—obliged, in short, to do everything
it lies in my power to do.
                    God knows,
I only wish I could.
                But it just so happens
that I arrived in Argos in a weakened way—
devoid of support—my allies have dwindled away—
myself exhausted by our terrible ordeal,
and barely able to count on even a fraction   690
of my former friends.
               Under the circumstances—
as I think you will agree—the obvious notion
of beating Argos to her knees by a show of strength   695
is quite out of the question.
                Let me be frank.
We are weak, and therefore our weapons must be
diplomacy and tact. Inadequate,
I admit, but not perhaps quite hopeless.
Whereas even to suggest a show of strength
as a way out, given our present weakness,
is palpable folly.
             Look at it this way, my boy.
Mobs in their emotions are much like children,

subject to the same tantrums and fits of fury.
But this anger must be treated with great patience,
rather like a fire that gets out of control.
Hands off is best. You sit quietly by,
watching and waiting, patiently biding your time
while their fury runs its course unchecked.
With any luck, it quickly burns itself out,
and in the lull, while the wind is shifting,   700
anything you want is yours for the asking.
Anger, however, is only one of their moods;
pity is another—but precious assets both,
if you know what you're doing.

                              Now this is my plan.
I'll go and smooth matters over
with Tyndareus and the city and persuade them   705
to moderate their tone.

                    As with sailing,
so with politics: make your cloth too taut,
and your ship will dip and keel, but slacken off
and trim your sails, and things head up again.
The gods, you know, resent being importuned
too much; in the same way the people dislike
being pushed or hustled. Too much zeal offends
where indirection works. And our only chance
of saving you at all lies in skill and tact,   710
not in force, as you perhaps imagine.
But these are the facts. On my own
I lack the men and strength your rescue requires;
and the Argives, I know, are not the sort of men
to be overawed by threats.

                    No, if we're wise,
we will do what we must and accept the facts.   715
We have no other choice.

                    (*Exit Menelaus attended by his retinue.*)

Orestes

You cheap traitor!
What in god's name have you ever done
but fight a war to bring your wife back home?
So now you turn your back and desert me,
do you?

This is the end, this is the last
of the house of Agamemnon.   720

My poor father—
even in his grave, deserted by his friends....
And now my last hope, my only refuge
from death is lost....

See, there it goes—
that traitor Menelaus was my final hope.
But wait—

Look! I see Pylades!
My best friend, Pylades, on his way   725
from Phocis!

Thank god! What a sight!
A friend, a loyal friend, in my despair.
No sailor ever saw a calm more greedily
than I now see my friend—

Pylades!

(Enter Pylades.)

Pylades

I seem to have reached here none too soon, Orestes.
As I was coming through town, I saw the Argives meeting   730
and with my own ears heard them discussing some proposal
to execute your sister and you.

In the name of heaven,
what has happened here? What does all this mean?

Orestes

It means this: we are ruined.

Pylades
                              Include me in that "we."   735
    Friends share and share alike.

Orestes
                        That traitor Menelaus—
    he betrayed my sister and me.

Pylades
                        I am not surprised.
    A vicious husband for a vicious wife.

Orestes
                                By coming home
    he helped my cause as much as if he'd stayed in Troy.

Pylades
    Then the rumor *was* true? He really has returned?

Orestes
    Somewhat late. His treachery, on the other hand,   740
    was promptness itself.

Pylades
                    What about that bitch Helen?
    Did he bring her home?

Orestes
                        No, the other way around.
    She brought him.

Pylades
                    Where is she hiding now?
    Where is that woman who murdered so many Argives?

Orestes
    In my house—if I have any right to call it mine.

Pylades
    What did you ask Menelaus?

Orestes

To intercede for us   745
and save our lives.

Pylades

By god, what did he say to that?
This I want to hear.

Orestes

Oh, patience, caution, and so on.
The usual rot that traitors talk.

Pylades

But what was his excuse?
That tells me everything.

Orestes

We were interrupted.
That old man came. You know the man I mean—   750
the father of those precious daughters.

Pylades

Tyndareus himself?
Furious with you, I suppose, because of your mother?

Orestes

You've hit it. So Menelaus took the old man's side
against my father.

Pylades

He refused to help you at all?

Orestes

Oh, he's no soldier—though he's quite the man
with the ladies.

Pylades

As matters now stand, your death is certain?   755

Orestes

They vote on our sentence today.

Pylades

I dread your answer,
but what will their verdict be?

Orestes

Life or death.
Little words with large gestures.

Pylades

Take Electra
and try to make your escape.

Orestes

No. Impossible.   760
There are sentries posted everywhere.

Pylades

I remember now.
Armed men were patrolling the streets.

Orestes

We are surrounded
like a city under siege.

Pylades

Ask what happened to me.
I have suffered too.

Orestes

Your troubles on top of mine?
What happened?

Pylades

My father Strophius banished me from Phocis.   765

Orestes

Banished you? On his authority as your father?
Or did he take you to court on a formal indictment?

Pylades

For aiding and abetting the murder of your mother—
that "shocking crime," as he calls it.

Orestes

                                        Heaven help me,
if you must suffer on my account!

Pylades

                              I am no Menelaus.
I can take it.

Orestes

                    But aren't you afraid of the Argives?   770
Suppose they decide to put you to death with me?

Pylades

They have no jurisdiction. I am a Phocian.

Orestes

Don't be too certain. In the hands of vicious men,
a mob will do anything.

Pylades

                              But under good leaders
it's quite a different story.

Orestes

                    By god, that's *it!*
We must speak to them ourselves.

Pylades

                                        But why should we?

Orestes

Suppose, for instance, I went to the meeting myself   775
and told them—

Pylades

                    That you were completely justified?

Orestes

That I avenged my father.

Pylades

                         They'd arrest you with pleasure.

Orestes

But what am I supposed to do? Sit here and sulk?
Die without saying a word in my own defense?

Pylades

A coward's act.

Orestes

               Then, for god's sake, what *should* I do?

Pylades

Do you have anything to gain from staying here?

Orestes

Nothing whatsoever.

Pylades

               And if you go to the meeting?

Orestes

Something might be gained.

Pylades

               Then, clearly, you have to go.   780

Orestes

Good enough. I'll go.

Pylades

               You may be killed, of course,
but at least you'll die fighting.

Orestes

               And escape a coward's death.

Pylades

Better than by staying here.

Orestes

               And my cause is just.

Pylades

Pray heaven that it seem that way to them.

Orestes

Besides, they may pity me—

Pylades

Yes, your high birth.

Orestes

Or they may feel indignation at my father's murder.   785

Pylades

Then our course is clear.

Orestes

Absolutely. I must go.
I refuse to die a coward's death.

Pylades

Spoken like a man.

Orestes

Wait. Should we tell Electra?

Pylades

Great heavens, no!

Orestes

There'd probably be tears.

Pylades

Which wouldn't be auspicious.

Orestes

Clearly silence is best.

Pylades

And will save no little time.

Orestes

One strong objection still remains.

Pylades

What's that?   790

Orestes

My madness. If I have an attack—

Pylades

Have no fear.

You are in good hands.

Orestes

Madmen are hard to handle.

Pylades

I will manage.

Orestes

But if my madness strikes you too?

Pylades

Forget it.

Orestes

You're certain then? You're not afraid?

Pylades

Afraid? Fear in friendship is an ugly trait.

Orestes

Then lead on, helmsman.

Pylades

Love leads you. Follow me.   795

Orestes

Take me first to my father's grave.

Pylades

What for?

Orestes

To implore his help.

Pylades

Agreed. This pilgrimage is good.

Orestes

But don't, for god's sake, let me see my mother's grave!

Pylades

No. She hated you.
                     But hurry. We must go now,
or the Argives may have voted before we arrive.
Here, lean yourself on me.
                          Now let the people jeer!   800
I'll lead you through the city, proud and unashamed.
What is my friendship worth unless I prove it now
in your time of trouble?

Orestes

                      "Provide yourself with friends
as well as kin," they say. And the proverb tells the truth.
One loyal friend is worth ten thousand relatives.   805

                            (*Exeunt Orestes and Pylades.*)

Chorus

Where, where are they now—
that glister of golden pride,
glory that camped at Troy
beside the Simois,
the boast of happiness
blazoned through Hellas?
Back and back they ebb,   810
a glory decays,
the greatness goes
from the happy house of Atreus.
Beneath the proud facade
the stain was old already—
strife for a golden ram,
and the long stain spread
as the curse of blood began—
slaughter of little princes,   815
a table laid with horror,
a feast of murdered sons.
And still corruption swelled,

murder displacing murder,
as through the blooded years
the stain spread on in time
to reach at last
the living heirs of Atreus.

And what had seemed so right,
as soon as done, became
evil, monstrous, wrong!
A mother murdered—
her soft throat slashed   820
by the stabbing sword,
and the blade raised high
while the brandished blood
fell warm from the steel,
staining, defiling
the sun's immaculate light.
Damnable, awful crime!
Sacrilege of madness born!
In horror, in anguish,
before she died,
his mother screamed—   825
No, no, my son, no!
Do not kill your mother
to revenge your father!
Do not make your life
an eternity of shame!   830

What madness like this?
What terror, what grief
can compare with this?
Hands, hands of a son,
stained with mother's blood!
Horror too inhuman
for mortal mind to bear.
The man who slew his mother
murdered and went mad.   835

Raving Furies stalk him down,
his rolling eyes are wild—
mad eyes that saw
his mother bare her breast   840
over her cloth of gold—
saw, and seeing, stabbed,
avenging his father
with his mother's murder!

> (*Electra appears from the palace and is startled
> to find Orestes gone.*)

Electra

But where is Orestes? For god's sake, women,
where did he go? Has he had another attack?   845

Coryphaeus

No, Electra. He went to the Argive meeting
to stand his trial and speak in his own defense.
Upon what happens there your life depends.

Electra

But *why?* And who persuaded him?

Coryphaeus

                Pylades.
But I think I see a messenger on the way.   850
He can answer your questions.

> (*Enter Messenger, an old peasant.*)

Messenger

              Lady Electra,
poor daughter of our old general Agamemnon,
I bring you bad news.

Electra

              If your news is bad,   855
I hardly need to guess: we must die.
The sentence is death.

Messenger
                              Yes. The Argives have voted
that you and your brother must die today.

Electra
                                        Death. . . .
But I expected no less. For a long time now
I dreaded in my heart that this would happen.   860
But what did they say? What were the arguments
that condemned us to death?
                              And how are we to die,
my brother and I? By being stoned to death   865
or by the sword?

Messenger
                    By strange coincidence, ma'am,
I'd just now come into town from the country,
thinking to get some news of how things stood
with you and Orestes. Your family, you see,
always took good care of me and, for my part,
I stood by your father to the very end.
I may be only a poor peasant, ma'am,
but when it comes to loyalty, I'm as good   870
as any man.
                    Well then, I saw a crowd
go streaming up to take their seats on the hill—
the same place where they say old Danaus
held the first public meeting in Argos
when Aegyptus stood his trial.
                              But anyhow,
seeing all that crowd, I went up and asked,
"What's happening here? Is there a war?   875
What's all this excitement for?"
                              "Look down,"
says someone. "Don't you see Orestes there?
He's on his way to stand trial for his life."
Then I saw a sight I never saw before,

and one whose likes I never hope to see
again:
       Orestes and Pylades together,   880
the one hunched down with sickness and despair,
the other sharing his troubles like a brother
and helping him along.
                In any case,
as soon as the seats were filled, a herald rose.
"Who wishes," he cried, "to speak to the question?   885
What is your wish? Should the matricide Orestes
live or die?"
         Then Talthybius got up—
the same man who fought with your father at Troy.
But he spoke like the toady he always was:
a two-faced speech, compliments for your father   890
in contrast to Orestes, cheap malicious stuff
puffed out with rolling phrases. And the gist?
Orestes' example was dangerous for parents.
But, needless to say, he was all smiles and sweetness
for Aegisthus' cronies.
         But that's your herald for you—   895
always jumping for the winning side, the friend
of any man with influence or power.
              After him
prince Diomedes spoke. It was his opinion
that you both should be banished, not killed,
since, by so doing, Argos would be guiltless   900
of your blood. The response, however, was mixed:
some applauded, others booed.
           The next speaker
was one of those cocky loudmouths, an Argive
but not from Argos—if you take my meaning—
anybody's man—for a price, of course—
sure of himself and reckless in his bluster,   905
but glib enough to take his hearers in.
He moved that Orestes and you should be stoned

to death, while Tyndareus sat cheering him on, 915
and even spoke to that effect.
     But at last
someone stood up to take the other side.
Nothing much to look at, but a real man;
not the sort one sees loafing in the market
or public places, ma'am, but a small farmer,
part of that class on which our country depends; 920
an honest, decent, and god-fearing man,
and anxious, in the name of common sense,
to say his bit.
     Now in this man's opinion,
Orestes deserved a crown. What had he done,
after all, but avenge his father's murder
by killing a godless, worthless, adulterous woman? 925
A woman, what was more, who kept men from war,
kept them at home, tormented by the fear
that if they left, those who stayed behind
would seduce their wives and destroy their families
and homes.
    He seemed to convince the better sort, 930
but no one spoke.
     Then Orestes rose.
"Men of Argos," he said, "it was for your sake
as much as for my father that I killed my mother.
But if you sanction this murder of husbands by wives, 935
you might as well go kill yourselves right now
or accept the domination of your women.
But you *will not*, you *must not*, do it.
As things now stand, my father's unfaithful wife
is dead. But if you vote that I must die, 940
then the precedent my act establishes
must fall, and you are all as good as dead,
since wives will have the courage of their crimes."
In short, a fine speech, and yet he failed;
while that cheap blabber, by playing to the mob,

induced them to pass a sentence of death. 945
Poor Orestes was barely able to persuade them
not to stone him to death, and then only
by promising that you and he would kill yourselves
today.

       Pylades, in tears, is bringing him home 950
from the meeting, followed by a group of friends,
all weeping and mourning. Such is his return,
and a bitter sight it is.

            So prepare the ropes,
bring out the sword, for you must die
and leave the light. Neither your high birth
nor Apollo in his shrine at Delphi helped. No, 955
Apollo has destroyed you both.

Coryphaeus

             Poor wretched girl.
Look at her now, her head hung down,
dumb with grief, trembling on the verge of tears....

Electra

  O country of Pelasgia,
let me lead the cry of mourning! 960
  With white nails I furrow my cheeks,
beat my breast,
each blow struck
for the queen of the dead,
goddess Persephone underground!
Mourn, you Cyclopean earth! 965
Shear your hair, you virgins,
and raise the cry of pity,
pity for us who die,
heirs of the fighting men of Hellas! 970

Down and down, my house.
Pelops' line is ended,

the ancient happy house,
its envied greatness gone.
Envy and resentment
out of heaven struck.
Envy was the vote   975
the men of Argos took.

O generations of men,
fleeting race of suffering mankind,
look, look on your hopes!
Look at your lives,
all those happy hopes
cut down with failure and crossed with death.
See, in endless long parade,
the passing generations go,
changing places, changing lives.   980
The suffering remains.
Change and grief consume our little light.

O gods in heaven, take me,
lift me to heaven's middle air
where the great rock,
shattered from Olympus,
swings and floats on golden lines!
Lift me, take me there
and let me cry my grief to Tantalus,   985
founder of my house,
father of my fathers,
who saw the curse begin—
saw the wingèd race
as Pelops' swerving car
spurred along the sea,
Myrtilus hurled in murder down,   990
the body tossed
from the hurtling car
where the boiling surf
pounds and batters on Geraestos!

And saw the curse drive on
and the spreading stain of blood—   995
the sign appear
in Hermes' flocks,
a ram with golden fleece,
portending terror,
doom to Atreus, breeder of horses,   1000
the quarrel in the blood
that drove the golden sun awry,
forced the glistering car
westward through the sky
where lonely Dawn drives down
her solitary steed.
And Zeus, in horror of that crime,
changed the paths   1005
where the seven Pleiades turned and flared.
And still the spreading stain,
murder displacing murder,
betrayal and broken faith,
Thyestes' feast of horror
and the adulterous love
of Aërope of Crete.   1010
And now the curse comes home,
the inescapable taint,
finding fulfilment at last
in my brother and me!

Coryphaeus

And here your brother comes
under his sentence of death.
And with him comes Pylades,
most loyal of his friends,   1015
guiding like a brother
poor Orestes' stumbling steps.

> (*Enter Orestes, supported by Pylades.*
> *Electra bursts into tears.*)

Electra

Orestes—
       O gods, to see you standing there,
so close to death, the grave so near—
O gods, I cannot bear it! To see you now   1020
for the last, last time. . . . No! No! No!

Orestes

Enough, Electra. No more of these womanish tears.
Resign yourself. It is hard, I know,
but we must accept our fate.

Electra

                    How *can* I stop?   1025
Look, look at this light, this gleaming air
we shall never see again!

Orestes

                    No more, Electra.
Isn't it enough that the Argives have killed me?
Must you kill me too? For god's sake,
no more tears.

Electra

                    But you are so young,
so young to die! You should live, Orestes! *Live!*   1030

Orestes.

In god's name, stop it! These cries of yours
will make me a coward.

Electra

                    But to *die*, Orestes!
Life is sweet, sweet! No one wants to die.

Orestes

No, but we have no choice. Our time has come.   1035
We merely have to choose the way in which we die:
by the sword or the rope.

Electra
                              Kill me yourself then,
Orestes. Don't let some Argive disgrace
the daughter of Agamemnon.

Orestes
                              I have my mother's blood
upon my hands. I will not have yours too.   1040
Do it in any way you wish, but you must do it
yourself.

Electra
          If I must, then I must. But, Orestes,
don't die before I do! Please. O gods,
let me hold you. . . .

Orestes
                    What is it worth,
this poor hollow pleasure—if those who die
have any pleasure left?

Electra
                    Oh, my brother,
dearest, sweetest name I know—my life—   1045

Orestes
      O gods, this breaks my heart—
                              With all my love
I hold you in my arms.
                              What shame on earth
can touch me any more?
                              Oh, my sister,
these loving words, this last sweet embrace
is all that we shall ever know in life   1050
of marriage and children!

Electra
                    If only one sword
could kill us both! If we could only share
one coffin together—

Orestes
>   Then death might be sweet.
But how little now of all our family is left   1055
to bury us.

Electra
>   Menelaus did nothing at all?
He betrayed our father like the coward he is?

Orestes

No, not once did he so much as show his face.
Not once. His eyes were glued upon the throne;
oh, he was careful not to help.
>   But come,
we must die as we were born—well,   1060
as the children and heirs of Agamemnon should.
I shall show the city of what blood I come
by falling on my sword. As for you,
follow my example and die bravely.
>   Pylades,
be the umpire of our deaths; then lay us out   1065
when we are dead, and make us both one grave
beside my father's tomb.
>   And now, goodbye.
I go to do what must be done.

Pylades
>   Wait!
Stop, Orestes. I have one reproach to make.
How could you think that I would want to live   1070
once you were dead?

Orestes
>   Why should my dying
mean that you should die?

Pylades
>   You can ask me that?
How can I live when my only friend is dead?

Orestes

It was I who murdered my mother, not you.

Pylades

We murdered together, and it is only just
that I share the cost with you.

Orestes

No,   1075

Pylades. Live; go home to your father.
You still have a country you can call your own;
I do not. You have your father's house
and you inherit wealth, great wealth.
That marriage with Electra which, as my friend,
I promised you, has failed. But marry elsewhere;   1080
have children.

The bonds which bound us once
are broken now. And now goodbye, my friend,
my best, my only friend.

And good luck.
Luck at least is something you may have,
but I cannot. The dead have lost their luck.

Pylades

How little you seem to understand, Orestes.   1085
If I desert you now to save myself,
may this green and growing earth refuse
my ashes, this golden air shelter me no more!
I murdered with you, and I affirm it
proudly. And it was I who planned that crime   1090
for which you suffer now, and I should die
with you and her.

Yes, with her, I said.
She is my wife, the wife you promised me.
What would my story be when I go home
to Delphi and Phocis?

That when all was well,   1095
I was your firm friend, but my friendship withered
when your luck ran out?
                        No, Orestes,
I have my duty too.
                        But since we have to die,
let us think and see if there is any way
of making Menelaus suffer too.

Orestes

Let me see that sight and I could die   1100
content.

Pylades

            Then do what I ask you and wait now.

Orestes

With pleasure, if only I can be revenged.

Pylades

                (*Drawing Orestes back out of hearing of the Chorus.*)
Whisper. Those women there—I don't trust them.

Orestes

They're all right. They're friends.

Pylades

                        Then listen.
We'll murder Helen. That will touch   1105
Menelaus where it hurts.

Orestes

                But how?
If we can manage it, I'm more than willing.

Pylades

A sword in the throat. Unless I'm mistaken,
she's hiding in your house now.

Orestes

Oh yes,
and putting her seals on everything we own.

Pylades

But not for long. Hades wants her, I think.

Orestes

But how can we do it? She has a retinue   1110
of slaves.

Pylades

Slaves? Is that all she has?
I'm not afraid of any Trojan slaves.

Orestes

Creatures who manage her perfume and mirrors!

Pylades

Gods! Did she bring those Trojan gewgaws home?

Orestes

Oh, Hellas is far too small to hold that woman now.

Pylades

What are slaves worth in a fight with men   1115
who were born free?

Orestes

If we can bring this off,
I'll gladly die twice.

Pylades

And so would I,
to get revenge for you.

Orestes

But describe your plan.
Every step.

Pylades
    First of all, we go inside
on the pretext of killing ourselves.

Orestes
         Good enough.   1120
  But then?

Pylades
    Then we make a great show of tears
and tell her how much we suffer.

Orestes
        At which, of course,
she'll burst into tears. But she'll be laughing inside.

Pylades
  Why then, so will we—exactly the same.

Orestes
  But how do we kill her?

Pylades
      We'll carry swords   1125
  hidden in our robes.

Orestes
      But what about her slaves?
We must kill them first.

Pylades
      No, we'll lock them up
  in different rooms.

Orestes
     But if they scream for help,
then we'll kill them.

Pylades
     And once we're through with them,
the way is clear. Right?

Orestes

Death to Helen!

That will be our motto.

Pylades

Now you have it.

But observe the beauty of my plan.

First,

if we killed a better woman than Helen,
it would be plain murder.

This is not.

No, we punish her in the name of all Hellas
whose fathers and sons she murdered, whose wives
she widowed.

Mark my words, Orestes.

There will be bonfires and celebrations in Argos;
men will call down blessings on our heads,
thank us, congratulate us for doing away
with a vicious, worthless woman. No longer
shall they call you "the man who murdered his mother."
No, a fairer title awaits you now,
the better name of "the killer of Helen
who killed so many men."

And why, in god's name,

should Menelaus prosper when you, your sister,
and your father have to die?—I omit your mother
with good reason. If, through Agamemnon,
Menelaus has his wife, he *shall* not, *must* not,
have your house.

For my part, let me die

if I do not lift my sword against that woman!
But should we fail, should she escape our hands,
we'll burn this house around us as we die!
One way or another, Orestes, we shall not be cheated
of glory.

Honor is ours if we die;

fame, if we escape.

1130

1135

1140

1145

1150

Coryphaeus

                    Every woman
loathes and despises the name of Helen, the woman
who disgraced her sex.

Orestes

                    Nothing in this world   1155
is better than a friend. For one good friend
I would not take in trade either power or money
or all the people of Argos. It was you,
my best friend, who planned our murder of Aegisthus.
You shared the risks with me, and once again,
good friend, you give me my revenge   1160
and all your help.

                    But I say no more,
lest I embarrass you by praising you
so much.

                    I have to die. Very well then,
but above all else I want my death
to hurt the man I hate. He betrayed me,   1165
he made me suffer, so let him suffer now
for what he did to me.

                    Am I or am I not
the son of Agamemnon, the man who ruled all Hellas,
not as a tyrant, but almost as a god,
with godlike power?

                    And I shall not shame him
by dying like a slave. No, I die free,
and I shall have my free revenge on you,   1170
Menelaus!

                    That revenge alone
would make me happy. If—which I doubt—
we could murder Helen and then escape,
so much the better. But this is a dream,
a prayer, a futile hope. It cheers the heart,   1175
but nothing more.

Electra
> Orestes, I have the answer!
A way out for us all!

Orestes
> That would take a god.
But go ahead, Electra. I know your shrewdness   1180
of mind.

Electra
> Listen then. You too, Pylades.

Orestes
Go on. Good news would make pleasant hearing now.

Electra
Do you remember Helen's daughter, Hermione?

Orestes
That little girl our mother took care of?

Electra
> Yes.
She has gone now to Clytemnestra's tomb.   1185

Orestes
What for? And what if she has?

Electra
> She went
to pour libations on our mother's grave.

Orestes
> And so?
What does this have to do with our escape?

Electra
Seize her as a hostage when she comes back.

Orestes
What good will that do?

Electra

Listen, Orestes.   1190
Once Helen is dead, Menelaus may attempt
to hurt one of us three—you or him or me—
though it hardly matters who: we are all one here.
Well, let him try. You merely set your sword
at Hermione's throat and warn him you will kill her
at the first false move. If then, seeing Helen   1195
lying in a pool of blood, he decides he wants
his daughter's life at least and agrees to spare you,
let the girl go. On the other hand,
if he tries to kill you in a frantic burst of rage,
you slit the girl's throat. He may bluster   1200
in the beginning, but he'll soon see reason,
I think. The man's a coward, as you know:
he won't fight.
                    And there you have my plan
for making our escape.

Orestes

                    What a woman!
The mind of a man with a woman's loveliness!   1205
If ever a woman deserved to live, not die,
that woman is you.
                    What do you say now,
Pylades? Will you forfeit a woman like this
by dying, or will you live, marry her,
and be happy?

Pylades

                    Nothing would please me more.
My dearest wish is to go home to Phocis
with Electra as my bride.

Orestes

                    Electra, I like your plan   1210
in every respect—provided we can catch
the traitor's cub. How soon, do you think,
will Hermione return?

Electra
                        Any moment now.
The time at least is exactly right.

Orestes
                              Perfect.   1215
Electra, you stay here outside the house
and wait for her. Make certain that no one,
and especially no friend of her father,
slips into the house. But if someone does,   1220
beat with your fist on the door or raise a cry,
but let us know.
                    You and I, Pylades—
I know I can count on your help now, my friend—
will go inside, get our swords and make ready
to settle our score with Helen.

                    (*He raises his arms in prayer and invokes
                        the ghost of Agamemnon.*)

                        O my father,   1225
ghost who walks the house of blackest night,
your son Orestes calls upon your help
in his hour of need! It is for you, Father,
I suffer. For you I was condemned to death
unjustly! And your own brother has betrayed me,
though what I did was right. Come, Father,
help me to capture his wife! Help me kill her!   1230
O Father, help us now!

Electra
                        O my father,
if you can hear our prayers beneath the earth,
come, rise in answer! We die for you!

Pylades
    O Agamemnon, kinsman of my father,
    hear my prayers!
                    Help us! Save your children!

Orestes

I murdered my mother!

Pylades

                   I held the sword that killed!   1235

Electra

I encouraged them! I made them brave!

Pylades

Hear our reproaches and save your children now!

Orestes

I offer my tears to you—

Electra

                And I my grief.

Pylades

Enough.
        We must be about our business now.   1240
If prayers can penetrate this earth below,
he hears.
        —O Zeus, Zeus of our fathers,
great power of justice, help us now,
help us to victory!
               Three friends together,
one common cause, one right,
and together we shall live or die!   1245

           (*Orestes and Pylades enter the palace.*)

Electra

Women of Mycenae, noble women of Argos,
a word with you, please.

Coryphaeus

             What is it, my lady?
For you are mistress still in the city of Argos.   1250

Electra

  I want half of you to watch the highway.
  The rest of you will stand guard over here.

Coryphaeus

  But why, lady?

Electra

             A premonition. I am afraid   1255
  there may be murderers lurking about the house.
  Fresh blood may be spilt.

          (*The Chorus divides into two sections, each section led by a
          Parastate, and goes to opposite sides of the orchestra.*)

First Parastate

             To your posts, women!
  I'll watch the road to the east.

Second Parastate

             And I'll watch here   1260
  on the westward side.

Electra

          Keep a close lookout
  on both sides now. Look all around you.

Coryphaeus

  We obey.

Electra

        Stay alert now. Look sharp.   1265

First Parastate

  Someone is coming! Look—a peasant
  approaching the palace.

Electra

          Then this is the end.   1270
  He'll betray our ambush to our enemies.

First Parastate

No. A false alarm. The road is empty.
There's no one there.

Electra

You on the other side,
is all well? Is there anyone in sight?   1275

Second Parastate

All's well here. You watch there.
Not an Argive in sight anywhere here.

First Parastate

Nor here either. Not a soul in sight.   1280

Electra

Wait then. I'll go and call in at the door.

(*She goes to the palace and calls inside.*)
Why are you so quiet?
Why this delay?
For god's sake, kill her!
They don't answer.   1285
Not a sound. O gods, what has happened?
Has her loveliness blunted their swords?
In a few minutes the soldiers will be here
to rescue her, rushing up with drawn swords!   1290
Back to your posts.
Look sharper than ever.
This is no time for napping.

Coryphaeus

I'm watching.   1295

Helen (from within)

Help me, Argos! Help! They'll murder me!

First Parastate

Did you hear her scream? They're killing her!

Second Parastate

    That awful cry! That was Helen screaming!

Electra

    O Zeus, Zeus, send us strength!
    Come, O Zeus! Help them now!   1300

Helen (from within)
    Help me, Menelaus! Help! I'm dying—

Electra

    Murder!
           Butcher!
                 Kill!
    Thrust your twin swords home!
    Slash, now slash again!
    Run the traitress through,
    kill the whore who killed   1305
    so many brave young men—
    the wounded and the dead,
    those for whom we mourn,
    those murdered and dying
    where the waters of Scamander
    eddy and roar!   1310

Coryphaeus

    Wait, Electra.
                I hear the sound of footsteps.
    Someone is coming.

Electra

                It must be Hermione.
    Yes, it is! It is! Hermione herself,
    at the very moment of murder.
                   But not a sound.
    Look at her—walking straight for our trap,   1315
    and a sweet catch she is, if I can take her.
    Quick, back to your posts.

Seem natural
and unconcerned; don't give us away.
I had better have a sullen sort of look,
as though nothing had happened here.   1320

(*Enter Hermione.*)

Ah,
have you been to Clytemnestra's grave, dear?
Did you wreathe it with flowers and pour libations?

Hermione

Yes, I gave her all the dues of the dead.
But, you know, I was frightened coming home.
I thought I heard a scream in the distance.   1325

Electra

A cry?

Really? But surely we have every right
to cry a little.

Hermione

Not *more* trouble, Electra?
What has happened now?

Electra

Orestes and I
have been sentenced to death.

Hermione

God forbid!
You, my own cousins, must die?

Electra

We must.
This is necessity whose yoke we bear.   1330

Hermione

Then that was why I heard that cry?

Electra

Yes.
He went and fell at Helen's knees—

Hermione
> Who went?

I don't understand.

Electra
> Orestes. To implore Helen

to save our lives.

Hermione
> Then well might the palace   1335

have rung with your cries.

Electra
> What better reason

could there be?
> But if you love us, dear,

go now, fall at your mother's feet
and beg her, implore her by her happiness
to intercede with Menelaus now
on our behalf. My mother nursed you in her arms: 1340
have pity on us now and save our lives.
Go plead with her. You are our last hope.
I will take you there myself.

Hermione
> Oh yes, yes!

I must go quickly! If it lies in my power,   1345
you are saved.

> *(Exit Hermione into the palace. Electra*
> *follows her to the door.)*

Electra
> For god's sake, Orestes,

Pylades! Lift your swords and seize your prey!

Hermione (from within)
Who are these men?
> *Help!*
> *Save me!*

Orestes (from within)

            Silence,
 girl.
   You are here to save us, not yourself.

Electra

 Hold her, seize her!
        Put your sword to her throat   1350
 and stop her screaming.
        Let Menelaus learn
 with whom he has to deal now. Show him
 what it means to fight with men, not cowards
 from Troy. Make him suffer for his crimes!

    (Electra enters the palace, closing the great doors behind her.
       From the palace comes the sound of commotion,
          scuffling, cries, and muffled screams.)

Chorus

 —Quick, raise a shout!

 —   A cry!

 —Drown the sound of murder in the palace!

 —A shout, before the Argives hear   1355
  and come running to the rescue!

 —Before they come, first let me see
  dead Helen, lying in her blood,
  or hear the story from her slaves.

Coryphaeus

 Some horror has happened; but what I do not know.   1360

Chorus

 —God's vengeance on Helen,
  justice crashing from heaven!

—Justice for Helen
who made all Hellas mourn,
mourn for her lover's sake—

—For Paris, bitter curse of Ida,   1365
Paris, who led all Hellas to Troy!

Coryphaeus
Hush. Be still.
              The bolts on the great doors
are sliding—someone is coming out—
some slave who can tell us what has happened.

              (Breathless and incoherent with terror, a Phrygian
                      slave bursts from the palace.)

Phrygian
Greekish sword—kill dead!
Trojan scared, oh.
              Run, run,
jump in slippers, fast, fast,   1370
clop-clop clamber over roof.
Hole in beams, inside court,
jump down
        boom!
            below.
Oh, oh.
            Where can run, where go?   1375
Mebbe foreign ladies know?
                Up, up,
soar in air, him shimmer nothing?
Swim in sea—mebbe? mebbe?—
where godbull ocean cradles world
flowing water with?

Coryphaeus
In god's name, speak, servant of Helen!   1380

Phrygian

> Oh, oh,
> > Ilium, Ilium, Troy, Troy!
> Holy hill of Ida, green one, O growing!
> *Ai ai,*
> > Ilium, Troy,
> hear the dirge I cry,
> > > *ai ai,*   1385
> death by Helenbeauty brought,
> eye of doom,
> of birdborn loveliness the eye,
> lovely eye of swan of Zeus,
> swan that sank in Leda's lap,
> eye of passion, glancing death,
> eye of love
> that broke the burnished walls of Troy!   1390
> Pity, pity, I cry
> for Ganymede of Troy,
> > > *ai ai,*
> ravished to bed
> by Zeus the rider!

Coryphaeus

> Tell us what happened as clearly as you can.

Phrygian

> *Ailinos!*   1395
> > *Ailinos!*
> *Ailinos!* the dirge begins,
> the dirge we cry
> for royal blood and princes dead
> by sword, by sword!
> > > *Ai ai!*
> But ladies, I tell you all
> and how come happen.

         Into palace came   1400
a pride of lions, Greekers, twins.
One of general Agamemnon, son;
other Pylades, man of plots, evil, *bad;*
Odysseus kind of, bluffer, cheater,
loyal, yes, and bold, bold,   1405
skills for war, of killer-snake.
God darn him dead
for plotty sneaks,
           I hope.
But walk they in. Tears, tears.
Sobs for Helen Pariswife.   1410
Oh so humble, sit 'em down,
one on left, one on right.
But swords too!
           And then—*well!*
Put their hands on lady's *knee,*
begging life.
             Slaves are scared.   1415
Terror, terror, skitter, scatter.
One man say, "Hey, treachery!"
"Look out, lady!" someone cry.
No no no guess other slaves,
but some are thinking,
               "Hey,   1420
snake who killed his mother
lady Helen tangled has
in webbery of plot."

Coryphaeus
   And where were you? Or had you run away?   1425

Phrygian
   No, no, no.
           In Eastern way   1430
   with foreign fan of feathers, yes,

fan the hair of lady Helen,
rippling air, to and fro,
gently over cheeks of ma'am.
And while I fan,
        slow, slow,
Helen's fingers wind the flax.
Spindle turning, fingers moving,
round and round the flax on floor,
Trojan spoils for cloth of purple,   1435
gift, yes, for sister's tomb.
Oh, oh.
      Orestes speaks:
"Deign, O ma'am, child of Zeus,
down from dais, please to step.
Stand by ancient Pelops' altar,   1440
hear my talk, but private, please."
So he led her, lady go,
poor suspecting nothing Helen.
Meanwhile, yes, evil friend,
partner Pylades of crime,   1445
is doing work.
        "Go, go!" he shout,
"Trojan cowards, slaves, slaves!"
Oh, and then he lock them up,
some in stables, others rooms,
here, there,
      oh oh,
from lady Helen barred away!   1450

Coryphaeus

  And then what happened? Go on.

Phrygian

  Oh! Oh! Oh!
        O Mother Ida!
  Horror, horror, oh, and crime!

What I saw in house of princes!
Never, never.
                    Out of hiding,   1455
out of purply cloaks
they drew their swords!
And eyes of them! Oh, going round
to see if danger anywhere.   1460
And then they came.
                    Oh, boars
they were, yes, boars attacking,
screaming, shouting,
                    "Die! Die!
Die for traitor husband, coward
who betrayed his brother's son,
who left him to die in Argos!"
Lady screamed,
                    ah, ah,   1465
snow-white arms, flailing, flailing,
beating bosom, beating breast!
Hair she tore, in sandals goldy
leaped to run!
                    But after, after,
came Orestes
                    Caught her, oh,   1470
winding fingers in her hair
and neck forced back,
                    down, down,
against her shoulder
Lifted, ah, sword to strike—

Coryphaeus

But where were her servants? Couldn't you help?

Phrygian

Oh, we shout, yes!
                    We batter doors

with iron bars, break down panels   1475
where we are!
            Then run, run,
rescue, rescue! Some with stones,
with swords, with spears.
                    But *then!*
Pylades came on—ooh, brave!
Hectorlike or Ajax with his helms of triple   1480
(I saw him once in Priampalace).
Steel on steel together meet,
but soon we see
Trojan men no match for Greek.   1485
Ai ai,
        one run, one dead,
wounded this and begging that.
So quick, quick, run, hide!
Falling some, dying others,
staggering is one with wounds.
And then, oh!
            Hermione came in   1490
as mother Helen sank to die.
Men stop, yes, Bacchantes,
dropping wands for seizing prey,
snatch at girl, then turn back
to kill, kill madam dead.   1495
But then, oh then—
suddenly, ah, ah!
madam vanish,
fly through roof
as though some magic mebbe mebbe
or robbery of thiever gods!
O Earth! O Zeus! O Night!
What then happen I not know.
No, no, run, I ran!
But Menelaus, *ai*—
all his suffer, all his hurt   1500

to bring the lady Helen home,
ah ah,

       nothing is.

Coryphaeus

On and on it goes, strangeness to strangeness
succeeding, horror to horror.

             And look—
here Orestes comes rushing from the palace   1505
with drawn sword!

          (Enters Orestes in haste, his sword drawn.)

Orestes

       Where is that coward slave
who ran from my sword inside?

Phrygian

          I bow down, yessir.
I kiss the ground, lord. Is Eastern custom, yes.

Orestes

This is Argos, fool, not Troy.

Phrygian

         But anywhere
wise man wants to live, not die.

Orestes

        And those screams of yours?
Admit it: you were shouting to Menelaus for help.   1510

Phrygian

Oh no, nosir. Not I. For you I was screaming.
You needed help.

Orestes

     Did Helen deserve to die?

Phrygian

Oh, yessir. Three times cut madam's throat,
and I not object.

Orestes

　　　　This is cowardly flattery.
You don't believe it.

Phrygian

　　　　Oh sir, I believe, sure.
Helen ruin Hellas, yes, kill Trojans too.　　　　　　　　1515

Orestes

Swear you're telling me the truth or I'll kill you.

Phrygian

Oh, oh! By life I swear—if life can have mebbe?

Orestes

　　　　(*Lowering his sword still closer to the Phrygian's throat.*)
Were all the Trojans as terrified by cold steel
as you?

Phrygian

　　　　Ooh, please, please, not so close!
All shiny bloody!

Orestes

　　　　What are you afraid of, fool?
Is it some Gorgon's head to turn you into stone?　　　　1520

Phrygian

Not stone, corpse yes. But this Gorgon thing
I do not know.

Orestes

　　　　What? Nothing but a slave
and afraid to die? Death might end your suffering.

Phrygian

Slave man, free man, everybody like to live.

Orestes

Well spoken. Your wit saves you. Now get inside.

Phrygian

You will not kill me?

Orestes

I spare you.

Phrygian

Oh, thank you, thank you.   1525

Orestes

Go, or I'll change my mind.

Phrygian

I no thank you for that.

(*Exit Phrygian.*)

Orestes

Fool, did you think I'd dirty my sword on your neck?
Neither man nor woman—who could want your life?
No, I came to stop your frightened screams. This city
of Argos is quickly roused to arms by any cry   1530
for help.
            Not that I'm afraid of Menelaus either.
No, let him come. His glory is his golden curls,
not his sword.
            But if he brings the Argives here
and in revenge for Helen's death refuses his help
to my sister, my friend and helper, or myself,   1535
then his daughter too shall join his wife in death.

(*Exit Orestes into palace, bolting the doors behind him.*)

Chorus

O gods! Murder!
Grief comes down once more
upon the house of Atreus!

First Parastate

What should we do? Send to the city for help,
or keep silent?

Second Parastate

Silence is the safer course. 1540

(*A lurid red glare suffused with billowing smoke
suddenly lights up the roof of the palace.*)

First Parastate

Look! Look up there on the roof—the smoke
pouring, billowing up!

Second Parastate

And the glare of torches!
They are burning the house, the ancestral house!
They shrink from nothing, not even murder!

Chorus

—God works his way with man. 1545

—The end is as god wills.

—Great is the power of god.

—And great it has been here

—where the fiend of vengeance drives,

—blood for blood, against this house,

—in vengeance for Myrtilus!

Coryphaeus

Wait. I see Menelaus coming this way
in great haste. He must have heard some news
of what has happened here.

Stand your guard, 1550
inside the house! Quick, bolt the palace doors.
Beware, Orestes.

This man in his hour of triumph
is dangerous. Take care.

(Enter Menelaus with armed attendants.)

Menelaus
> I have come
> to investigate a tale of incredible crimes   1555
> committed by two lions—I cannot bring myself
> to call them men.
>   I am also told that Helen
> is not dead, but has disappeared, vanished
> into thin air, the idiotic fiction
> of a man whose mind was almost crazed with fear
> or, more probably, as I suspect, the invention
> of the matricide and patently absurd.   1560
> Inside there, open the doors!

> > > > > > > > *(Dead silence.)*
>   Very well.
> Men, break down that door so I can rescue
> my poor daughter from the hands of these murderers
> and recover Helen's body.
>   In revenge for her,   1565
> I personally shall put these men to death.

*(Dimly visible in the swirling smoke, Orestes and Pylades appear
on the roof, with Hermione between them. Orestes holds
a sword at Hermione's throat. Farther back stands
Electra with torches blazing.)*

Orestes
> You there, don't lay a finger on that door.
> Yes, I mean *you*, Menelaus, you braggart!
> Touch that door and I'll rip the parapet
> from this crumbling masonry and smash your skull.   1570
> The doors have been bolted down with iron bars
> on purpose to keep you out.

Menelaus
> > > > > Gods in heaven!
> Torches blazing—and people standing on the roof

like a city under siege, and—*no!*
A man holding a sword at my daughter's throat!   1575

Orestes

Do you want me to ask the questions, Menelaus,
or would you prefer that I do the talking?

Menelaus

                      Neither.
But I suppose I must listen.

Orestes

                 For your information,
I am about to kill your daughter.

Menelaus

               Her too?
Wasn't it enough that you murdered her mother?

Orestes

No, heaven stole her and robbed me of the pleasure.   1580

Menelaus

This is mockery. Do you deny you killed her?

Orestes

It pains me to deny it. Would to god I had!

Menelaus

Had what? This suspense is torture.

Orestes

             Killed her.
Struck down the whore who pollutes our land.

Menelaus

Let me have her body. Let me bury her.   1585

Orestes

Ask the gods for her carcass. In the meanwhile
I will kill your daughter.

Menelaus

The mother-killer
murders again!

Orestes

His father's avenger
and betrayed by you.

Menelaus

Wasn't her death enough?

Orestes

I can never have my fill of killing whores.   1590

Menelaus

But you, Pylades! Are you his partner
in this murder too?

Orestes

His silence says he is.
But I speak for him.

Menelaus

If I catch you,
you will regret this act.

Orestes

We won't run away.
In fact, we'll burn the house.

Menelaus

Burn the house!   1595
Burn the palace of your fathers?

Orestes

To keep it from you.
But your daughter dies. First the sword,
then the fire.

Menelaus
         Kill her. I shall get revenge.

Orestes
  Very well.

Menelaus
       No, wait! *For god's sake, no!*

Orestes
  Silence. You suffer justly for what you did.

Menelaus
  Can justice let you live?

Orestes
              Live—and reign too!   1600

Menelaus
  Reign where?

Orestes
      Here in Argos.

Menelaus
           You?
  You officiate as priest?

Orestes
        And why not?

Menelaus
  Or sacrifice for war?

Orestes
        If you can, I can too.

Menelaus
  My hands are clean.

Orestes
        Your hands, yes, but not your heart.

Menelaus
  Who would speak to you?

Orestes

Those who love their fathers.   1605

Menelaus

And those who love their mothers?

Orestes

Were born lucky.

Menelaus

That leaves you out.

Orestes

Yes. I loathe whores.

Menelaus

Then keep that sword away from her!

Orestes

Guess again,

traitor.

Menelaus

Could you kill my child?

Orestes

Ah, the truth

at last!

Menelaus

What do you want?

Orestes

Persuade the people—   1610

Menelaus

Persuade them of what?

Orestes

To let us live.

Menelaus

Or you will kill my child?

Orestes

It comes to that.

Menelaus

   O gods, my poor wife—

Orestes

                  No pity for me?

Menelaus

   —brought home to die!

Orestes

                 Would to god she had!

Menelaus

   All my countless labors—

Orestes

                 Nothing done for me.   1615

Menelaus

   All I suffered—

Orestes

            Is irrelevant to me.

Menelaus

   I am trapped.

Orestes

           Trapped by your own viciousness.
All right, Electra, set the house on fire!
You there, Pylades, most loyal of my friends,
burn the roof! Set those parapets   1620
to blazing!

Menelaus

         Help, help, people of Danaus,
knights of Argos!
             To arms! To arms!
This man with mother's blood upon his hands
threatens our city, our very lives!

(General alarm. Suddenly Apollo appears ex machina *above the palace. Behind him on the same level stands Helen.)*

Apollo

Stop,   1625
Menelaus. Calm your anger.

It is I,
a god, Phoebus Apollo, son of Leto,
who speak.

You too, Orestes, standing there
with drawn sword over that girl, hear
what I say.

Helen is here with me—
yes, that same Helen whom you tried to kill   1630
out of hatred for Menelaus. This is she
whom you see enfolded in the gleaming air,
delivered from death. You did not kill her.
For I, so commanded by Zeus the father,
snatched her from your sword.

Helen lives,
for being born of Zeus, she could not die,   1635
and now, between the Dioscuri in the swathe
of air, she sits enthroned forever, a star
for sailors.

Menelaus must marry again,
since the gods by means of Helen's loveliness
drove Trojans and Greeks together in war   1640
and made them die, that earth might be lightened
of her heavy burden of mortality.
So much for Helen.

I now turn to you,
Orestes.

It is your destiny to leave this land
and go in exile to Parrhasia for a year.   1645
Henceforth that region shall be named for you,
called Oresteion by the Arcadians and Azanians.
From there you must go to the city of Athena

and render justice for your mother's murder
to the three Eumenides.

Gods shall be your judges, 1650
sitting in holy session on the hill of Ares,
and acquitting you by sacred verdict.

Then,
Orestes, you shall marry Hermione,
the girl against whose throat your sword now lies.
Neoptolemus hopes to make her his wife, 1655
but never shall, for he is doomed to die
when he comes to Delphi seeking justice
for his father's death.

Give Electra in marriage
to Pylades as you promised. Great happiness
awaits him.

Let Orestes reign in Argos, 1660
Menelaus. But go yourself and be king in Sparta,
the dowry of Helen, whose only dowry yet
has been your anguish and suffering.

I myself
shall reconcile the city of Argos to Orestes,
for it was I who commanded his mother's murder. 1665
I compelled him to kill.

Orestes

Hail, Apollo,
for your prophetic oracles! True prophet,
not false!

And yet, when I heard you speak,
I thought I heard the whispers of some fiend
speaking through your mouth.

But all is well, 1670
and I obey.

See, I now release Hermione,
and we shall marry if her father gives
his blessing and consent.

Menelaus
                    Farewell, Helen,
daughter of Zeus! I envy you your home
and happiness among the gods.
                              Orestes,   1675
I now betroth my only child to you,
as Apollo commands.
                    We come of noble birth
and nobly may this marriage bless us both.

Apollo
    Let each one go to his appointed place.
    Now let your quarrels end.

Menelaus
                    I obey, lord.

Orestes
    And I. Menelaus, I accept our truce   1680
    and make my peace with Apollo and his oracle.

Apollo
        Let each one go his way.
        Go and honor Peace,
        loveliest of goddesses.
        Helen I now lead
        to the halls of Zeus,
        upon the road that turns
        among the blazing stars.   1685
        There with Hera she shall sit,
        with Heracles and Hebe throned,
        a goddess forever,
        forever adored—
        there between her brothers,
        the sons of Zeus,
        reigning on the seas,
        a light to sailors.   1690

*(Exeunt Menelaus and retinue, Orestes arm in arm
with Hermione, Pylades and Electra,
as the Chorus files out.)*

Chorus

Hail, O Victory!
Preserve my life
and let me wear the crown!

IPHIGENIA IN AULIS

Translated and with an Introduction by Charles R. Walker

INTRODUCTION TO
IPHIGENIA IN AULIS

THE *Iphigenia in Aulis* was produced, together with the *Bacchae* and the *Alcmaeon*, at the Great Dionysia in March, 405 B.C., a few months after Euripides' death. It seems probable that Euripides' son (some say his nephew) produced the play and perhaps filled in parts of the script which Euripides had left incomplete at the time of his death.

The play is full of invention and dramatic reversals. Some classical critics, dubbing it pure melodrama, have felt that it represented a woeful falling-off from the sterner standards of Greek tragedy. Most students of dramatic literature find it an exciting "transition piece," for it is an obvious bridge between classical tragedy and postclassical drama. But whatever else it may be, for the majority of readers, both scholarly and other, it is still tragic, still Greek, and still Euripides.

Euripides here, more than ever, takes liberties with his legendary material. The legend briefly is this: Iphigenia, daughter of Agamemnon, is sacrificed to the goddess Artemis, to persuade her to grant the Greek ships a favoring wind on their way to conquer Troy. But the great heroes of Homer are cut down to size, or below, to human, almost modern, politicians preparing to fight a war out of ambition or fear. In Homer, Agamemnon, "king of men," while not as glamorous a hero as Hector or Odysseus, is nevertheless a man of courage, a first-rate commander, a king. In the *Iphigenia* he has become an ambitious politician, wavering in his motives, and a moral, if not a physical, coward. Menelaus is also of doubtful character. Achilles, to be sure, has something of the hero about him, but it is the heroism of a very human youth, not of an adult Homeric warrior. As to Iphigenia, her character has been transformed from an unwilling victim into a true saint. She does not appear in Homer, but tradition pictures Iphigenia as a gagged, unwilling victim, appealing with her eyes, even at the moment of her death, for pity. This, for example, is the Iphigenia of Aeschylus' *Agamemnon*. Euripides remolds her character and so the plot he derives from the legend. In this play, she gives her life (much as Joan of Arc did) in accordance with what she regards as the "divine will" and the needs of her country.

I have suggested that the play is more modern than most Greek tragedies; perhaps it is more modern than any of them. But in what sense is it modern? First of all in techniques of the theater: it is full of new dramatic devices as well as a concentration of old ones. Instead of the formal Euripidean prologue giving the audience background for the plot, there is a lively duologue full of dramatic tension between Agamemnon and a servant. (An old-style prologue also exists and in this version is integrated into the dialogue, ll. 49–114.) The chorus is no longer essential to the dramatic action but it often establishes the mood. It consists in this play of women who have crossed over from their native Chalcis to Aulis, apparently as sightseers to see the heroes and the famous Greek fleet. Their vivid description of the army and the ships in the first chorus seems comparable in function to scenery in the modern theater or to background shots in a motion picture. Part of the role of the normal chorus appears to have been taken over by an increase in the number and significance of solos, or arias. As to the plot, it is tight; the action, rapid and full of surprises. Aristotle found Iphigenia's quick change in attitude toward her destiny hard to believe. Most modern readers, or hearers of the play, do not. Finally, in several scenes there are intimate conversations and expressions of what we would call "sentiment."

The text of *Iphigenia* is unusually corrupt, and there is by no means agreement among scholars as to what should be attributed to Euripides and what to later interpolators. But on many strategic passages there is general agreement. In this connection the present translator had a revealing experience. Being thoroughly familiar with the play but only slightly familiar with the conclusions of textual commentators, he prepared an acting version in English for the modern stage. This necessitated some cutting from choruses and dialogue of passages which to him seemed padded, irrelevant, or undramatic. In comparing the acting version with what the textual commentators had been saying, he found that he had dropped most of the spurious passages. In short, it is here suggested that there has come to us *from the hand of Euripides* a highly playable script. This translation, it should be said, is based on the *whole* text. The spurious ending, or exodus, together with a few lines omitted as either spurious or interfering with the dramatic tension, is given in the Appendix.

Here, then, we have a play which in action, mood of disillusioned realism, number of heroic characters "debunked," and in intimate, even domestic, dialogue appears very modern indeed. And yet, the plot is woven around an angry goddess who won't let the winds blow the Achaean ships to the sack of Troy unless a king's daughter is slain in human sacrifice! Can such a play be credible to modern readers and theatergoers? How indeed could it have been credible in Euripides' time to Greeks who had outgrown human sacrifice centuries before? One obvious answer is that, as in all Greek tragedies, the dramatist is skilful enough to make the audience accept the conditions of the tragic dilemma as set forth in the myth. But the second reason—related to the first—is that the play really is not about the institution of human sacrifice at all. It might have been, but it isn't. What then is the play about?

One way to approach this question is to start with the characters, especially the two with whom Euripides was obviously deeply involved—the women of the play. There are two of them, in a sense three, though the third never appears. She is Helen of Troy, whom the dramatist never tires of depicting and denouncing both in his dialogue and in his choruses. These characters, all three, sharply contrast with one another. Helen, through selfish love, has brought "travail and trouble" upon all the Greeks. Iphigenia, by selfless sacrifice, rescues the Greek expedition from futility and becomes, so both she and the other characters believe, a "true savior of Greece." Perhaps there is a hint of the meaning of the play in this contrast of the two women. Again the reader or spectator will inevitably compare Iphigenia, the girl who loves her father in spite of his weakness and his intention to kill her, with Clytemnestra, who hates her husband and will one day kill him (as the legend tells us) when he returns from Troy.

Clytemnestra in her speeches of anger and supplication reveals herself in her full tragic stature. Iphigenia's scenes with her father are in a wholly different mood—intimate, affectionate, and pathetic. But they perhaps also point toward what Euripides was saying in the play. She is wholly blind to his weakness. To her—and to her alone in the play—he is a great man, committing her to her death for the sake of Greece. Her attitude toward him is one of love throughout. In an early scene, for example, when father and daughter meet after long absence, she is full of affection and gaiety. But even when she pleads for her life (before she decides to die willingly), her plea is in terms of love and intimacy, not indignation or fear. At the turning point in the play, when she announces her resolve to die, she uses Agamemnon's own words in defense of the war for which she is to die. Finally, in the last scene with her mother, as the play moves toward its tragic end, she asks Clytemnestra not to hate her husband.

Let me clear up one possible misunderstanding. Did Euripides then condone Agamemnon's crime and the injury visited upon his wife Clytemnestra by consenting to the sacrifice of his daughter? Certainly not. No student of this or of his other plays could believe that he did. But perhaps he believed that Iphigenia and Clytemnestra were both "right."

These are, of course, only guesses as to what interested Euripides in this version of the Iphigenia story. Perhaps, somewhere in the death and sacrifice of youth that has occurred in all wars from Troy to Korea lies the meaning—and the mystery—of the play. But how can that be? The sacrifice here is to a divinity "delighting in human blood," and the expedition is led by a wavering and ambitious ruler. Certainly the war will be fought from very mixed motives, some patriotic, some ignoble. All of this was without a doubt also a part of what Euripides was saying, but not all of it, I believe. There is also a blaze of devotion in the play and the mystery of young and *voluntary* dying that has occurred in all periods of human history. Euripides has brought the same theme into other plays but never as the center of dramatic action. As in Shaw's *Saint Joan*, it is as much what Iphigenia's sacrifice does to others as what it does to herself that makes the dramatic moments in the play. This is strikingly true in the scene with Achilles, as well as in the final tragic parting between mother and daughter.

As it has come down to us, the end of the play presents us with a riddle and a challenge. The legendary material contains a variant, probably a later one in mythic history, by which Iphigenia is rescued at the last moment. Miraculously, she is snatched away to live—for a time, at least—in fellowship with the gods, and a hind is slain on the altar instead. In other words, she is not really sacrificed. This "happy ending" has been added by a later interpolator to the text of Euripides' play and appears in all editions. I have followed the practice of most modern translators (Schiller among them) in omitting this happy ending. The whole force of the play collapses if the heroine is hastily caught up to heaven at the last minute. And incidentally, the scene of rescue as reported by the messenger is not only undramatic and unconvincing but spurious. Scholars are unanimous that it is by a later interpolator.

The reader may recall another story of divine rescue of a human victim, the moving story of Abraham and Isaac. But why should that story appear serious and convincing to most people, regardless of their religious faith, but the snatching of Iphigenia as fantasy or fake, as it has to most readers of the play? The reason, I believe, is a fairly obvious one. The Abraham story concerns the problem of faith—faith in Jehovah and utter surrender to his will. But this is only superficially true of Euripides' play. Euripides never for a moment suggests that the goddess should be obeyed out of love or piety. All the arguments for the sacrifice are purely practical, when they are not cynical and self-seeking. It is quite clear that to the playwright it was a crime for Agamemnon to accede to the goddess'— or her priest's—demands. (It is not even clear whether he believes that Artemis has demanded the sacrifice or whether he regards the whole thing as the invention of Calchas, the priest.) The nobility and worth of Iphigenia's action, therefore, is quite independent of either the worthiness of the cause or the motives of those who send her to her death. Her sacrifice is a kind of absolute good that transcends all the rational cynicism around her.

Unhappily this does not rid us of the whole difficulty. There is good evidence that, although the "messenger ending" is spurious, there was once another authentic ending, or "exodus" as the Greeks

called the last scene, in which Euripides brought in Artemis herself
to resolve the issues of the play and perhaps to explain why a hind
was to be substituted for a girl. But what did Euripides actually tell
his audience through the mouth of the goddess? We shall probably
never know. I am certain, however, that, whatever Euripides wrote,
his exodus did not "explain away," as does the interpolated ending,
the poetry, the power, or the mystery of the play.

CHARACTERS

Agamemnon, commander-in-chief of the Greek army

Old Man, servant of Agamemnon

Chorus of women of Chalcis who have come to Aulis to see the Greek fleet

Menelaus, brother of Agamemnon, husband of Helen

Clytemnestra, wife of Agamemnon

Iphigenia, daughter of Agamemnon

Orestes (silent)

Messenger

Achilles, future hero of the Trojan war

Attendants, armor-bearers

IPHIGENIA IN AULIS

SCENE: *In front of the tent of Agamemnon, commander of the Greek armies;*
on the shore of Aulis' gulf where all the Greek ships lie becalmed.
Agamemnon walks in front of his tent.
TIME: *Night, just before dawn.*

Agamemnon

Old man, come out in front of the tent.

Old Man (*entering*)

I'm coming—
What new plan have you got in your head,
My lord Agamemnon?

Agamemnon

Hurry up!

Old Man

I'm hurrying—and I'm not asleep.
Sleep rests light on these old eyes.
I can look sharp.   5

Agamemnon

(*Continues to pace up and down for several*
seconds as the Old Man watches him.)

Well, what is that star
That moves across the sky?

Old Man

That's Sirius, next to the seven Pleiades.
It's still the hour when it rides
Right in the middle of heaven.

Agamemnon

(*Taking his eyes from the sky and listening.*)

No voice is there of birds even,
Or of the seas' waves.

The silence of the winds   10
Holds hushed the river.

Old Man

Yes, but why have you been rushing
Up and down, my lord Agamemnon,
Outside your tent? There's peace
And quiet still over at Aulis
And the guards are quiet too—
Over on the walls of the fort.
They don't move at all. Can we   15
Not go inside now?

Agamemnon

            I envy you, old man,
I am jealous of men who without peril
Pass through their lives, obscure,
Unknown; least of all do I envy
Those vested with honors.

Old Man

Oh, but these have a glory in their lives!   20

Agamemnon

Ah—a glory that is perilous, and
Will trip them as they walk.
High honors are sweet
To a man's heart, but ever
They stand close to the brink of grief.
Many things can bring calamity.
At one time, it is an enterprise
Of the gods which, failing,
Overturns a man's life. At another,   25
The wills of men, many and malignant,
Ruin life utterly.

Old Man

            I don't like words
Like these from a king. Agamemnon,

Atreus begat you, but not to have
All good things in your life. No,   30
It is necessary and it is fated
That you be glad and that you
Be sad too, for you were born
Human, and whether you like it or not,
What the gods will comes true.

                                                   (Pause.)

But you've lit your lamp and
Been writing a letter, haven't you?   35
You still have it in your hand—
With those same words you've
Been putting together. You seal
The letter up—and then tear
The seal open. You've been doing it
Over and over again. Then you
Throw the torch on the ground,
And bulging tears come down out   40
Of your eyes. My lord, you act
Helpless, and mad! What is the pain,
What is the new thing of agony,
O my king! Tell it to me, for I
Am a good man and a loyal servant;
So you can speak. Remember? It was I   45
Who was in the bridal train—
Long ago in the beginning. I was given
To your wife, part of the wedding dowry,
And Tyndareus picked me for this service
Because I was honest.

Agamemnon

            (Explaining the whole situation to the Old Man.)

    Three girls were born to Leda, daughter of Thestius: Phoebe,
Clytemnestra, who is my wife, and Helen. The young men, fore-   50
most in fortune, from all Greece came as Helen's suitors. And each
of them uttered terrible threats against the others, each swearing
he would murder his fellow suitors if he himself failed to

win the girl. Here was her father's dilemma, whether he could   55
best escape disaster at fate's hands by *giving* her or by *not giving* her
in marriage. Then this idea came to him, to bind the suitors by
oath to make a treaty one with another—and seal it with a burnt   60
offering—that whoever won as wife Helen, the child of Tyndareus, that man all the others would defend. If any man should
drive her husband away and steal her from her house, all must
make war upon him and sack his town, whether the town were   65
Greek or barbarian. When they had sworn this, the old man—
tricking them with his strategy—gave his daughter permission to
choose that suitor to whom the sweet breath of love turned her
her heart. So she chose Menelaus—would to God she had not   70
chosen him. Then from Phrygia to Sparta came Paris, who was the
judge of the goddesses—so the Argives have the story. He came
with his garments flowered in gold and his dress blazoned with
barbaric gems. He loved Helen and was loved by her. Then, when   75
her husband was out of the country, he stole her and carried her
off to the herd lands of Ida. Menelaus, stung into fury, ranged
through Greece and invoked that old oath sworn to Tyndareus,
the oath claiming help to avenge this wrong. So all the Greeks   80
sprang to arms, and now they have come to the narrows of Aulis
with all their armament, their ships, their shields, chariots and
horses. And since I am Menelaus' brother, for his sake they chose   85
me as commander-in-chief. Would to God another man had won
that honor.

After the army was mustered in here at Aulis, we were delayed
by the dead calm. It was then the prophet Calchas spoke to all of
us in despair at the weather and urged that my daughter, Iphige-   90
nia, be sacrificed to the goddess of this place. He predicted that
if she were sacrificed we would sail and take and overthrow utterly the land of Troy. But if she were not sacrificed none of these
things would happen. So when I heard this, I ordered our herald,
Talthybius, to make a loud proclamation and dismiss the whole   95
army. I would never have the cruel brutality to kill my own
daughter! After that my brother bore down upon me with arguments of every kind, urging me to commit this horror. Then I

wrote a letter, folded and sealed it, dispatched it to my wife asking
her to send our daughter to be married to Achilles. And in the 100
letter I praised his reputation as a hero and said he would not sail
unless a bride came from our family here to Phthia. I contrived
this deception about the maid's marriage to persuade my wife. Of 105
the Achaeans who know, there are Calchas, Odysseus, and Menelaus, only.

I did this wrong! Now in this letter I rewrite the message and
put down the truth. This I was doing when you saw me in the
dark unsealing the letter and sealing it again. But take the dispatch 110
at once. You must go to Argos! Of the message folded here I will
tell you all, since you are loyal both to my wife and to my house.

Old Man

Tell me then and show me—so that 115
The words I speak with my tongue
Will say these words in the letter.

Agamemnon

(Nods and reads.)

Child of Leda, Clytemnestra:
This letter will bring you
A new message, and different
From the other. Do not send your daughter
To the calm beach of Aulis, here
On the Euboean harbor. For we must 120
Wait another season before we can
Celebrate our child's marriage.

Old Man

But when Achilles loses his bride—
Won't his heart blow up in fierce 125
Anger against you and against
Your wife? Oh, this is
A threatening thing! Tell me
What you mean by it.

Agamemnon
                        I'll tell you—
Not in fact but in name only
Is there a marriage with Achilles.
He knows nothing of it or of our plan
Or that I have said I would give him   130
My daughter as his bride.

Old Man

To bring her here a victim then—
A death offering—you promised   135
Her to the son of the goddess!
Oh, you have dared a deed of horror,
My lord Agamemnon!

Agamemnon

My mind is crazed, I fall in ruin!
No—you must get on your way and run.
Forget that your legs are old.

Old Man

I will hurry, my lord.   140

Agamemnon

                  (*Putting his hands on the Old Man's shoulders.*)

Don't rest by those forest springs
Or give in to sleep.

Old Man
                  No, no!

Agamemnon

When you come to the fork in the road
Look keenly both ways and be sure   145
The carriage doesn't pass quickly—
When you are not looking—and so
Bring my daughter right to

The Greek ships. And if you
Meet her and her escort,
Turn them back! Yes, take the reins   150
And shake them, send them back
To Argos, back to the city of Cyclops.

Old Man

I will, my lord!

Agamemnon

Now, go out from the gates.

Old Man

Wait. When I say these things,
Tell me, what will make your wife
And your daughter trust me?   155

Agamemnon

This seal. Keep it. It is
The same as the seal on the letter.
Now go! The dawn is here, and
The sun's chariot already is
Making the day bright. Go—
And help me out of my trouble.   160

(Old Man goes out.)

No mortal man has happiness
And fortune to the end. He is
Born, every man, to his grief!

(Agamemnon goes out.)
(Enter Chorus.)

Chorus

I have come to the shore
And the sea sands of Aulis   165
Over Euripus' waters
And the sea narrows sailing—
From Chalcis, my city,

Chalcis, nurse to the fountain
Arethusa, sea surrounded   170
And shining—to see this host
Of noble Achaeans, with their oar-borne ships
Of heroes, whom Menelaus, the yellow-haired   175
And Agamemnon, nobly born—our husbands tell—
Had sent in a thousand galleys
To seek out Helen and seize her;
Helen, whom Paris the herdsman   180
Took from the banks of the river,
Reedy Eurotas, where Aphrodite bestowed her—
On the day when the Cyprian held—
After her dewy bath—
A battle of beauty
With Hera and Pallas Athene.
Through the grove of the victims   185
Artemis' grove I came swift running;
At my eagerness, my cheeks
Reddened with shame—at my yearning to see
The Danaans' fence of shields,
The war gear by each tent,   190
And the great host of armored horsemen.
And now those two whose names are Ajax
I looked upon,
The son of Oileus and Telamon's child
Who is the crown and pride
Of Salamis. Squatting they played at draughts,
Delighting in its trickery.
With them was Protesilaus,   195
With them Palamedes the sea god's son.
Another hurled the discus, Diomedes,   200
And took great joy in it.
Nearby Meriones, Ares' kin,
At whom all mortals marvel.
And from his mountainous island came
Laertes' son and Nireus, goodliest seeming
Of all the Achaeans.   205

Swift-footed Achilles I saw—
His feet like the stormwind—running,
Achilles whom Thetis bore, and
Chiron trained into manhood.
I saw him on the seashore,   210
In full armor over the sands racing.
He strove, his legs in contest
With a chariot and four,
Toward victory racing and rounding
The course. And Eumelus, the Pheretid
Charioteer cried forth in frenzy.   215
I saw his handsome horses there,
Gold-wrought in bits and harness.
Eumelus with his goad struck them,   220
The yoke horses dappled gray,
Their manes white-flecked, and the
Trace horses which flanked them.
Clearly I saw these as they grazed
The post at the end of the race course—   225
They were bays, with their fetlocks
Spotted. And always beside them Peleus' son
Hurled himself onward,
Right by the chariot's car rail,
Right by the spinning axle.   230
And then I came upon the fleet,
An indescribable wonder, so that
With joy my woman's eyes were filled.
The armament of Myrmidons from Phthia
Were there on the right, swift ships, fifty of them.   235
Upon their sterns set high in gold,
The divine daughters of the sea lord   240
Carved as symbols of Achilles' host.
Keel by keel beside them
Lay the Argive ships
Commanded by Mecistes' son,
Whose father Talaus fostered him to manhood.   245
And there was Sthenelus, Capaneus' son.

And leader of the Attic ships in number sixty,
The son of Theseus, who had anchored them
In an even line, and with insignia,
Pallas Athene in her winged car   250
Drawn by the horses of uncloven hoof,
A blessed sign to mariners.

In Boeotia's naval squadron
I counted fifty ships
Fitted with blazonry;   255
Cadmus on each of them
With his golden dragon
High on their poops lifted.
It was Leitus the earth-born
Who commanded the squadron.   260
Next from the land of Phocis
Captain of Locrian ships,
Equal in number was the son of Oileus,
Who had embarked from Thronium,   265
Illustrious city.

From Mycenae, walled by the Cyclops,
The son of Atreus sent his ships,
A hundred galleys in order;
With him his brother,
Commander and friend,
Sailing to wreak revenge on her
Who had fled his hearth   270
To accomplish a foreign marriage.
From Pylus, Gerenian Nestor's
Ships I beheld;
On their poops emblazoned
Bull-bodied Alpheus,   275
Alpheus, the river that runs by his home.
Twelve Aenian ships were there
With Gouneus the king as captain.

Hard by the lords of Elis   280
Whom all men call Epeians;
Their ships Eurytus led,
And led too the Taphian squadron—
Oars gleamed white in the sunlight—
Whose king is Meges, Phyleus' son.   285
They had set sail from the Echinad isles
A rocky terror to mariners.

Ajax, Salamis born,
Linked the right wing of the navy to the left,   290
Knitting together nearest and farthest
Of galleys. And for that linkage
Moved his own twelve ships, easy to pilot.
So the line was unbroken—
Of ships and of shore and of people.   295
No home-going will there be
For any barbarian craft
Which grapples with him there.

The navy's setting forth   300
I've seen it on this day,
So when at home I hear men speak of it,
My vision of the marshaled ships
Will live in memory.

                (Menelaus and the Old Man enter quarreling.)

Old Man

  Menelaus! You have dared a fearful thing
  That goes against all conscience.

Menelaus

                          Stand back!
  You're a slave—*too* loyal to your master!

Old Man

  The insult you've given is honorable.   305

Menelaus

Keep your place—or you'll pay for it in pain.

Old Man

(*Shouting.*)

You had no right to open the letter I carried!

Menelaus

Nor had you the right to carry a message
That brings evil and disaster to all Greece.

Old Man

I'll argue that with others—give me the letter.

Menelaus

I will not give it.   310

Old Man

And I won't let it go!

Menelaus

This stick will beat your head into a bloody pulp.

Old Man

To die for my lord would be a good death.

Menelaus

Hands off—you talk too much for a slave.

(*Enter Agamemnon.*)

Old Man

O my king, look how I am wronged!
He took me by force—and tore your letter   315
From my hand. Now, he won't listen to right
Or to reason.

Agamemnon

What is this—a brawl
And argument right at my own door?

Menelaus

Before this man is heard I have the right
To speak.

Agamemnon

      What brought you into the scuffle—
And why abuse him with such violence?

                            (*The Old Man goes out.*)

Menelaus

First, look upon my face, Agamemnon,   320
Then I will begin to tell my story.

Agamemnon

I am the son of Atreus. Do you think
He shrinks from *your* eye, Menelaus?

Menelaus

                              (*Impatiently.*)

This letter carries a message of treason!

Agamemnon

I see the letter—First, give it to me—

Menelaus

Not till I've shown its message to all Greeks.

Agamemnon

So now you know what you have no right   325
To know. You broke the seal!

Menelaus

                   Yes, I broke it
And to your sorrow. You'll suffer now
For the evil you secretly plotted!

Agamemnon

Where did you find him? Oh, you have no shame!

Menelaus

    I was watching to see if your daughter
    Had arrived at the camp out of Argos.

Agamemnon

    It's true—you have no shame. What reason
    Have you for spying in my affairs?

Menelaus

                        My own desire
    Urged me. I am not a slave of yours.   330

Agamemnon

    Can there be any outrage like this?
    You won't allow me to rule in my own house!

Menelaus

    No, for your mind is treacherous. One day
    You plan one thing, another day another,
    Tomorrow you will shift again.

Agamemnon

                     You frame
    The lies neatly. Oh, I hate a smooth tongue!

Menelaus

    Agamemnon,
    A disloyal heart is false to friends and
    A thing of evil. Now *you* I want to question,   335
    And don't, because you are angry, turn your face
    From the truth—I shall not rack you too hard.
    Have you forgotten when you were eager
    And anxious to lead the Greek army to Troy,
    Wanting to appear unambitious but in your heart
    Eager for command? Do you remember how humble
    You were to all the people, grasping the hand,
    Keeping open the doors of your house, yes,   340

Open to all, granting to every man, even the lowly,
The right to address and to hail you by name?
These ways and tricks you tried, to buy
In the market advancement, but when at last
You won power, then you turned these habits
Of your heart inside out. Now were you
No longer loving to your friends of yesterday.
No—the old ones could not reach you, but,
Unapproachable, you were seldom found at home.   345
Oh, it is vile for a man, if he be noble,
And when he has won to the heights of power,
To put on new manners for old and change
His countenance. Far more when he's in fortune
And able truly to succor, must he hold
Firmly to old friends. This is the good man's
Character. So I blame you for these things
Where first I found you ignoble. And then
You came to Aulis with the army—   350
The Panhellenic host! And suddenly—
From being all, you became nothing,
Confounded by a fate God-given, lacking
But this one thing: a favoring wind
To dispatch the fleet. So the Danaans urged
That you send back every ship and at Aulis
Put an end to this toil without meaning.
I remember your face then, bewildered,
Unhappy, fearing you would never captain
Your thousand ships or fill up with spears   355
The fields of Priam's Troy. Then you called me
Into council. What shall I do? you asked me.
What scheme, what strategy can I devise
That will prevent the stripping-off
Of my command and the loss of my glorious name?

Calchas spoke: Sacrifice on the altar
Your own daughter to Artemis, and the Greek ships

Will sail. At that instant your heart filled up
With gladness and happily, in sacrifice,   360
You promised to slay the child. So you
Sent willingly to your wife, not by compulsion—
You cannot deny that—that she send the girl
Here, and for pretext, that she come to marry
Achilles. This is the very air which heard
These words from your mouth. But then, turning
Your mind about, in secret you recast
The message. So now your story?—you will
Never be your daughter's murderer! I tell you   365
Thousands have done what you have done. Willingly
Worked and striven up to the peaks of power,
Then in the flush of attainment, they fail
And fall in ignominy. Now in some instances
The populace is responsible out of stupidity,
But with other men the failure is in them,
Impotent—like you—to lead or protect
The state. Oh, chiefly in this present case
I groan for Greece in her affliction,   370
For she was ready to act with honor,
But on account of your girl and you,
She lets the barbarians, even the basest
Of them, slip from her grasp and make her name
A mockery! O may I never make
Any man ruler of my country or
Commander of her armies because I am
In debt to him. No, a general
Must have wit; and a ruler, understanding.   375

Chorus

Terrible are these fighting words which lead
Brothers into strife with one another.

Agamemnon

Now will I give you briefly *my* reproach.
Nor will my looks grow haughty with contempt,

But looking and speaking I'll be temperate,
As it befits a brother and as a good man   380
To another shows decency and respect.
Your eyes are bloodshot—and what
Dire threats are these? Tell me, who
Has wronged you, what do you want? Are you
Burning to possess a virtuous wife? Well,
I can't procure her for you. The one you had
You governed foully. Should I pay the price
For these your sins, when I am innocent?
Or is it my advancement that bites your heart?   385
No, you've thrown to the winds all reason
And honor, and lust only to hold a lovely woman
In your arms. Oh, the pleasures of the base
Are always vile. And now—if yesterday
I was without wit or wisdom, but today
Have counseled with myself well and wisely—
Does that make me mad? Rather are you crazed,
For the gods, being favorable, rid you of
A wicked wife, and now you want her back!   390
As to the suitors, marriage-mad, with evil
In their hearts, they swore an oath to Tyndareus.
Yes, I grant that, but a crazed hope which
I believe a god inspired effected all,
Not any influence or strength in you.
Make war with them—they'll join you in their folly!   395
But in heaven there is intelligence—it can
Perceive oaths bonded in evil, under compulsion
Sworn. *So I will not kill my children.*
Nor will your enterprise of vengeance upon
An evil wife prosper against all justice.
If I did commit this act, against law, right,
And the child I fathered, each day, each night,
While I yet lived would wear me out in grief
And tears. So these are my few words, clear   400
And easily understood. You may choose madness,
But I will order my affairs in decency and honor.

Chorus

How different are these words from those you spoke
Before—but it is good to save the child.

Menelaus

O gods—so now I have *no* friends.

Agamemnon

And you'll have none while you try to destroy them.   405

Menelaus

Where is the proof you are our father's son,
My brother?

Agamemnon

        I am brother to you
When you are sane, not mad.

Menelaus

              Should not
A friend share with friends his grief?

Agamemnon

Speak when you have befriended me,
Not done me injury.

Menelaus

           Greece is in grief   410
And in trouble. Isn't it right that you
Should bear a part of the hardship?

Agamemnon

This is what I think—Greece, like yourself,
Some god has driven mad.

Menelaus

            You have a king's
Scepter—boast of it and puff yourself up!

To me you are a traitor, so I'll turn
To other means and other friends.

(Enter Messenger.)

Messenger

O commander of all the armies of Greece,
King Agamemnon, I am here to bring   415
To you your daughter, Iphigenia,
And her mother who is with her,
The queen, Clytemnestra.
And the boy Orestes is here—you've been
So long from home that, seeing him, delight
Will fill your heart.

Now after weary travel, beside a stream   420
Free flowing, the ladies rest and bathe
Their feet. So do the horses! On the green
Meadow we've turned them loose to browse.

I have come, running ahead of the others
To prepare you with this information:
Rumor travels fast and by now the army   425
Knows that your daughter has arrived in Aulis.
In fact, crowds from the camp already have come
On the run for a sight of the maiden.
For the highborn are glorious and all men
Gaze at them. Now they are saying: Is it
A marriage, or what happens now?   430
Has King Agamemnon so yearned in love
For his daughter that now he has brought her
To Aulis? This too you could hear them say:
Men make the marriage offering to Artemis,
Aulis' queen, but who will be the bridegroom?

(He smiles.)

Shall we prepare barley for sacrifice?   435
Let us crown our heads with garlands, and you,
King Menelaus, start the bridal hymn!

Oh, let the lutes be played, and there should be
Dancing within the pavilion, since for
The maid this day should dawn in happiness.

Agamemnon

(Stiffly.)

You are thanked for your news. Now you may go   440
Within the pavilion. As to the rest—
It will go well as the fates will it.

(The Messenger goes out.)

O God, how can I find words or begin
To speak in the face of this, my disaster?
Fallen into the pit, fate chains me there.
I forged a conspiracy, but shrewder far
A hundred times were the stratagems   445
Which Fate invented. O fortunate men of mean,
Ignoble birth, freely you may weep and
Empty out your hearts, but the highborn—
Decorum rules our lives and we, by service
To the mob, become its slaves.   450

                    Look at me, brother.
I am ashamed of these tears. And yet
At the extremity of my misfortune
I am ashamed not to shed them. What words
Can I utter to my wife or with what countenance
Receive and welcome her when she appears,   455
Unsummoned, in the midst of my disaster?
Yet coming she only obeys nature,
Following a daughter here to do love's services,
And give the bride away. So doing, she
Shall find me out the author of this evil.

And the unhappy maiden! Maiden, no—   460
Soon, it seems, Hades will marry her.
Oh, piteous fate! I hear her cries to me;

O Father, why do you kill me? May Death
Be your bride also and betroth
All of your dear ones as he has plighted me!
Beside her, Orestes the infant will cry out   465
Meaningless words, but full of meaning
To my heart!
O Paris, Helen, it is your marrying
Which has wrought these things
And my damnation!

Chorus

And I too grieve, so far as a stranger may,
Over a king's misfortune.   470

Menelaus

My brother, grant me this, to grasp your hand—

Agamemnon

Here it is. You have won the mastery.
I now face the ordeal of my defeat.

Menelaus

No! I swear by Pelops, father of our
Father, and by Atreus, who begat us both,
That truly now I do not speak toward
Any end but inwardly and from my heart.   475
When I saw tears bursting from your eyes
Tears started in mine and a great pity
Seized me. I am no longer terrible   480
To you, or any more your enemy.
All the words spoken I now withdraw, and
From them I retreat. I stand in your place
And beseech you do not slay the child
To prosper me and to destroy yourself.
It is against all justice that you should
Groan from the same cause that makes me

Fortunate or that your daughter die while
All my children live and face the sun.
What do I want? Could I not obtain 485
A perfect marriage elsewhere, if I longed for
Marrying? But a brother whom I should
Most cherish, I was about to forfeit
To gain a Helen, so bartering excellence
For evil. I was witless and adolescent
Until, crowding upon the deed, I saw and knew
All that it meant to kill the child. 490
Besides this, thinking upon our kinship,
Pity for the girl in her harsh agony
Swept over me: she would be killed
On account of my marriage. But what has Helen
To do with this girl of yours? Disband
The host, I say, let it go from Aulis, 495
And so cease drowning your eyes in tears
Or summoning me to grieve and weep for you.
As to your share and mine in the oracle
Concerning your daughter's destiny, I
Want no part in it; my share I give to you.
And so I've turned my threatening words 500
Into their opposites! But it is fitting;
I have changed because I love a brother.
To seek, as here I have done, always
For the best action in the case is *not*
The character of an evil man!

Chorus

O King, you honor your forefathers— 505
A speech worthy of Tantalus, Zeus' son.

Agamemnon

I thank you, Menelaus, that now
Beyond my hopes you have spoken justly,
With right reason, worthy of yourself.

These quarrels between brothers spring from
Many things, over a woman, for instance,
Or out of greed for the inheritance.
I loathe them all. Such kinships pour bitterness   510
Into both hearts. But we have arrived
At a fatal place: A compulsion absolute
Now works the slaughter of the child.

Menelaus

What do you mean? Who will force you to kill her?

Agamemnon

The whole concourse of Achaean armies.

Menelaus

No—not if you send her back to Argos.   515

Agamemnon

I might do it secretly—but from the army
I could not keep the secret.

Menelaus

                      You are wrong
To fear the mob so desperately.

Agamemnon

Listen to me. To the whole Greek army
Calchas will report the prophecy.

Menelaus

No, not if Calchas, the prophet, is first dead,
And that will be quite simple to accomplish.

Agamemnon

How arrogant they are! The whole race of prophets—   520
A curse upon this earth.

Menelaus
>   They're of no value
> To man, or use whatever, especially when alive.

Agamemnon
>   Menelaus, do you feel none of the terror
>   Which creeps into my heart?

Menelaus
>   How can I know
>   Your fear if you do not name it?

Agamemnon
>   Odysseus,
>   Son of Sisyphus, *knows* all these things.

Menelaus
>   Odysseus is not such a man or personage   525
>   That he can harm you or me.

Agamemnon
>   He is cunning
>   In his tactics always and his ear
>   Is close to the mob.

Menelaus
>   It's his ambition,
>   An evil and a cursed thing, piercing
>   His very soul.

Agamemnon
>   I agree—so will he not
>   Stand up in the midst of the army and
>   Tell the prophecy which Calchas spoke
>   And how I promised to sacrifice   530
>   My victim to Artemis—and how I then
>   Annulled my promises? Oh, with these words
>   Will he arouse and seize the very soul

Of the army, order them to kill you
And me—and sacrifice the girl.

If I should escape to Argos they then
Would follow me there, and even to
The Cyclopean walls to raze them
To the earth and the land destroy utterly.   535
Such is the terrible circumstance in which
I find myself. Now in my despair I am
Quite helpless, and it is God's will.

(He bows his head for a moment
in despair, then looks up.)

Do this one thing for me, Menelaus,
Go to the army, take all precaution
That Clytemnestra learn nothing of this
Till after I have seized the child and   540
Sent her to her death. So I may do
This evil—which I have to do—
With fewest tears. And you, ladies, who are
Our guests, see that you guard your lips.

(Agamemnon and Menelaus go out.)

Chorus

O blest are those who share
In Aphrodite's gifts   545
With modesty and measure,
Blest who escape the frenzied passion.
For Eros of the golden hair
Shoots his two arrows of desire,
And the one brings happiness   550
To man's life, the other ruin.
O Cypris, loveliest of goddesses
In heaven, keep this frenzied arrow
From my heart.
Keep modest my delights

All my desires lawful,   555
So may I have my part in love
But not in passion's madness.

Many are the natures of men,
Various their manners of living,
Yet a straight path is always the right one;   560
And lessons deeply taught
Lead man to paths of righteousness;
Reverence, I say, is wisdom
And by its grace transfigures—
So that we seek virtue
With a right judgment.   565
From all of this springs honor
Bringing ageless glory into
Man's life. Oh, a mighty quest
Is the hunting out of virtue—
Which for womankind
Must be a love in quietness,
But, for men, infinite are the ways   570
To order and augment
The state.
O Paris, you returned to
The land which reared you,
Herdsman of white heifers
Upon Ida's mountains; where   575
Barbarian melodies you played
Upon a Phrygian flute
And echoed there once more
Olympus' pipe.

Full-uddered cattle browsed
When the goddesses summoned you   580
For this trial of beauty—
Trial which sent you
To Greece, to knock at the doors
Of ivory palaces; it was there

Looking into Helen's eyes
You gave and took the ecstasies of love.   585
So from this quarrel came
The assault by Greeks
With ship and spear
Upon Troy's citadel.

(Turning, they see Queen Clytemnestra
and Iphigenia in a chariot,
approaching.)

O august ladies,   590
Daughters of the mighty of the earth,
How blest you are! Behold
Iphigenia, the king's daughter,
And Clytemnestra, queen,
Daughter of Tyndareus.
They, sprung from the mighty ones,
Ride on to highest destiny.   595
The gods themselves, bestowers of happiness,
They are not more august
Than these
The fortunate amongst mankind.

Now let us stand here, children of Chalcis,
Let us receive the queen
Out of her chariot
And keep her step from stumbling   600
To the earth.

(Enter, riding in a chariot, Clytemnestra, Iphigenia,
and the young child, Orestes. Attendants
accompany them.)

Gently, but with good will,
And with our hands
We will help you down.
O noble daughter of Agamemnon,
Newly come to Aulis, have no fear!

For to you, stranger from Argos— 605
Gently and without clamor
We who are strangers too
Give you our welcome.

Clytemnestra

I shall think of this as a good omen—
Your kindness and good words—for I am here,
Hopefully, to lead this young girl 610
Into a noble and a happy marriage.
Now, will you take the dowry from the wagon—
All of her bridal gifts which I have brought.
Carry them into the pavilion carefully.
And you, daughter, put down your pretty feet
And get out of the carriage. All of you
Maidens take her into your arms and help 615
Her down.

(*Smiling and matter of fact.*)

And now, will someone lend me
The support of an arm, that with greater
Ease I may dismount—stand in front, please,
Of the horses' yoke—see the colt's eyes are 620
Wild with terror!

(*After the horse has been steadied.*)

Now, this is Agamemnon's son.
Take him—his name is Orestes—and he's
Still quite a helpless baby. My baby,
Are you still asleep from the rolling wheels?
Wake up and be happy. This is your sister's
Wedding day! You are noble, and so
You will have a nobleman as kin, 625
The godlike child of the Nereid.
My child, Iphigenia, come sit next to
Your mother. Stay close beside me and show
All these strangers here how happy and how

Blessed I am in you! But here he comes—
Your most beloved father. Go, give him welcome.   630

(Enter Agamemnon.)

Iphigenia

O Mother, don't be angry if I run
Ahead and throw myself into his arms.

(Attendants go out, one of them carrying
Orestes in her arms.)

Clytemnestra

Mightiest and most honored, Lord Agamemnon,
Obedient to your command, we are here.

Iphigenia

Father!
I long to throw myself before anyone   635
Into your arms—it's been so long a time—
And kiss your cheek! Oh, are you angry, Mother?

Clytemnestra

No my child, this is rightful, and it is
As it has always been. Of all the children
I have borne your father, you love him most.

Iphigenia

Father, what a desperate age since I   640
Saw you last! But now, seeing you again,
I am happy.

Agamemnon

                    And I, seeing you,
Am happy. You speak for both of us, Iphigenia.

Iphigenia

(Smiling and laughing.)

Hail! O Father, it is a good and
Wonderful thing you have done—bringing me here!

« 325 »

Agamemnon

    I do not know how to answer what you say,
    My child.

Iphigenia

            Oh? You say you are glad to see me,
    But your eyes have no quiet in them.

Agamemnon

    I have cares—the many cares of a general   645
    And a king.

Iphigenia

            Oh, turn away from all of them,
    My father—be here and mine only, now!

Agamemnon

    I am. Now I am nowhere but in this place,
    And with you utterly, my darling.

Iphigenia

                   Oh then,
    Unknit your brow.

                       (*Putting her hand on his forehead.*)
           And smooth your face for love.

Agamemnon

    Now see my joy as I look at you—

Iphigenia

                 And yet,
    The tears—a libation of tears—are there   650
    Ready to pour from your eyes.

Agamemnon

             Well,
    There is a long parting about to come
    For both of us—

Iphigenia
> I don't understand,
> Dear Father—I don't understand—

Agamemnon
> And yet
> You do seem to speak with understanding,
> And I am the more grieved.

Iphigenia
> I'll speak foolishly
> If that will please you more.

Agamemnon

(*To himself.*)

> How hard to curb my tongue!   655

(*Aloud.*)

> Yes, do.

Iphigenia
> Now for a time, Father dear, won't you stay
> At home with your children?

Agamemnon
> O that I might!
> This willing and not doing will crack my heart.

Iphigenia
> Menelaus' wrongs and his spearmen—O
> That they'd disappear!

Agamemnon
> He and his wrongs
> Will destroy others first—then ruin me.

Iphigenia

(*Still preoccupied with her absence from him.*)

> Father, you've been so long in Aulis' gulf!   660

Agamemnon

I must

Equip and dispatch the armies, I am still
Hindered and held up.

Iphigenia

Where is it they say
These Trojans live, my father?

Agamemnon

In the country
Where Paris, the son of Priam, dwells, and
Would to heaven he had never lived at all!

Iphigenia

You're going on a long voyage, *leaving me!*

Agamemnon

(Speaking to himself.)

But your situation is like mine, my daughter—   665
You're going on a long voyage—leaving your father.

Iphigenia

Oh—on this voyage of *yours* I only wish
It were right for you to take me with you!

Agamemnon

It is ordained that you too take a long
Sailing, my daughter, to a land where—where
You must remember me!

Iphigenia

Shall I go
On this voyage with my mother, or alone?

Agamemnon

Alone—Cut off and quite separated
From both your father and your mother.

Iphigenia

A new home you make for me, Father,   670
Where will it be?

Agamemnon

                    Now stop—it's not right
For a girl to know all of these things.

Iphigenia

Father, over there when you have done
All things well, hurry back to me from Troy!

Agamemnon

                            (*Driven by an inner compulsion to speak
                            what he knows he must conceal.*)

I will, but first, right here, in Aulis
I must offer sacrifice.

Iphigenia

                    Oh yes, of course,
With sacrifices we must pay homage to heaven.

Agamemnon

                            (*Hypnotized by his own thoughts.*)

You shall see this one, for you are to stand   675
By the basin of holy water.

Iphigenia

Then round the altar shall I start the dance?

Agamemnon

O for this happy ignorance that is yours!
Now go into the pavilion and be
Alone with your maidens. Give me a kiss
Of pain and your right hand, for soon you go
To live apart from your father. And this   680
Will be too long a parting!

(*Holding her in his arms.*)

O breast and cheeks! O golden hair!
What bitter burden Helen and her Troy city
Have laid upon you! I must stop, for as I
Touch you my eyes are water springs—the tears
Start their escape. Go into the pavilion!   685

(*Iphigenia goes out.*)

Oh, forgive me, child of Leda, for this
Self-pity! Here am I giving in marriage
My daughter to Achilles! Such partings
Bring happiness but prick the heart of a father
Who, after all his fostering care, must give
Away a daughter to another's home.   690

Clytemnestra

I am not unfeeling, nor do I reproach
Your grief. For I, too, shall sorrow
As I lead her and as the marriage hymn is sung.
But time and custom will soften sadness.
His name to whom you have betrothed   695
Our child I know. Now tell me
His home and lineage.

Agamemnon

Asopus had a daughter, Aegina—

Clytemnestra

Yes, who married her, god or a mortal?

Agamemnon

Zeus married her. Aeacus was their son
And he became Oenone's husband.

Clytemnestra

Tell me,
Which child of Aeacus received the inheritance?   700

Agamemnon

    Peleus—he married Nereus' daughter.

Clytemnestra

    Did the gods bless their marriage
    Or did he take her against their will?

Agamemnon

    Zeus betrothed her and the lord Nereus
    Gave her away in marriage.

Clytemnestra

                  Tell me—
    Where did he marry her? Under the sea's waves?

Agamemnon

    No, on the holy foothills of Pelion,   705
    Where Chiron lives.

Clytemnestra

               It is there the tribes
    Of Centaurs make their home?

Agamemnon

                       Yes, and it was there
    The gods gave Peleus a marriage feast.

Clytemnestra

    Will you tell me this—did Thetis rear
    Achilles or his father?

Agamemnon

              Chiron taught him,
    That he might never learn the customs of
    Evil men.

Clytemnestra

           I would say a wise teacher, but
    Peleus giving him that teacher was wiser still.   710

Agamemnon

　So, such a man is your daughter's husband.

Clytemnestra

　A perfect choice! Where is his city in Greece?

Agamemnon

　It is within Phthia; and beside
　The river Apidanus—

Clytemnestra

　　　　　　　　And it's there
　That you will bring your child and mine?　　　　　　715

Agamemnon

　That should be her husband's care.

Clytemnestra

　Well, I ask heaven's blessings upon them—
　What is the day set for the marriage?

Agamemnon

　When the full moon comes, to bring them good luck.

Clytemnestra

　Now I ask this, have you slain the victims
　To Artemis, the goddess, for our child?

Agamemnon

　I shall, I have made all the preparations.

Clytemnestra

　And then you will hold the marriage feast?　　　　　　720

Agamemnon

　When I've sacrificed to the gods their due.

Clytemnestra

And where do *I* make the women's feast?

Agamemnon

Here, by these proud sterns of our ships.

Clytemnestra

By the anchors and hawsers? Well,
May good fortune come of it?

Agamemnon

My lady,

This you must do—Obey!   725

Clytemnestra

That is no revelation—

I am accustomed to it.

Agamemnon

So here

Where the bridegroom is I will—

Clytemnestra

Do what?

You'll take what office that is mine?

Agamemnon

I shall

Give the child away—with the Danaan's help.

Clytemnestra

And meantime, where must *I* be staying?   730

Agamemnon

In Argos, where you must take care
Of your younger daughters.

Clytemnestra

Leaving the child?

Who then will lift the marriage torch?

Agamemnon

    Whatever torch is fitting, I will raise it.

Clytemnestra

    Against all custom! And you see
    Nothing wrong in that?

Agamemnon

                I see that it is
    Wrong for you to stay, mingling with the host   735
    Of the army—

Clytemnestra

          I think it *right*
    A mother give away her daughter.

Agamemnon

    But wrong, I tell you, to leave the maidens
    Alone in our halls.

Clytemnestra

           In maiden chambers
    They are safe and well guarded.

Agamemnon

              Obey me!

Clytemnestra

    No! by the Argive's goddess queen!
    You go outside and do your part, I indoors   740
    Will do what's proper for the maid's marrying.

                       (Clytemnestra goes out.)

Agamemnon

    Oh, I have rushed madly into this and failed
    In every hope: desiring to send my wife
    Out of my sight—I a conspirator
    Against my best beloved and weaving plots

Against her. Now I am confounded   745
In all things. Yet to the priest Calchas
I will go, with him to ask the goddess' pleasure
Though that should spell my doom,
And for Greece toil and travail.
A wise man keeps his wife at home
Virtuous and helpful—or never marries.   750

(Agamemnon goes out.)

Chorus

Now will they come to Simois
And the silvery swirl of her waters—
The Greeks mighty in assembly
With their ships and their armor;
To Ilium, to the plains of Troy   755
Sacred to Phoebus Apollo,
Where Cassandra is prophet, I hear,
Her head green crowned with the laurel—
And wildly she flings her golden hair
As the god breathes in her soul   760
The frenzy of foresight.

Upon the battle towers of Troy,
Around her walls, Trojans will stand
When Ares in harness of bronze
On these stately ships over the sea   765
Moves to the runnels of Simois.
Oh, he'll come desiring the seizure of Helen
To hale her from Priam's palace,   770
She whose brothers are Zeus' sons—
Dioscuri are their name stars in heaven—
To hale Helen to the land of Greece
By toil of battle
And the shields and spears of Achaeans.

Pergamus with walls of stone, Phrygia's town,
He will encircle in bloody battle,   775

Cutting the defenders' throats,
To drag their bodies headless away;
Then from the citadel's top peak to earth
He will sack all the dwellings in Troy city.
So every maiden will wail loudly,
And with them Priam's queen.   780
And Helen too, who is daughter of Zeus,
She will cry aloud,
Who in the years gone had forsaken her husband.
Oh, we who are women of Chalcis
May this fate never be ours   785
Or that of our children's children!
To be as the golden Lydian ladies,
Or the Phrygian wives—
To stand before their looms
And wail to one another:

"Who will lay hands on my shining hair,   790
When tears flood my eyes,
And who will pluck me a flower
Out of my country's ruin?
Oh it is on account of *you*,
Child of the arch-necked swan,
If the story is to be believed,
The story that Leda bore you to a winged bird,   795
To Zeus himself transformed!
But perhaps this is a fable
From the book of the Muses
Borne to me out of season,   800
A senseless tale."

                                        (*Achilles enters.*)

Achilles

Where is the commander-in-chief?
Will one of his aides give him this message
That Achilles, the son of Peleus is here
At the door of his pavilion.

*(After a pause, turns and speaks what
is on his mind to the Chorus.)*

This delay by the river Euripus
Is not alike for all, let me tell you.
Some of us are unmarried. We've simply   805
Abandoned our halls and sit here idly
On the beaches. Others have left at home
Their wives and children, all because
A terrible passion has seized all Greece
To make this expedition—not without
Heaven's contrivance. Whatever others
May argue, I'll tell *my* righteous grievance!   810
I left Pharsalia and my father Peleus,
And here by the Euripus I must wait—
Wait because here these light winds blow—
And curb my own troops, my Myrmidons.
They are forever urging me and saying:
We are the army for Troy! How many months   815
Must we drag out here? Act if you are going
To act, if not, wait no longer upon
Atreus' sons and on their dallyings
But lead the army home.

(Clytemnestra enters from the pavilion.)

Clytemnestra

Son of the Nereid, I come to greet you—
I heard your voice inside the tent.   820

Achilles

O august lady—Whom do my eyes meet,
A woman peerless in her loveliness!

Clytemnestra

It is not marvelous that you do not know me
Since into my presence you never came before.

(Smiling.)

But I praise your respect for modesty.

Achilles

Who are you? And why, lady, have you come   825
To the mustering-in of the Greek army—
You, a woman, into a camp of armed men?

Clytemnestra

I am the daughter of Leda, Clytemnestra.
Agamemnon is my husband.

Achilles

             My lady,
You have spoken what was fitting
With brevity and beauty, but for me
I may not rightly hold converse here   830
With you or any woman—

                  (*He starts to leave.*)

Clytemnestra

Oh wait! Why rush away? With your
Right hand clasp mine and let this be
The beginning of a blest betrothal.

Achilles

What are you saying, Queen Clytemnestra?
I take your right hand in mine? That is
Wrongful—I would be ashamed before the king.

Clytemnestra

It is wholly right, child of the Nereid,   835
Since soon you will marry my daughter.

Achilles

                What!
What marriage do you speak of, my lady?

             (*After a moment's pause.*)

I have no word to put into my answer,
Unless this I say—from some strange frenzy
Of your mind you have conceived this story—

Clytemnestra

By nature all men are shy, seeing new
Kinsmen, or hearing talk of marriage.   840

Achilles

My lady, never have I courted your daughter,
Or from the sons of Atreus either
Has ever word of this marriage come to me.

Clytemnestra

(*Deeply troubled.*)

I do not understand—I am amazed at your words—

Achilles

Let's search this out together for there may   845
Be truth in what we both have said.

Clytemnestra

Oh, I have been horribly abused!
The betrothal which I came here to find,
At Aulis, never existed here or anywhere
But is a lie—Oh, I am crushed with shame!

Achilles

My lady, perhaps it is only this:
Someone is laughing at us both.
But I beg of you: take any mockery
Without concern, and bear it lightly.   850

Clytemnestra

Farewell! Deceived as I am, humiliated,
I can no longer lift my eyes to yours.

Achilles

I too bid you farewell, my lady,
And go now into the tent to seek your husband.

Old Man

(Calling from within the tent.)

Sir, wait! I'm calling to you there—O   855
Grandson of Aeacus, child of the goddess,
And you, my lady, daughter of Leda!

Achilles

Who shouts through the open door—and in terror?

Old Man

I am a slave. I cannot boast to you
Of my position—that is my fate.

Achilles

Whose slave? Not mine, he would not be here
In Agamemnon's retinue.

Old Man

                I belong
To the lady who stands before this tent   860
A gift to her from her father, Tyndareus.

Achilles

I wait. Now say why you hold me here.

Old Man

Are both of you alone before the doors?

Achilles

We are. Speak and come out from the royal tent.

Old Man (entering)

May Fate and my good foresight rescue you!

Achilles

(To Clytemnestra.)

The man's story—it tells something   865
About to happen and I think important—

« 340 »

Clytemnestra

Speak, old man, don't wait to kiss my hand.

Old Man

You know who I am, my lady, loyal
To you and to your children?

Clytemnestra

Yes, I know,
You were an old house servant in the palace.

Old Man

King Agamemnon took me as a portion
In your dowry.

Clytemnestra

Yes, yes, and coming to Argos   870
With us, you have been mine ever since.

Old Man

That is the truth, and I am more loyal
To you than to your husband—

Clytemnestra

Now the mystery
You have been guarding, out with it!

Old Man

(*Trembling as he speaks.*)

I'll tell you quickly. Her father plans
With his own hand to kill your child.

Clytemnestra

What words of a crazed mind
Have come out of your mouth, old man.

Old Man

It is true—with a knife at her white throat   875
He will kill her.

Clytemnestra

> Oh, how miserable am I!
> He has been stricken, then, with madness?

Old Man

> No. In all other things, my queen,
> Your lord is sane except in this obsession
> Toward you and toward the child.

Clytemnestra

> Why? *Why?* What is the demon of vengeance
> Which drives him to this horror?

Old Man

> The oracle is the demon, the oracle
> Which Calchas spoke telling how the fleet may sail—

Clytemnestra

> Her father will kill her! O gods, what a fate   880
> And affliction for me and for the child.
> You say the fleet? Where will it sail?

Old Man

> To the lords of Troy and to their halls
> So that Menelaus may bring Helen back.

Clytemnestra

> Oh, fate then has bound Helen's homecoming
> To my daughter and to her death.

Old Man

> You know all of the mystery now, and that
> It is to Artemis that her father
> Will sacrifice the child.

Clytemnestra

(Her voice hard and full of hate.)

And the marriage,
That was the pretext which he invented
To bring me from Argos.

Old Man

Yes, and the king
Calculated that you would bring her gladly   885
To be the bride of Achilles.

Clytemnestra

O Daughter,
We have been escorted, you and with you
Your mother, to death and to destruction.

Old Man

The fate of the child is pitiable
And yours too, my queen. The king
Has dared a deed of horror.

Clytemnestra

Now, I cannot
Hold them back, these streams of tears. I am lost,
Utterly.

Old Man

What greater cause, my lady,
For grieving than a child taken away?
Weep, weep.

Clytemnestra

(Suddenly controlling herself.)

These plans—how do you know them   890
For the truth? Where did you find out these things,
Old man?

Old Man

   I'll tell you. I was on my way, running
   To bring you the letter, a second to
   Follow the first from my lord Agamemnon—

Clytemnestra

   And my husband's word to bring the girl—
   To bring her to her death—did he confirm
   The message?

Old Man

          No. He said *not* to bring her,
   For this second time he wrote sanely and
   In his right mind.

Clytemnestra

          Oh, why didn't you deliver *that* letter?

Old Man

   Because Menelaus tore it out of my hand,   895
   And he is the cause of all our ruin.

Clytemnestra

                  (Turning to Achilles.)

   Child of the Nereid, Peleus' son, do you hear?

Achilles

   I hear the story of your fate and misery
   And I cannot bear my part in it.

Clytemnestra

   They use this trick of your marriage
   To slaughter my child!

Achilles

          Now lady, let me
   Hurl *my* reproach upon your husband—

Clytemnestra

(Falling on her knees to him.)

Oh, you were born of a goddess, I—
I am mortal but I am not ashamed   900
To clasp your knees or to do eagerly
This or anything that will bring succor
For my daughter's sake. Protect us both—
Me from my evil fate, and she, defend her
Who is your betrothed, even though the
Marriage may never be. In name only
Is she your bride, and yet, I led her here
To be your wife and crowned her head   905
With a bride's wreath.

                    Oh, I have brought her
Not for marrying but for death and sacrifice!
Son of the goddess, a shameful reproach
Will be yours if you do not shield her!
Although no marriage yokes you
To the unhappy girl, yet to all men,
You are her lord and her dear husband.
Listen to me—since through your name   910
You have brought my undoing and my end,
I beg you, by your beard, your right hand, and
By your mother's name—O cleanse your own
Name of this reproach!

Child of the goddess, I have no altar
To which I can flee for safety except
To your knees, and I have no friends to help me
In this distant place. You have heard
The strategy, which is savage and shameless,
Of Agamemnon the king, and you see
How I have come, a woman and helpless,
Into a camp of men, sailors of the fleet,
Eager for any violence and yet

Strong to save and help if it come
Into their hearts. Oh—if you have the courage,   915
Now stretch out your hand and surely I am
Saved, but if you do not dare it—I am lost!

Chorus

Oh, what a power is motherhood, possessing
A potent spell. All women alike
Fight fiercely for a child.

Achilles

At your words in pride and in anger
My soul is lifted up.[1]
Our generals, the Atreidae, I obey
When their command is righteous, but
When evil, I shall not obey, and here
As in Troy, I shall show my nature free   930
To fight my enemy with honor.

But you, lady, suffer things savage and cruel
Even from those you love, so with my compassion
Which I put around you like a shield
I shall make right these wrongs abominable
As far as a young man can.
I tell you—never will your daughter   935
Who is my betrothed—die murdered by
Her father's hand. Nor to this conspiracy
Of your husband will I offer my name or
My person. He has planned it guiltily
In this fashion that though my sword
Is not drawn, my name, my name only
Will kill the child. Oh, then forever
Defiled would be my blood, if through me,   940
And through my marriage, the maiden die!
Then in dishonor, undeserved, incredible,

[1] See Appendix for omitted passage: lines 920–27.

She'd suffer intolerable wrongs—
And I would be the basest of all Greeks,
No more a man than Menelaus,   945
No son of Peleus but a fiend's child,
If for his sake my name should do this butchery.

No! By Nereus, fostered by ocean's
Waves, by the father of Thetis who bore me,
By him I swear, never will Agamemnon
Lay hands upon your daughter—nor even   950
With his finger tips touch the fringe
Of her robe.[2] Calchas, the prophet, when next
He makes sacrifice will find bitter and   955
Accursed the barley and holy water.
What sort of man is a soothsayer or prophet?
I will tell you: If he is lucky
In his guessings even then he'll speak
A flock of lies and little truth, but
When his guess is wrong and unlucky,
Poof! like smoke he is nothing.
Now must I tell you, it is not on account
Of this marriage I have said these things—
No—there are many girls for marrying,   960
But I cannot endure the insult and injury
Which the lord Agamemnon has heaped upon me!

                              (*More calmly.*)

What would have been fitting, if he had wanted
This snare and pretext, then he should
Have requested from me the use of my name.
As it was, I knew nothing, and so
To your husband, chiefly through faith in me,
You surrendered your daughter.

           (*In a lower voice, after thinking the matter over.*)

Perhaps—I might have granted him use   965
Of my name—for the sake of Greece—

[2] See Appendix for omitted passage: lines 952–54.

If so the ships could sail. Nor would
I have denied help to the common cause
Of those with whom I march.

(Angry again and his voice rising.)

But now
I am nothing and nobody in the eyes
Of the army chiefs! At their convenience
They do me honor or injury. I tell you
If anyone tries to tear or separate
Your daughter from me now I will fight him.
Yes—before I go to Troy this sword
Shall know his blood in death.   970
                              But you, lady,
Be calm now and comforted. I make myself
Known to you as though I were a god, mighty
And strong to help. Well, I am no god, and yet—
To save the girl—I shall be godlike now!

Chorus

You have spoken, Peleus' son, words worthy   975
Of yourself and of the dread sea goddess.

Clytemnestra

How can I praise and yet not overpraise
Or stint my words to lose your graciousness?
The noble, being praised, in an odd fashion
Hate those who laud them—if too much.   980
I am ashamed to tell my piteous story;
The affliction is mine, not yours—
And yet, a good man, though he be free
From trouble, succors the unfortunate.
Have mercy—my sorrow is worthy of it.   985
For first I thought that you would be my son,
And cherished in my heart an empty dream!
But now death threatens my child, an ill omen
Perhaps for your own marriage! so

You must protect yourself as well as me!
Again and again you have said this truth   990
That if you willed, my daughter would be saved.
Do you desire that she come to clasp your knees?
It would transgress a maiden's character,
But if you wish it she shall come
And blushing lift her innocent eyes to yours.
But if I can win you without her coming,   995
In maiden pride she shall remain indoors. We
Should, as far as we may, reverence modesty.

Achilles

Oh, do not bring her here for me to see!
Let us avoid foolish scandal, for the troops
Being crowded, idle, and away from home,   1000
Love filthy gossip and foul talk.
If your daughter comes a suppliant, or never,
It is the same. This enterprise is mine—
Believe my words—to rid you of these evils.   1005
Oh may I die if I mock you in this
And only live if I shall save the girl!

Clytemnestra

Heaven bless you for helping the unfortunate.

Achilles

Listen to me and you'll succeed in this—

Clytemnestra

What do you mean? I *must* listen to you.   1010

Achilles

Then once more let us persuade her father
To a saner mood.

Clytemnestra

        Terror of the army—
This base fear is in him.

Achilles

> Reason can wrestle
And overthrow terror.

Clytemnestra

> My hopes are cold on that.
>
> *(Pause.)*
>
> What must I do?

Achilles

> First this, beseech him like a suppliant   1015
> Not to kill his daughter. If he resists
> Then come to me you must. But if he yields
> To your deep wish—why then—
> I need not be a party to this affair.
> His very yielding will mean salvation.
>
> So, if I act by reason and not violence,
> I'll be a better friend and, too, escape   1020
> The troops' reproach. So without me you and
> Those dear to you may succeed in all.

Clytemnestra

> You've spoken wisely. What seems good to you
> I'll do. But if we fail in my great hope,   1025
> Where can I find and see you once again,
> In desperation seeking your hand and help.

Achilles

> I'll be on watch—and like a sentinel—
> But we'll appoint a place—and so avoid
> Your frantic search among the troops for me.   1030
> Do nothing to demean your heritage;
> Tyndareus' house deserves a fair report,
> Being a high name among all Greeks.

Clytemnestra

> These things shall be as you have spoken them.
> Rule me—it is my compulsion to obey.

If there are gods, you, being righteous,
Will win reward in heaven; if there are none,   1035
All our toil is without meaning.

(Clytemnestra and Achilles go out.)

Chorus

Oh what bridal song with Libyan flute,
With lyre dance-loving,
With reeds pipe-pealing,
Rang forth on the air,
When to Pelion came lovely haired   1040
The Graces to feast with the gods;
Gold-sandaled their feet
Stamping the ground;
On to the marriage of Peleus and Thetis,
Over the hills of the Centaurs,
Down through Pelion's woodlands,
To magnify with music's praise,   1045
The son of Aeacus.
And Phrygian Ganymede, Dardanus' child,   1050
Of Zeus favored and loved,
Into a golden bowl
Poured the libation, while
Near on the glistening sea sands, circling,   1055
The daughters of Nereus
Wove the marriage dance.

With lances of pine and a leafy crown
The reveling Centaurs and riders came   1060
To the gods' feast, and the bowls brimming
With Bacchus' gift.

Wildly they cried, "Hail Nereus' daughter,
Hail to your son, a bright light blazing
For Thessaly." So sang the prophet
Of Phoebus. And foreknowing,   1065
Chiron proclaimed his birth,
Birth of him who would come with an army

Of Myrmidons, spear-throwers,
Into Troyland for the sacking   1070
Of Priam's glorious city.
And he—they sang—will put upon his body
The armor wrought by Hephaestus,
Gift of his goddess mother,
Thetis who bore him.   1075
So the gods sang this wedding hymn
Blessing the marriage
Of Peleus, noble in birth,
And of the most favored
Of Nereus' daughters.

But you, Iphigenia, upon your head   1080
And on your lovely hair
Will the Argives wreathe a crown
For sacrifice.
You will be brought down from the hill caves
Like a heifer, red, white, unblemished,
And like a bloody victim
They will slash your throat.

You were not reared   1085
To be drawn to slaughter
By the music
Of a herdsman's pipe
But by your mother's side
Fostered to marry kings.

Oh, where now has the countenance
Of modesty or virtue   1090
Any strength,
When the blasphemer rules,
And heedless men
Thrust righteousness behind them,
When lawlessness rules law,

And no man—or his neighbor—
Fears the jealousy of God?

Clytemnestra

(*Entering and speaking to the Chorus.*)

I have come from the pavilion seeking
My husband. For he left our tent
And has been absent long. My unhappy
Child now weeps her heart out, first moaning   1100
Soft, then crying aloud, for she has heard
Of the death her father plots against her—
I speak of Agamemnon, and he comes. Now
In an instant he will be found guilty
Of this unholy crime against his child!   1105

(*Agamemnon enters.*)

Agamemnon

O daughter of Leda, I am glad
To find you now outside our tent,
For at this moment I must speak to you
Of several things not proper for a bride to hear.

Clytemnestra

What things fit so perfectly this moment?

Agamemnon

Send for the child from the pavilion   1110
To join her father. But first listen to me:
The lustral waters have now been prepared
And the barley to throw on cleansing fire;
Bridal victims are ready—their black blood
Soon to flow in honor of Artemis.

Clytemnestra

Speaking, you give all these things fair names.   1115
But for the deed of your intention—
I can find no good name for that.

(*Calling.*)

Come outside, my daughter; the will
Of your father you now know fully and well.
Come and bring your brother Orestes,
Child, and cover him with your robe.

> (*Enter Iphigenia with Orestes in her arms*
> *followed by an attendant.*)

Behold she is here, and in her coming   1120
To you now she is obedient, but as to the rest
Of this business, on her behalf and mine
I shall now speak.

Agamemnon

                    Child, why are you crying?
Why do you look upon the ground and hood
Your eyes from me with your robe?

Clytemnestra

                              I do not know
How I can make a beginning of my story
To you, since in equal measure the beginning,   1125
The middle, and the end is sorrow.

Agamemnon

                              What has happened?
Why do you both look at me with trouble
And with terror in your eyes?

Clytemnestra

                    My husband,
Answer my question with the courage of a man.

Agamemnon

Go on—I am willing. There is no need   1130
To command an answer from me.

Clytemnestra

Your child and mine—do you intend to kill her?

> (*Iphigenia, distraught, turns from her father.*
> *Attendant takes the child Orestes*
> *from her arms.*)

Agamemnon

What a horrible speech! To hold such
Accusation in the mind is vile—

Clytemnestra

Stop! Give me first an answer to this question.

Agamemnon

A reasonable question I will answer.

Clytemnestra

I ask this only—answer it.

1135

Agamemnon

> (*After a pause in which he stares at her in growing*
> *fear and agony, finally it bursts from him.*)
> Oh, my fate,

August and awful! My misfortune.
Oh, what an evil demon is mine

Clytemnestra

Yours? Mine and hers! One evil fate for three
And misery for us all.

Agamemnon

> (*Turning on her suddenly.*)
> Whom have I wronged?

Clytemnestra

You ask me this—your mind has lost its reason!

Agamemnon

(To himself.)

I am destroyed—my secret is betrayed.   1140

Clytemnestra

Listen, I know every part of this history
For I have sought it out and I know fully
Your intention. Even now your silence
Makes confession and this great groan of yours,
So with few words speak out.

Agamemnon

Then I would give you
A lie and lying would add shame   1145
To my misfortune. I will be silent.

Clytemnestra

Hear me now—
For I shall give you open speech and no
Dark saying or parable any more.
And this reproach I first hurl in your teeth,
That I married you against my will, after
You murdered Tantalus, my first husband,   1150
And dashed my living babe upon the earth,
Brutally tearing him from my breasts.
And then, the two sons of Zeus, my brothers,
On horseback came and in white armor made
War upon you. Till you got upon your knees
To my old father, Tyndareus, and he   1155
Rescued you. So you kept me for your bed.

But after that I became reconciled
To you and to your house, and you will bear
Witness that I, as your wife, have been
Blameless, modest in passion, and in honor
Seeking to increase your house so that   1160

Your coming-in had gladness and
Your going-out joy. A rare spoil for a man
Is the winning of a good wife; very
Plentiful are the worthless women.
And so I bore you this son and three daughters.
Now one of these you would tear from me.   1165
If any man should ask you why, why
Do you kill your daughter? What answer will
You make? Or must your words come from my mouth?
I kill her, you must answer, that Menelaus
May win Helen back. And so our child,
In her beauty, you pay as price for a woman
Of evil. So you buy with our best beloved   1170
A creature most loathed and hated.

But think now. If you leave me and go
To this war, and if your absence there
From me is stretched over the years,
With what heart shall I keep your halls in Argos?
With what heart look at each chair and find it
Empty of her; at her maiden chamber   1175
And it empty always; or when I sit
Down with tears of loneliness and for
A mourning that will have no end.

O child!

I shall then cry out. Who brought you to this death?
It was your father—he and no other,
And by no other's hand! This is the shame,
Agamemnon, and the retribution
You leave in your house.

Here am I

And the children you have left me. Oh, only
A little more do we need of pretext   1180
And provocation so that upon your

Homecoming we give you the welcome that
Is wholly due. No! by the gods, do not
Force me to become a woman of evil!
Or to betray you! And you, against me
Do not commit this sin! Tell me now,
After the sacrifice of your child, what prayer   1185
Can your mouth utter? What things of good
Can you ever pray for when you have
Slain the girl?

    Now you go from your home,
And if this going-out be shameful, will not
The return be evil? Tell me, in all
Conscience, how can I ask heaven to give
You any blessing? We must think the gods
Fools, if we ask blessing for the killers   1190
Of our children!

    When you return at last
To Argos, after the war, will you embrace
And kiss your daughters and your son? God forbid!
It would be sacrilege. For do you suppose
Any child of yours, when you have sent
A sister to her death, would ever look
Upon your face again, or in your eyes?

Speak to me—have you ever taken account
Of such things in any wise? Or is your thought
And need only to brandish scepters and   1195
Lead armies? Well then, here is a righteous
Offer you should have made to the army!
Achaeans, you are eager to sail for Troy—
Then cast lots to find whose daughter must die!
This would be justice—rather than slay
Your own child, a victim to the army.   1200
Or—let Menelaus—for this is his affair—

Kill *his* daughter for her mother's sake.
For look, my girl is torn from me, from me
Who have been faithful to my marriage,
But she who has sinned against her husband's bed—
She will return to prosper, and bring   1205
Her daughter home. And now at last answer me
If in anything I have failed to speak
Justly, but if my words are fair and
Truly spoken, be no longer mad, but wise.
Repent! And do not kill the girl—who is
Your child and mine.

Chorus

Agamemnon, yield to her! It is good
That you together save the child. No man
Can rightly speak against this word of mine.   1210

Iphigenia

                                    O my father—

If I had the tongue of Orpheus
So that I could charm with song the stones to
Leap and follow me, or if my words could
Quite beguile anyone I wished—I'd use
My magic now. But only with tears can I   1215
Make arguments and here I offer them.
O Father,
My body is a suppliant's, tight clinging
To your knees. Do not take away this life
Of mine before its dying time. Nor make me
Go down under the earth to see the world
Of darkness, for it is sweet to look on
The day's light.
I was first to call you father,   1220
You to call me child. And of your children
First to sit upon your knees. We kissed
Each other in our love. "O child,"

You said, "surely one day I shall see you
Happy in your husband's home. And like
A flower blooming for me and in my honor."   1225
Then as I clung to you and wove my fingers
In your beard, I answered, "Father, you,
Old and reverent then, with love I shall
Receive into my home, and so repay you
For the years of trouble and your fostering   1230
Care of me." I have in memory all these words
Of yours and mine. But you, forgetting,
Have willed it in your heart to kill me.

Oh no—by Pelops
And by Atreus, your father, and
By my mother who suffered travail
At my birth and now must suffer a second   1235
Time for me! Oh, oh—the marriage
Of Paris and Helen—Why must it touch
My life? Why must Paris be my ruin?
Father, look at me, and into my eyes;
Kiss me, so that if my words fail,   1240
And if I die, this thing of love I may
Hold in my heart and remember.

                                        (*Turning to Orestes.*)

My brother, so little can you help us
Who love you, but weep with me and
Beg our father not to kill your sister.
Oh, the threat of evil is instinct,
Even in a child's heart. See, even
Without speech, he begs you, Father,   1245
Pity and have mercy on my sister's life.
Yes, both of us beseech you, this little child
And I, your daughter grown. So these words
Are all my argument. Let me win life
From you. I must. To look upon the world
Of light is for all men their greatest joy—   1250

The shadow world below is nothing.
Men are mad, I say, who pray for death;
It is better that we live ever so
Miserably than die in glory.

Chorus

O wicked Helen, through you, and through your
Marriage, this terrible ordeal has come
To the sons of Atreus and to the child.

Agamemnon

My daughter and my wife, I know what calls
To me for pity and compassion, and   1255
What does not. *I love my children!*
Did I not I would be mad indeed.
Terrible it is to me, my wife, to dare
This thing. Terrible not to dare it.

Here is my compulsion absolute:
Behold the armies, girt about by the fleet,
And with them over there, the kings of Greece   1260
With all their bronzen armor at their feet—
None of them can sail to Ilium's towers
Nor sack the famous bastion of Troy
Until, as the prophet Calchas has decreed,
I make you the victim of this sacrifice.

O child, a mighty passion seizes
The Greek soldiers and maddens them to sail
With utmost speed to that barbarian place   1265
That they may halt the plunder of marriage beds
And the rape and seizure of Greek women.
The army, angered, will come to Argos,
Slaughter my daughters, murder you and me
If the divine will of the goddess
I annul. It is not Menelaus

Making a slave of me—Nor am I here
At Menelaus' will, but Greece lays upon me   1270
This sacrifice of you beyond all will
Of mine. We are weak and of no account
Before this fated thing.

O child,

Greece turns to you, to me, and now,
As much as in us lies she must be free.[3]

[3] For omitted passage, lines 1274–75, see Appendix.

(*Agamemnon goes out. Attendant who holds Orestes
leaves the stage. Iphigenia turns
to her mother.*)

Clytemnestra

O maidens who are friendly to us—O my child,
What a terrible dying is yours.
Your father, betraying you to death,
Has fled away.

Iphigenia

Oh, pitiable am I, Mother!
The selfsame grieving song
Is ours, fallen from fate's hands.   1280
Life is no longer mine,
Nor the dayspring's splendor.
O snow-beaten Phrygian glen and Ida's
Hill: there on a day was the tender suckling thrown,   1285
Priam's child, from his mother torn,
For the doom of death; it was the herdsman
Of Ida, Paris of Ida,
So named, so named in his Trojan city.   1290
Would God they had never reared him,
Reared Alexander, herdsman of cattle,
To dwell by the silvery waters,
By the nymphs and their fountains,   1295

By that meadow green and abundant
With roses and hyacinths
Gathered for goddesses.

There on that day came Pallas   1300
And Cypris the beguiling,
Hera, and Hermes, God's messenger—
Cypris, who crushes with desire,
Pallas with her spear,   1305
And Hera, Zeus' royal wife and queen—
They came for the judging,
For the hateful battle of beauty
Which to me brings death, O maidens,
But to the Danaans glory.   1310

O my mother, my mother,
Artemis has seized me, for Ilium
A first sacrifice!
He who began my life
Has betrayed me in misery
To a lonely dying.
Oh, my wretchedness,   1315
As I see her,
Helen, doom-starred and evil;
Bitter, bitter
Is the death you bring me!
Murdered by my father—
Accursed butchery,
For I shall be slain
By his unholy hands.

Oh, if only Aulis had not taken   1320
To the bosom of her harborage
These, our ships—
With their wings of pine,
Their beaks of bronze!

Oh, if only
The breath of Zeus had not swept them
To the roadstead that faces the river.
Zeus' breath—it brings delight—
And doom—to mortals;   1325
At one time the sails laugh
In a favoring breeze,
At another, Zeus the Almighty
Blows down upon mortals
Delay and doom.
O toil-bearing race, O toil-bearing   1330
Creatures living for a day—
Fate finds for every man
His share of misery.
O Tyndareus' daughter,
What burden you have laid
Upon the Danaans   1335
Of anguish and disaster!

Chorus

I pity you for your evil fate. Oh—
That it had never found you out!

Iphigenia

O Mother, there are men—I see them coming here.

Clytemnestra

It is Achilles, son of the goddess
For whom your father brought you here—

Iphigenia

Maidens, open the doors, so that I may   1340
Hide myself.

Clytemnestra

        Why do you run away, child?

Iphigenia

I am ashamed to see him—to look
On the face of Achilles.

Clytemnestra

But why?

Iphigenia

Oh, my unlucky marriage—I am ashamed—

(Covering her face with her hands.)

Clytemnestra

In this crisis, daughter, you can't afford
These delicate feelings. So stay—this
Is no time for modesty—if we can—

*(Threatening shouts of the army are heard
off stage. Enter Achilles.)*

Achilles

Woman of misery and misfortune,   1345
Leda's daughter—

Clytemnestra

Yes, you have said what is true.
I am she.

Achilles

(Pauses for a moment.)

The Argives are shouting
A thing of terror.

Clytemnestra

What are they shouting?

Achilles

It is about your daughter.

Clytemnestra

Oh, the words
Of ill omen—you have said them now.

Achilles

Yes, they are shouting she must be slaughtered
In sacrifice.

Clytemnestra
                    And was there no one
On the other side to argue against them?

Achilles

Yes, I spoke to the yelling crowd and so
Was in danger.

Clytemnestra
                    In danger of what?
Achilles

Of death by stoning.

Clytemnestra
                    Oh—and because you
Tried to save my child?   1350

Achilles
                              Yes, for that.

Clytemnestra
                                        (*Incredulous.*)

But who would have dared to lay a hand on you?

Achilles
                                        (*Bitterly.*)

Every Greek soldier.

Clytemnestra
                              (*Still not believing him.*)

                    But your own legion
Of Myrmidons, they were there at your side?

Achilles

And the first to threaten my death.

Clytemnestra

O my child—

Now we are lost.

Achilles

(*Bitterly.*)

They mocked me, they shouted
That I had become a slave of this marriage.

Clytemnestra

What did you say?

Achilles

I answered that they
Would never slaughter my bride.   1355

Clytemnestra

Oh, a right answer!

Achilles

My bride, whom her father had pledged to me.

Clytemnestra

Yes, and brought to you from Argos.

Achilles

They drowned my voice by their yelling
And cried me down.

Clytemnestra

Oh, the mob—what a terror
And an evil thing!

Achilles

But I will defend you!

Clytemnestra

(*Almost scornful.*)

You—one man fighting a thousand!

(*Enter two armor-bearers.*)

Achilles

Look!

These men are bringing me armor for that battle.

Clytemnestra

May the gods bless your courage—

Achilles

I shall be blest!

Clytemnestra

The child then shall *not* be killed?   1360

Achilles

Not if I live!

Clytemnestra

But tell me now, who will come here and try
To seize the girl?

Achilles

Men by thousands will come—
Odysseus will lead them.

Clytemnestra

Sisyphus' son?

Achilles

Yes!

Clytemnestra

Of his own will, or chosen by the army?

Achilles

He will be chosen, but glad of his appointment.

Clytemnestra

Chosen for evil, for bloodshed and murder!

Achilles

But I will keep him from the girl!   1365

Clytemnestra

                                        (*Suddenly hysterical.*)

Will he, if she resists, drag her away?

Achilles

There is no doubt—and by her golden hair!

Clytemnestra

What *then* must I do?

Achilles

                        Hold fast to the child—

Clytemnestra

And so save her from murder—

Achilles

                                It comes to this—

Iphigenia

                        (*Who for some minutes has not heard them,
                                breaks from her revery.*)

Mother, now listen to my words. I see
Your soul in anger against your husband.
This is a foolish and an evil rage.
Oh, I know when we stand before a helpless
Doom how hard it is to bear.   1370

                                (*Pause.*)

                        But hear me now.
It is rightful and good that we thank and
Praise our friend for his eager kindness.
But you must be careful and see that he
Is not blamed by the army. Such a thing
Would win us nothing but would bring him
Utter ruin. And now hear me, Mother,
What thing has seized me and I have conceived
In my heart.

            I shall die—I am resolved—   1375
And having fixed my mind I want to die

Well and gloriously, putting away
From me whatever is weak and ignoble.
Come close to me, Mother, follow my words
And tell me if I speak well. All Greece turns
Her eyes to me, to me only, great Greece
In her might—for through me is the sailing
Of the fleet, through me the sack and overthrow
Of Troy. Because of me, never more will
Barbarians wrong and ravish Greek women,   1380
Drag them from happiness and their homes
In Hellas. The penalty will be paid
Fully for the shame and seizure of Helen.

                             And all
These things, all of them, my death will achieve
And accomplish. I, savior of Greece,
Will win honor and my name shall be blessed.
It is wrong for me to love life too deeply.   1385
I am the possessed of my country
And you, Mother, bore me for all Greece,
Not for yourself alone.

                         Wrong and injury
Our country suffers, and so thousands
Of men arm themselves, thousands more in these ships
Pick up their oars. They will dare very greatly
Against the enemy and die for Greece.
These are thousands, but I with my one life
To save, am I to prevent all? Where is   1390
The judgment of justice here? To the soldiers
Who die is there a word we can answer?
None. But consider further, is it right
For this man to make war upon all the Greeks
For one woman's sake and surely die?
Rather in war is it far better that
Many women go to their death, if this

Keep one man only facing the light
And alive.

       O Mother, if Artemis
Wishes to take the life of my body,   1395
Shall I, who am mortal, oppose
The divine will? No—that is unthinkable!
To Greece I give this body of mine.
Slay it in sacrifice and conquer Troy.
These things coming to pass, Mother, will be
A remembrance for you. They will be
My children, my marriage; through the years
My good name and my glory. It is
A right thing that Greeks rule barbarians,   1400
Not barbarians Greeks.

             It is right,
And why? They are bondsmen and slaves, and we,
Mother, are Greeks and are free.

Chorus

    Child, you play your part with nobleness.
    The fault is with the goddess and with fate.

Achilles

                O child of Agamemnon—
If I had won you as my bride, if only—   1405
I would have sworn a god had given me
Happiness. I envy Greece because you
Are hers, not mine. And you too I envy
Because Greece has chosen you, not me,
To die. Of our country with honor too
You have spoken. You gave up the fight
Against God's will and chose the thing that was
Good and was fated. And yet the more I
See of your nature—for it is noble—

Desire for our marriage overcomes   1410
My spirit.

        Listen to me, listen.
For I want to serve you and help you. Yes,
And to carry you home as my bride.
O Thetis, goddess mother, witness this
Is the truth. I am in agony to throw
Myself into battle with all the Greeks
To save you. Consider again how
Terrible a thing and how evil is death!   1415

Iphigenia

I speak this as one past hope and fear,
So listen to me. It is enough that
Helen, daughter of Tyndareus, because
Of her body hurls men into war
And to slaughter. But you, stranger and my friend,
You must not die for me or kill any man;
Only let me, if I have the strength, save Greece.   1420

Achilles

O noble heart! How can I ever add
Words of mine to these of yours, since you
Have fixed your will to die. Your soul is noble—
Who would not speak this truth! But yet—it is
Possible you will repent and alter
Your fixed mind. Then know my proposal   1425
And offer—for I come with these arms and
Shall place them by the altar directly.
I shall come, but not like the others
To suffer, but to prevent your death
And sacrifice. Oh, in a flash you can
Turn to me and prove my promises! Yes,
Even at the final second when you
See the sword thrust at your throat. For this is

A rash and hasty impulse; I will not   1430
Let you die for it. So, I shall arrive
With these arms at the goddess' altar,
And there wait and watch till you come.

(Achilles goes out, Iphigenia turns to her mother.)

Iphigenia

You make no sound, but you are weeping.
Why do you weep for me?

Clytemnestra

                Is not this sorrow
Terrible enough to break my heart?

Iphigenia

Stop! And trust me in all of this, Mother.   1435
Do not make a coward of me.

Clytemnestra

              Daughter,
I do not want to wrong or hurt you.
Tell me what I must do.

Iphigenia

            Here is one thing I ask:
Don't shear from your head the lock of hair
Or dress yourself in mourning for my sake.

Clytemnestra

What are you saying, child? When I have lost
You forever—

Iphigenia

        No! I am not lost
But saved! And you too, through me, will be   1440
Remembered gloriously.

Clytemnestra

           Oh, what do you mean?
Is it not right that I mourn your death?

Iphigenia

No! For I say no funeral mound is
To be heaped up for me.

Clytemnestra

What? Isn't it
Ordained and rightful that there be a burying
For the dead?

Iphigenia

The altar of the goddess,
Mother, who is Zeus' daughter, will be
My grave and my monument.

Clytemnestra

O my child,
Yours are the good words and the right ones.   1445
I will obey you.

Iphigenia

That will be my memorial
As one favored by fate because I brought
Help to Greece.

Clytemnestra

Your sisters—what message
Shall I take them?

Iphigenia

O Mother, do not dress
Them in mourning.

Clytemnestra

                                                        (*Nodding.*)
But have you some last word
Of love that I may speak to them?

Iphigenia

                                                        (*Slowly.*)
Only this—
I say goodbye to them now. That is all.

(Thinking.)

Orestes—do this, nurture him and see   1450
That he comes to strength and manhood for my sake.

Clytemnestra

Embrace and look at him for the last time.

Iphigenia

(Taking him in her arms.)

Dearest—you tried to help as best you could!

Clytemnestra

(Speaking with difficulty.)

O my child, when I go home to Argos
Is there something I can do to bring you joy?

Iphigenia

(Turning her eyes slowly upon her mother.)

Yes. Do not hate *him*. Do not hate my father
Who is your husband.

Clytemnestra

Oh! Oh! Your father
Must run a course of agony and terror   1455
For your sake.

Iphigenia

Running against his will,
For the sake of Greece, he has committed me
To death.

Clytemnestra

By a treacherous plot! Unkingly
And unworthy of Atreus!

Iphigenia

(No longer listening.)

Who will lead me
To the altar, before they seize me
And drag me by my hair?

Clytemnestra

                        I—I will come with you.

Iphigenia

  No, no, that is wrong!

Clytemnestra

                   I'll go—just my hand
  On your robe—

Iphigenia

              Mother, trust me,   1460
  Here you must stay, which will be better
  For you and for me also. Let it be
  One of my father's attendants who brings me
  To the meadow of Artemis and to the place
  Where I shall be killed.

Clytemnestra

                 Oh, child,
  You are going now—

Iphigenia

             Yes.
  And not to come back again.

Clytemnestra

                     Leaving your mother—   1465

Iphigenia

  Oh, you see how hard—

Clytemnestra

               Oh, stay.
  Don't leave me, child!

                      (*She bursts into a flood of tears.*)

Iphigenia

  Stop! I forbid your crying out or any tears!

O lift up your voices,
Lift them to Artemis
In honor of my fate
And of my dying;
Shout a paean of glory
To the daughter of Zeus.
And let the host of Danaans be silent,
As the priest takes
From the basket the barley;   1470
So may the fire blaze
With the meal of purification,
And my father will turn to the right
And encircle the altar.
Then I will come
And bring to Greece
Her salvation
And a crown of victory!
Lead me on
For the sack and overthrowing   1475
Of Troy city
And the Phrygian land.
Put on my hair a wreath
Of garlands
And on my head a crown.
O drench me with the waters,
The waters of purification.
About the altar of Artemis,
About her temple,
Dance!
Let us dance in honor of Artemis,   1480
Goddess, queen and blest.
With my own blood
In sacrifice
I will wash out
The fated curse of God.
O Mother, my lady mother,   1485

Now I give you my tears
For when I come to the holy place
I must not weep. 1490
Now maidens let us join
In praise of Artemis,
Artemis in her temple
Across Chalcis strait,
Where now in Aulis gulf,
And by the narrows,
Spears are flung fiercely
In my name. 1495
O motherland Pelasgia,
Mycenae, my Mycenae
Who fostered me—

Chorus

Do you call on Perseus' citadel 1500
Wrought by the hands of the Cyclops?

Iphigenia

You fostered me
A light to Greece
I do not refuse to die for you.

Chorus

Never will your glory pass away.

Iphigenia

O dayspring 1505
Torch of God
And glorious light!
To another world I go
Out of this place
Out of time
To dwell.
And now, and now,

Beloved light
Farewell!

(Iphigenia goes out.)

FINAL CHORUS

O look at the girl who walks   1510
To the goddess' altar
That Troy may be brought low
And the Phrygian die.
Behold, she walks
With her hair in garlands of honor,
And flung upon her body the lustral waters.
To the altar she goes
Of the goddess of bloody mind
Where she shall drip
With streams of flowing blood   1515
And die,
Her body's lovely neck
Slashed with a sword to death.
Oh, the waters await you,
The waters of purification;
Your father will pour them.
And the army too awaits you,
The mighty host of the Greeks
Awaits eagerly your death
For their sailing to Troy.   1520
But now all hail to the daughter of Zeus,
All hail to Artemis, goddess queen,
For from this maiden's death
You bring a prosperous thing!
Goddess,
You who joy in human blood,
Now be our guide and send
The armies of all the Greeks
To the land of Phrygia   1525
And to the citadel of treacherous Troy;

There give to Greece and to her spearmen
A crown of victory.
And for the king,
Agamemnon,
O touch his head   1530
With a glory everlasting.[4]

[4] See Appendix for omitted passage, lines 1532–1629.

APPENDIX TO
IPHIGENIA IN AULIS

APPENDIX

Lines 920–27

Achilles

—And yet I've learned to curb   920
My vaunting spirit, when I face disaster,
Just as I don't immoderately rejoice
When triumphs come. Certainly a man schooled
Well in reason may live out his life
Calling his soul his own. At times, of course,
It's pleasant not to be overwise. Yet when
One can hold firm the will—that's profitable.   925
I was educated by the most god-fearing
Amongst all men, Chiron, and it was from him
I've learned to act in singleness of heart.

Lines 952–54

Achilles

That would reverse all values—you could then
Persuade me that Sipylus, the barbarian
Border town, is a Greek city and besides
Birthplace of all our chieftains! Or,
The opposite absurdity, that Phthia is
A name unknown to the world of men.

Lines 1274–75

Agamemnon

No longer by the barbarians in their violence
Must Greeks be robbed of their wives.   1275

Lines 1532–1629

Messenger (entering)

O daughter of Tyndareus, Clytemnestra,
Come outside the pavilion and receive
My message.

Clytemnestra (entering)

> Hearing your voice calling, I am here,
> Wretched, fearful, and in terror that you   1535
> Have come to add a new disaster
> To my present grief.

Messenger

> It is about your child—
> I must recount a thing of awe and wonder.

Clytemnestra

> Then don't delay, but tell it as quickly
> As you can.

Messenger

> I shall, and everything, dear mistress,   1540
> You shall learn clearly from the beginning
> Unless my whirling thoughts trip up my tongue.
> When we came to Artemis' grove and to
> The flowered meadow of Zeus' daughter,
> Leading your child to the mustering ground
> Of the Achaeans, then quickly the army   1545
> Of Argives assembled.
> And when King Agamemnon saw his girl
> Walk into the grove for the sacrifice
> He groaned bitterly, and turning his head
> Wept, drawing his robe across his eyes.   1550
> But she, standing beside her father, spoke:
> "O Father, I am here at your command—
> Willingly I give my body to be   1555
> Sacrificed for my country, for all Greece.
> If it be the will of heaven, lead me
> To the goddess' altar. Prosper, I say;
> Win victory in this war and then return
> To our fatherland. But let no Argive
> Touch me with his hand. Silent, unflinching,

I offer my neck to the knife." These words   1560
She spoke, and every man hearing her wondered
At the maid's courage and nobility.
Then Talthybius, standing in the midst,
According to his office spoke, proclaiming
A holy silence to the army,
And Calchas, the prophet, unsheathing   1565
With his hand the sharp knife, laid it
In the golden basket. Then he crowned
The head of the girl. And the son of Peleus,
Taking the barley and the lustral waters,
Ran round the goddess' altar and cried out:
"O child of Zeus, O slayer of wild beasts,   1570
You who turn your disk of shining light
Through the night's shadows, receive this sacrifice
Which we make to you—we the Achaean host
And the king Agamemnon—unblemished blood
From the neck of a fair girl. And grant
That ungrieved now the fleet may sail;   1575
And grant this too that we and our spears spoil
The battlements of Troy." Then Atreus' sons
And the whole army stood with eyes bent on
The earth. And the priest, taking the knife,
Uttered his prayer, and scanned her neck to strike
His blow. Oh, then I stood with my head
Bowed, and a great anguish smote my heart—   1580
But suddenly a miracle came to pass.
Clearly all heard the blow strike home—
But after, with no man knowing where or how,
The maiden vanished from the earth.
Then the priest with a great voice cried aloud
And the whole army echoed him—this when
They saw the portent which a god had sent   1585
But no man had foreknown. Though our eyes saw,
It was a sight incredible, for a
Panting hind lay there on the earth, great

To behold and fair indeed; the goddess'
Altar freely ran with the creature's blood.
At this Calchas spoke and with joy you must   1590
Believe: "O commanders of the allied
Armies, behold this victim which the goddess
Has laid upon the altar, a mountain hind
Rather than the maid; this victim she receives
With joy. By this no noble blood   1595
Stains her altar. Gladly she accepts
This offering and grants a fair voyage
For the attack on Troy. Let every sailor
Then be glad, and go to the galleys,
For on this day we must leave the hollow   1600
Bays of Aulis, and cross the Aegean sea."
Then when the victim had been burned
Wholly to cinder in Hephaestus' flame,
He prayed for the army's safe return.
After all this King Agamemnon sent me
To report to you and tell what fortune   1605
Had come from heaven and what deathless glory
He had won for Greece. And I who saw
This thing, being present, report it now to you.
Clearly your child was swept away to heaven;
So give over grief and cease from anger
Against your husband. No mortal can foreknow   1610
The ways of heaven. Those whom the gods love
They rescue. For think, this day beheld
Your child die, and come alive again.

Chorus

  With what gladness I hear the messenger's
  Report! Your child he tells us is alive
  And with the gods in heaven.

Clytemnestra

  O child! what god has stolen you from me?   1615
  How can I ever call to you? How know

That this is not a story merely told
That I may have relief from bitter pain?

Chorus

Behold King Agamemnon comes to us,
And the same story he will tell to you.   1620

(*Enter Agamemnon.*)

Agamemnon

My lady, may we now be happy
In our daughter's destiny. Truly she
Dwells now in fellowship with the gods.
Now must you take this little son of ours
And journey home. The army's eyes are on
The fleet. It will be long, long,
Before my greeting comes to you again   1625
On the return from Troy. Meantime
May all go well with you!

Chorus

With joy, son of Atreus, sail on
To the Phrygian land,
With joy return,
Bringing glorious spoil from Troy!

ELECTRA

Translated and with an Introduction by Emily Townsend Vermeule

INTRODUCTION TO *ELECTRA*

The *Electra* was almost certainly produced in 413 B.C., between the sailing of the relief expedition to Sicily which the Dioscuri are rushing to protect (l. 1347) and the fleet's destruction in September. It thus falls squarely in Euripides' middle group of unorthodox Trojan War "tragedies" and contains elements of all their qualities: the bitter pathos of *Trojan Women* (415 B.C.), the romantic melodrama of *Iphigenia among the Taurians* (414 B.C.), the farce of *Helen* (412 B.C.). It also looks back to *Andromache* (419 B.C.) and forward to *Orestes* (408 B.C.) as a study in war-bred delinquency and is tempered by its own special quality as a tabloid thriller.

With this mixture of dramatic tones, *Electra* has received equally mixed critical notices, from Schlegel's "a singular monument of poetical, or rather unpoetical, perversity" to Murray's "close-knit, powerful . . . intellectual, rebellious." The play is undoubtedly perverse; it is also undoubtedly well constructed (better than *Choephoroe* or Sophocles' *Electra*). It is fast-paced, logical, exciting. The main offense is in the characters, and, secondarily, the choral *embolima*, which generally seem irrelevant, the careless repetition of words, the falling out of character in long speeches, and the lack of poetic grandeur.

At first reading, many points of style and content seem so deliberately in bad taste that one suspects an entire parody of tragedy in the high style, apart from the mockery of *Choephoroe* in the tokens scene. To the unsympathetic it can seem enormously funny, and prohibitive to tragic response, when Aegisthus is nervous that Electra may have a baby even if kept under lock and key, when she makes her tragic entrance with a water pot, when Orestes asks if the Farmer finds her too unattractive to sleep with, when Electra sends Orestes off to death and slaughter like Mabel in *The Pirates of Penzance*, when she complains that no one likes her well enough to be her midwife (which is not surprising if she washes as little as she says). Yet all this grows out of Euripides' chosen characterization of Electra, based firmly on Sophocles' conception of that model heroine: unwashed, in rags, a slave princess, longing for attention and some emotional outlet, morbidly attached to her dead father, powerfully jealous of Clytemnestra, vindictive and efficient.

Euripides adds new insights, mainly Electra's failure to distinguish right from wrong; her daydreams limited to clothes, marriage, money; her subtle streak of nymphomania. But, while exposing her psychology with a ruthless scalpel and pushing Sophocles' character to its logical extreme, he has lost sight of the spiritual strength with which Sophocles endowed her, and so sacrifices that sympathy for the protagonist which is essential to tragedy. Again from Sophocles, Orestes takes on some of Chrysothemis' ethos, as a foil to Electra, with the added spice of having to pay for her decisions while she goes free. The Pedagogue has split into Euripides' Farmer and Old Man, the former full of rustic aphorisms and kindness, the latter again strategic co-ordinator for his emotional charges. Clytemnestra owes something to Sophocles' portrayal of middle-class grandeur, but with less imagination and authority, more vanity and torment. Aegisthus we see from two angles: in Electra's prejudiced testimony, as a drunken bully and seducer; in the Messenger's account of his death, as an affable and pious host. Indeed this double vision is true of the whole play, as Electra's image of the truth, and the truth itself, stubbornly refuse to match.

The astigmatism is deliberate. While inspired by Sophocles' power of characterization, Euripides apparently disapproves of his freeing the protagonists from the painful aftereffects of murder and so reverts to Aeschylus in matters like the blood-curse, the Furies, and the trial, recapitulating *Eumenides* in his Epilogue. But Aeschylean morality is somehow missing, and by the end of the play we see that Euripides has been playing falsely with both his sources, and, by jamming the characters of Sophocles into the framework of Aeschylus, has destroyed the validity of both. There emerges a true Euripidean demonstration that life resists formula and that even a moral situation as clear as the one confronting the heirs of Agamemnon is chaotic when seen from the inside.

The abstract moral justification for murdering Clytemnestra and Aegisthus is the same as earlier; it is even more cogent here, with a blood-price set on Orestes' head, new children to usurp the dynasty,

Electra's forced marriage to a peasant. But the strength of the moral position depends on the characters involved. When the protagonists are as unsympathetic as here, when the victims are hit from behind at a sacrifice or ambushed in the role of compassionate grandmother, must we shift our moral judgments or acknowledge the justice of the murders while admitting that we personally find them a little hard to take? If Hadas feels that "Electra is a self-pitying slattern, Orestes a timid ruffian, Clytemnestra a suburban clubwoman, Aegisthus a courteous and popular ruler, the murders as dastardly as conceivable," or Rose calls Orestes and Electra "fanatical monomaniacs," they have fallen into Euripides' trap. He is challenging the audience to maintain moral clarity in the face of extreme distaste for the agents of justice, who do irreparable damage out of confused and flippant motives with the guidance of heaven. *Electra* is another phase in his campaign against Apollo, the morality of the gods, and tender-minded human champions of "justice"—a concept in fact cold and difficult, admirable in the abstract, ugly in concrete situations.

The double vision of character is Euripides' demonstration tool, a technique of seducing the audience into sympathy with the protagonists and then destroying that sympathy by a display of wanton brutality. This is familiar from *Medea, Hecuba, Heracles, Bacchae.* The play begins along orthodox melodramatic lines: injured innocents, lost birthright and love, cruel usurpers, the dead calling for vengeance. But gradually we realize that neither Electra nor Orestes is capable of serious thought. Orestes relies on Apollo's oracle until actually faced with his mother and a knife; when he tries to withdraw in emotional chaos, Electra drives him on. She has no oracle, only a lust for revenge. Both children are more concerned with their standard of living than with morality; their lost ancestral home looms largest in their minds as a paradise of rugs, good food, money; to Electra the fact that Clytemnestra saved her from death at Aegisthus' hands means less than the clothes of the Trojan slaves. Electra never realizes, Orestes only dimly, that they are committing exactly the same atrocity for which they want to punish their elders. With the confused thinking characteristic of obsessive neurotics, they believe that killing their mother will somehow make her love them again, so that they can settle down and be happy. Their surprise at the results is more disturbing than their pain.

Orestes scarcely mentions his father. Electra has a genuine attachment to him, which Clytemnestra notes she showed as a child and which has doubtless grown stronger since his death. But when she comes to condemn Clytemnestra, her tirade is almost entirely in terms of her mother's sexual escapades and femininity, which Electra envies while refusing to imitate. Jealousy of her mother rather than love for her father drives her on, so that we hear a good deal about Clytemnestra's looks and clothes and her two marriages, while Electra's fiancé was unfairly translated to godhead, her other suitors turned from the door, and her present husband scarcely what she wishes in terms of breeding, money, or marital affection. The content of her nocturnal brooding is clear from the way she taunts dead Aegisthus with his looks and adulteries and refuses to have him as a husband. This is objectively irrelevant, since he had other interests and is dead, but psychologically revealing, for she must have watched him closely during her period of forcibly extended virginity. Orestes' suggestion that Aegisthus expects another child (l. 626) puts the false-baby notion in her mind, an unconscious perfect choice of bait for Clytemnestra. Her fear of Orestes' touch, her insistence to complete strangers on her married virginity, her first reaction to the murder: Who will marry me now?—all underline the frustration implicit in her name.

The characterization may be ugly, but it is brilliant and convincing. It is deliberately calculated to alienate us from "the right side"; Electra's initial suffering explains but does not excuse her subsequent viciousness. The victims have been alienated by their cruelty, vanity, and sordid private lives, which their flickering kindness does not sufficiently relieve. Apollo is alienated by a label of brutal ignorance. There is no focus of sympathy left, only a pervasive bad taste which leads to disgust with all forms of violence.

The question is whether Euripides enjoyed the psychological exploration of suffering for its own sake, or had a moral purpose. In the first case, one tags the play with *pathei pathos* or "suffering brutalizes," and shelves it as a work of uncomfortable insight. In the second case one is forced to consider Euripides' theme that good and evil bear no relation to human character, are beyond the reach of simple formula, possibly do not exist at all. In either case *Electra* cannot be dismissed as wilful or perverse. It is a planned demonstration that personal relationships, human or divine, are inescapably fraught with indecency and that justice can be as ugly as crime.

The text followed is J. D. Denniston's Oxford edition (1939), based on Murray. I have omitted lines 899 and 1097–1101 (= fragment 464, *Cretan Women*) and changed the order of speakers at 677–81 to accord with Denniston's tentative suggestion.

ELECTRA

CHARACTERS

Farmer, a Mycenaean

Electra

Orestes

Pylades, a mute character

Chorus of Argive peasant women

Old Man

Messenger

Clytemnestra

Dioscuri: Castor, and Polydeuces, a mute character

ELECTRA

SCENE: *A high bare slope of the Argive hills commanding a view of the road to Argos, stage left, and the southern passes toward Sparta, right. A square timber-and-mudbrick cottage stands in the center. The time is the end of night with stars still in the sky. The Farmer stands looking down toward the river valley and the sea.*

Farmer

Argos, old bright floor of the world, Inachus' pouring
tides—King Agamemnon once on a thousand ships
hoisted the war god here and sailed across to Troy.
He killed the monarch of the land of Ilium,
Priam; he sacked the glorious city of Dardanus;   5
he came home safe to Argos and high on the towering shrines
nailed up the massive loot of Barbary for the gods.
So, over there he did well. But in his own house
he died in ambush planned for him by his own wife
Clytemnestra and by her lover Aegisthus' hand.   10
    He lost the ancient scepter of Tantalus; he is dead.
Thyestes' son Aegisthus walks king in the land
and keeps the dead man's wife for himself, Tyndareus' child.
As for the children he left home when he sailed to Troy,
his son Orestes and his flowering girl Electra,   15
Orestes almost died under Aegisthus' fist,
but his father's ancient servant snatched the boy away,
gave him to Strophius to bring up in the land of Phocis.
Electra waited motionless in her father's house.
But when the burning season of young ripeness took her,   20
then the great princes of the land of Greece came begging
her bridal. Aegisthus was afraid. Afraid her son
if noble in blood would punish Agamemnon's death.
He held her in the house sundered from every love.
Yet, even guarded so, she filled his nights with fear   25
lest she in secret to some prince might still bear sons;

he laid his plans to kill her. But her mother, though
savage in soul, then saved her from Aegisthus' blow.
The lady found excuse for murdering her husband
but flinched from killing a child, afraid of the world's contempt.　30
Later Aegisthus framed a new design. He swore
to any man who captured Agamemnon's son
running in exile and murdered him, a price of gold.
Electra—he gave her to me as a gift, to hold
her as my wife.

　　　　　　Now, I was born of Mycenaean　35
family, on this ground I have nothing to be ashamed of,
in breeding they shone bright enough. But in their fortune
they ranked as paupers, which blots out all decent blood.
He gave her to me, a weak man, to weaken his own fear,
for if a man of high position had taken her　40
he might have roused awake the sleeping Agamemnon's
blood—justice might have knocked at Aegisthus' door.
I have not touched her and the love-god Cypris knows it:
I never shamed the girl in bed, she is still virgin.
I would feel ugly holding down the gentle daughter　45
of a king in violence, I was not bred to such an honor.
And poor laboring Orestes whom they call my brother—
I suffer his grief, I think his thoughts, if he came home
to Argos and saw his sister so doomed in her wedding.

　Whoever says that I am a born fool to keep　50
a young girl in my house and never touch her body,
or says I measure wisdom by a crooked line
of morals, should know he is as great a fool as I.

　　　　　(*Electra enters from the cottage carrying a water jar on
　　　　　　　　her head and talking to herself.*)

Electra

　O night, black night, whose breast nurses the golden stars,
　I wander through your darkness, head lifted to bear　55
　this pot I carry to the sources of the river—
　I am not forced, I chose this slavery myself

to illuminate Aegisthus' arrogance for the gods—
and cry my pain to Father in the great bright air.
For my own mother, she, Tyndareus' deadly daughter,   60
has thrown me out like dirt from the house, to her husband's joy,
and while she breeds new children in Aegisthus' bed
has made me and Orestes aliens to her love.

Farmer

Now why, unhappy girl, must you for my sake wrestle
such heavy work though you were raised in luxury?   65
Each time I mention it you flash into rebellion.

Electra

I think you equal to the gods in kindliness,
for you have never hurt me though I am in trouble.
It is great fortune for men to find a kind physician
ot suffering, which I have found in finding you.   70
Indeed without your bidding I should make the labor
as light as I have strength for; you will bear it better
if I claim some share with you in the work. Outdoors
you have enough to do; my place is in the house,
to keep it tidy. When a man comes in from work   75
it is sweet to find his hearthplace looking swept and clean.

Farmer

Well, if your heart is set on helping, go. The spring
is not so distant from the house. At light of dawn
I will put the cows to pasture and start planting the fields.
A lazy man may rustle gods upon his tongue   80
but never makes a living if he will not work.

*(They go off together, stage right. Enter Orestes and Pylades
from the mountain road, quickly but cautiously, and as-
sure themselves the coast is clear.)*

Orestes

Pylades, I consider you the first of men
in loyalty and love to me, my host and friend.

You only of my friends gave honor and respect
to Orestes, suffering as I suffer from Aegisthus.   85
He killed my father—he and my destructive mother.
I come from secret converse with the holy god
to this outpost of Argos—no one knows I am here—
to counterchange my father's death for death to his killers.
During the night just passed I found my father's tomb,   90
gave him my tears in gift and sheared my hair in mourning
and sprinkled ceremonial sheep's blood on the fire,
holding the rite concealed from the tyrants who rule here.
   I will not set my foot inside the city walls.
I chose this gatepost of the land deliberately,   95
compacting a double purpose. First, if any spy
should recognize me I can run for foreign soil,
second, to find my sister. For they say she married
and, tamed to domestic love, lives here no longer virgin.
I want to be with her and take her as my partner   100
in the work and learn precise news from behind the walls.
   And now, since lady dawn is lifting her white face,
smooth out our footprints from the path and come away.
Perhaps a field-bound farmer or some cottage wife
will meet us on the road, and we can ask discreetly   105
whether my sister lives anywhere in these hills.
   Quick now! I see some sort of serving girl approach
with a jar of fountain water on her shaven head—
it looks heavy for her. Sit down here, let us question
the slave girl. Pylades, perhaps at last we shall hear   110
the news we hoped for when we crossed into this land.

                    (*They hide behind the altar in front of the cottage. Electra*
                              comes back along the path with her jar, singing
                                                  aloud, half dancing.)

Electra

   Quicken the foot's rush—time has struck—O
   walk now, walk now weeping aloud,
          O for my grief!

I was bred Agamemnon's child,   115
formed in the flesh of Clytemnestra
   Tyndareus' hellish daughter,
Argos' people have named me true:
      wretched Electra.
Cry, cry for my labor and pain,   120
   cry for the hatred of living.
Father who in the halls of death
lie hacked by your wife and Aegisthus, O
   help, Agamemnon!

Come, waken the mourning again,   125
bring me again the sweetness of tears.

Quicken the foot's rush—time has struck—
walk now, walk now weeping aloud,
    O for my grief!
In what city and in what house, O   130
brother of grief, do you walk a slave?
   You left me locked in the cursed
palace chambers for doom to strike
    your sister in sorrow.
Come, loose me from labor, come   135
   save me in pity, O Zeus,
Zeus, for our father's hate-spilled blood
help storm the wicked and harbor our lost
    voyager in Argos.

Set this vessel down from my head, O   140
take it, while I lift music of mourning
    by night to my father.
Father, the maenad song of death
   I cry you among the dead
beneath the earth, the words I pour   145
   day after day unending
as I move, ripping my flesh with sharp

nails, fists pounding my clipped
    head for your dying.

Ai, ai, tear my face!   150
I, like the swan of echoing song
in descant note at the water's edge
who calls to its parent so dearly loved
and dying now in the hidden net
of twisted meshes, mourn you thus   155
    in agony dying,

body steeped in the final bath,
lull most pitiful, sleep of death.
    O for my grief!
Bitter the ax and bitter the gash,   160
   bitter the road you walked
from Troy straight to their plotted net—
   your lady did not receive you
with victor's ribbons or flowers to crown you,
but with double-edged steel she made you
savage sport for Aegisthus, gave you   165
    to her shifty lover.

                 (*The chorus of Argive peasant women enters from the*
                   Mycenae road to confront Electra.)

Chorus
    Princess, daughter of Agamemnon,
    we have come to your country court,
        Electra, to see you.
    There passed, passed me a man
        bred on the milk of the hills,
    a Mycenaean mountaineer   170
    who gave me word that on the third
    day the Argives herald abroad
    a holy feast, when all the girls
    will pass in procession up to the temple of Hera.

Electra

Dear friends, not for shimmering robes,   175
not for twisted bracelets of gold
   does my heart take wing in delight.
I am too sad, I cannot stand
   in choral joy with the maidens
or beat the tune with my whirling foot;   180
   rather with tears by night
and tears by day shall I fill my soul
   shaking in grief and fear.
Look! think! would my filthy locks
and robe all torn into slavish rags   185
do public honor to Agamemnon's
   daughter, the princess?
honor to Troy which will never forget
   my conquering father?

Chorus

Great, great is the goddess. Come,   190
I will lend you a dress to wear,
   thick-woven of wool,
and gold—be gracious, accept—
             gold for holiday glitter.
Do you think your tears and holding back
honor from god will ever hurt   195
your haters? Not by sounding lament
but only by prayer and reverent love
for the gods, my child, will you learn to live gentler days.

Electra

Gods? Not one god has heard
my helpless cry or watched of old   200
   over my murdered father.
Mourn again for the wasted dead,
   mourn for the living outlaw

somewhere prisoned in foreign lands
   moving through empty days,
passing from one slave hearth to the next   205
   though born of a glorious sire.
And I! I in a peasant's hut
waste my life like wax in the sun,
thrust and barred from my father's home
   to a scarred mountain exile   210
while my mother rolls in her bloody bed
   and plays at love with a stranger.

Chorus

Like Helen, your mother's sister—Helen charged and found
guilty of massive pain to Greece and all your house.

Electra

Oh, oh! women, I break from my deathbound cry.   215
Look! there are strangers here close to the house who crouch
huddled beside the altar and rise up in ambush.
Run, you take the path and I into the house
with one swift rush can still escape these criminals.

Orestes

Poor girl, stand still, and fear not. I would never hurt you.   220

Electra

Phoebus Apollo, help! I kneel to you. Do not kill me.

Orestes

I hope I shall kill others hated more than you.

Electra

Get out; don't touch. You have no right to touch my body.

Orestes

There is no person I could touch with greater right.

Electra

Why were you hiding, sword in hand, so near my house?   225

Orestes

Stand still and listen. You will agree I have rights here.

Electra

I stand here utterly in your power. You are stronger.

Orestes

I have come to bring you a spoken message from your brother.

Electra

Dearest of strangers, is he alive or is he dead?

Orestes

Alive. I wish to give you all the best news first.   230

Electra

God bless your days, as you deserve for such sweet words.

Orestes

I share your gift with you that we may both be blessed.

Electra

Where is he now, attempting to bear unbearable exile?

Orestes

He is wrecked, nor can conform to any city's code.

Electra

Tell me, he is not poor? not hungry for daily bread?   235

Orestes

He has bread, yet he has the exile's constant hunger.

Electra

You came to bring a message—what are his words for me?

Orestes

"Are you alive? Where are you living? What is your life?"

Electra

I think you see me. First, my body wasted and dry—

Orestes

Sadness has wasted you so greatly I could weep.   240

Electra

Next, my head razor-cropped like a victim of the Scythians.

Orestes

Your brother's life and father's death both bite at your heart.

Electra

Alas, what else have I? I have no other loves.

Orestes

You grieve me. Whom do you think your brother loves but you?

Electra

He is not here. He loves me, but he is not here.   245

Orestes

Why do you live in a place like this, so far from town?

Electra

Because I married, stranger—a wedding much like death.

Orestes

Bad news for your brother. Your husband is a Mycenaean?

Electra

But not the man my father would have wished me to marry.

Orestes

Tell me. I am listening, I can speak to your brother.   250

Electra

This is his house. I live quite isolated here.

Orestes

A ditch-digger, a cowherd would look well living here.

Electra

He is a poor man but well born, and he respects me.

Orestes

Respects? What does your husband understand by "respect"?

Electra

He has never been violent or touched me in my bed.   255

Orestes

A vow of chastity? or he finds you unattractive?

Electra

He finds it attractive not to insult my royal blood.

Orestes

How could he not be pleased at marrying so well?

Electra

He judges the man who gave me had no right to, stranger.

Orestes

I see—afraid Orestes might avenge your honor.   260

Electra

Afraid of that, yes—he is also decent by nature.

Orestes

Ah.
You paint one of nature's gentlemen. We must pay him well.

Electra

We will, if my absent brother ever gets home again.

Orestes

Your mother took the wedding calmly, I suppose?

Electra

Women save all their love for lovers, not for children.   265

Orestes

What was in Aegisthus' mind, to insult you so?

Electra

He hoped that I, so wedded, would have worthless sons.

Orestes

Too weak for undertaking blood-revenge on him?

Electra

That was his hope. I hope to make him pay for it.

Orestes

This husband of your mother's—does he know you are virgin?   270

Electra

No, he knows nothing. We have played our parts in silence.

Orestes

These women listening as we talk are friends of yours?

Electra

Good enough friends to keep our words kindly concealed.

Orestes

How should Orestes play *his* part, if he comes to Argos?

Electra

If he comes? ugly talk. The time has long been ripe.   275

Orestes

Say he comes, still how could he kill his father's killers?

Electra

As Father suffered let our enemies suffer too.

Orestes

Mother and lover both? are you bold for that killing?

Electra

Mother by the same ax that cut Father to ruin.

Orestes

May I tell him what you say and how determined you are?   280

Electra

Tell him how gladly I would die in Mother's blood.

Orestes

O, I wish Orestes could stand here and listen.

Electra

Yet if I saw him I should hardly know him, sir.

Orestes

No wonder. You were both very young when you were parted.

Electra

I have only one friend who might still know his face.   285

Orestes

The man who saved him once from death, as the story goes?

Electra

Yes, old now and old even when he nursed my father.

Orestes

When your father died did his body find some burial?

Electra

He found what he found. He was thrown on the dirt outdoors.

Orestes

I cannot bear it. What have you said? Even a stranger's   290
pain bites strangely deep and hurts us when we hear it.
Tell me the rest, and with new knowledge I will bring
Orestes your tale, so harsh to hear and so compelling
when heard. Uneducated men are pitiless,
but we who are educated pity much. And we pay   295
a high price for being intelligent. Wisdom hurts.

Chorus

The same excitement stirs my mind in this as yours—
I live far from the city and I know its troubles
hardly at all. Now I would like to learn them too.

Electra

I will tell if I must—and must tell you who love me—   300
how my luck, and my father's, is too heavy to lift.
Since you have moved me to speak so, stranger, I must beg
that you will tell Orestes all my distress, and his.
First tell him how I am kept like a beast in stable rags,
my skin heavy with grease and dirt. Describe to him   305
this hut—*my* home, who used to live in the king's palace.
I weave my clothes myself and slavelike at the loom
must work or else walk naked through the world in nothing.
I fetch and carry water from the riverside,
I am deprived of holy festivals and dances,   310
I cannot talk to women since I am a girl,
I cannot think of Castor, who was close in blood
and loved me once, before he rose among the gods.
My mother in the glory of her Phrygian rugs
sits on the throne, while circled at her feet the girls   315
of Asia stoop, whom Father won at the sack of Troy,
their clothes woven in snowy wool from Ida, pinned
with golden brooches, while the walls and floor are stained
still with my father's black and rotting blood. The man
who murdered him goes riding grand in Father's chariot,   320

with bloody hands and high delight lifting the staff
of office by which Father marshaled the Greek lords.
The tomb of Agamemnon finds no honor yet,
never yet drenched with holy liquids or made green
in myrtle branches, barren of bright sacrifice.   325
But in his drunken fits, my mother's lover, brilliant
man, triumphant leaps and dances on the mound
or pelts my father's stone memorial with rocks
and dares to shout against us with his boldened tongue:
"Where is your son Orestes? When will that noble youth   330
come to protect your tomb?" Insults to empty space.
   Kind stranger, as I ask you, tell him all these things.
For many call him home again—I speak for them—
the voices in our hands and tongues and grieving minds
and heads, shaven in mourning; and his father calls.   335
All will be shamed if he whose father captured Troy
cannot in single courage kill a single man,
although his strength is younger and his blood more noble.

Chorus

Electra! I can see your husband on the road.
He has finished his field work and is coming home.   340

(*The Farmer enters from the left to confront the group by his house.*)

Farmer

Hey there! who are these strangers standing at our gates?
What is the errand that could bring them to our rough
courtyard? Are they demanding something from me? A nice
woman should never stand in gossip with young men.

Electra

My dearest husband, do not come suspecting me.   345
You shall hear their story, the whole truth. They come
as heralds to me with new tidings of Orestes.
Strangers, I ask you to forgive him what he said.

Farmer

What news? Is Orestes still alive in the bright light?

Electra

So they have told me, and I do not doubt their words.   350

Farmer

Does he still remember his father, and your troubles?

Electra

We hope so. But an exile is a helpless man.

Farmer

Then what are these plans of his? What have they come to tell?

Electra

He sent them simply to see my troubles for themselves.

Farmer

What they don't see themselves I imagine you have told them.   355

Electra

They know it all. I took good care that they missed nothing.

Farmer

Why were our doors not opened to them long ago?
Move into the house, you will find entertainment
to answer your good news, such as my roof can offer.
Servants, pick up their baggage, bring their spears indoors.   360
Come, no polite refusals. You are here as friends
most dear to me who meet you now. Though I am poor
in money, I think you will not find our manners poor.

Orestes

By the gods! is this the man who helps you keep your marriage
a fiction, who has no desire to shame Orestes?   365

Electra

This is the man they know as poor Electra's husband.

Orestes

Alas,
we look for good on earth and cannot recognize it
when met, since all our human heritage runs mongrel.
At times I have seen descendants of the noblest family
grow worthless though the cowards had courageous sons;   370
inside the souls of wealthy men bleak famine lives
while minds of stature struggle trapped in starving bodies.

How then can man distinguish man, what test can he use?
the test of wealth? that measure means poverty of mind;
of poverty? the pauper owns one thing, the sickness   375
of his condition, a compelling teacher of evil;
by nerve in war? yet who, when a spear is cast across
his face, will stand to witness his companion's courage?
We can only toss our judgments random on the wind.

This fellow here is no great man among the Argives,   380
not dignified by family in the eyes of the world—
he is a face in the crowd, and yet we choose him champion.
Can you not come to understand, you empty-minded,
opinion-stuffed people, a man is judged by grace
among his fellows, manners are nobility's touchstone?   385
Such men of manners can control our cities best,
and homes, but the well-born sportsman, long on muscle, short
on brains, is only good for a statue in the park,
not even sterner in the shocks of war than weaker
men, for courage is the gift of character.   390
Now let us take whatever rest this house can give;
Agamemnon's child deserves it, the one here and the one
absent for whom I stand. We have no choice but go
indoors, servants, inside the house, since our poor host
seems eager to entertain us, more than a rich man might.   395
I do praise and admire his most kind reception
but would have been more pleased if your brother on the crest

of fortune could have brought me to a more fortunate house.
Perhaps he may still come; Apollo's oracles
are strong, though human prophecy is best ignored.   400

(Orestes and Pylades go into the house.)

Chorus

   Now more than ever in our lives, Electra, joy
makes our hearts light and warm. Perhaps your fortune, first
running these painful steps, will stride to the goal in glory.

Electra

   You are thoughtless. You know quite well the house is bare;
why take these strangers in? They are better born than you.   405

Farmer

   Why? Because if they are the gentlemen they seem,
will they not treat the small as gently as the great?

Electra

   Small is the word for you. Now the mistake is made,
go quickly to my father's loved and ancient servant
who by Tanaos' river, where it cuts the hills   410
of Argos off from Spartan country, goes his rounds
watching his flocks in distant exile from the town.
Tell him these strangers have descended on me; ask
him to come and bring some food fit for distinguished guests.
He will surely be happy; he will bless the gods   415
when he hears the child he saved so long ago still lives.
Besides, we cannot get any help from Father's house,
from Mother—our news would fly to her on bitter wings,
bold though she is, if she should hear Orestes lives.

Farmer

   Well, if you wish it, I can pass your message on   420
to the old man. But you get quick into the house
and ready up what's there. A woman when she has to
can always find some food to set a decent table.

(Electra goes into the cottage.)

The house holds little, yet it is enough, I know,
to keep these strangers choked with food at least one day.   425
   In times like these, when wishes soar but power fails,
I contemplate the steady comfort found in gold:
gold you can spend on guests; gold you can pay the doctor
when you get sick. But a small crumb of gold will buy
our daily bread, and when a man has eaten that,   430
you cannot really tell the rich and poor apart.

(The farmer goes off right, toward the hills.)

Chorus

O glorious ships who sailed across to Troy once
   moving on infinite wooden oars
guarding the circling choir of Nereid dancers
where the dolphin shook in love at the flute-   435
   melody and about the sea-
   blue prows went plunging
as he led the goddess Thetis' son,
light-striding Achilles, on his way
with Agamemnon to Ilium's cliffs   440
   where Simois pours in the sea.

Of old the Nereids passed Euboea's headlands
   bringing the heavy shield of gold,
forged on Hephaestus' anvil, and golden armor.
Up Mount Pelion, up the jut   445
   of Ossa's holy slopes on high,
   up the nymphs' spy-rocks
they hunted the aged horseman's hill
where he trained the boy as a dawn for Greece,
the son of Thetis, sea-bred and swift-   450
   lived in the Atreid wars.

Once I heard from a Trojan captive known to the port
   in Nauplia close to Argos
   of your brilliant shield, O goddess'
child, how in its circled space   455

these signs, scenes, were in blazon warning,
  mourning, for Phrygia:
running in frieze on its massive rim,
Perseus lifting the severed head
cut at the neck—with Gorgon beauty   460
he walks on wings over the sea;
Hermes is with him, angel of Zeus,
  great Maia's
child of the flocks and forests.

Out of the shield's curved center glittered afar the high
  shining round of the sun   465
    driving with wingèd horses,
and the chorused stars of upper air—
Pleiads, Hyads—Hector eyed them,
  swerving aside.
Over the helmet of beaten gold   470
Sphinxes snatch in hooking nails
their prey trapped with song. On the hollow
greave, the lioness' fire breath
flares in her clawed track as she runs,
  staring back
at the wind-borne foal of Peirene.   475

All along the blade of the deadly sword, hooves pounding,
horses leap; black above their backs the dust blows.
  Still this prince of arms and men
  you killed by lust of sex and sin   480
  of mind, Tyndarid Helen.
For this the sons of heaven will send
you yet among the dead; some far
day I shall still see your blood fall   485
red from your neck on the iron sword.

(Enter the Old Man, alone, from the right,
out of breath after climbing.)

Old Man

Where is my young mistress and my lady queen,
the child of Agamemnon, whom I raised and loved?
How steep this house seems set to me, with rough approach,
as I grow old for climbing on this withered leg.   490
But when your friends call, you must come and drag along
and hump your spine till it snaps and bend your knees like pins.

(Electra enters from the cottage.)

Why there she is—my daughter, look at you by the door!
I am here. I have brought you from my cropping sheep
a newborn lamb, a tender one, just pulled from the teat,   495
and flowers looped in garlands, cheese white from the churn,
and this stored treasure of the wine god, aged and spiked
with a pungent smell—not much of it, but sweet, and good
to pour into the cup with other weaker wine.
Let someone carry all this gear to the guests indoors,   500
for I have cried a little and would like to dry
my face and eyes out here on my cloak—more holes than wool.

Electra

Old uncle, father, why is your face so stained with tears?
After so long has my grief stirred your thoughts again,
or is it poor Orestes in his running days   505
you mourn for, or my father, whom your two old hands
once nursed and helped without reward for self or love?

Old Man

Reward, no. Yet I could not stop myself, in this:
for I came past his tomb and circled from the road
and fell to the earth there, weeping for its loneliness,   510
and let it drink, tapping this winesack for your guests
in brief libation, and I wreathed the stone in myrtle.
And there I saw on the burning-altar a black-fleeced
sheep, throat cut and blood still warm in its dark stream,
and curling locks of bright brown hair cut off in gift.   515

I stopped, quiet, to wonder, child, what man had courage
to visit at that tomb. It could not be an Argive.
    Is there a chance your brother has arrived in secret
and paused to stare upon his father's shabby tomb?
Look at the lock of hair, match it to your own head,   520
see if it is not twin to yours in color and cut.
Often a father's blood, running in separate veins,
makes the two bodies almost mirrors in their form.

Electra

Old man, I always thought you were wiser than you sound
if you really think my brother, who is bright and bold,   525
would come to our land in hiding, frightened by Aegisthus.
Besides, how could a lock of his hair match with mine?
one from a man with rugged training in the ring
and games, one combed and girlish? It is not possible.
You may find many matching birds of the same feather   530
not bred in the same nest, old man, nor matched in blood.

Old Man

At least go set your foot in the print of his hunting boot
and see if it is not the same as yours, my child.

Electra

You make me angry. How could rocky ground receive
the imprint of a foot? And if it could be traced,   535
it would not be the same for brother and for sister,
a man's foot and a girl's—of course his would be bigger.

Old Man

Is there no sign then, if your brother should come home...
of loom or pattern by which you would know the cloth
you wove, I wrapped him in, to rescue him from death?   540

Electra

You know quite well Orestes went away in exile
when I was very small. If a little girl's hand

could weave, how could a growing boy still wear that cloth
unless his shirt and tunic lengthened with his legs?

    Some pitying stranger must have passed the tomb and cut   545
a mourning-lock, or townsmen slipping past the spies. . . .

Old Man

    Where are the strangers now? I want to look them over
and draw them out with conversation of your brother.

                   (*Orestes and Pylades enter from the cottage.*)

Electra

    Here they come striding lightly from the cottage now.

Old Man

    Well. They look highborn enough, but the coin may prove   550
false. Often a noble face hides filthy ways.
Nevertheless—
             Greetings, strangers, I wish you well.

Orestes

    And greetings in return, old sir.
                        Electra, where,
to what friends of yours, does this human antique belong?

Electra

    This is the man who nursed and loved my father, sir.   555

Orestes

    What! the one who saved your brother once from death?

Electra

    Indeed he saved him—if indeed he still is safe.

Orestes

    Ah, so!
Why do you stare upon me like a man who squints
at the bright stamp of a coin? Do I stir your memory?

Electra

Perhaps just happy seeing Orestes' twin in age. 560

Orestes

Dear Orestes. Why does he walk round me in circles?

Electra

Stranger, I am astonished too as I look at him.

Old Man

Mistress, now pray. Daughter Electra, pray to the gods.

Electra

For what of the things I have, or all I never had?

Old Man

For a treasure of love within your grasp, which god reveals. 565

Electra

As you please; I will pray the gods. What was in your mind?

Old Man

Look now upon this man, my child—your dearest love.

Electra

I have been looking rather at you; is your mind disturbed?

Old Man

My mind not steady when my eyes have seen your brother?

Electra

What have you said, old man? what hopeless impossible word? 570

Old Man

I said I see Orestes—here—Agamemnon's son.

Electra

How? What sign do you see? What can I know and trust?

Old Man

    The scar above his eye where once he slipped and drew
    blood as he helped you chase a fawn in your father's court.

Electra

    I see the mark of a fall, but—I cannot believe—   575

Old Man

    How long will you stand, hold yourself back from his arms and
        love?

Electra

    I will not any longer, for my heart has trust
    in the token you show.
                O Brother so delayed by time,
    I hold you against hope—

Orestes

                Time hid you long from me.

Electra

    I never promised myself—

Orestes

                I had abandoned hope.   580

Electra

    And are you he?

Orestes

             I am, your sole defender and friend.
    Now if I catch the prey for which I cast my net—

Electra

    I trust you and trust in you. Never believe in god
    again if evil can still triumph over good.

Chorus

    You have come, you have come, our slow, bright day,   585
        you have shone, you have shown a beacon-

lit hope for the state, who fled of old
your father's palace, doomed and pained,
    drifting in exile.

Now god, some god restores us strong   590
   to triumph, my love.
Lift high your hands, lift high your voice, raise
prayers to the gods. In fortune, fortune
your brother shall march straight to the city's heart.   595

Orestes

Enough. I find sweet pleasure in embrace and welcome,
but let us give ourselves over to pleasure later.
Old man, you came on the crest of opportunity—
tell me what I must do to punish the murderer
and purify my mother from adultery.   600
Have I in Argos any strong measure of friends
or am I bankrupt in backing as I am in fortune?
Whom shall I look to? Shall it be by day or night?
What hunting-track will lead me toward my enemies?

Old Man

My son, you lost your friends when luck deserted you.   605
That would indeed be luck met on the road for you,
someone to share both good and evil without change.
But you from root to leaf-top have been robbed of friends
who, leaving, left you no bequest of hope. Hear me:
in your own hand and the grace of god you hold all poised   610
to capture back your city, place, and patrimony.

Orestes

But what should we be doing now to strike our target?

Old Man

Kill him. Kill Thyestes' son. And kill your mother.

Orestes

Such the triumphal crown I came for, yet—how reach it?

Old Man

Not inside the city even if you were willing.   615

Orestes

Is he so strongly fenced by bodyguards and spears?

Old Man

You know it. The man's afraid of you and cannot sleep.

Orestes

Let that go, then. Tell me another way, old man.

Old Man

Yes—you shall hear, for something came to me just now.

Orestes

I hope your plan and my reaction are equally good.   620

Old Man

I saw Aegisthus as I hauled my way up here.

Orestes

Good, that sounds hopeful. Where am I to find him now?

Old Man

Close, down in the meadows where his horses graze.

Orestes

What is he doing? Out of despair I see new light.

Old Man

Offering a banquet to the goddess Nymphs, I think.   625

Orestes

To keep his children safe? For a child soon to be born?

Old Man

I know only that he is prepared to kill a bull.

Orestes

How many men are with him? simply alone with servants?

Old Man

No citizens were there; a handful of palace servants.

Orestes

No one who might still recognize my face, old man?   630

Old Man

They are his private servants and have never seen you.

Orestes

And would they, if we conquered, be, ah—kindly disposed?

Old Man

That is characteristic of slaves, and luck for you.

Orestes

How would you suggest my getting close to him?

Old Man

Walk past where he will see you as he sacrifices.   635

Orestes

He has his fields, I gather, right beside this road?

Old Man

And when he sees you he will ask you to join the feast.

Orestes

He shall find a bitter banquet-fellow, if god wills.

Old Man

What happens next—you play it as the dice may fall.

Orestes

Well spoken. The woman who gave me birth is—where?   640

Old Man

In Argos. She will join her husband for the feast.

Orestes

But why did she—my mother—not start out with him?

Old Man

The gossip of the crowd disturbs her. She held back.

Orestes

Of course. She feels the city watching her on the sly.

Old Man

That's how it is. Everyone hates a promiscuous wife.   645

Orestes

Then how can I kill them both at the same time and place?

                         (Electra comes forward.)

Electra

I will be the one to plan my mother's death.

Orestes

Good—then fortune will arrange the first death well.

Electra

Let our single friend here help us with both deaths.

Old Man

It shall be done. What death have you decided for her?   650

Electra

Old uncle, you must go to Clytemnestra; tell her
that I am kept in bed after bearing a son.

Old Man

Some time ago? or has your baby just arrived?

Electra

Ten days ago, which days I have kept ritually clean.

Old Man

And how will this achieve the murder of your mother?   655

Electra

She will come, of course, when she hears about the birth.

Old Man

Why? Do you think she cares so deeply for you, child?

Electra

Yes—and she can weep about the boy's low breeding.

Old Man

Perhaps. Return now to the goal of your design.

Electra

She will come; she will be killed. All that is clear.   660

Old Man

I see—she comes and walks directly in your door.

Electra

From there she need walk only a short way, to death.

Old Man

I will gladly die too, when I have seen her die.

Electra

But first, old man, you ought to guide Orestes down—

Old Man

Where Aegisthus holds his sacrifices to the gods?   665

Electra

Then go face my mother, tell her all about me.

Old Man

    I'll speak so well she'll think it is Electra speaking.

Electra (to Orestes)

    Your task is ready. You have drawn first chance at murder.

Orestes

    Well, I would go if anyone could show me where.

Old Man

    I will escort you on your way with greatest joy.   670

Orestes

    O Zeus of Our Fathers, now be Router of Foes.

Electra

    Have pity on us, for our days are piteous.

Old Man

    Pity them truly—children sprung of your own blood.

Electra

    O Hera, holy mistress of Mycenae's altars—

Orestes

    Grant us the victory if our claim to victory is just.   675

Old Man

    Grant them at last avenging justice for their father.

Electra

    O Earth, ruler below, to whom I stretch my hands—

Orestes

    And you, O Father, dwelling wronged beneath the earth—

Old Man

    Protect, protect these children here, so dearly loved.

Electra

    Come now and bring as army all the dead below—   680

Orestes

    Who stood beside you at Troy with the havoc of their spears—

Old Man

    All who hate the godless guilty defilers here.

Electra

    Did you hear us, terrible victim of our mother's love?

Old Man

    All, your father hears all, I know. Time now to march.

Electra

    I call to you again and say *Aegisthus dies!*   685
    And if Orestes in his struggle falls to death
    I too am dead, let them no longer say I live,
    for I will stab my belly with a two-edged sword.
      I will go in and make our dwelling fit for the outcome:
    then if a message of good fortune comes from you   690
    the whole house shall ring out in triumph. If you die
    triumph will shift to desolation. This is my word.

Orestes

    I understand you.

Electra

                Make yourself fit man for the hour.
    You, my women, with your voices light a fire-
    signal of shouting in this trial. I shall stand guard,   695
    a sword raised ready for the issue in my hand.
    Even in defeat I shall not grant to those
    I hate, the right to violate my living flesh.

          (*Orestes, the Old Man, and Pylades go off toward*
             Mycenae; Electra withdraws into the house.)

Chorus

 The ancient tale is told
  in Argos
 still—how a magic lamb   700
 from its mother gay on the hills
 Pan stole, Pan of the wild
 beasts, kind watcher, Pan
 who breathes sweet music to his jointed reed.
 He brought it to show the gold   705
 curls of its wool. On the stone
 steps a standing herald called:
 To the square, to the square, you men
 of Mycenae! Come, run, behold
  a strange and lovely thing   710
 for our blessed kings. Swiftly the chorus in dance
  beat out honor to Atreus' house.

 The altars spread their wings
  of hammered
 gold, fire gleamed in the town
 like the moon on Argos' stones   715
 of sacrifice, lotus flutes
 tended the Muses, lilting
 ripples of tune. The dance swelled in desire
 tense for the lamb of gold—
 whose? Quick, Thyestes' trick:
 seducing in the dark of sleep   720
 Atreus' wife, he brought
 the strange lamb home, his own.
  Back to the square he calls
 all to know how he holds the golden beast,
  fleece and horn, from Atreus' house. 725

 That hour—that hour Zeus
 changed the stars on their blazing course,
 utterly turned the splendid sun,

turned the white face of the dawn 730
so the sun drives west over heaven's spine
    in glowing god-lit fire,
the watery weight of cloud moves north,
the cracked waste of African Ammon
dries up, dies, never knowing dew, 735
robbed of the beautiful rain that drops from Zeus.

Thus it is always told.
I am won only to light belief
that the sun would swerve or change his gold
chamber of fire, moved in pain 740
at sorrow and sin in the mortal world,
    to judge or punish man.
Yet terrible myths are gifts
which call men to the worship of god.
You lost god when you killed your lord, 745
forgot the gods and the blood of your glorious brothers.

Listen, listen.
Friends, did you hear a shout? or did anxiety
trick me? a shout deep-rolling like the thunder of Zeus?
Again it comes! The rising wind is charged with news.
Mistress, come out! Electra, leave the house! 750

(*Electra appears at the door.*)

Electra

Dear friends, what is it? How do we stand now in our trial?

Chorus

I do not know yet—only a voice is crying death.

Electra

I hear it too. It is still faint, far. But I hear it.

Chorus

It comes from a great distance, yet it seems so close.

Electra

It is the Argives groaning there—or is it our friends?   755

Chorus

I cannot tell; the note of clamoring is slurred.

Electra

So you announce my death by sword. Why am I slow?

Chorus

Lady, hold back until you learn the outcome clearly.

Electra

Not possible. We are beaten. Where are the messengers?

Chorus

They will come soon. To kill a king is not quick or light.   760

(*Enter a Messenger in excitement.*)

Messenger

Hail maidens of Mycenae, beautiful in triumph!
Orestes is victor! I proclaim it to all who love him.
The murderer of Agamemnon lies on the earth
crumpled in blood, Aegisthus. Let us thank the gods.

Electra

Who are you? Why should I think your message is the truth?   765

Messenger

You do not know your brother's servant? You have seen me.

Electra

Dearest of servants! out of fear I held my eyes
shaded from recognition. Now indeed I know you.
What was your news? my father's hated murderer dead?

Messenger

Dead, dead. I will say it twice if that is pleasing.   770

Electra

O gods! O Justice watching the world, you have come at last.
How did he die? what style of death did Orestes choose,
to kill Thyestes' son? Give me the details.

Messenger

When we rose from your cottage and walked down the hill
we came across a beaten double wagon-track,   775
and there we found the famous master of Mycenae.
He happened to be walking in the water-meadow,
scything young green shoots of myrtle for his hair.
He saw us and called out: "You are most welcome, strangers.
Who are you? Have you traveled far? Where is your home?"   780
Orestes answered, "We are Thessalians on our way
toward Alpheus' valley where we shall sacrifice to Zeus
of Olympia." When Aegisthus heard, he called again,
"Now you must stop among us as our guests and share
our feast. I am at the moment slaughtering a bull   785
for the Nymphs. Tomorrow morning you shall rise refreshed
and lose no time on the road. Come with me to the shrine—"
while he was still talking he took him by the hand
and led us off the road—"I will take no refusal."
When we had reached his garden hut he gave commands: 790
"Quick, someone fill a bowl of water for the strangers
so their hands will be clean to make lustration at the altar."
But Orestes interrupted: "We are clean enough.
We washed ourselves just now in the clear river water.
If citizens need strangers for your sacrifice   795
we are here, Aegisthus. We shall not refuse you, prince."
    After this they broke off public conversation.
Now the king's bodyguard laid down their spears
and sprang all hands to working.
Some brought the lustral bowl and baskets of holy grain,   800
some laid and lit the fire or around the hearth
set up the sacred ewers—the whole roof rang with sound.
Your mother's lover took the barley in his hands

and cast it on the altar as he said these words:
"Nymphs of the Rocks, I have killed many bulls for you,   805
and my wife, Tyndareus' child, has killed often at home.
Guard us in present fortune, ruin our enemies."
(Meaning you and Orestes.) But my master prayed
the utter reverse, keeping his words below his breath,
to take his dynastic place again. Aegisthus raised   810
the narrow knife from the basket, cut the calf's front lock,
with his right hand dedicated it to the holy fire,
and, as his servants hoisted the beast upon their shoulders,
slashed its throat.
          Now he turns to your brother and says,
"One of your great Thessalian virtues, as you boast,   815
is to be a man of two skills: disjointing bulls
and taming horses. Stranger, take the iron knife,
show us how true Thessalian reputation runs."
Orestes caught the beautifully tempered Dorian blade,
loosened his brooch, flung his fine cloak back from his shoulders,   820
chose Pylades as his assistant in the work,
and made the men stand off. Holding the beast by its foot,
he laid the white flesh bare with one pass of his hand.
He stripped the hide off whole, more quickly than a runner
racing could double down and back the hippodrome course,   825
and loosened the soft belly. Aegisthus scooped the prophetic
viscera up in his hands.
          The liver lobe was not
there. Unhidden, the portal-vein and gall-sac showed
disaster coming at him even as he peered.
His face darkened, drew down. My master watched and asked,   830
"What puts you out of heart?" "Stranger, I am afraid.
Some ambush is at my door. There is a man I hate,
an heir to Agamemnon and his war on my house."
He answered, "You can scarcely fear a fugitive's
tricks when you control the state? Now to appease us   835
with sacrificial flesh, will someone bring a knife—
Phthian, not Dorian—and let me split his breast?"

He took it and struck. Aegisthus heaped the soft parts, then
sorted them out. But while his head was bent above them,
your brother stretched up, balanced on the balls of his feet,   840
and smashed a blow to his spine. The vertebrae of his back
broke. Head down, his whole body convulsed, he gasped
to breathe, writhed with a high scream, and died in his blood.

    The servingmen who saw it flashed straight to their spears,
an army for two men to face. And yet with courage   845
they stood, faced them, shook their javelins, engaged—
both Pylades and Orestes, who cried, "I have not come
in wrath against this city nor against my people.
I have only paid my father's killer back in blood.
I am injured Orestes—do not kill me, men   850
who helped my father's house of old."

                         They, when they heard
his words, lowered their spears, and he was recognized
by some old man who used to serve the family.
Swiftly they crowned your brother's head with flower wreaths,
shouting aloud in joy and triumph. He comes to you   855
bringing a head to show you—not a Gorgon horror,
only Aegisthus whom you loathe, who was in debt
for blood and found the paying bitter at his death.

Chorus

Come, lift your foot, lady, to dance
    now like a fawn who in flying   860
arcs leaps for joy, light, almost brushing the sky.
    He wins a garland of glory
more great than those Alpheus' glades grant to the perfect,
your own brother; now, in the hymn strain,
praise the fair victor, chant to my step.   865

Electra

O flame of day and sun's great chariot charged with light,
O earth below and dark of night where I watched before,
my eyes are clear now, I can unfold my sight to freedom,

now that Aegisthus, who had killed my father, falls.
Bring me my few belongings, what my house keeps treasured   870
as ornaments of splendor for the hair, dear friends,
for I will crown my brother as a conqueror.

Chorus

Lay now the bright signs of success
    over his brow, as we circle
our chorused step, dancing to the Muses' delight.   875
    Now again in our country
our old and loved kings of the blood capture the power,
in high justice routing the unjust.
Raïse to the flute's tune shouts of our joy.

(Enter Orestes, Pylades, and servants with corpse.)

Electra

O man of triumph sprung of our triumphant father   880
who fought and won below the walls of Troy—Orestes!
Take from my hands these twisted lock-rings for your hair.
You come, a runner in no trifling race, but long
and challenging, to your home goal, killing Aegisthus
who was your enemy, who once destroyed our father.   885
    And you, companion of the shield, Pylades, son
of a most reverend father, please receive your crown
from my hand, for you have won an equal share of glory
in this stark trial. May I see your fortune always high.

Orestes

You must believe, Electra, that the gods have been   890
first founders of our luck; then you may turn to praise
me as the simple servant of both god and luck.
I come to you the killer of Aegisthus, not
in words but action. You know this, but more than this
I have here in my hands the man himself, though dead.   895
You may want to display him for the beasts to eat
or as a toy for carrion birds born of bright air
or stick his head upon a stake. He is all yours.

Electra

　I am ashamed to speak and yet I wish to speak.　　　　　900

Orestes

　What is it? Speak your mind and so emerge from fear.

Electra

　I am ashamed to insult the dead; some hate may strike me.

Orestes

　There is no man on earth, nor will be, who could blame you.

Electra

　Our state is harsh to please and takes delight in slander.

Orestes

　Speak as you need to, Sister. We were joined to him　　905
　in bonds of hatred which could know no gentle truce.

Electra

　So be it.
　　　　　Which of our sufferings shall I speak in prelude,
　which shall I make finale, or marshal in the center?
　And yet through rising nights I never once have missed
　calling aloud what I wished to tell you to your face　　910
　if only I were liberated from my fears
　of old. We are at the point now. I give you the full
　tale of ruin I hoped to tell you in your life.
　　You killed me, orphaned me, and him too, of a father
　we loved dearly, though he had done no harm to you.　　915
　In ugliness you bedded my mother, killed her man
　who captained the Greeks abroad while you skulked far from
　　　Phrygia.
　You climbed such heights of stupidness that you imagined
　your marriage to my mother would not marry you
　to cuckoldry, though your own success in Father's bed　　920

was criminal. You should know, when a man seduces another's
wife in secret sex and then is forced to keep her,
he heads for disaster if he thinks that she, unchaste
to her first husband, will suddenly turn chaste for him.

Your household life was painful though you could not see it;   925
you knew in your heart that you had made a godless marriage,
and Mother knew she had acquired a godless man,
so each in working pain shouldered the other's load
for mutual help: she got your evil, you got hers.
Every time you walked outdoors in Argos, you heard,   930
"There goes the queen's husband." It was never "the king's wife."
O what perversion, when the woman in the house
stands out as master, not the man. I shake in hate
to see those children whom the city knows and names
not by their father's name but only by their mother's.   935
It marks the bridegroom who has climbed to a nobler bed;
when no one mentions the husband, everyone knows the wife.

Where you were most deceived in your grand unawareness
was your boast to be a man of power since you had money.
Wealth stays with us a little moment if at all;   940
only our characters are steadfast, not our gold,
for character stays with us to the end and faces
trouble, but wealth which lives with us on terms of crime
wings swiftly from the house after brief blossoming.

The women in your life I will not mention—a maiden   945
ought not—but only hint that I know all about them.
You played it haughty since you lived in a grand palace
and were handsome enough. But let me have a husband
not girlish-faced like you but graceful in male courage
whose sons would cling bold to the craggy heights of war;   950
your looks were only ornamental at the dance.

Die then. You paid your debt, never knowing that time
stripped your disguises bare. So should no criminal
who starts his race without a stumble vainly believe
that he has outrun Justice, till in the closing stretch   955
he nears the finish line and gains the goal of death.

Chorus

He wrought horrors, yet has paid in horror to you
and your brother. Justice has enormous power.

Electra

Enough now. Women, take his body out of sight,
conceal it well in darkness so that when she comes   960
my mother sees no corpses till her throat is cut.

                    (*The corpse is carried into the cottage.*)

Orestes

Hold off a little; we might find another plan.

Electra

What's there? I see some allies racing from Mycenae.

Orestes

Not allies. You are looking at my mother who bore me.

Electra

How beautifully she marches straight into our net;   965
see how grandly she rides with chariot and escort.

Orestes

What—what is our action now toward Mother? Do we kill?

Electra

Don't tell me pity catches you at the sight of her.

Orestes

O god!
How can I kill her when she brought me up and bore me?

Electra

Kill her just the way she killed my father. And yours.   970

Orestes

O Phoebus, your holy word was brute and ignorant.

Electra

Where Apollo is ignorant shall men be wise?

Orestes

He said to kill my mother, whom I must not kill.

Electra

Nothing will hurt you. You are only avenging Father.

Orestes

As matricide I must stand trial. I was clean before.   975

Electra

Not clean before the gods, if you neglect your father.

Orestes

I know—but will I not be judged for killing Mother?

Electra

And will you not be judged for quitting Father's service?

Orestes

A polluted demon spoke it in the shape of god—

Electra

Throned on the holy tripod? I shall not believe you.   980

Orestes

And I shall not believe those oracles were pure.

Electra

You may not play the coward now and fall to weakness.
Go in. I will bait her a trap as she once baited one
which sprang at Aegisthus' touch and killed her lawful husband.

Orestes

I am going in. I walk a cliff-edge in a sea   985
of evil, and evil I will do. If the gods approve,
let it be so. This game of death is bitter, and sweet.

(Orestes goes slowly into the house with Pylades, without looking back.
Up the road by which he had just come with Aegisthus' corpse, en-
ter Clytemnestra in a chariot, attended by Trojan slave girls.)

Chorus

    Hail! hail!
Queen and mistress of Argos, hail,
   Tyndareus' child,
sister in blood to the lordly sons   990
of Zeus who dwell in starred and flaming
air, saviors adored by men
   in the roar of the salt sea.
Hail! I honor you like the gods
for your looming wealth and brilliant life.   995
The time to guard and heal your doom
   is now, O Queen. Hail!

Clytemnestra

    Get out of the carriage, Trojan maidens; hold my hand
tight, so I can step down safely to the ground.

               (Looking around somewhat embarrassed.)
Mostly we gave the houses of our gods the spoils   1000
from Phrygia, but these girls, the best in Troy, I chose
to ornament my own house and replace the child
I lost, my loved daughter. The compensation is small.

Electra

    Then may not I, who am a slave and also tossed
far from my father's home to live in misery,   1005
may I not, Mother, hold your most distinguished hand?

Clytemnestra

    These slaves are here to help me. Do not trouble yourself.

Electra

    Why not? You rooted me up, a casualty of war;
my home was overpowered; I am in your power,
as they are too—left dark, lonely, and fatherless.   1010

Clymnestra

And dark and lonely were your father's plots against
those he should most have loved and least conspired to kill.
I can tell you—no. When a woman gets an evil
reputation she finds a bitter twist to her words.
This is my case now, not a pretty one. And yet,   1015
if you have something truly to hate, you ought to learn
the facts first; then hate is more decent. But not in the dark.
    My father Tyndareus gave me to your father's care,
not to kill me, not to kill what I bore and loved.
And yet he tempted my daughter, slyly whispering   1020
of marriage with Achilles, took her from home to Aulis
where the ships were stuck, stretched her high above the fire
and, like pale field grass, slashed Iphigenia's throat.
If this had been to save the state from siege and ruin,
if it had helped his home and spared his other children   1025
to rack one girl for many lives, I could have forgiven.
But now for the sake of Helen's lust and for the man
who took a wife and could not punish her seducer—
for their lives' sake he took the life of my dear child.
I was unfairly wronged in this, yet not for this   1030
would I have gone savage so, nor killed my husband so,
but he came home to me with a mad, god-filled girl
and introduced her to our bed. So there we were,
two brides being stabled in a single stall.
    Oh, women are fools for sex, deny it I shall not.   1035
Since this is in our nature, when our husbands choose
to despise the bed they have, a woman is quite willing
to imitate her man and find another friend.
But then the dirty gossip puts us in the spotlight;
the guilty ones, the men, are never blamed at all.   1040
If Menelaus had been raped from home on the sly,
should I have had to kill Orestes so my sister's
husband could be rescued? You think your father would
have borne it? He would have killed me. Then why was it fair
for him to kill what belonged to me and not be killed?   1045

I killed. I turned and walked the only path still open,
straight to his enemies. Would any of his friends
have helped me in the task of murder I had to do?
 Speak if you have need or reason. Fight me free;
demonstrate how your father died without full justice.   1050

Chorus

 Justice is in your words but justice can be ugly.
 A wife should give way to her husband in all things
 if her mind is sound; if she refuses to see this truth
 she cannot enter fully counted to my thought.

Electra

 Keep in mind, Mother, those last words you spoke,   1055
 giving me license to speak out freely against you.

Clytemnestra

 I say them once again, child; I will not deny you.

Electra

 But when you hear me, Mother, will you hurt me again?

Clytemnestra

 Not so at all. I shall be glad to humor you.

Electra

 Then I speak—and here is the keynote of my song.   1060
 Mother who bore me, how I wish your mind were healthy.
 Although for beauty you deserve tremendous praise,
 both you and Helen, flowering from a single stalk,
 you both grew sly and lightweight, a disgrace to Castor.
 When she was raped she walked of her own will to ruin,   1065
 while you brought ruin on the finest man in Greece
 and screened it with the argument that for your child
 you killed your husband. The world knows you less well than I.
 You, long before your daughter came near sacrifice,
 the very hour your husband marched away from home,   1070

were setting your brown curls by the bronze mirror's light.
Now any woman who works on her beauty when her man
is gone from home indicts herself as being a whore.
She has no decent cause to show her painted face
outside the door unless she wants to look for trouble.   1075
　　Of all Greek women, you were the only one I know
to hug yourself with pleasure when Troy's fortunes rose,
but when they sank, to cloud your face in sympathy.
You needed Agamemnon never to come again.
And yet life gave you every chance to be wise and fine.   1080
You had a husband scarcely feebler than Aegisthus,
whom Greece herself had chosen as her king and captain;
and when your sister Helen—did the things she did,
that was your time to capture glory, for black evil
is outlined clearest to our sight by the blaze of virtue.   1085
　　Next. If, as you say, our father killed your daughter,
did I do any harm to you, or did my brother?
When you killed your husband, why did you not bestow
the ancestral home on us, but took to bed the gold
which never belonged to you to buy yourself a lover?   1090
And why has *he* not gone in exile for your son
or died to pay for me who still alive have died
my sister's death twice over while you strangle my life?
If murder judges and calls for murder, I will kill
you—and your own Orestes will kill you—for Father.   1095
If the first death was just, the second too is just.

Clytemnestra

　　My child, from birth you always have adored your father.   1102
This is part of life. Some children always love
the male, some turn more closely to their mother than him.
I know you and forgive you. I am not so happy   1105
either, child, with what I have done or with myself.
　　How poorly you look. Have you not washed? Your clothes are
　　　　bad.
I suppose you just got up from bed and giving birth?

O god, how miserably my plans have all turned out.
Perhaps I drove my hate too hard against my husband.   111

Electra

Your mourning comes a little late. There is no cure.
Father is dead now. If you grieve, why not
recall the son you sent to starve in foreign lands?

Clytemnestra

I am afraid. I have to watch my life, not his.
They say his father's death has made him very angry.   111.

Electra

Why do you let your husband act like a beast against us?

Clytemnestra

That is his nature. Yours is wild and stubborn too.

Electra

That hurts. But I am going to bury my anger soon.

Clytemnestra

Good; then he never will be harsh to you again.

Electra

He has been haughty; now he is staying in my house.   1120

Clytemnestra

You see? you want to blow the quarrel to new flames.

Electra

I will be quiet; I fear him—the way I fear him.

Clytemnestra

Stop this talk. You called me here for something, girl.

Electra

I think you heard about my lying-in and son.
Make me the proper sacrifice—I don't know how—   1125

as the law runs for children at the tenth night moon.
I have no knowledge; I never had a family.

Clytemnestra

This is work for the woman who acted as your midwife.

Electra

I acted for myself. I was alone at birth.

Clytemnestra

Your house is set so desolate of friends and neighbors?   1130

Electra

No one is willing to make friends with poverty.

Clytemnestra

Then I will go and make the gods full sacrifice
for a child as law prescribes. I give you so much
grace and then pass to the meadow where my husband rests
praying to the bridal Nymphs. Servants, take the wagon,   1135
set it in the stables. When you think this rite
of god draws to an end, come back to stand beside me,
for I have debts of grace to pay my husband too.

Electra

Enter our poor house. And, Mother, take good care
the smoky walls put no dark stain upon your robes.   1140
Pay sacrifice to heaven as you ought to pay.

> (*Clytemnestra walks alone into the house; the
> Trojan girls withdraw with the chariot.*)

The basket of grain is raised again, the knife is sharp
which killed the bull, and close beside him you shall fall
stricken, to keep your bridal rites in the house of death
with him you slept beside in life. I give you so   1145
much grace and you shall give my father grace of justice.

> (*Electra goes into the cottage.*)

Chorus

Evils are interchanging. The winds of this house
shift now to a new track. Of old in the bath
my captain, mine, fell to his death;
the roof rang, the stone heights of the hall echoed loud   1150
to his cry: "O terrible lady, will you kill me now
newly come home to love at the tenth cycle of seed?"

. . . .

Time circles back and brings her to the bar,   1155
she pays grief for love errant. She, when her lord
came safe home, after dragging years,
where his stone Cyclops' walls rose straight to the sky, there with
    steel
freshly honed to an edge killed him, hand on the ax. O wretched   1160
husband, most wretched suffering must have turned her then:
a lioness mountain-bred, ranging out
from her oak-sheltered home, she sprang. It was done.

Clytemnestra (from inside the house)

O children—O my god—do not kill your mother—no.   1165

Chorus

Do you hear her cry trapped in the walls?

Clytemnestra

O, O, I am hurt—

Chorus

I also am hurt to hear you in your children's hands.
Justice is given down by god soon or late;
you suffer terribly now, you acted terribly then   1170
against god and love.

(*Orestes, Electra, and Pylades emerge from the house, and the
doors open to reveal the corpses of Aegisthus and
Clytemnestra lying together.*)

Behold them coming from the house in robes of blood
newly stained by a murdered mother, walking straight,
living signs of triumph over her frightful cries.
There is no house, nor has there been, more suffering   1175
or more at war than this, the house of Tantalus.

Orestes

O Earth and Zeus who watch all work
men do, look at this work of blood
and corruption, two bodies in death
lying battered along the dirt   1180
under my hands, only to pay
for my pain.

Electra

Weep greatly for me, my brother, I am guilty.
A girl flaming in hurt I marched against
the mother who bore me.

Chorus

Weep for destiny; destiny yours   1185
to mother unforgettable wrath,
to suffer unforgettable pain
beyond pain at your children's hands.
You paid for their father's death as the law asks.

Orestes

Phoebus, you hymned the law in black   1190
melody, but the deed has shone
white as a scar. You granted us rest
as murderers rest—to leave the land
of Greece. But where else can I go?
What state, host, god-fearing man   1195
will look steady upon my face,
who killed my mother?

Electra

O weep for me. Where am I now? What dance—
what wedding may I come to? What man will take
   me bride to his bed?   1200

Chorus

Circling, circling, your wilful mind
veers in the blowing wind and turns;
you think piously now, but then
thoughtless you wrought an impious thing,
dear girl, when your brother's will was against you.   1205

Orestes

You saw her agony, how she threw aside her dress,
how she was showing her breast there in the midst of death?
   My god, how she bent to earth
the legs which I was born through? and her hair—I touched it—

Chorus

I know, I understand; you have come   1210
through grinding torment hearing her cry
   so hurt, your own mother.

Orestes

She cracked into a scream then, she stretched up her hand
toward my face: "My son! Oh, be pitiful my son!"   1215
   She clung to my face,
suspended, hanging; my arm dropped with the sword—

Chorus

Unhappy woman—how could your eyes
bear to watch her blood as she fought
   for her breath and died there?   1220

Orestes

I snatched a fold of my cloak to hood my eyes, and, blind,
   took the sword and sacrificed
my mother—sank steel to her neck.

Electra

    I urged you on, I urged you on,
    I touched the sword beside your hand.   1225

Chorus

    Working a terrible pain and ruin.

Orestes

    Take it! shroud my mother's dead flesh in my cloak,
        clean and close the sucking wounds.
    You carried your own death in your womb.

Electra

    Behold! I wrap her close in the robe,   1230
    the one I loved and could not love.

Chorus

    Ending your family's great disasters.

        (The Dioscuri appear on the roof over the scene of mourning.)

    Whom do I see high over your house
    shining in radiance? Are they divinities
    or gods of the heavens? They are more than men   1235
    in their moving. Why do they come so bright
        into the eyes of mortals?

Dioscuri (Castor speaking for both)

    O son of Agamemnon, hear us: we call to you,
    the Twins, born with your mother, named the sons of Zeus,
    I Castor, and my brother Polydeuces here.   1240
    We come to Argos having turned the rolling storm
    of a sea-tossed ship to quiet, when we saw the death
    of this our murdered sister, of your murdered mother.
    Justice has claimed her but you have not worked in justice.
    As for Phoebus, Phoebus—yet he is my lord,   1245
    silence. He knows the truth but his oracles were lies.

Compulsion is on us to accept this scene, on you
to go complete the doom which fate and Zeus decreed.
　Give Pylades Electra as a wife in his house,
and leave Argos yourself. The city is not yours　　　　　　1250
to walk in any longer, since you killed your mother.
The dreadful beast-faced goddesses of destiny
will roll you like a wheel through maddened wandering.
But when you come to Athens, fold the holy wood
of Pallas' statue to your breast—then she will check　　　1255
the fluttering horror of their snakes, they cannot touch you
as she holds her Gorgon-circled shield above your head.
　In Athens is the Hill of Ares, where the gods
first took their seats to judge murder by public vote,
the time raw-minded Ares killed Halirrhothius　　　　　　1260
in anger at his daughter's godless wedding night,
in anger at the sea-lord's son. Since then this court
has been holy and trusted by both men and gods.
There you also must run the risk of trial for murder.
But the voting-pebbles will be cast equal and save you,　　1265
you shall not die by the verdict: Loxias will take
all blame on himself for having asked your mother's death,
and so for the rest of time this law shall be established:
When votes are equal the accused must have acquittal.
The dreadful goddesses, shaken in grief for this,　　　　　1270
shall go down in a crack of earth beside the Hill
to keep a dark and august oracle for men.
Then you must found a city near Arcadian
Alpheus' stream, beside the wolf-god's sanctuary.
and by your name that city shall be known to men.　　　　1275
　So much I say to you. Aegisthus' corpse the men
of Argos will hide, buried in an earth-heaped tomb.
Menelaus will bury your mother. He has come just now
to Nauplia for the first time since he captured Troy.
Helen will help him. She is home from Proteus' halls,　　1280
leaving Egypt astern. She never went to Troy.
Zeus fashioned and dispatched a Helen-image there

to Ilium so men might die in hate and blood.
    So. Let Pylades take Electra, girl and wife,
and start his journey homeward, leaving Achaea's lands;   1285
let him also to his Phocian estates escort
your "brother," as they call him—set him deep in wealth.
    Turn your feet toward Isthmus' narrow neck of earth,
make your way to the blessed hill where Cecrops dwells.
When you have drained the fulness of a murderer's doom   1290
you may again be happy, released from these distresses.

Chorus

Sons of Zeus, does the law allow us
to draw any closer toward your voice?

Dioscuri

The law allows, you are clean of this blood.

Electra

Will you speak to me too, Tyndaridae?   1295

Dioscuri

Also to you. On Phoebus I place all
   guilt for this death.

Chorus

Why could you, who are gods and brothers
   of the dead woman here,
not turn her Furies away from our halls?   1300

Dioscuri

Doom is compelling, it leads and we follow—
doom and the brutal song of Apollo.

Electra

And I? What Apollo, what oracle's voice
ordained I be marked in my mother's blood?

Dioscuri

>You shared in the act, you share in the fate: 1305
>   both children a single
>curse on your house has ground into dust.

Orestes

>O Sister, I found you so late, and so soon
>I lose you, robbed of your healing love,
>and leave you behind as you have left me. 1310

Dioscuri

>She has a husband, she has a home, she
>needs no pity, she suffers nothing
>   but exile from Argos.

Electra

>Are there more poignant sorrows or greater
>than leaving the soil of a fatherland? 1315

Orestes

>But I go too, I am forced from my father's
>home, I must suffer foreigners' judgment
>for the blood of my mother.

Dioscuri

>   Courage. You go
>to the holy city of Pallas. Endure. 1320

Electra

>Hold me now closely breast against breast,
>   dear Brother. I love you.
>But the curses bred in a mother's blood
>dissolve our bonds and drive us from home.

Orestes

>Come to me, clasp my body, lament 1325
>as if at the tomb of a man now dead.

Dioscuri

Alas, your despair rings terribly, even
    to listening gods;
pity at mortal labor and pain still
lives in us and the lords of heaven.   1330

Orestes

I shall not see you again.

Electra

I shall never more walk in the light of your eye.

Orestes

Now is the last I can hear your voice.

Electra

Farewell, my city.
Many times farewell, fellow citizens.   1335

Orestes

O loyal love, do you go so soon?

Electra

I go. These tears are harsh for my eyes.

Orestes

Pylades, go, farewell; and be kind to   1340
    Electra in marriage.

Dioscuri

Marriage shall fill their minds. But the hounds
are here. Quick, to Athens! Run to escape,
for they hurl their ghostly tracking against you,
serpent-fisted and blackened of flesh,   1345
offering the fruit of terrible pain.
We two must rush to Sicilian seas,
rescue the salt-smashed prows of the fleet.

As we move through the open valleys of air
we champion none who are stained in sin,   1350
but those who have held the holy and just
dear in their lives we will loose from harsh
   sorrow and save them.
So let no man be desirous of evil
nor sail with those who have broken their oaths—   1355
   as god to man I command you.

Chorus

Farewell. The mortal who can fare well,
not broken by trouble met on the road,
   leads a most blessèd life.

THE PHOENICIAN WOMEN

Translated and with an Introduction by Elizabeth Wyckoff

INTRODUCTION TO
THE PHOENICIAN WOMEN

THIS is a translation of the play which came down to later antiquity as Euripides' *Phoenician Women*, a play first produced in one of the years 411–409 B.C. What it actually is, is that play, as added to by fourth-century producers. The play in its original form undoubtedly covered, in its episodic action and in its reminiscences of the past and prophecies for the future, more stages of the Oedipus legend than one would have thought a single play could hold. The producers improved on this situation. Their additions brought in everything really memorable in the dramatic tradition of Oedipus which Euripides had left out, drawing freely on earlier plays from the *Seven against Thebes* to the *Oedipus at Colonus*. (This last, of course, Euripides had been unable to draw on, as he died before it was produced.) They also went in for heightening the melodrama, which took some doing.

This has been recognized ever since Valckenaer's edition of 1755, and there are three long passages which modern critics are pretty well agreed in rejecting as the work of Euripides. The first two are easily recognized. One is the messenger's description of the Argive heroes (ll. 1104–40). The second is the report of Eteocles' challenge, and the arming of the brothers for battle (ll. 1221–58). The reader of this translation will not be able to judge the linguistic points which furnish much of the evidence for setting them aside. But I think he can see the extent to which the first is extraneous. Euripides did as much as he wanted to with the Seven in lines 119–81. And the second passage is, among other things, a patchwork of bits from the *Children of Heracles*. These two I have bracketed, to warn the reader.

The third long interpolation begins at line 1582 and may include all the rest of the play.

It seems likely enough that besides the lyric lamentations there was some dialogue between Creon, Oedipus, and Antigone, pointing ahead to the next stages of the story. But the Creon-Oedipus-Antigone scene we have is certainly not the one Euripides wrote.

Note, for one thing, that Antigone is apparently planning both to go into exile, at once, with Oedipus and, in defiance of Creon, to bury Polyneices. This is impossible, but the author is simply assimilating his figure to both Sophoclean Antigones.

However, I am not as sure as some critics are that everything from line 1582 on is invented, or even everything in lines 1582–1709. I think what we may well have here is a Euripidean groundwork, once self-consistent, to which have been added references to those portions of the later story which Euripides chose to omit. (And of course this reworker probably had to do some deleting.) I am unable to disentangle the Euripidean strands in what I suspect to be a collaboration rather than a simple insertion and have therefore bracketed nothing, simply warning the reader here.

Finally, it is obvious that a play which has been so freely handled in gross would probably be tinkered with in detail. This has happened; single lines and short passages have been inserted here and there. For example, line 11 looks very much as if someone wanted to get Creon into the program notes as soon as possible, even though this interrupts Jocasta's identification of herself. Lines 141–44 clear up the sort of point that might have bothered a prompter, and borrow from lines 95–98 to do it. Line 1225 is one of many lines of which the scholiast says, "In many copies this line does not occur." Line 1346 was originally omitted in four manuscripts.

In these, and all analogous cases, I have not troubled the reader with brackets. Editors disagree. However, I have tried to play fair and not to weave an inorganic line into context. Therefore even a reader confined to this translation can join centuries of scholars in spotting the inconsistencies and redundancies. However, he should remember that many of them may well be Euripides' own. Anyone who wishes to pursue these questions further might start with D. L. Page's *Actors' Interpolations in Extant Greek Tragedy* and the Preface to J. U. Powell's edition of this play.

The translation was made from Murray's Oxford text of 1909. The places where I have departed from his readings are these:

Line 22: †(obelus) βρέφος, manuscripts, Murray; λέχος Schoene, Powell.

Line 1533: ἐπὶ, manuscripts, Murray (who obelizes the passage); ἐπί "anonymus," quoted by Wecklein, Powell.

Line 1606: I read this as a single line, without the lacuna which Murray assumes.

Line 1740: I give this line to Oedipus, with the manuscripts and Powell, rather than to Antigone, with Murray (who had evidence from the scholiast).

THE PHOENICIAN WOMEN

CHARACTERS

Jocasta

Pedagogue

Antigone

Chorus of young women from Phoenicia

Polyneices

Eteocles

Creon

Teiresias

Menoeceus

Two Messengers

Oedipus

THE PHOENICIAN WOMEN

Jocasta

   You who cut your way through heaven's stars,
   riding the chariot with its welded gold,
   Sun, with your swift mares whirling forth our light,
   evil the shaft you sent to Thebes that day
   when Cadmus came here, leaving Phoenicia's shore,   5
   he who wed Cypris' child, Harmonia,
   fathering Polydorus, who in turn
   had Labdacus, they say, and he had Laius.
   Now I am known as daughter of Menoeceus,   10
   Creon my brother by the selfsame mother,
   my name Jocasta, as my father gave it,
   Laius my husband. When he still was childless
   after long marriage with me in the palace,
   he went to Phoebus asking and beseeching   15
   that we might share male children for the house.
   But he said, "Lord of Thebes and its famed horses,
   sow not that furrow against divine decree.
   For if you have a child, him you beget
   shall kill you, and your house shall wade through blood."   20
   But Laius, in his lust, and drunk beside,
   begot a child on me, yet when he had,
   knowing his sex was sin, as God had said it,
   he gave the child to shepherds to expose   25
   in Hera's field, high on Cithaeron's rock,
   when he had pinned its ankles with sharp iron
   (and this is why Greece called it Oedipus).
   Then Polybus' herdsman-riders took the child
   and brought it home and gave it to their mistress.
   She took my labor's fruit to her own breast   30

and told her husband that it was her own.
When his red beard was growing, my young son,
who had guessed or heard the truth, set off to learn,
at Phoebus' house, his parents. So did Laius,   35
seeking to learn if the child he had exposed
were still alive. They met in middle journey
at the same spot in the split road of Phocis.
Then Laius' runner ordered him away:
"Stranger, yield place to princes." But he came on,   40
silent, in pride. So with their sharp-edged hooves
the mares of Laius bloodied up his feet.
And so—why give the detail of disaster?—
son slew his father, and he took the team
to give to Polybus, his foster parent.
When the Sphinx bore down our city with her raids,   45
my husband gone, Creon proclaimed my marriage:
whoever might guess the clever maiden's riddle,
to him I should be wed. And so it happened.
It was Oedipus, my son, who guessed her song.   50
So he became the ruler of this land
and got the scepter of this realm as prize.
The wretch, unknowing, wedded with his mother;
nor did she know she bedded with her son.
And to my son I bore two further sons,   55
Eteocles and mighty Polyneices,
and daughters two. Her father named Ismene
while I before had named Antigone.
When Oedipus learned I was his wife and mother,
he had endured all suffering, and he struck   60
with terrible gory wounding his own eyes,
bleeding the pupils with a golden brooch.
When his sons' beards had grown, they shut him up
behind the bolts that this fate might be forgotten
which needs too much intelligence to explain it.   65
There in the house he lives, and struck by fate
he calls unholy curses on his children.

They shall divide this house with sharpened steel.
They were afraid that if they lived together   70
the gods might grant his prayers. So they agreed
that Polyneices should go, a willing exile,
while Eteocles stayed in this land and held the scepter,
to change though, year by year. Yet when Eteocles
sat safe on high, he would not leave the throne,
but keeps his brother exiled from this land.   75
He went to Argos, married Adrastus' daughter,
and brings the Argive force he has collected
against these very seven-gated walls,
seeking his share of the land, and his father's scepter.   80
I have persuaded son to come to son
under a truce before they take to arms.
I hope for peace. The messenger says he'll come.
O Zeus who lives in heaven's shining folds
save me and let my sons be reconciled.   85
If you are wise you should not leave a mortal
constantly wretched throughout all of life.

(Jocasta returns to the palace. Enter, from the palace,
Antigone and the old Pedagogue.)

Pedagogue

Antigone, flower of your father's house,
your mother has said you may leave the maiden's room
to climb the very steepest of the roof   90
and see the Argive army, as you asked.
But wait, that I may track the road before you
in case some citizen is in the way.
Then some slight blame would come on me the slave,   95
worse on your highness. Since I know, I'll tell
all that I saw and heard among the Argives
when I went there from here to make the truce
with your brother's army, and came back again.

(The Pedagogue goes up the steps to the house roof.)

No citizen is near the house at all.
Try the old cedar ladder with your feet,   100
look over the plain and see by Ismenus' stream
and Dirce's spring how great the enemy host.

(Antigone goes up the stairs and speaks at the top.)

Antigone

Reach your old hand to my young one. Help me step
up from the stairs.   105

Pedagogue (pulling her up)

Take hold, my girl. You're here, but just in time.
The Argive army is moving, the companies part.

Antigone

Hecate, Leto's child! The lightning-shine   110
of bronze all over the plain!

Pedagogue

Polyneices comes no trifler to this land.
He brings the clamor of many horse and foot.

Antigone

The gates, and their locks! Are the brazen bolts
holding firm Amphion's wall of stone?   115

Pedagogue

Take heart, all's well and safe inside the city.
Look at the first man, if you want to mark him.

Antigone

Who is he with the crest of white
who comes at the head of the host and lightly shakes   120
the brazen shield on his arm?

Pedagogue

A captain, lady.

Antigone

Yes, but who, and whence?
Speak out his name, old man.

Pedagogue

He boasts his birth from Mycenae and he lives   125
by Lerna's waters, lord Hippomedon.

Antigone

How prideful, how hateful to see!
Like an earth-born giant hurling flame in a picture,   130
not like the race of day.

Pedagogue

Do you see the one who is crossing Dirce's stream?

Antigone

How strange, how strange his arms! And who is he?

Pedagogue

Tydeus, the warrior from far Aetolia.

Antigone

Is this the one who has married the very sister   135
of Polyneices' bride?
How strange his arms, half-barbarous to see!

Pedagogue

All the Aetolians carry such a shield
and hurl light lances so they hit the mark.   140

Antigone

Old man, how did you learn all this so well?

Pedagogue

I knew them, for I saw their arms before
when I went from here to there to make the truce
with your brother's army. I know them in their harness.

Antigone

> Who comes by Zethus' tomb with falling curls,   145
> a youth, and frightful to see?
> Some captain, since an armed crowd follows on.

Pedagogue

> Parthenopaeus, Atalanta's son.   150

Antigone

> I hope that Artemis, ranging the hills with his mother,
> strikes with her shaft and destroys him
> who comes to plunder my town.

Pedagogue

> I hope so, child. But the right is on their side.
> And I am afraid the gods may see things clear.   155

Antigone

> And where is he whom my selfsame mother bore
> to a painful fate?
> Dear ancient, tell me, where is Polyneices?

Pedagogue

> He stands with Adrastus, close by the maidens' tomb,
> Niobe's seven daughters. You see him now?   160

Antigone

> Not clearly, but enough to guess his shape.
> Oh, could I run on my feet like a wind-swift cloud through the
>   sky
> to my own dear brother, and throw my arms round his neck,   165
> poor exile—but how he shines in his golden arms
> ablaze with the light of dawn.

Pedagogue

> He is coming to this house, you may be glad.   170
> Under a truce.

Antigone

But who comes here, old man?
Who mounts and drives a chariot of white?

Pedagogue

That is the prophet Amphiaraus, lady,
bringing the victims whose blood shall please this land.

Antigone

Selene, daughter of shining-girdled Sun,   175
you with your round gold light, how calm he comes,
how gently prods his horses!
—Where is the man who insulted us so fiercely?

Pedagogue

Capaneus? There he marks the approaches out,   180
takes the walls' measures up and down the towers.

Antigone

Nemesis, and you, deep thunder of Zeus,
and shining flare of the lightning, it is for you
to put his boasting to sleep.
He said he would bring the Theban girls   185
as slaves to Mycenae's women,
would give them to Lerna's triple fount,
slaves to Poseidon's lover's waters.
Artemis, golden-locked, child of Zeus, may I never   190
endure that slavery.

Pedagogue

Child, back into the house, and stay inside
your maiden chamber. You have had the joy
of that desired sight you wished to see.   195
Noise in the city proves a crowd of women
is pressing toward the royal palace now.
The female sex is very quick to blame.

If one of them gets a little launching place,
far, far she drives. There seems to be some pleasure   200
for women in sick talk of one another.

> (*Antigone and the Pedagogue go into the palace. Enter,
> from the side, the Chorus of Phoenician women.*)

Chorus

I came, I left the wave of Tyre
the island of Phoenicia,
as prize for Loxias, slave to Phoebus' house,   205
to rest by Parnassus' snowy ridge.
I came on a ship through the Ionians' sea,
over the fruitless plain,   210
though the west wind rushed from Sicily,
a beautiful blast from heaven.
Chosen most beautiful of my town,
an offering to Apollo,   215
I came to Cadmus' land, as I am Agenor's kin,
sent to Laius' kindred towers.
I might, like the golden statue-girls,   220
have served Phoebus by now.
But Castalia's water is waiting still
to wet my hair for his service.   225

O rock that shines in the fire,
double gleam on the heights
where Dionysus dances,
and vine who distils the daily wealth,   230
the fruitful cluster of grapes,
holy cave of the serpent, mountain rocks
where the gods keep watch, O sacred mountain of snow,
may I, unfearing, dance the Immortal's dance   235
by Phoebus' central hollow with Dirce left behind.

Now before the walls
savage Ares comes   24
kindling the fiame of death

for this city—may it not happen.
Shared are the griefs of friends,
shared; if she must suffer,
this seven-gated land, then does Phoenicia share it.   245
Common blood, common children,
through Io who wore the horns.
I also have my part in this.

A cloud about the town,   250
a close cloud of shields,
kindles the scheme of death.
Soon shall Ares know
that he brings to Oedipus' sons
the curse of the very Furies.   255
Ancestral Argos, I fear your strength,
and I fear the gods' part too.
For this man at arms
comes against our home with justice.

(Enter, from the side, Polyneices, with drawn sword.)

Polyneices

The warders' bolts have let me through the walls
with ease, and so I fear once in the net
I won't get out unbloodied. Thus I look   265
hither and yonder, watching for a trick.
My hand that holds this sword shall prove my courage.
    Ah, who is there? Or do I fear a noise?
All things seem terrible to those who dare   270
when they set foot upon the enemy's land.
I trust my mother, and I do not trust her
who brought me here under a pledge of truce.
Defense is close. The sacrificial hearths   275
are near, nor is the palace desolate.
I'll thrust my sword in the darkness of its case
and ask who are these women by the house.
    Ladies, what land was it you left to come
to our Hellenic halls?

Chorus

> It was Phoenicia reared me. Agenor's grandsons   280
> have sent me here a captive, prize for Phoebus.
> And while the sons of Oedipus delayed
> to send me on to Loxias' oracle
> there came the Argives' war against this city.   285
> Give answer in return, you who have come
> to the gated fortress of the Theban land.

Polyneices

> My father is Oedipus, Laius' son, my mother
> Jocasta, daughter of Menoeceus.
> The Theban people call me Polyneices.   290

Chorus

> Kin of Agenor's children who are my lords,
> who sent me here—
>
> Master, I fall on my knees,
> the humble habit of home.
> At last you have come to your father's land.   295
> Queen, queen, come forth,
> open the gates!
> Mother who bore him, do you hear us now?
> Why your delay in leaving the halls
> and taking your son in your arms?

> > (*Enter Jocasta from the palace.*)

Jocasta

> I heard your Phoenician cry,
> girls, and my poor old feet,
> trembling, have brought me out.
> My child, my child, at last I see you again.   305
> Embrace your mother's breast with your arms,
> stretch forth your face and your dark curly hair,
> to shadow my throat.

Oh, oh, you have barely come,
unhoped for, unexpected, to your mother's arms.   310
What shall I say, how phrase the whole
delight in words and actions
that compasses me about.   315
If I dance in my joy shall I find the old delight?
Child, you went as an exile; your father's house
was left in desolation, your brother's doing.
But your own yearned after you   320
Thebes itself yearned.
And so I weep, and cut my whitened hair.
No longer, child, do I wear white robes,
I have changed to these dark gloomy rags.   325
And the old man in the house, the blind old man,
since the pair of you left the house,
clings to his weeping desire. He seeks the sword   330
for death by his own hand, he casts a noose
over the roof beams mourning his curse on his children.
He is hidden in darkness and steadily wails his woe.   335
And I hear that you have paired yourself in marriage,
the joy of making children.
In a stranger's house you have taken a stranger bride,   340
a curse to your mother and Laius who was of old.
Doom brought by your wedding.
I did not light your wedding torch
as a happy mother should.   345
Ismenus gave no water to the marriage;
your coming to your bride was never sung in Thebes.
May the cause of these sufferings perish, be it the steel   350
or strife, or your father, or a demon-rout
in Oedipus' house.
For all their grief has fallen upon me.

Chorus

Childbirth is terrible for womankind.   355
Therefore all women love their children so.

Polyneices

Mother, with reason, unreasoning have I come
among my enemies. But all men must still
love their own country. Who says something else
enjoys his talk while thinking far away.   360
I was so scared, had gone so far in fear
lest brother's craft might kill me on the way,
that through the town I came with sword in hand,
turning my face about. Just one thing helped,   365
the truce—and your own pledge which led me on
through the ancestral walls. I came in tears
seeing at last the halls and the gods' altars,
the playing fields that reared me, Dirce's spring,
which I have left unjustly and now live
in a stranger town, blurring my eyes with tears.   370
I come from grief and find you grief indeed.
Your hair is shorn; your garments are of black.
Alas, alas, my sorrows and myself!
Mother, how frightful is the strife of kindred,
and reconciling hard to bring about!   375
What does my father do within the house,
he who sees darkness? What of my two sisters,
do they, poor girls, lament my exile now?

Jocasta

Some god is ruining all of Oedipus' children.
The beginning was my bearing outside law.   380
It was wrong to marry your father and to have you.
But what of this? The god's will must be borne.
Still, I must ask you, fearing it may sting,
one question for whose answer I am yearning.

Polyneices

Ask openly, leave nothing out at all.   385
Your wish is mine, my mother.

Jocasta

So now I ask what first I wish to know.
What is it to lose your country—a great suffering?

Polyneices

The greatest, even worse than people say.

Jocasta

What is its nature? What so hard on exiles?   390

Polyneices

One thing is worst, a man cannot speak out.

Jocasta

But this is slavery, not to speak one's thought.

Polyneices

One must endure the unwisdom of one's masters.

Jocasta

This also is painful, to join with fools in folly.

Polyneices

One must be a slave, for gain, against one's nature.   395

Jocasta

The saying is that exiles feed on hopes.

Polyneices

Lovely to look at, but they do delay.

Jocasta

And doesn't time make clear that they are empty?

Polyneices

They have their charm in troubles.

Jocasta

How were you fed before your marriage fed you?   400

Polyneices

Sometimes I'd have a day's worth, sometimes not.

Jocasta

Your father's foreign friends, were they no help?

Polyneices

Hope to be rich! If you are not—no friends.

Jocasta

Your high birth brought you to no lordly height.

Polyneices

Want's the bad thing. My breeding did not feed me.   405

Jocasta

It seems one's country *is* the dearest thing.

Polyneices

You couldn't say in words how dear it is.

Jocasta

How did you get to Argos, and with what plan?

Polyneices

Apollo gave Adrastus a certain answer.

Jocasta

What sort? Why mention this? I cannot guess.   410

Polyneices

To marry his daughters to a boar and a lion.

Jocasta

What has my son to do with wild beasts' names?

Polyneices

    I do not know. He was calling me to my fate.

Jocasta

    For the god is wise. How did you meet your marriage?

Polyneices

    It was night; I came upon Adrastus' portal.   415

Jocasta

    A wandering exile, looking for a bed?

Polyneices

    Just so—and then another exile came.

Jocasta

    And who was he? Wretched as you, no doubt.

Polyneices

    That Tydeus who is named as Oeneus' son.

Jocasta

    But why did Adrastus think you were those beasts?   420

Polyneices

    Because we fought over the pallet there.

Jocasta

    And then he understood the oracle?

Polyneices

    And gave us two his daughters two to wed.

Jocasta

    Were you happy or unhappy in these weddings?

Polyneices

    Right to this day we have no fault to find.   425

Jocasta

How did you lure the army to follow you here?

Polyneices

Adrastus promised his two sons-in-law,
Tydeus and me—Tydeus is now my kinsman—
that both should be brought home, but I the first.
So many Mycenaean chiefs are here   430
and many Danaans, doing me a favor
which hurts me, though I need it. My own town
I fight against. I call the gods to witness
against my will I fight my willing kindred.
But—you can possibly undo these troubles—   435
Mother, you reconcile these kindred-friends,
save you and me and the city from these sorrows.
This has been sung before, but I shall say it:
"Men honor property above all else;
it has the greatest power in human life."   440
And so I seek it with ten thousand spears.
A beggar is no nobleman at all.

Chorus

Here comes Eteocles to hold his parley.
Jocasta, as their mother, it's for you
to say the words to reconcile your sons.   445

                                            (*Enter Eteocles.*)

Eteocles

Mother, I'm here. I came to do a favor
for you. Now what's to come? Let someone speak.
I have broken off my ambushing of chariots
about the walls that I might hear from you
that arbitration for which I have admitted   450
this one within the walls—at your persuasion.

Jocasta

Check for a moment. Swiftness brings not justice.
It is slow speech that brings the greatest wisdom.

Check your dread glare, the seethings of your spirit.
It is not Gorgon's severed head you see;   455
you look upon your brother who has come.
And you, Polyneices, look upon your brother,
for if you look upon his face once more
you will speak better and will hear him better.
I want to give you both some good advice.   460
When friend falls out with friend and they come together
looking at one another, let them look
at that for which they came, forget old wrongs.
Son Polyneices, you may speak the first.   465
For you have come, and brought the Argive army,
as one who claims a wrong. Now may some god
be judge and reconciler of these griefs.

Polyneices

The word of truth is single in its nature;
and a just cause needs no interpreting.   470
It carries its own case. But the unjust argument
since it is sick, needs clever medicine.
I took good foresight for our father's house,
for him, and for myself, hoping to flee
those curses with which once our father cursed us.   475
So willingly myself I left this land,
leaving the rule to him for a year's circle,
so that I myself might take the rule in turn.
Thus we should not fall into hate and envy
doing and suffering evil—but that has happened.   480
For he who swore this, and called the gods to witness,
did nothing of what he promised and still holds
the tyranny and his share of my own house.
And now I am ready, if I get my own,
to send away the army from this land,   485
to take my own house for my proper turn,
and yield it back to him for equal time,
so not to plunder my fatherland nor besiege

her towers with the scaling ladder's steps.
But if I get not justice I shall try   490
to do just this. I call the gods to witness
I have done all in justice, now most unjustly
I am robbed of my fatherland, an offense to heaven.
The facts I've told you, Mother, without heaping
great twists of argument. The clever and the humble   495
alike can see that I have spoken right.

Chorus

I think, though I am not a Hellene born,
that what you say is argued very well.

Eteocles

If all men saw the fair and wise the same
men would not have debaters' double strife.   500
But nothing is like or even among men
except the name they give—which is not the fact.
I'll speak to you, Mother, without concealment:
I'd go to the stars beyond the eastern sky
or under earth, if I could do one thing,   505
seize tyranny, the greatest of the gods.
I will not choose to give this good thing up
to any other, rather than keep it myself.
It's cowardice to let the big thing go
and settle for the smaller. Besides, I should be shamed   510
that he should come in arms and sack the land,
and so achieve his purpose. This would be for Thebes
real shame, if fearing spearmen from Mycenae
I yielded up my scepter for him to hold.
He should not seek his truce with arms in hand,   515
for argument can straighten out as much
as enemy steel can do.
If he will live here on some other terms,
he can. But what he asks I will not yield.
When I can rule should I become his slave?   520

So—on with fire, on with swords of war,
harness the horses, fill the plain with chariots,
knowing that I will never yield my rule.
If one must do a wrong, it's best to do it
pursuing power—otherwise, let's have virtue.   525

Chorus

It isn't right to speak so well of evil.
This is no good thing, but a bitterness to justice.

Jocasta

My son Eteocles, old age is not
a total misery. Experience helps.
Sometimes we can speak wiser than the young.   530
Why do you seek after the goddess Ambition?
The worst of all; this goddess is Injustice.
Often she comes to happy homes and cities,
and when she leaves, she has destroyed their owners,
she after whom you rave. It's better, child,   535
to honor Equality who ties friends to friends,
cities to cities, allies to allies.
For equality is stable among men.
If not, the lesser hates the greater force,
and so begins the day of enmity.   540
Equality set up men's weights and measures,
gave them their numbers. And night's sightless eye
equal divides with day the circling year.
While neither, yielding place, resents the other.   545
So sun and night are servants to mankind.
Yet you will not endure to hold your house
in even shares with him? Where's justice then?
Why do you honor so much tyrannic power
and think that unjust happiness is great?   550
It's fine to be looked up to? But it's empty.
You want to have much wealth within your halls,
much trouble with it?

And what is "much"? It's nothing but the name.
Sufficiency's enough for men of sense.
Men do not really own their private goods;   555
we simply care for things which are the gods',
and when they will, they take them back again.
Wealth is not steady; it is of a day.
Come, if I question you a double question,
whether you wish to rule, or to save the city,   560
will you choose to be its tyrant? But if he wins
and the Argive spear beats down the Theban lance,
then you will see this town of Thebes subdued
and many maidens taken off as slaves,
assaulted, ravished, by our enemies.   565
Truly the wealth which now you seek to have
will mean but grief for Thebes; you're too ambitious.
So much for you.
                  Your turn now, Polyneices:
ignorant favors has Adrastus done you,
and you have come in folly to sack your city.   570
Come, if you take this land—heaven forbid it—
by the gods, what trophies can you set to Zeus?
How start the sacrifice for your vanquished country,
and how inscribe your spoils at Inachus' stream?
"Polyneices set these shields up to the gods   575
when he had fired Thebes?" Oh, never, Son,
be this, or such as this, your fame in Greece!
If you are worsted and his side has best,
how shall you go to Argos, leaving here
thousands of corpses? Some will surely say:
"Adrastus, what a wedding for your daughter!   580
For one girl's marriage we have been destroyed."
You are pursuing evils—one of two—
you will lose the Argives or fail in winning here.
Both of you, drop excess. When double folly
attacks one issue, this is worst of all.   585

Chorus

O gods, in some way yet avert these evils
and make the sons of Oedipus agree!

Eteocles

Mother, it's too late for talking, and this intermission time
has been wasted; your good purpose can accomplish nothing now.
For we cannot come to terms except as I have laid them down: 590
that I shall hold the scepter of power in this land.
Leave off your long advisings, now Mother, let me be.
And *you*—outside these walls now, or surely you shall die.

Polyneices

What invulnerable someone will lay a sword on me
for slaughter and not bring away a murder for himself?   595

Eteocles

Near enough, he hasn't left you. Do you see these hands of mine?

Polyneices

Oh, I see you. Wealth's a coward and a thing that loves its life.

Eteocles

Then why come you with so many for a battle with a no one?

Polyneices

Oh, a prudent captain's better than a bad one in the war.

Eteocles

You can boast, when we've a truce that saves you from your   600
death.

Polyneices

So can you. Again I'm claiming rule and sharing of this land.

Eteocles

No use to ask. My house shall still be ruled by none but me.

Polyneices

Holding more than is your sharing?

Eteocles

Yes. Now leave this land at
once.

Polyneices

Altars of our fathers' worship—

Eteocles

which you come to plunder now

Polyneices

hear me!

Eteocles

Which of them will hear you when you fight your   605
fatherland?

Polyneices

Temples of the gods who ride white horses—

Eteocles

and who hate you.

Polyneices

I am driven from my country—

Eteocles

for you came to ruin it.

Polyneices

wrongfully, O gods.

Eteocles

Don't call on these gods, but Mycenae's!

Polyneices

Impious by nature!

Eteocles

Never have I been my country's foe.

Polyneices

who drive me off without my portion.

Eteocles

And I'll kill you yet, be- 610
sides.

Polyneices

Oh, my father, hear my sorrow!

Eteocles

And he hears what you are doing.

Polyneices

and you, Mother!

Eteocles

It's indecent that you speak of her at all.

Polyneices

O my city!

Eteocles

Go to Argos, and call on Lerna's stream.

Polyneices

I'm going, never worry. Thank you, Mother.

Eteocles

Leave the land!

Polyneices

I am going, but our father, let me see him.

Eteocles

You shall not. 615

Polyneices

Or the girls our sisters.

Eteocles

Never shall you look on them again.

Polyneices (calling)
   O my sisters!

Eteocles
                  Now why call them when you are their enemy?

Polyneices
   Fare you very well, my mother.

Jocasta
                     Well, I suffer very much.

Polyneices
   I'm no longer son of yours.

Jocasta
                  I was born for suffering.

Polyneices
   For this man has done me insult.

Eteocles
                     And I stand insulted back.   620

Polyneices
   Where'll you be before the towers?

Eteocles
                  And why should you ask
      that?

Polyneices
   I shall stand against, to kill you.

Eteocles
                  I desire the selfsame thing.

Jocasta
   Oh, woe is me, my children, what will you do?

Polyneices
                     You'll see.

« 484 »

Jocasta

Won't you flee your father's cursings?

Eteocles

                          Let the whole house fall

   to ruin.

Polyneices

Soon my bloody sword no longer shall be lazy in its sheath.   625
By the land herself who bore me and her gods I now do swear
that dishonored, badly treated, I am thrust outside the land
like a slave, as if I were not son of Oedipus, as he is.
O my city, if you suffer, lay the blame on him, not me:
I attack against my will, I was thrust away unwilling.   630
Apollo of the roadways and rooftrees, fare you well,
and my friends of youth and statues of the gods we fed with
   honey.
I don't know if I can ever speak a word to you again.
But I still have hope that somehow if the gods are on my side
I shall kill him and be master of this our Theban land.   635

Eteocles

Leave this place; your name means "quarrel" and our father
   named you well.

        (*Jocasta returns to the palace and Polyneices leaves.*)

Chorus

Tyrian Cadmus came to this land.
Here the heifer bent her legs and fell,   640
proved the oracle, told him here to build
his house on the fertile plain,
where comes the moisture of fair-flowing waters,   645
Dirce's water over the furrows green that take the seed,
where his mother bore Bacchus after her marriage with Zeus.   650
He was still a child when the twining ivy came,
green tendrils and all, to cover him over,

to be part of the Bacchic dances of Theban girls   655
and the women who call his name.

And there the bloody dragon was,
savage monster who guarded Ares' spring,
looked with his roving eyes on its running stream.
The beast was slain with a boulder
when Cadmus came seeking water of lustration,
and struck the bloody head with the blows of his monster-slaying
    arm,
sowing its teeth in the furrows deep, at unmothered Pallas' bid-
    ding.
Then earth sent up armed terror over its surface.
Iron-hearted slaughter sent them back again,
and their blood bedewed the land which had briefly showed them
to the shining winds of heaven.

On you also I call, Io's child,
Epaphus, son of our mother, and of Zeus,
—with foreign cry, with foreign prayers—   680
come, come to this land!
It was your descendants who founded it,
and the two-named goddesses own it, Kore and dear Demeter,   685
who is ruler of all, nurse of all, the earth.
Epaphus, send us the goddesses of the torch,
defend this land, for the gods all things are easy.

Eteocles (to an attendant)

Go, and bring here Creon, Menoeceus' son,   690
the brother of Jocasta, my own mother,
saying I would consult him on private matters
and state affairs before I go to war.
    But he has saved your trouble; here he is.   695
For now I see him coming to my house.

(*Enter, from the side, Creon.*)

Creon

> I've traveled far, trying to see you, King
> Eteocles; round the Cadmean gates
> and all their guards I went, to hunt you down.

Eteocles

> Creon, be sure I wished to see you too.   700
> I found the terms of peace from Polyneices,
> when we discussed them, far from what we need.

Creon

> I've heard that he desires more than Thebes,
> trusting his new connection and his army.
> But this we must leave hanging on the gods.   705
> I've come to tell you what's immediate.

Eteocles

> What's this? I do not know what you will tell.

Creon

> We have a prisoner from the Argive side.

Eteocles

> What does he say that's new from over there?

Creon

> He says the Argive host will shortly circle,   710
> armor and all, the old Cadmean town.

Eteocles

> Then Cadmus' town must hurry out her arms.

Creon

> But where? Are you too young to see what's needed?

Eteocles

> Over the trenches, where they are to fight.

Creon

This land is few in numbers, they are many.   715

Eteocles

And well I know that they are bold—in speech.

Creon

Well, Argos has a swelling fame in Greece.

Eteocles

Fear not. I'll fill the plain up with their blood.

Creon

I hope so. But I see much labor here.

Eteocles

So I'll not coop my army within walls.   720

Creon

To take good counsel—this is victory.

Eteocles

You want that I should turn to other roads?

Creon

All of them, lest our fate depend on one.

Eteocles

Should we lay ambush and attack at night?

Creon

So, if you failed, you would come safe again.   725

Eteocles

Night holds all even, but favors more the daring.

Creon

It's dread to have ill luck under the darkness.

Eteocles

A spear-attack while they are at their dinner?

Creon

A brief surprise—but we need victory.

Eteocles

But Dirce's stream is deep for their retreat.   730

Creon

Nothing's as good as holding on to safety.

Eteocles

Suppose we rode against the Argive camp?

Creon

They're well walled in, with chariots around.

Eteocles

What shall I do? Give enemies the town?

Creon

No, but take counsel, though you are so clever.   735

Eteocles

And what forecounsel's cleverer than mine?

Creon

They say that seven men, as I have heard—

Eteocles

What's their assignment? This is a small force.

Creon

will lead their companies to assault the gates.

Eteocles

What shall we do? Not wait till I am helpless?   740

Creon

You also choose out seven for the gates.

Eteocles

To take command of troops, or fight alone?

Creon

With troops, when they have chosen out the best.

Eteocles

I see—to ward off scalings of the walls.

Creon

And choose lieutenants; one man can't see all.   745

Eteocles

Choosing for courage or for prudent minds?

Creon

Both. Neither's any good without the other.

Eteocles

So be it. To the seven-gated town
I'll go, and set the captains as you say
in even numbers against their enemies.   750
It would take long, long talk to give each name,
now while the enemy camps outside our walls.
But I will go, my arm shall not be idle.
I hope my brother may be my opponent,
that I may fight and take him with my spear   755
and kill him who came to sack my fatherland.
The marriage of Antigone, my sister,
and your son Haemon, will be your affair
if I should fail. Their earlier betrothal
I ratify, as I move off to war.   760
You are my mother's brother. I need not tell you

to care for her, for my sake and your own.
My father bears the weight of his own folly,
self-blinded. I won't praise this, and his curse
may kill his sons if it is brought to pass.   765
One thing we haven't done. We should find out
if seer Teiresias has some word for us.
I'll send your son Menoeceus after him,
the boy who has your father's name, to bring him.   770
With kindness will he come to speak to you,
but I have blamed his seercraft and he hates me.
I lay one charge on you, and on the city,   775
if our side wins, let never Polyneices
be buried here in Theban earth. If someone
tries burial, he must die, though he be dear.
So much to you. And now to my own followers:
bring out my arms and armor. To the fight
which lies before me now I go with Justice,   780
who will bring victory. And I pray to Prudence,
kindest of gods, that she will save this city.

                                        (*Exit Eteocles.*)

Chorus

Ares, who brings us trouble, lover of blood and death,
why do you love them, why stand away from Bromios' feasts?   785
Never, when dances are fair and the girls are crowned,
do you loosen your locks and sing to the breath of the flute
which the Graces have given for dancing. No, you rouse the host,
the armed host of Argos against our Thebes with blood.   790
You dance first in the dance that knows no music.
Not when the thyrsus whirls and the fawns are there
do you come to Ismenus' stream.
But with sound of chariots, clatter of bits and hooves,
you urge the Argives against our earth-sown race,   795
a dancing crowd in arms that swells with shields,
decked in bronze to batter our walls of stone.
Strife is a terrible god, she who has planned
these sufferings for our rulers, the Labdacid kings.   800

O glade with the holy foliage, loved by the many beasts,
Artemis' own Cithaeron that wears the snow,
would you had never taken Jocasta's child
and brought to rearing Oedipus, child cast out of his house,
marked by the golden pins. And would that the wingèd maid,   805
the mountain portent of grief had never sung her songs,
the Sphinx whose music was no music at all,
who climbed over our walls with hoof and claw
and dragged our youth on high
to heaven's height untrodden, she whom Hades sent   810
against the people of Cadmus. And another evil strife,
the strife of Oedipus' children, comes on the town and its homes.
Evil is never good, nor are these lawless sons,   815
their mother's travail, their father's shame.
She came to her kinsman's bed. . . .
    [A few words are missing at the end of this antistrophe.]

Earth, you bore, you bore
—I heard the news in my foreign home, I heard it well—
the race that grew from the teeth of the crimson-crested monster,   820
Thebes' noblest shame.
And the sons of heaven they came to Harmonia's marriage,
the walls of Thebes they rose to Amphion's lyre,
midway between the streams   825
which pour their moisture over the rich green plain
from Dirce and Ismenus.
And Io, my hornèd mother, was also mother to kings of Thebes.
This city has shifted from one rule to another, but ever   830
has stood on high, decked with the crowns of war.

(*Enter the prophet Teiresias, led by his young
daughter, accompanied by Menoeceus.*)

Teiresias

Now lead me on, my daughter. You're the eye
for my blind steps, as star is to a sailor.   835
Now set my path upon the level plain

and lead me lest I stumble. Your father's weak.
Guard my lot-tablets with your maiden hand
which on my holy seat of prophecy   840
I drew when I had marked the oracle-birds.
O young Menoeceus, Creon's son, now tell me,
how far is still our journey to the town,
and to your father? My knees begin to buckle.
I've come so far I hardly can go on.

Creon

Take courage. You have come to harbor now,   845
among your friends. Now hold him up, my son.
Mule cars, and old men's feet, they need the help
of someone else's hand.

Teiresias

Ah, we are here. Why did you want me, Creon?

Creon

I've not forgotten. But collect your strength,   850
and draw your breath; forget your laboring road.

Teiresias

I am fatigued, since only yesterday
I came from labor for Erechtheus' sons.
There they had war against Eumolpus' spear,
and I gave Cecrops' children victory.   855
So, as you see, I wear a golden crown,
as first fruit of their plunder from the foe.

Creon

I'll take your crown of victory as an omen.
We're in mid-wave of danger, as you know,
Danae's sons against us, strife for Thebes.   860
Our king is gone, dressed in his warrior-arms,
against Mycenae's force, Eteocles.

But he enjoined me to find out from you
what we should do in hope to save our city.

Teiresias

As far as he goes, I'd have locked my mouth,   865
withheld the oracles, but at your asking,
I'll tell you. Creon, the land has long been sick,
since Laius made a child against heaven's will,
and begot poor Oedipus, husband to his mother.
The bloody ruin of his peering eyes   870
is the gods' clever warning unto Greece.
And Oedipus' sons who tried to cloak this up
with passage of time, as if to escape the gods,
erred in their folly, since they gave their father
neither his rights nor freedom to depart.   875
And so they stung the wretch to savage anger.
Therefore he cursed them terribly indeed,
since he was ailing and, besides, dishonored.
What did I not do, what did I not say?
All the result was hatred from those sons.
Death by their own hands is upon them, Creon;   880
and many corpses fallen over corpses,
struck with both Argive and Cadmean shafts,
will give the Theban land a bitter mourning.
You, my poor city, will be buried with them,
if no one is persuaded by my words.   885
This would be best, that none of Oedipus' house,
live in the land as citizen or lord,
since the gods hound them on to spoil the state.
But since the bad is stronger than the good
there is one other way to save the town.   890
But even for me it is not safe to say
that which is bitter to the man in power
who yet could save this city. Fare you well.
One among many, I will take what comes.
What else to do?   895

Creon

Stay here, old man.

Teiresias

Do not lay hands on me.

Creon

Now wait! Why flee?

Teiresias

Luck flees you, not myself.

Creon

Speak the salvation of the town and townsmen.

Teiresias

Now you may wish it; soon you'll wish it not.

Creon

I could not fail to wish my country's safety.   900

Teiresias

You really want to hear, and you are eager?

Creon

What should I be more earnest for than this?

Teiresias

Soon you will hear about my prophecies.
—But first there's something that I need to know.
Where is Menoeceus, he who brought me here?   905

Creon

He isn't far away, he's close to you.

Teiresias

Let him withdraw, far from my prophecies.

Creon

He is my son and will not talk at large.

Teiresias

You wish that I should speak while he is here?

Creon

Yes. He'll be glad to hear of what will save us.   910

Teiresias

Then shall you hear the way of prophecy,
what you must do to save the Theban town.
You must kill Menoeceus for his country's sake,
your child—since you yourself have asked your fate.

Creon

What are you saying? What's your word, old man?   915

Teiresias

Just what it is, and this you needs must do.

Creon

Oh, you have said much evil in short time.

Teiresias

Evil to you, great safety to your city.

Creon

I wasn't listening, I didn't hear.
City, farewell.

Teiresias

This is no more the man he was. He dodges.   920

Creon

Go, and goodbye. I do not need your seercraft.

Teiresias

Has truth now died because you are unhappy?

Creon

Oh, by your knees and by your old man's beard—

Teiresias

Why fall before me? What you ask is ruin.

Creon

be quiet; don't reveal this to the town.   925

Teiresias

You tell me to do wrong; I won't keep quiet.

Creon

What will you do? You plan to kill my child?

Teiresias

Others must deal with action. I must speak.

Creon

Why is this curse on me, and on my son?

Teiresias

You are right to ask, and bring me to debate.   930
He must, in that chamber where the earth-born dragon
was born, the watcher over Dirce's streams,
be slaughtered, and so give libation blood
for Cadmus' crime, appeasing Ares' wrath,
who now takes vengeance for his dragon's death.   935
Do this, and Ares will be your ally.
If earth gets fruit for fruit, and human blood
for her own offspring, then this land shall be
friendly to you, she who sent up the crop
of golden-helmeted Sown Men. One of their race,
child of the dragon's jaws, must die this death.   940
You are the one survivor of the Sown,
pure-blooded, on both sides, you and your sons.
Haemon's betrothal saves him from the slaughter.
For he is not unwedded, though still virgin.   945
This boy, who belongs to none but to the city,
if he should die, might save his fatherland,

make harsh homecoming for Adrastus and the Argives,
casting the dark of night upon their eyes,   950
and make Thebes famous. There you have your choice,
to save your city or to save your son.
    Now you have all I know. Child, take me home.
A man's a fool to use the prophet's trade.
For if he happens to bring bitter news   955
he's hated by the men for whom he works;
and if he pities them and tells them lies
he wrongs the gods. No prophet but Apollo
should sing to men, for he has nought to fear.

                (Exeunt Teiresias and his daughter.)

Chorus

    Creon, why are you silent, holding your tongue?   960
    But I myself am stricken and amazed.

Creon

    What can one say? But my response is clear.
    I'll never walk into such wretchedness
    as to give my city the slaughter of my son.
    It's part of human life to love one's children.   965
    No one would give his own son up to death.
    Let no one praise me who would kill my sons!
    Though I, since I am in the prime of life,
    am ready to die to set the country free.
    Up, son, before the whole town learns of this,   970
    pay no attention to these wanton bodings,
    fly quickly, get yourself outside this land.
    For he will tell this to the chiefs and captains
    making the rounds of the gates and their commanders.
    If we anticipate him, you are safe.   975
    If you come second, we're destroyed, you die.

Menoeceus

    Where shall I flee, what city and what friend?

Creon

As far away from here as you can get.

Menoeceus

You'd better tell me where, and I will do it.

Creon

Go beyond Delphi—

Menoeceus

        and where on beyond? 980

Creon

into Aetolia.

Menoeceus

      And where after that?

Creon

Thesprotia's plain.

Menoeceus

      Where holy Dodona stands?

Creon

Yes.

Menoeceus

    What protection will that be for me?

Creon

The god will guide you.

Menoeceus

      And for my supplies?

Creon

I'll give you gold.

Menoeceus

    Thank you for that, my father. 985
Go get it then. I'll go to see your sister
Jocasta, she who nursed me at her breast,

when my mother died and I was left an orphan.
I'll go to see her, and I'll save my life.
—Please hurry, Father, *you* don't want to keep me.   990

(*Exit Creon. Menoeceus addresses the Chorus.*)

Women, how well I've taken away his fear,
cheating with words, to get what I desire.
He'd steal me out, robbing the state of safety,
give me to cowardice. This can be forgiven
an ancient, but not pardoned in myself,   995
that I should so betray my fatherland.
Know well, I'm going, and I'll save the town,
and give my life to death to save the land.
How shameful if men who are not under omens,
and so constrained by heaven's necessity,   1000
stand at their shields and do not shrink at death,
fighting before the towers for fatherland,
while I, betraying my father and my brother
and my own city, leave the land a coward.
Wherever I'd live, I'd show myself a weakling.   1005
By Zeus, among the stars, and bloody Ares,
who set the sprouting offspring of this land
to be its rulers, I am going now.
I'll take my stand on the high battlements
over that precinct where the dragon lived,
there slay myself above its gloomy depths   1010
that the seer spoke of; so I'll free the land.
I've said my say, and now I go to give
my city no mean gift. I'll cure this ailing land.
If every man would take what good he can   1015
and give it to his city's common good,
cities would suffer less, be happy from now on.

(*Exit Menoeceus.*)

Chorus

You came, you came,
you wingèd thing, earth's offspring, monster's child,   1020

to seize the sons of Cadmus.
Half a maiden, a fearful beast,
with roving wings and claws that fed on blood.   1025
You who snatched the youths from Dirce's plain,
crying your Fury's shriek,
the song that knows no music,
you brought, you brought sorrows upon our land,   1030
bloody ones—and bloody was the god
who brought these things about.
Mournings of the mothers,
mournings of the maidens,
filled our homes with grief.   1035
Groan and cry ran back and forth
from one to another through the town,
and thunder groaned as they did   1040
each time the wingèd bird seized one of the city's men.

In time there came
by Pythian sending Oedipus the wretched,
here to this land of Thebes.   1045
Then were we glad, but later we grieved.
He conquered the riddle; poor wretch, he wed his mother.
He stained the town and through slaughter he came to strife, 1050
casting the curse on his sons.
We praise him who goes,
we praise the man who is dying to save his land.   1055
Groaning he leaves to Creon.
But the seven-gated town,
her he makes to conquer.
Pallas, make us mothers   1060
of sons as good as this,
you who checked the dragon-blood,
by the rock you urged Cadmus to throw.
Yet from this saving came   1065
a curse of God on this land, and slaughter with it.

(Enter, from the side, an armed messenger.)

Messenger

You there, whoever's watching at the gate,
open, and bring Jocasta from the house.
Open, I say! You've waited long, but now
come forth and hear, famed wife of Oedipus,   1070
leaving your wailing and your tears of grief.

(Enter Jocasta from the palace.)

Jocasta

Dear friend, you haven't come to tell disaster,
Eteocles' death, you who march by his shield,
constantly keeping off the enemy shafts.
What is the new word that you bring to me?   1075
Is my son alive or dead? Now tell me true.

Messenger

He lives, so tremble not, that fear is gone.

Jocasta

How is the circuit of the seven gates?

Messenger

They stand unbroken, the city is not plundered.

Jocasta

Were they endangered by the Argive spear?   1080

Messenger

Right on the verge. But our Cadmean Ares
was stronger than the Mycenaean spear.

Jocasta

By the gods, tell one thing more! What do you know
of Polyneices? I care for his life too.

Messenger

    Both of your sons are living to this moment.   1085

Jocasta

    God bless you! How, when you were sore besieged,
    did you force back the Argives from the gates?
    Tell me, that I may please the blind old man,
    sitting inside, with news of the city's saving.

Messenger

    When Creon's son, who died to save the city,   1090
    on the highest tower standing, had thrust his sword
    through his own throat and saved this land of ours,
    your son sent seven companies and their captains,
    to the seven gates, to keep the Argives off.
    Horses against the horsemen did he set,   1095
    foot against infantry, so where the wall
    was weak against assault, he guarded it.
    From the high citadel we saw the host,
    white-shielded men of Argos. They left Teumesus,   1100
    they rushed the ditch to set the town on fire.
    Then the paean and the trumpet played together,
    from there, and from our walls.
    [Then first attacked were the Neitian gates
    by a company bristling with its thick-set shields.   1105
    Parthenopaeus led them, the huntress' child,
    whose family sign was blazing on his shield,
    Atalanta with her distant-ranging arrows
    killing Aetolia's boar. Against the gate
    of Proetus, came the man of sacrifice,
    carrying victims on his car, no signs   1110
    of insolence on his shield. Wisely, his arms were blank.
    Against the Ogygian gate the lord Hippomedon
    came with a sign in middle of his shield,
    the All-Seeing one, with eyes all over him,   1115

some eyes that look forth as the stars come up,
others that hide among the setting stars,
and will look later when that man has died.
Against the next gate Tydeus took his stand.
He bore a lion's hide upon his shield   1120
with bristling mane. And there Prometheus held
in his right hand the torch to burn the town.
Your Polyneices by the Gate of Springs
led on the war. Upon his shield the fillies
of Potniae raged and ran in panic-fear,   1125
worked by the pivots near the handle-grip.
They did seem mad indeed.
And he who loves war even as Ares does
Capaneus led against the Electran gate.
The iron markings on his shield were these: 1130
an earth-born giant carried on his shoulders
a whole town wrenched away from its foundations,
this to suggest what our town is to suffer.
Adrastus himself was at the seventh gate.
A hundred snakes were drawn upon his shield.   1135
Yes, on his left arm rode the Argive Hydra.
And from our walls these snakes, with snatching jaws,
were taking Cadmus' children.
Now all these things I very well could see
since it was I who took the password round.]   1140
So first we fought with arrows and throwing-spears
and far-flung slingshots and the crash of stones.
When we had won this fighting, Tydeus cried,
sudden, so did your son, "O Danaan men,
do not delay, before their shafts have stunned you,   1145
fall on the gates, light-armed, and horse, and chariots."
And when they heard the cry, no man was slow
and many fell, their heads bedaubed with blood.
On our side too you might have seen as many   1150
dive to the plain and breathe their life away.
They dewed the dry earth with their streams of blood.

Then that Arcadian, Atalanta's son,
no Argive, rushed upon the gates a storm,
crying for double-axes and for fire,
meaning to overturn our town, but then   1155
the sea-god's son, Periclymenus, cast a stone,
a wagon's load, from the high cornice-top,
broke up his yellow head, shattered the joinings
of bone on bone; straightway his blushing face   1160
blushed with his blood. He'll not return his life
to the queen of archers, his mother, the mountain maid.
When he had seen that this gate was defended,
your son went on, I followed, and I saw
Tydeus, and many shieldmen him beside   1165
dashing Aetolian spears against the front
of our defenses, so that many fled
the outer battlements. But against him too
your son brought on the crowd as a huntsman does
and saved the towers. So to the next gate   1170
we hurried on, having stopped the sickness there.
How can I tell you how Capaneus raged?
For he came with the steps of a long ladder.   1175
This was his boast, that Zeus's awful fire
could not hold him back from overturning the city.
He cried this as they threw the stones against him,
and still climbed up, cowered within his shield,
step after step, the ladder rung by rung.
Just as he reached the cornice of the wall   1180
Zeus struck with lightning, and the earth rang out
so all were frightened. From the ladder he fell,
limbs whirling like a sling. His hair streamed high;
his blood fell down to earth. His arms and legs
went spinning like Ixion on his wheel.   1185
He fell upon the ground a flaming corpse.
When Adrastus saw Zeus was his enemy,
he drew his army back behind the ditch.
But we, who saw the omen on our side,

horsemen and chariots and foot rushed out.   1190
We crashed our spears into their very center;
ruin was everywhere. They died, they fell
down from the chariot's rim. The wheels rebounded.
Axle on axle, corpse on corpse was heaped.   1195
This land's defenses have been kept from ruin
this day. The gods must see if this our land
shall still be fortunate, for some god has saved her.

Chorus

How fair is victory! If the gods have still   1200
a better plan, I'll hope for my own fortune.

Jocasta

The gods and fortune both have served us well.
My sons are alive. The country has escaped.
But Creon, he has reaped a mournful harvest,   1205
who married me to Oedipus. Gone is his son:
good fortune for the town, a grief to him.
Go on and tell me what my son will do.

Messenger

Let be the rest. So far your fortune holds.

Jocasta

Suspicious sayings. This I'll not allow.   1210

Messenger

What more do you want than to know your sons are saved?

Jocasta

To hear if I have happiness in the future.

Messenger

Let me go. Your son's near helper is not with him.

Jocasta

You hide some evil and cover it up in dark.

Messenger

I would not add your sorrows to your gains.   1215

Jocasta

You must, unless you fly away to heaven.

Messenger

Alas, why not have let me leave good news?
Why force me to the bad?
Your sons intend—Oh shamefulness of daring!—
a single combat, severed from the host.   1220
[And they have said to Argives and Cadmeans
words which should never have been said at all.
Eteocles began. High on a tower,
he ordered that the army be called to silence
and said, "O leaders of the land of Hellas,   1225
lords of the Danaans, you who here have come,
and Cadmus' people, not for Polyneices
nor for myself should you exchange your lives.
For I myself, putting this danger off,
alone will join in battle with my brother.   1230
If I kill him, I'll hold my house alone;
if I am worsted, to him alone I'll yield it.
Give up the fight, Argives, and leave the land;
of the Sown Men there are already dead enough.   1235
So much he said, and your son Polyneices
straightway leapt up and praised what he had said.
And all the Argives shouted their approval,
and Cadmus' people, for they thought it just.
So truce was made. In no man's land the chiefs   1240
took solemn oath they would abide by it.
Then did they cover their bodies with brazen arms,
the two young sons of the old Oedipus.
Their friends were dressing them. The Theban lords
saw to our captain, the Argive chiefs the other.   1245
Then they stood shining, and they had not paled.

And from about their friends came up to them,
cheered them with speech and said such words as this:
"Polyneices, now you can set up for Zeus   1250
his triumph-statue and make Argos famed."
To Eteocles: "Now you are fighting for your city,
now if you conquer, you will hold the rule."
Such things they said, exhorting them to battle.
The seers slew sheep and marked the points of flame,   1255
its cleavages, any damp signs of evil,
and that high shining which may have two meanings,
a mark of victory, or of the losing side.]
If you have help or any words of wisdom
or spells of incantation, go, hold back   1260
your children from dread strife. The danger's great.
Your dreadful prize will only be your tears
if you should lose both sons this very day.

(*Exit the messenger.*)

Jocasta

My child Antigone, come outside the house.
No help for you in maidens' works and dances.   1265
The gods have set it so. But those brave men
your brothers, who are rushing on their death,
you and your mother must keep from mutual murder.

(*Enter Antigone from the palace.*)

Antigone

Mother, what new terror for your own   1270
do you cry out before the palace front?

Jocasta

Daughter, your brothers' lives are falling fast.

Antigone

What do you say?

Jocasta

                    They're set for single fight.

Antigone

What will you tell me?

Jocasta

Hard words. Follow me.

Antigone

Where, as I leave my chamber?

Jocasta

To the armies.   1275

Antigone

I fear the crowd.

Jocasta

Modesty will not help.

Antigone

What shall I do?

Jocasta

Undo your brothers' strife.

Antigone

But how?

Jocasta

Prostrate, with me, before them.

Antigone

Lead, Mother, to the plain. We can't delay.

Jocasta

Then hurry, hurry, daughter. If I catch them   1280
before they hurl their spears, my life's in light.
But if they die, I'll lie with them in death.

(*Exeunt Jocasta and Antigone.*)

Chorus

Alas, alas, my shuddering heart!
Pity, pity goes through my flesh.   1285

as I think of that wretched mother.
Which of her children will kill her child
—Oh, the sufferings, Zeus, Oh earth—   1290
cutting his brother's throat, spilling his brother's breath?
and I, poor soul, which corpse shall I lament?

Woe, oh woe, twin beasts!
Bloody spirits, shaking the spear,
how soon they will work their murders!
Unhappy that ever they came to this duel.   1300
With foreign wailings I'll mourn the dead.
The fortune of death is near, the light will show what comes.
Murder the Furies have wrought is a fate beyond all fates.   1305

But I see Creon coming to the house
with clouded face, and break off this lament.

(Enter, from the side, Creon, and attendants
carrying the body of Menoeceus.)

Creon

What shall I do? And do my tears lament   1310
myself, or this poor city, held in gloom
as if it traveled over Acheron.
My child has perished, dying for the land.
The name he leaves is noble, but sad for me.
Just now I took him from the dragon-rocks,   1315
took in my arms my son who killed himself.
My whole house mourns. And I, in my old age,
I come for my old sister, Queen Jocasta,
to lay my son out for his funeral.
For to the dead we who are not yet dead   1320
should pay respect, honoring the god below.

Chorus

Gone is your sister, Creon, from the house.
And with her went the maid Antigone.

Creon

    Where? And what trouble called them? Tell me now.

Chorus

    She heard her sons were planning single fight   1325
    with spear and shield over the royal house.

Creon

    What are you saying? This I had not heard,
    since I was caring for my own son's corpse.

Chorus

    Your sister left the house some time ago.
    I think the mortal combat of those sons,   1330
    Oedipus' sons, is at an end by now.

Creon

    Alas, indeed I see a sign of that.
    The dark and scowling face of one who comes
    to bring the news of everything that's happened.

                        (Enter a messenger, from the side.)

Messenger

    Woe is me, how tell my story or the groaning that I bring?   1335

Creon

    We are ruined, I can tell it from the gloom with which you start.

Messenger

    "Woe is me," I cry again, for the trouble I bring is great.

Creon

    To be heaped upon the suffering we had suffered. What's your
      news?

Messenger

    Creon, your sister's children are no longer in the light.

Creon

Alas! 1340
Great is the sorrow you bring, for me and for the state.
O house of Oedipus, have you heard the news?
Your sons have perished, both in one disaster.

Chorus

The house might weep, if it could understand.

Creon

Alas, disaster, born of heavy fate! 1345
Ah, for my sorrows, how I suffer now!

Messenger

Then do you know the further misery?

Creon

How could there be a worser fate than this?

Messenger

Your sister died along with her two sons.

Chorus

Lead off the wailing, batter your head in mourning 1350
with your fair white arms!

Creon

Jocasta, what an ending to your life,
and to your marriage which that riddle made.
Tell me about the slaughter of the sons,
the working-out in fight of Oedipus' curse. 1355

Messenger

You know our first good fortune before the towers,
for the girdle walls are not so far away
you couldn't see the things that happened there.

When they were ordered in their shining arms,
the two young sons of Oedipus the old,   1360
they rose and went into the middle plain,
the two commanders, the pair of generals,
for the struggle of the single fight in arms.
Looking toward Argos Polyneices prayed,
"O lady Hera, yours I am, since wed   1365
to Adrastus' child and living in your land.
Grant I may kill my brother, so my hand
show sign of victory, my opponent's blood."
He asked a shameful crown, his brother's death.
Tears came to many at fate's monstrosity.   1370
Men slipped their eyes about among the crowd.
Eteocles prayed, looking toward the house
of golden-shielded Pallas, "Daughter of Zeus,
grant me to cast my spear in victory
against my brother's breast from this my arm,   1375
to kill the one who comes to sack my land."
Then the Tyrrhenian trumpet-blast burst forth,
like fire, as the signal for the fight;
they ran a dreadful race at one another
and like wild boars that sharpen their savage teeth   1380
drew close, both foaming slaver down their beards.
Both shook their spears, but drew within their shields
so that the steel might spend itself in vain.
If either saw the other's eye peer up
above the rim, he darted with his spear,
hoping to catch him quickly with its point.   1385
But both were clever, peering through the shield-slits,
so neither's spear was any use at all.
We who were watching sweated more than they,
all fearful for our friends.
Eteocles slipped a little on a stone
that turned beneath his foot. One leg came out   1390
around the shield; and Polyneices struck,

seeing the mark thus offered to his steel.
The Argive spear went cleanly through his calf
and all the Danaan army cried in joy.
And then Eteocles saw his brother's shoulder
bare in the struggle, and he struck at that.
Thebans rejoiced; the spearhead broke off short.
His spear no use, he fell back step by step, 1400
then seized and hurled a rugged rock which broke
his brother's spear, so now on even terms
they stood, since neither had a lance in hand.
Then snatching at the handles of their swords
they came together, and they clashed their shields, 1405
pushed back and forth, and frightful was the noise.
Eteocles, who'd been to Thessaly,
had learned and used a fine Thessalian trick.
He disentangled from their present struggle,
fell with his left foot back, watching his mark 1410
in his foe's belly. Then he jumped ahead
on his right foot and struck him in the navel.
The sword went through and stuck right in the spine.
Stooped over his belly Polyneices falls 1415
with gasps of blood. The victor stuck his sword
into the earth, began to strip his arms.
Not mindful of himself, only of that.
This was his finish. The other had some life left,
had kept his sword all through his painful fall, 1420
scarcely he managed, but he thrust that sword,
he the first-fallen, through his brother's liver.
They bit the dust and lie near one another;
the two did not divide their heritage.

Chorus

O Oedipus, how much I mourn your woes. 1425
It seems a god has now fulfilled your curse.

Messenger

Hear now the woe that followed upon these.
Just as her fallen children left this life
their mother came upon them in her haste,
she in her hurry, with her daughter too.   1430
And when she saw them with their mortal wounds,
she groaned, "O children, I bring help too late."
Falling upon her children, each in turn,
she wept, she mourned them, all her wasted nursing.
Their sister at her side like a warrior's helper   1435
cried, "O supporters of our mother's age,
you have betrayed my marriage, dearest brothers."
Eteocles' hard dying breath was coming
out from his chest, and yet he heard his mother,
laid his damp hand on hers. He could not speak.
But tears fell from his eyes in sign of love.   1440
The other had breath, and looking toward his sister
and his old mother, Polyneices said:
"Mother, we're dead. I pity you indeed,
and this my sister and my brother corpse,   1445
my friend turned enemy, but still my friend.
Mother, and you, my sister, bury me
in my own land. Persuade the angry state
to grant me this much of my father's soil,
though I got not our house. Close up my eyes,   1450
Mother," he said, and put her hand upon them.
"Farewell, the darkness now is closing in."
So both together breathed out their sad lives.
But their mother, when she looked on this disaster   1455
snatched a sword off the corpses and she did
a dreadful deed. Straight through her neck she drove
the steel. So now she lies among her own.
In death her arms are cast about them both.
Then did the people rush to strife of words,   1460
we claiming that my master won the day,

and they the other. The captains quarreled too.
Some claimed that Polyneices' spear struck first,
the others that dead men have no victory.
Meanwhile, Antigone had left the armies.   1465
They rushed for weapons, but by prudent forethought
the Theban host had halted under arms.
So we fell on them not yet in their armor,
swooping upon the Argive host in haste.
No one withstood us, they fled, and filled the plain.   1470
Blood flowed from myriad corpses slain by spears.
When we had conquered, some set up for Zeus
his trophy-statue, others stripped the corpses
and sent the shields as spoil within the walls.   1475
And others, with Antigone, bring the dead
so their own friends may give them mourning here.
Of these sad contests, some have ended well
for this our city, others ill indeed.

> (*Exit the messenger. Enter Antigone with attendants
> bearing the bodies of the brothers and Jocasta.*)

Chorus

No longer for hearing alone   1480
is the city's grief. You may see
the three dead on their way
move to the palace, they who found
together their darkened end.

Antigone

No veil now covers the curls on my delicate cheek,   1485
nor in maiden shame have I hidden the blush on my face,
I come as a bacchant, celebrating death.
I have thrown the veil from my hair, my saffron robe hangs loose. 1490
I bring on the dead with my groans.
O Polyneices, you followed your quarreling name.
Woe it was for Thebes; and your strife which was more than
    strife,   1495

but ended as murder on murder has brought the end
of Oedipus' house in blood.
What singer, what singers, O house,   1500
shall I call for this song of grief,
I who bring three kindred bloodily dead,
mother and children, the Fury's delight?
Delight of her who has ruined the house entire,
Oedipus' house; and the ruin began
when he unriddled the riddling song
of the singing Sphinx and slew her dead.   1505

O Father, woe for you!
What Greek or foreign man of a noble race   1510
in the course of our brief day's life
has suffered so many griefs so clear to see?

My poor self, how my song rings out!
What bird that sits in the oak or the high twigs of the olive   1515
will join my lamenting, alone, without my mother,   1520
helping the song of my grief.
Woe for the wailings with which I mourn,
I who shall live my life alone
among my falling tears.

On which of them first shall I cast my shorn-off hair?   1525
On my mother's breasts where I drew my milk,
or the horrible wounds of my brethren?

Oh, oh, come forth from the house,   1530
with your blinded face,
old father Oedipus, show your wretched age,
you who drag out long life
there in the house after casting the dark on your eyes.   1535

(*Enter, from the palace, Oedipus.*)

Oedipus

Why have you brought me forth to the light,   1540
dragging my blindness along on a stick,

with your pitiful tears, from my bed in the dark,
a gray, invisible ghost of the air, a corpse, a flying dream?   1545

Antigone

You must hear the telling of dreadful news.
Father, your sons are dead.
And so is the wife who tended and guided your stumbling steps,
O Father, woe is me.   1550

Oedipus

Woe for my frightful griefs. One must moan, one must cry aloud.
Three lives gone! My child,
how did they leave the light, what was the fate that fell?

Antigone

Not in reproach do I say it, nor glad at your grief,   1555
but in simple sorrow: the venging power of your curse,
heavy with swords and fire and wicked fightings, fell,
Father, on your sons.

Oedipus

Alas!

Antigone

Why this lament?   1560

Oedipus

My children!

Antigone

You are in grief.
But, Father, if you could see the chariot of the sun
and cast your eyes on these corpses!

Oedipus

It's clear what disaster came on my sons.   1565
But what doom struck down my wife?

Antigone

She showed all men her groaning tears.
She went to her sons as a suppliant, to adjure them by her breast.
Wielding their spears in war with each other,
their mother she found them like lions wild.
There in the flowering meadow, beside Electra's gate,   1570
they were fighting and wounded; already the blood
was running to make them cold.   1575
Hades' libation, which Ares grants.
So taking the bronze-hammered sword from the dead,
she plunged it in flesh, and in grief for her sons,
she fell on her sons.
The god who brought this about
has brought together all of these griefs for our house,   1580
Father, in one short day.

Chorus

This day has started very many sorrows
for Oedipus' house. May later life be better!

Creon

Cease from your mourning. Now it is the time
to think of burial. Oedipus, hear this speech: 1585
Eteocles, your son, gave me the rule
over this land, and made that rule the dowry
for Haemon's marriage with Antigone.
I will not let you live here any more,
for clearly has Teiresias said that never,   1590
while you are here, can the city prosper well.
So, on your way! This proclamation comes
not as an insult, nor am I your enemy.
I simply fear that the Avengers who pursue you
may yet do damage to our fatherland.

Oedipus

O fate, you bred me wretched from the start,   1595
for suffering, if ever mortal was.
Before I came to light from my mother's womb
Apollo prophesied that I, the unborn,
should kill my father—suffering indeed.
Once I was born, the father who begot me,
counting me as his enemy, tried to kill me   1600
since he must die through me, and so he sent me,
still a breast-loving baby, to be food
for the wild beasts.
There was I saved. Cithaeron, you should sink
in the depthless chasms of the underworld,   1605
you who did not destroy me, but your spirit
gave me in servitude to Polybus.
So when, ill-fated, I had killed my father,
I came into my wretched mother's bed
and begot brothers whom I now have killed,   1610
passing on to my children Laius' curse.
For I am not so foolish in my nature
as to do what I did to my eyes, and to their lives,
if it were not some god who had contrived it.
Well, what's to do now with my wretched self?   1615
Who is to guide the blind man? She who's dead?
Full well I know, were she alive, she would.
Or my good pair of sons? They are no more.
Am I still young enough to make my living?
From what? Creon, why kill me utterly?
For you are killing me if you cast me out.   1620
Yet I'll not clutch your knees and prove a coward.
Even in misery, I won't betray my birth.

Creon

It is well thought of not to grasp my knees;   1625
I could not let you live within this land.
Now, of these dead, the one must straight be taken

into the house. The other, he who came
to sack his fatherland with alien help,
that Polyneices do you cast unburied
beyond the boundaries of his fatherland.   1630
And this shall be proclaimed to all the Thebans:
"Whoever lays a wreath upon this corpse
or buries him, shall find reward in death.
Leave him unwept, unburied, food for the birds."
And you, Antigone, leave your triple dirge   1635
and come within the house. For one more day
you shall be maiden, but tomorrow Haemon
and marriage are for you.

Antigone

Father, what wretchedness is on us now!
I mourn for you still more than for the dead.   1640
For yours is not mixed grief heavy and light;
but you are perfect in your misery.
    But you, new ruler, I would ask you this:
Why wrong my father, sending him from the land?
Why lay down laws against this pitiful corpse?   1645

Creon

Eteocles' this decision, and not mine.

Antigone

Senseless. And you a fool to follow it.

Creon

Is it not right to do what is commanded?

Antigone

Not when wrong deeds are wickedly laid down.

Creon

Is it not right to give him to the dogs?   1650

Antigone

The punishment you seek is not the law's.

Creon

It is, for a foe who should have been our friend.

Antigone

Therefore he yielded up his life to fortune.

Creon

And therefore let him yield his burial.

Antigone

What wrong, if you should give him his share of earth?   1655

Creon

Be sure, this man is going to lie unburied.

Antigone

Then I shall bury him, though the state forbids.

Creon

Then will you bury yourself close by that corpse.

Antigone

It's glorious that two friends should lie together.

Creon

Lay hold on her and take her to the house.   1660

Antigone

Oh no! I will not loose my hold on him.

Creon

The gods' these judgments, and not yours, my girl.

Antigone

And it is not judged right to assault a corpse.

Creon

No one shall lay the damp dust over him.

Antigone

They must. I pray it for Jocasta's sake. 1665

Creon

You work in vain. You cannot get your wish.

Antigone

At least allow me but to bathe his body.

Creon

This too shall be forbidden by the state.

Antigone

But then to bandage up his savage wounds.

Creon

There is no tendance you may give this corpse. 1670

Antigone

O dearest, but at least I kiss your mouth.

Creon

Don't mar your marriage with these lamentations.

Antigone

Do you think that living I will wed your son?

Creon

You'll be forced to it. What refuge from his bed?

Antigone

That night will make me one with the Danaids. 1675

Creon (to Oedipus)

Do you see the daring of her insolence?

Antigone

    Let the steel know. My oath is by the sword.

Creon

    Why do you wish so to avoid this marriage?

Antigone

    I'll go to exile with my wretched father.

Creon

    You show nobility, as well as folly.   1680

Antigone

    And know you well that I will die with him.

Creon

    Go! You'll not kill my son. Now leave the land.

                     (Exit Creon into the palace.)

Oedipus

    Daughter, I praise your loving zeal for me.

Antigone

    How could I marry and send you alone to exile?

Oedipus

    Stay and be happy. I will bear my woes.   1685

Antigone

    But you are blind. Who'll care for you, my father?

Oedipus

    Where fate decides it I will fall and lie.

Antigone

    Ah, where is Oedipus and his famous riddle?

Oedipus

Perished. One day, my fortune and my fall.

Antigone

Should I not have some part in all your troubles?   1690

Oedipus

Exile with a blind father is disgrace.

Antigone

Not for the dutiful. Then it is an honor.

Oedipus

Now lead me forward, that I may touch your mother.

Antigone

There. Lay your hand upon your aged dear.

Oedipus

O Mother, O unhappy wife of mine!   1695

Antigone

She lies there piteous, having suffered all.

Oedipus

Where is Eteocles' corpse, and Polyneices'?

Antigone

Here lie they, stretched out close to one another.

Oedipus

Put my unseeing hand upon their faces.

Antigone

There. Lay your hand upon your sons in death.   1700

Oedipus

O dear dead sons, unhappy as your father!

Antigone

    O Polyneices, dearest name to me.

Oedipus

    Now Loxias' doom is working to its end.

Antigone

    What is it? Further woes on top of woes?

Oedipus

    That, wandering, I shall die on Attic soil.   1705

Antigone

    Where? Which of Athens' forts will shelter you?

Oedipus

    It will be Colonus, where the horse-god lives.
    But come, help your blind father on his way,
    since you are eager to be exiled with me.

Antigone

    On to our exile. Father, stretch out your hand.   1710
    I help your steps as the wind helps on the ship.

Oedipus

    I come, I come.
    Oh my poor child, now lead me.

Antigone

    I do, I do, most wretched I,
    of all the girls of Thebes.

Oedipus

    Where shall I set my old foot?   1715
    Daughter, give me my staff.

Antigone

> This way, this way, with me.
> Like this, like this, your feet.   1720
> Your strength is like a dream.

Oedipus

> Oh you, Oh you, who are driving an ancient man
> in exile from his land.
> What terrible things I have suffered!   1725

Antigone

> Why of your suffering speak? Justice regards not the wicked.
> She gives no prizes for folly.

Oedipus

> And I am the one who reached the heights of song.
> When I found out the maiden's riddle, no fool was I. 1730

Antigone

> You go back to the Sphinx, and our shame.
> Stop speaking of past good fortune.
> There awaits you pitiful suffering   1735
> and, somewhere, an exile's death.
>
> And I leave tears for the girls my friends
> as I part from my fatherland
> to wander, unmaidened.

Oedipus

> Alas for your honest heart!   1740

Antigone

> It will give me fame as great as my father's sorrows.
> I mourn for your wrongs, and for those which are done my
>   brother,
> who goes from the house a corpse to lie unburied.

Father, even if I must die,
in secret I'll bury that body.   1745

Oedipus

Return again to your friends!

Antigone

My own laments are enough.

Oedipus

You can pray to the holy altars.

Antigone

They have had enough of my troubles.   1750

Oedipus

Then go to Bacchus' shrine in the hills
where none but the Maenads are!

Antigone

To go where once I went
in Theban fawnskin clad,
and danced in Semele's holy choir!
It would be no grace I should do the gods.

Oedipus

You that live in my ancestral Thebes, behold this Oedipus,
him who knew the famous riddles and who was a man most
    great.
It was I alone put down the murdering power of the Sphinx.   1760
Now it's I who go dishonored in sad exile from the land.
Yet why do I lament these things and mourn for them in vain?
The constraint the gods lay on us we mortals all must bear.

Chorus

O great Victory, stay with me
all my life.
Nor cease to give me crowns!

THE BACCHAE

Translated and with an Introduction by William Arrowsmith

INTRODUCTION TO *THE BACCHAE*

In 408, at the age of seventy, apparently bitter and broken in spirit, Euripides left Athens for voluntary exile at the court of Archelaus in Macedon; and there, in 406, he died. After his death his three last plays—*The Bacchae, Iphigenia at Aulis,* and the (lost) *Alcmaeon at Corinth*—were brought back to Athens by the dramatist's son, Euripides the Younger, and produced, winning for their dead author the prize so frequently denied him during his lifetime.

Of itself *The Bacchae* needs neither apology nor general introduction. It is, clearly and flatly, that unmistakable thing, a masterpiece; a play which, for dramatic turbulence and comprehensiveness and the sheer power of its poetry, is unmatched by any except the very greatest among ancient and modern tragedies. You have to go to the *Oedipus Tyrannus* or the *Agamemnon* or *Lear* to find anything quite like it in range and power, and even then it remains, of course, unique. But like those plays, *The Bacchae* is finally a mysterious, almost a haunted, work, stalked by divinity and that daemonic power of necessity which for Euripides is the careless source of man's tragic destiny and moral dignity. Elusive, complex and compelling, the play constantly recedes before one's grasp, advancing, not retreating, steadily into deeper chaos and larger order, coming finally to rest only god knows where—which is to say, where it matters.

At the very least then *The Bacchae* requires of its critics gentleness in approaching it and humility in handling; the reader who is not willing to follow where the play, rather than his prejudice, leads him forfeits his quarry. But *sophrosunē* is not a common critical virtue, and despite the critic's clear warning in the fate of Pentheus, the play has suffered more than most from the violence of its interpreters. Perhaps this was only to be expected; because *The Bacchae* is concerned with extreme religious experience, it has naturally engaged the liveliest prejudices of its readers. Thus, apart from the pathologies of criticism, we find a long strain of (peculiarly Christianizing) interpretation which insists, against all probability and the whole experience of the play, that *The Bacchae* is to be understood as a deathbed conversion to the mysteries of Dionysus—Euripides' palinode, as it were, for a lifetime of outspoken hostility to the Olympian system. In revenge, this absurd view was challenged by an even absurder one which, by casting Dionysus as a devil and Pentheus as a noble martyr to human enlightenment, turned the play into a nineteenth-century rationalist tract on the evils of religion. Alternatively, the play has been viewed as a stark schematic conflict between any two of a variety of contrasted abstractions apparently symbolized by Pentheus and Dionysus: reason vs. the irrational; aristocratic skepticism vs. popular piety; civilized order and routine vs. the eruptive force of nature and life. What, in my opinion, vitiates these interpretations is that they are all, or nearly all, incomplete perceptions masking as the whole thing. And like all partial perceptions or half-truths, these are maintained by rejecting whatever in the experience of the play cannot accommodate them; in this way the true power that stalks the play has mostly been expelled or shrouded in a fresh and imposed chaos. Taken in their ensemble, however, these partial perceptions help to round out the whole. For look at the play again and surely what one sees is neither a rationalist tract nor Euripides' dying *confiteor* to Olympus but a play which is moved by profoundly religious feeling and which also happens to display Euripides' familiar hostility to received religion. The inconsistency is only apparent; for in the nature of god as it is defined by the action of the play, the contradictions vanish. Or so I see it. And yet there is more there too.

A few cautions will perhaps be in order. The subject of *The Bacchae* is a (dimly) historical event, the invasion of Hellas by the rites of Dionysus, while the story of Pentheus is Euripides' re-enactment of a myth which doubtlessly embodied Dionysiac ritual.[1] Despite this, *The Bacchae* is neither a study of Dionysiac *cultus* nor a cautionary essay on the effects of religious hysteria; nor, for that matter, however faithfully it may present the *hieros logos* or sacred myth of Dionysiac ritual, is it best read as an anthropological passion-play of the mystical scapegoat or the Year-Daimon. Dionysiac religion is the field on which the action of the play takes place, *not* what

[1] The story of Pentheus provided the subject of several ancient tragedies, including a trilogy by Aeschylus.

it is deeply about, and although the play requires a reasonable knowledge about the phenomena of religious ecstasy we call Dionysiac,[2] for the most part it supplies the necessary information and dictates the meaning of its own terms. If we understand that the rewards of the Dionysiac life are here and now, that the frenzied dances of the god are direct manifestations of ecstatic possession, and that the Bacchante, by eating the flesh of the man or animal who temporarily incarnates the god, comes to partake of his divinity, we are in a position to understand the play. One should also perhaps be aware that the view of Dionysiac worship presented by this play is a special one, clearly shaped by the dramatist's needs and modified accordingly; indeed he elaborately warns his fifth-century contemporaries that they must not confound their own experience of Dionysiac worship with that of the play. Thus, for example, against the suspicions of his contemporaries that the Dionysiac mountain-rites were frequently orgiastic in the modern sense of that word, Euripides insists that *his* Bacchae are chaste, and this must be taken as final for the play. Elsewhere he deliberately intrudes anachronism, allowing Teiresias to describe Dionysus pretty much as the fifth century knew his worship: its human sacrifices purged away, its wildness tamed by being fused with Olympian worship and set under state supervision. Beyond this, one should, of course, be aware of the intentional ritual irony that underlies the death of Pentheus—he dies as a scapegoat and a living substitute for the god he rejects. This, however, is an irony of the play, not its meaning, and it is overshadowed by the greatest irony of them all—that this terrible indictment of the anthropomorphic Dionysus that *The Bacchae* makes should have been acted out in the *hieros logos* of the god and presented in the Theater of Dionysus.

Like a number of other Euripidean plays, *The Bacchae* tends to converge about a single central controlling moral term whose meaning is constantly invoked by the action and at the same time altered by it, modified and refreshed under dramatic pressure. This key term is the concept of *sophia* (and its opposite, *amathia*). Constantly

[2] Those interested should consult the Introduction to the Commentary of E. R. Dodds on *The Bacchae* (Oxford, 1944).

thrown up by the action, informing it and guiding it, *sophia* is crucial to the play; but since it is impossible to convey its range of
meaning by a single English equivalent, the reader should know
what is involved when it occurs. At its broadest, *sophia* is roughly
translatable by the English concept of "wisdom"; *sophia*, that is, is
primarily a moral rather than an intellectual skill, based upon experience and expressed in significant judgment. But in the Greek—and
nowhere more strongly than in the choruses of this play—it implies
a firm awareness of one's own nature and therefore of one's place in
the scheme of things. In other words, it presupposes self-knowledge,
an acceptance of those necessities that compose the limits of human
fate; by contrast, the man of *amathia* acts out of a kind of unteach-
able, ungovernable ignorance of himself and his necessities; he is
prone to violence, harshness, and brutality. Thus, in the eyes of the
Chorus, Pentheus forfeits any claim to *sophia* because he wantonly,
violently, refuses to accept the necessity that Dionysus incarnates: he
is, in other words, *amathēs*.

Below the level of this broad sense of *sophia*, however, the range
of meaning in the Greek word is extremely wide. For if *sophia* is
generically what we mean by wisdom, it is also skill, craft, cleverness, know-how, cunning, smartness, and the specific craft of expedience (in this sense exactly matching one of the commoner uses
of the English word "wise"). And so the play exhibits the spectrum
of these various *sophiae* classified roughly in terms of the characters,
their pretensions and what others think of them. Thus Teiresias possesses the narrow professional *sophia* (i.e., skill, expertise) of the sage
and seer, and also shares with Cadmus the more general "wisdom"
of ripe old age and long experience. In the Chorus' eyes, Pentheus'
sophia is that of (mere) cleverness: the quick, articulate, argumenta-
tive, shallow cleverness of the trained sophist or "professional intellectual." And finally, lowest of all, there is the knowing animal
cunning of the practiced hunter, the cool eye and feline skill of
Dionysus stalking his intended victim. Elsewhere the Chorus dis-
tinguishes something called *to sophon* which it contrasts unfavorably
with high *sophia;* and I think we must understand this to be something like a rubric for the lower *sophiae* or whatever in them con-

tributes to compose the sense of "worldly wisdom," a calculating, shrewd, even opportunistic, skill of the worldly and ambitious, which blinds its possessor to the good that comes—to the Chorus' way of thinking—from acceptance here and now. But over the surface of these meanings of *sophia* the action plays endlessly, testing one *sophia* against another, matching opponents in a steady rage of exposure that in the end inverts all roles and pretensions and leaves the stage, desolate and bleak, to the suffering survivors confronted with the inexorable, pitiless necessity that Dionysus is. We witness, that is, a life and death struggle between rival shapes of *sophia* in the course of which each claimant betrays the thing he stands for: Pentheus' cleverness foundering terribly upon the force he refuses to accept; the *sophia* of the Dionysiac quest nakedly revealed as sheer animal cunning and brutality. We witness, in short, *sophia* becoming *amathia*. There, in *amathia*, the god and his victim meet.

Dramatically, the core of the play is an exquisitely constructed confrontation between the two major opponents, the young god Dionysus and the young man Pentheus. The contrasting itself seems almost schematic: the athletic Pentheus pitted against the languid god; traditional Greek dress contrasted with the outlandish Asiatic livery of the Bacchante; the angry, impetuous, heavy-handed young man as against the smiling, soft-spoken, feline effortlessness of Dionysus; the self-ignorant man confronted with the humanized shape of his necessity. Below the contrasts run the resemblances, for these young rivals, we need to remember, are first cousins and they share a family likeness. Thus each is deeply jealous of his own *personal* honor and ruthless in enmity; each is intolerant of opposition to his will. The god, of course, in the end prevails, but the drama of the god's gradual usurpation of his victim depends for its effectiveness and irony upon our understanding of the initial confrontation. For it is by playing upon Pentheus' vulnerability, his deep ignorance of his own nature, that the god is able to possess him, humiliate him and finally to destroy him. For Dionysus, the motives of humiliation and revenge are crucial; and Dionysus is a supreme artist in exact poetic vengeance. Thus, point for point, each of Pentheus' threats, insults, and outrages is revenged with ironic and ferocious precision as Pentheus goes off, waving his thyrsus, tricked out in woman's robes and a fawn-skin, to his death on the mountain as the sacrificial surrogate of the god. We see in his costume and madness not merely his complete humiliation but the total loss of identity the change implies. And so the reversal is complete, the hunter become the hunted and the hunted the hunter.

If we consider Pentheus in isolation, it should be immediately apparent that his is not the stuff of which tragic heroes are made. Nor, for that matter, is he a convincing candidate to symbolize reason against the Dionysiac irrational. He is, in fact, a deeply unreasonable man, intemperate in anger and utterly unconvinced by reasonable evidence. Around him cluster almost all the harsh words of the Greek moral vocabulary: he is violent, stubborn, self-willed, arbitrary, impatient of tradition and custom, impious, unruly, and immoderate. At times he evinces the traits of a stock tragedy-tyrant, loud with threats and bluster, prone to confuse the meaning of subject with slave. But so, I think, he must be shown in order to be presented for what he is: ignorant of himself and his nature, profoundly *amathēs*. Yet as he makes his entrance, breathing fury against the Maenads, I think we are meant to be struck by his extreme youth. Just how old he is, Euripides does not tell us; but since he is presented as still a beardless boy at the time of his death (see ll. 1185 ff.), he cannot very well be much more than sixteen or seventeen. And this youth seems to me dramatically important, helping to qualify Pentheus' prurient sexual imagination (for the voyeurism which in a grown man would be overtly pathological is at most an obsessive and morbid curiosity in a boy) and later serving to enlist our sympathies sharply on the side of the boy-victim of a ruthless god. Pentheus' *hybris*, of course, remains, for ignorance of one's identity and necessities is finally no excuse. And yet, in the Greek view of things, extreme youth should help to extenuate the offense. For the young are naturally susceptible to *hybris*, that simple overflow of the dangerous pride (or the suppressed strength) of the flesh and spirit into outrage and violence; and, being susceptible, they merit both understanding and lenience. *Sophia*, after all, is not a young man's virtue, and though necessity may be inflexible, our humanity is not. However much Pentheus' conduct may outrage sympathy, his youth and utter human helplessness before the awful shape of his necessity are addressed directly to our understanding and compassion.

But Pentheus is something more than a mere personification of suppressed necessity, and his *hybris* has social as well as sexual roots. At least it seems to me that Euripides has taken elaborate pains to show in Pentheus the proud iconoclastic innovator, rebelling against tradition, outside of the community's *nomos* (custom as law), and disdainful of any power above man. Ranged against him are Cadmus, Teiresias, and the Chorus, who all alike appeal to the massive authority of tradition and folk-belief and constantly invoke against the scoffer the full force of *dikē* (custom incarnate as justice) and *sophrosunē* (very roughly, humility). Thus in flat ominous opposition to Pentheus' lonely arrogance of the "exceptional" (*perissos*) individual, superior and contemptuous, defying the community's *nomos* in the name of his own self-will, is set the chorus' tyrannous tradition: "Beyond the old beliefs, no thought, no act shall go" (ll. 891–92). We have, that is, a head-on collision between those who, for all their piety, represent the full-blown tyranny of popular custom and conforming tradition and the arrogant exemplar of the ruthlessly antitraditional mind. Both sides are alike in the cruel and bigoted violence with which they meet opposition and the *sophrosunē* and *dikē* and *sophia* which they variously claim mock their pretensions and implicitly condemn their conduct. If in the end the conduct of the Chorus and Dionysus outrage our sympathies and enlist them on Pentheus' behalf, it is because, in the nature of things, the *amathia* of a man is less heinous than that of a god. But both are *amatheis*, Pentheus and Dionysus alike. Beyond this point certainty is impossible. But I suspect that the play employs Dionysus and Pentheus and the conflict between them as a bitter image of Athens and Hellas terribly divided between the forces that, for Euripides, more than anything else destroyed them: on the one side, the conservative tradition in its extreme corruption, disguising avarice for power with the fair professions of the traditional *aretai*, meeting all opposition with the terrible tyranny of popular piety, and disclosing in its actions the callousness and refined cruelty of civilized barba-

rism; on the other side, the exceptional individual, selfish and ego-
tistical, impatient of tradition and public welfare alike, stubborn,
demagogic, and equally brutal in action. This interpretation, however, should not be pressed; if it is there at all, it is tenuously, sugges-
tively there, informing the terms of a social conflict between Pentheus and Dionysus' followers which is otherwise unexplained.

Dionysus himself is a difficult figure only, I think, because he is
so clearly a transitional one, a figure which under dramatic pressure
is in the process of becoming something quite different from what he
was at the outset. What the divinity of Dionysus represents, however, should be clear enough from the play: the incarnate life-force
itself, the uncontrollable chaotic eruption of nature in individuals
and cities; the thrust of the sap in the tree and the blood in the veins,
the "force that through the green fuse drives the flower." As such,
he is amoral, neither good nor bad, a necessity capable of blessing
those who (like the Asian Bacchantes) accept him, and of destroying or maddening those who (like Pentheus) deny him. Like any
necessity, he is ambiguous, raw power: his *thyrsus* spurts honey for
the bands of the blessed but becomes a killing weapon when turned
against the scoffer. But to the question, Is Dionysus a traditional
"Olympian" deity or is he the amoral and daemonic personification
of the force he represents? the answer, I think, is clearly that he is,
at different times, both. If he begins the play as a conventional, anthropomorphic deity of the Homeric type, endowed with human
virtues and human passions, he undergoes a progress which more
and more forces him into the shape of the amoral necessity he represents and which culminates in his final epiphany as a pitiless, daemonic, necessitous power. In the withering of his traditional *sophia*
through the dramatic demonstration that his only *sophia* is the cunning of the hunter, his traditional divinity also withers. For divinity
divested of morality becomes daemonic (not devilish but the reality
of awful, inscrutable, careless power), like Dionysus here. Just so,.in
the *Hippolytus*, we can see coming into focus beneath the lineaments
of the Olympian Aphrodite the inexorable, amoral face of the nar-
rowly sexual necessity of man and nature. It needs, however, to be
insisted that these personified necessities of the Euripidean stage are

not mere naturalistic psychological symbols. They are precisely *daimones*, the great powers that stalk the world, real with a terrible reality, the source of man's very condition, the necessities which determine his life. And if the feelings stirred by what is limited before the unlimited are religious, then man's attitude toward these *daimones* is religious, the veneration and awe the fated must feel before the great gods of existence: Death, Life, Sex, Grief, Joy. *Sophia* accepts because it is a wisdom of experience, based on awe learned of both joy and bitter suffering.

Grouped about Dionysus and Pentheus, variously informing their struggle or suffering its consequences, stand the other characters of the play—Teiresias, Cadmus, Agave, and the Chorus of Asian Bacchantes. Of these Agave has been put here almost entirely to suffer, and the very extremity and brutality of what she suffers is unmistakably intended to expose the brutal ferocity of Dionysus. For it is in her person and through her words as she moves from the terrible irony of her triumphal entrance to one of the cruelest (and finest) recognition scenes in tragedy that the balance of sympathies shifts decisively against Dionysus, exposing him for what he is; *this*, she cries ecstatically, holding up the head of her dismembered son, is the quarry of the chase, the great Dionysiac hunt for "those great, those manifest, those certain goals, achieving which our lives are blest." Where Pentheus' passion ends, hers begins, even more terrible than his, driving us relentlessly on to the true epiphany of the god. What god, we want to know, no matter what provocation, could make a mother dismember her son and still retain his *sophia*? And the answer, of course, is: no god but necessity, which is not wise and, though divine, has no altars.

Teiresias and Cadmus, however, are more problematic. Each, as we have seen, claims a distinctive *sophia* and yet they fail to convince us. In part, this is due to the deliberate pathos and incongruity of their entrance: two doddering old men in fawn-skins off to the dances on the mountain. But although they hover on the edge of comedy, they are not funny but pathetic: two incongruous, shrewd old mummers of ecstasy. For they are not, we soon discover, among the number of those who dance in the sheer conviction of delight, their bodies possessed and compelled by the inward god—though they would like to convince both us and each other that they are so possessed. They dance in shrewd expedience, Cadmus realistically aware of the value of having a god in the family, Teiresias sensing the future greatness of the new religion and the opportunities for priestly expertise. Piously, self-righteously, they go through the motions of accepting their necessity; but if elated at first by their role and costume, they make their exit in a state of near exhaustion, propping each other up and limping off, a long way from ecstasy. And there is irony again, of course, when Teiresias, affecting the role of staunch traditionalist, lectures Pentheus on the nature of Dionysus with the pedantic etymologizing zeal of a professional sophist. But their function here is to occupy the mean of worldly wisdom (*to sophon*) between the *sophia* claimed by the Chorus and the *amathia* of Pentheus. They are trimmers and compromisers, true men of the mean, set in sharp contrast to Pentheus, who, contemptuous of any compromise, temperamentally inhabits extreme positions. As such they round out the range of attitudes which center on Dionysus: the utter possessed madness of the Theban women on the mountain which is typified by Agave; the calmer, more reflective worship of the Chorus of Asian Bacchae; the worldly compromising temper of the two old men, and the passionate and sweeping denial of the god by Pentheus.

The Chorus here deserves mention also, all the more since its role as Bacchante has necessarily been modified by its choral and dramatic functions. For it is from their lips—impressively confirmed and amplified by the two messengers—that we get what is so crucial to the play, the full poetic resonance of the Dionysiac life; in the sweep and beauty of their language we are meant to feel what Dionysus means for suffering mortality, the direct eruption of deity in blessing and miracle. Dionysus, as we have seen, is ambivalent: "most terrible, and yet most gentle, to mankind." The exodus of the play emphasizes the terrible aspect of the god, and so it is important for dramatic balance that the gentle side of Dionysus be given the fullest possible statement. Moreover, we can believe the Chorus, for, unlike the Maenads on the mountain, the Bacchantes of the Chorus are not possessed. A divinity, true, moves in their words, but less as a chaotic wildness than as a controlled and passionate conviction. Indeed, at times these foreign women seem to be surprisingly Hellenized and their sentiments indistinguishable from those of a standard tragic chorus. They tend to alternate, that is, between a feverish (Asiatic) hymning of the god and slow, reflective, traditional (Greek) gnomes on the nature of divinity and the dangers of disobedience. This duality *may* derive from their double role as dramatic Chorus and followers of Dionysus, or it may be that Euripides is anxious to set before us an image of that controlled Dionysiac experience with which the fifth century was familiar. For by means of this anachronism, he can, without deeply violating dramatic consistency, show the point at which the convinced (but not possessed) Bacchante can separate her humanity from the god. Just this, of course, takes place at the end of the play, and its importance should not be minimized. For, despite their having danced for joy at the death of Pentheus, the Chorus, when finally confronted by Agave bearing Pentheus' head on her *thyrsus*, is moved to unmistakable horror and pity. In their feelings, they clearly separate themselves from the god with whom they have hitherto identified themselves completely. Bacchantes they may be, the scene seems to say, but they are human first. Against Dionysus who shows himself utterly inflexible and ruthless to the end, their reaction is decisive. And the tone of pity sets the stage for the all-important exodus.

For what we see in the exodus is, I think, the discovery of compassion, and in this the exodus of *The Bacchae* follows good Euripidean precedent. One thinks of the *Hippolytus* (so much like *The Bacchae* in so many ways) where, under the yoke of another inflexible necessity, compassion and understanding flower between Theseus and the dying Hippolytus; or of *Heracles* and the same discovery of love and need between the anguished hero and his friend and his father in the face of the bleak necessity of a careless, ruthless heaven. So here, beneath the inexorable harshness of that necessity called Dionysus, out of their anguish and suffering, Agave and Cadmus discover compassion, the pity that is born from shared suffering. In this they declare their humanity and a moral dignity which heaven, lacking those limits which make men suffer *into* dignity and compassion, can never understand or equal. This is their moral victory, the only victory the doomed can claim over the necessities which make them suffer. But it is a great victory; for by accepting their necessities in anguish, they claim the uniquely human skill of *sophia*, the acceptance of necessity and doom which teaches compassion.[3] It is that faith and that fate which, in Euripides, makes man human, not mere god.

The text of my translation is the Oxford text of Gilbert Murray, supplemented by the brilliant commentary of E. R. Dodds.

[3] Cf. Euripides' *Electra*, ll. 294–95, where Orestes states that pity (*to oiktos*) is never found among the *amatheis* but only among the wise (*sophoisi*).

CHARACTERS

Dionysus (also called Bromius, Evius, and Bacchus)

Chorus of Asian Bacchae (followers of Dionysus)

Teiresias

Cadmus

Pentheus

Attendant

First Messenger

Second Messenger

Agave

Coryphaeus (chorus leader)

For Anne and George
ex voto
XAIPETE

THE BACCHAE

SCENE: *Before the royal palace at Thebes. On the left is the way to Cithaeron; on the right, to the city. In the center of the orchestra stands, still smoking, the vine-covered tomb of Semele, mother of Dionysus.*

Enter Dionysus. He is of soft, even effeminate, appearance. His face is beardless; he is dressed in a fawn-skin and carries a thyrsus (i.e., a stalk of fennel tipped with ivy leaves). On his head he wears a wreath of ivy, and his long blond curls ripple down over his shoulders. Throughout the play he wears a smiling mask.

Dionysus

I am Dionysus, the son of Zeus,
come back to Thebes, this land where I was born.
My mother was Cadmus' daughter, Semele by name,
midwived by fire, delivered by the lightning's
blast.
     And here I stand, a god incognito,
disguised as man, beside the stream of Dirce   5
and the waters of Ismenus. There before the palace
I see my lightning-married mother's grave,
and there upon the ruins of her shattered house
the living fire of Zeus still smolders on
in deathless witness of Hera's violence and rage
against my mother. But Cadmus wins my praise: 10
he has made this tomb a shrine, sacred to my mother.
It was I who screened her grave with the green
of the clustering vine.
          Far behind me lie
those golden-rivered lands, Lydia and Phrygia,
where my journeying began. Overland I went,
across the steppes of Persia where the sun strikes hotly
down, through Bactrian fastness and the grim waste   15
of Media. Thence to rich Arabia I came;

and so, along all Asia's swarming littoral
of towered cities where Greeks and foreign nations,
mingling, live, my progress made. There
I taught my dances to the feet of living men,
establishing my mysteries and rites
that I might be revealed on earth for what I am:
a god.
        And thence to Thebes.

                        This city, first   20
in Hellas, now shrills and echoes to my women's cries,
their ecstasy of joy. Here in Thebes
I bound the fawn-skin to the women's flesh and armed
their hands with shafts of ivy. For I have come   25
to refute that slander spoken by my mother's sisters—
those who least had right to slander her.
They said that Dionysus was no son of Zeus,
but Semele had slept beside a man in love
and fathered off her shame on Zeus—a fraud, they sneered,   30
contrived by Cadmus to protect his daughter's name.
They said she lied, and Zeus in anger at that lie
blasted her with lightning.
                        Because of that offense
I have stung them with frenzy, hounded them from home
up to the mountains where they wander, crazed of mind,
and compelled to wear my orgies' livery.
Every woman in Thebes—but the women only—   35
I drove from home, mad. There they sit,
rich and poor alike, even the daughters of Cadmus,
beneath the silver firs on the roofless rocks.
Like it or not, this city must learn its lesson:
it lacks initiation in my mysteries;   40
that I shall vindicate my mother Semele
and stand revealed to mortal eyes as the god
she bore to Zeus.
                        Cadmus the king has abdicated,
leaving his throne and power to his grandson Pentheus;

who now revolts against divinity, in *me;*   45
thrusts *me* from his offerings; forgets *my* name
in his prayers. Therefore I shall *prove* to him
and every man in Thebes that I am god
indeed. And when my worship is established here,
and all is well, then I shall go my way
and be revealed to other men in other lands.   50
But if the men of Thebes attempt to force
my Bacchae from the mountainside by threat of arms,
I shall marshal my Maenads and take the field.
To these ends I have laid my deity aside
and go disguised as man.

                   (*He wheels and calls offstage.*)

               On, my women,   55
women who worship me, women whom I led
out of Asia where Tmolus heaves its rampart
over Lydia!
           On, comrades of my progress here!
Come, and with your native Phrygian drum—
Rhea's drum and mine—pound at the palace doors   60
of Pentheus! Let the city of Thebes behold you,
while I return among Cithaeron's forest glens
where my Bacchae wait and join their whirling dances.

       (*Exit Dionysus as the Chorus of Asian Bacchae comes*
               dancing in from the right. They are dressed in
                  fawn-skins, crowned with ivy, and carry
                      thyrsi, timbrels, and flutes.)

Chorus

    Out of the land of Asia,
    down from holy Tmolus,   65
    speeding the service of god,
    for Bromius we come!
    Hard are the labors of god;
    hard, but his service is sweet.
    Sweet to serve, sweet to cry:
               Bacchus!   *Evohé!*

—You on the streets!
        —You on the roads!
                —Make way!
—Let every mouth be hushed. Let no ill-omened words   70
  profane your tongues.
              —Make way! Fall back!
                      —Hush.
—For now I raise the old, old hymn to Dionysus.

—Blessèd, blessèd are those who know the mysteries of god.
—Blessèd is he who hallows his life in the worship of god,
  he whom the spirit of god possesseth, who is one
  with those who belong to the holy body of god.   75
—Blessèd are the dancers and those who are purified,
  who dance on the hill in the holy dance of god.
—Blessèd are they who keep the rite of Cybele the Mother.
—Blessèd are the thyrsus-bearers, those who wield in their hands
  the holy wand of god.   80
—Blessèd are those who wear the crown of the ivy of god.
—Blessèd, blessèd are they: Dionysus is their god!

—On, Bacchae, on, you Bacchae,
  bear your god in triumph home!
  Bear on the god, son of god,
  escort your Dionysus home!   85
  Bear him down from Phrygian hill,
  attend him through the streets of Hellas!

—So his mother bore him once
  in labor bitter; lightning-struck,
  forced by fire that flared from Zeus,   90
  consumed, she died, untimely torn,
  in childbed dead by blow of light!
  Of light the son was born!

—Zeus it was who saved his son;   95
  with speed outrunning mortal eye,

bore him to a private place,
bound the boy with clasps of gold;
in his thigh as in a womb,
concealed his son from Hera's eyes.

—And when the weaving Fates fulfilled the time,   100
the bull-horned god was born of Zeus. In joy
he crowned his son, set serpents on his head—
wherefrom, in piety, descends to us
the **Maenads** writhing crown, her *chevelure* of snakes.

—O Thebes, nurse of Semele,   105
crown your hair with ivy!
Grow green with bryony!
Redden with berries! O city,
with boughs of oak and fir,   110
come dance the dance of god!
Fringe your skins of dappled fawn
with tufts of twisted wool!
Handle with holy care
the violent wand of god!
And let the dance begin!
He is Bromius who runs   115
to the mountain!
        to the mountain!
where the throng of women waits,
driven from shuttle and loom,
possessed by Dionysus!

—And I praise the holies of Crete,   120
the caves of the dancing Curetes,
there where Zeus was born,
where helmed in triple tier
around the primal drum
the Corybantes danced. They,   125
they were the first of all
whose whirling feet kept time

to the strict beat of the taut hide
and the squeal of the wailing flute.
Then from them to Rhea's hands
the holy drum was handed down;
but, stolen by the raving Satyrs,   130
fell at last to me and now
accompanies the dance
which every other year
celebrates your name:
    Dionysus!

—He is sweet upon the mountains. He drops to the earth   135
    from the running packs.
He wears the holy fawn-skin. He hunts the wild goat
    and kills it.
He delights in the raw flesh.
He runs to the mountains of Phrygia, to the mountains
    of Lydia he runs!   140
He is Bromius who leads us! *Evohé!*

— With milk the earth flows! It flows with wine!
It runs with the nectar of bees!

—Like frankincense in its fragrance
is the blaze of the torch he bears.   145
Flames float out from his trailing wand
    as he runs, as he dances,
    kindling the stragglers,
    spurring with cries,
and his long curls stream to the wind!   150

—And he cries, as they cry, *Evohé!*—
    On, Bacchae!
    On, Bacchae!
Follow, glory of golden Tmolus,
    hymning god   155
    with a rumble of drums,

with a cry, *Evohé!* to the Evian god,
with a cry of Phrygian cries,
when the holy flute like honey plays   160
the sacred song of those who go
to the mountain!

        to the mountain!   165

—Then, in ecstasy, like a colt by its grazing mother,
the Bacchante runs with flying feet, she leaps!

      (The Chorus remains grouped in two semicircles about the
      orchestra as Teiresias makes his entrance. He is in-
      congruously dressed in the bacchant's fawn-skin
      and is crowned with ivy. Old and blind,
      he uses his thyrsus to tap his way.)

Teiresias

Ho there, who keeps the gates?

               Summon Cadmus—   170
Cadmus, Agenor's son, the stranger from Sidon
who built the towers of our Thebes.

                 Go, someone.
Say Teiresias wants him. He will know what errand
brings me, that agreement, age with age, we made   175
to deck our wands, to dress in skins of fawn
and crown our heads with ivy.

      (Enter Cadmus from the palace. Dressed in Dionysiac
      costume and bent almost double with age, he is an
      incongruous and pathetic figure.)

Cadmus

            My old friend,
I knew it must be you when I heard your summons.
For there's a wisdom in his voice that makes
the man of wisdom known.

            But here I am,
dressed in the costume of the god, prepared to go.   180
Insofar as we are able, Teiresias, we must

do honor to this god, for he was born
my daughter's son, who has been revealed to men,
the god, Dionysus.
     Where shall we go, where
shall we tread the dance, tossing our white heads
in the dances of god?
     Expound to me, Teiresias.   185
For in such matters you are wise.
       Surely
I could dance night and day, untiringly
beating the earth with my thyrsus! And how sweet it is
to forget my old age.

Teiresias

     It is the same with me.
I too feel young, young enough to dance.   190

Cadmus

 Good. Shall we take our chariots to the mountain?

Teiresias

 Walking would be better. It shows more honor
to the god.

Cadmus

    So be it. I shall lead, my old age
conducting yours.

Teiresias

     The god will guide us there
with no effort on our part.

Cadmus

       Are we the only men   195
who will dance for Bacchus?

Teiresias

      They are all blind.
Only we can see.

Cadmus

But we delay too long.
Here, take my arm.

Teiresias

Link my hand in yours.

Cadmus

I am a man, nothing more. I do not scoff
at heaven.

Teiresias

We do not trifle with divinity.   200
No, we are the heirs of customs and traditions
hallowed by age and handed down to us
by our fathers. No quibbling logic can topple *them*,
whatever subtleties this clever age invents.
People may say: "Aren't you ashamed? At your age,
going dancing, wreathing your head with ivy?"   205
Well, I am *not* ashamed. Did the god declare
that just the young or just the old should dance?
No, he desires his honor from all mankind.
He wants no one excluded from his worship.

Cadmus

Because you cannot see, Teiresias, let me be   210
interpreter for you this once. Here comes
the man to whom I left my throne, Echion's son,
Pentheus, hastening toward the palace. He seems
excited and disturbed. Yes, listen to him.

(*Enter Pentheus from the right. He is a young man of
athletic build, dressed in traditional Greek dress;
like Dionysus, he is beardless. He enters
excitedly, talking to the attendants
who accompany him.*)

Pentheus

I happened to be away, out of the city,   215
but reports reached me of some strange mischief here,

stories of our women leaving home to frisk
in mock ecstasies among the thickets on the mountain,
dancing in honor of the latest divinity,
a certain Dionysus, whoever he may be!   220
In their midst stand bowls brimming with wine.
And then, one by one, the women wander off
to hidden nooks where they serve the lusts of men.
Priestesses of Bacchus they claim they are,
but it's really Aphrodite they adore.   225
I have captured some of them; my jailers
have locked them away in the safety of our prison.
Those who run at large shall be hunted down
out of the mountains like the animals they are—
yes, my own mother Agave, and Ino
and Autonoë, the mother of Actaeon.   230
In no time at all I shall have them trapped
in iron nets and stop this obscene disorder.

   I am also told a foreigner has come to Thebes
from Lydia, one of those charlatan magicians,
with long yellow curls smelling of perfumes,   235
with flushed cheeks and the spells of Aphrodite
in his eyes. His days and nights he spends
with women and girls, dangling before them the joys
of initiation in his mysteries.
But let me bring him underneath that roof
and I'll stop his pounding with his wand and tossing   240
his head. By god, I'll have his head cut off!
And *this* is the man who claims that Dionysus
is a god and was sewn into the thigh of Zeus,
when, in point of fact, that same blast of lightning
consumed him and his mother both for her lie   245
that she had lain with Zeus in love. Whoever
this stranger is, aren't such impostures,
such unruliness, worthy of hanging?

        (For the first time he sees Teiresias and
        Cadmus in their Dionysiac costumes.)

What!

But this is incredible! Teiresias the seer
tricked out in a dappled fawn-skin!

And *you*,

you, my own grandfather, playing at the bacchant   250
with a wand!

Sir, I shrink to see your old age
so foolish. Shake that ivy off, grandfather!
Now drop that wand. Drop it, I say.

(*He wheels on Teiresias.*)

Aha,

I see: this is *your* doing, Teiresias.   255
Yes, you want still another god revealed to men
so you can pocket the profits from burnt offerings
and bird-watching. By heaven, only your age
restrains me now from sending you to prison
with those Bacchic women for importing here to Thebes
these filthy mysteries. When once you see   260
the glint of wine shining at the feasts of women,
then you may be sure the festival is rotten.

Coryphaeus

What blasphemy! Stranger, have you no respect
for heaven? For Cadmus who sowed the dragon teeth?
Will the son of Echion disgrace his house?   265

Teiresias

Give a wise man an honest brief to plead
and his eloquence is no remarkable achievement.
But you are glib; your phrases come rolling out
smoothly on the tongue, as though your words were wise
instead of foolish. The man whose glibness flows
from his conceit of speech declares the thing he is: 270
a worthless and a stupid citizen.

I tell you,

this god whom you ridicule shall someday have

enormous power and prestige throughout Hellas.
Mankind, young man, possesses two supreme blessings.
First of these is the goddess Demeter, or Earth—   275
whichever name you choose to call her by.
It was she who gave to man his nourishment of grain.
But after her there came the son of Semele,
who matched her present by inventing liquid wine
as his gift to man. For filled with that good gift,
suffering mankind forgets its grief; from it   280
comes sleep; with it oblivion of the troubles
of the day. There is no other medicine
for misery. And when we pour libations
to the gods, we pour the god of wine himself
that through his intercession man may win   285
the favor of heaven.
                        You sneer, do you, at that story
that Dionysus was sewed into the thigh of Zeus?
Let me teach you what that really means. When Zeus
rescued from the thunderbolt his infant son,
he brought him to Olympus. Hera, however,
plotted at heart to hurl the child from heaven.   290
Like the god he is, Zeus countered her. Breaking off
a tiny fragment of that ether which surrounds the world,
he molded from it a dummy Dionysus.
This he *showed* to Hera, but with time men garbled
the word and said that Dionysus had been *sewed*   295
into the thigh of Zeus. This was their story,
whereas, in fact, Zeus *showed* the dummy to Hera
and gave it as a hostage for his son.
                        Moreover,
this is a god of prophecy. His worshippers,
like madmen, are endowed with mantic powers.
For when the god enters the body of a man   300
he fills him with the breath of prophecy.
                        Besides,

he has usurped even the functions of warlike Ares.
Thus, at times, you see an army mustered under arms
stricken with panic before it lifts a spear.
This panic comes from Dionysus.

       Someday   305
you shall even see him bounding with his torches
among the crags at Delphi, leaping the pastures
that stretch between the peaks, whirling and waving
his thyrsus: great throughout Hellas.

         Mark my words,
Pentheus. Do not be so certain that power   310
is what matters in the life of man; do not mistake
for wisdom the fantasies of your sick mind.
Welcome the god to Thebes; crown your head;
pour him libations and join his revels.

  Dionysus does not, I admit, *compel* a woman
to be chaste. Always and in every case   315
it is her character and nature that keeps
a woman chaste. But even in the rites of Dionysus,
the chaste woman will not be corrupted.

         Think:
you are pleased when men stand outside your doors
and the city glorifies the name of Pentheus.   320
And so the god: he too delights in glory.
But Cadmus and I, whom you ridicule, will crown
our heads with ivy and join the dances of the god—
an ancient foolish pair perhaps, but dance
we must. Nothing you have said would make me
change my mind or flout the will of heaven.   325
You are mad, grievously mad, beyond the power
of any drugs to cure, for you are drugged
with madness.

Coryphaeus
     Apollo would approve your words.
Wisely you honor Bromius: a great god.

Cadmus

My boy,

Teiresias advises well. Your home is here   330
with us, with our customs and traditions, not
outside, alone. Your mind is distracted now,
and what you think is sheer delirium.
Even if this Dionysus is no god,
as you assert, persuade yourself that he is.
The fiction is a noble one, for Semele will seem   335
to be the mother of a god, and this confers
no small distinction on our family.

You saw

that dreadful death your cousin Actaeon died
when those man-eating hounds he had raised himself
savaged him and tore his body limb from limb
because he boasted that his prowess in the hunt surpassed   340
the skill of Artemis.

Do not let his fate be yours.

Here, let me wreathe your head with leaves of ivy.
Then come with us and glorify the god.

Pentheus

Take your hands off me! Go worship your Bacchus,
but do not wipe your madness off on me.
By god, I'll make him pay, the man who taught you   345
this folly of yours.

(He turns to his attendants.)

Go, someone, this instant,

to the place where this prophet prophesies.
Pry it up with crowbars, heave it over,
upside down; demolish everything you see.
Throw his fillets out to wind and weather.   350
That will provoke him more than anything.
As for the rest of you, go and scour the city
for that effeminate stranger, the man who infects our women
with this strange disease and pollutes our beds.

And when you take him, clap him in chains 355
and march him here. He shall die as he deserves—
by being stoned to death. He shall come to rue
his merrymaking here in Thebes.

(*Exeunt attendants.*)

Teiresias

Reckless fool,
you do not know the consequences of your words.
You talked madness before, but this is raving
lunacy!

Cadmus, let us go and pray 360
for this raving fool and for this city too,
pray to the god that no awful vengeance strike
from heaven.

Take your staff and follow me.
Support me with your hands, and I shall help you too
lest we stumble and fall, a sight of shame,
two old men together.

But go we must, 365
acknowledging the service that we owe to god,
Bacchus, the son of Zeus.

And yet take care
lest someday your house repent of Pentheus
in its sufferings. I speak not prophecy
but fact. The words of fools finish in folly.

(*Exeunt Teiresias and Cadmus. Pentheus
retires into the palace.*)

Chorus

—Holiness, queen of heaven, 370
Holiness on golden wing
who hover over earth,
do you hear what Pentheus says?
Do you hear his blasphemy
against the prince of the blessèd, 375
the god of garlands and banquets,

Bromius, Semele's son?
These blessings he gave:
laughter to the flute   380
and the loosing of cares
when the shining wine is spilled
at the feast of the gods,
and the wine-bowl casts its sleep   385
on feasters crowned with ivy.

—A tongue without reins,
defiance, unwisdom—
their end is disaster.
But the life of quiet good,
the wisdom that accepts—   390
these abide unshaken,
preserving, sustaining
the houses of men.
Far in the air of heaven,
the sons of heaven live.
But they watch the lives of men.
And what passes for wisdom is not;   395
unwise are those who aspire,
who outrange the limits of man.
Briefly, we live. Briefly,
then die. Wherefore, I say,
he who hunts a glory, he who tracks
some boundless, superhuman dream,
may lose his harvest here and now
and garner death. Such men are mad,   400
    their counsels evil.

—O let me come to Cyprus,
island of Aphrodite,
homes of the loves that cast
their spells on the hearts of men!   405
Or Paphos where the hundred-
mouthed barbarian river

brings ripeness without rain!
To Pieria, haunt of the Muses,   410
and the holy hill of Olympus!
O Bromius, leader, god of joy,
Bromius, take me there!
There the lovely Graces go,
and there Desire, and there
the right is mine to worship   415
   as I please.

—The deity, the son of Zeus,
in feast, in festival, delights.
He loves the goddess Peace,
generous of good,
preserver of the young.   420
To rich and poor he gives
the simple gift of wine,
the gladness of the grape.
But him who scoffs he hates,
and him who mocks his life,
the happiness of those
for whom the day is blessed   425
but doubly blessed the night;
whose simple wisdom shuns the thoughts
of proud, uncommon men and all
their god-encroaching dreams.
But what the common people do,   430
the things that simple men believe,
   I too believe and do.

(As Penthus reappears from the palace,
enter from the left several attendants
leading Dionysus captive.)

Attendant

Pentheus, here we are; not empty-handed either.
We captured the quarry you sent us out to catch.   435
But our prey here was tame: refused to run

or hide, held out his hands as willing as you please,
completely unafraid. His ruddy cheeks were flushed
as though with wine, and he stood there smiling,
making no objection when we roped his hands   440
and marched him here. It made me feel ashamed.
"Listen, stranger," I said, "I am not to blame.
We act under orders from Pentheus. He ordered
your arrest."

           As for those women you clapped in chains
and sent to the dungeon, they're gone, clean away,   445
went skipping off to the fields crying on their god
Bromius. The chains on their legs snapped apart
by themselves. Untouched by any human hand,
the doors swung wide, opening of their own accord.
Sir, this stranger who has come to Thebes is full   450
of many miracles. I know no more than that.
The rest is your affair.

Pentheus

           Untie his hands.
We have him in our net. He may be quick,
but he cannot escape us now, I think.

        (While the servants untie Dionysus' hands, Pentheus
             attentively scrutinizes his prisoner. Then
             the servants step back, leaving Pentheus
                 and Dionysus face to face.)

           So,
you *are* attractive, stranger, at least to women—
which explains, I think, your presence here in Thebes.
Your curls are long. You do not wrestle, I take it.   455
And what fair skin you have—you must take care of it—
no daylight complexion; no, it comes from the night
when you hunt Aphrodite with your beauty.

                Now then,
who are you and from where?

Dionysus
                                    It is nothing   460
to boast of and easily told. You have heard, I suppose,
of Mount Tmolus and her flowers?

Pentheus
                                    I know the place.
It rings the city of Sardis.

Dionysus
                                    I come from there.
My country is Lydia.

Pentheus
                        Who is this god whose worship
you have imported into Hellas?

Dionysus
                                Dionysus, the son of Zeus.   465
He initiated me.

Pentheus
                        You have some local Zeus
who spawns new gods?

Dionysus
                            He is the same as yours—
the Zeus who married Semele.

Pentheus
                                How did you see him?
In a dream or face to face?

Dionysus
                            Face to face.
He gave me his rites.

Pentheus
                        What form do they take,   470
these mysteries of yours?

Dionysus

> It is forbidden
> to tell the uninitiate.

Pentheus

> Tell me the benefits
> that those who know your mysteries enjoy.

Dionysus

> I am forbidden to say. But they are worth knowing.

Pentheus

> Your answers are designed to make me curious.

Dionysus

> No: 475
> our mysteries abhor an unbelieving man.

Pentheus

> You say you saw the god. What form did he assume?

Dionysus

> Whatever form he wished. The choice was his,
> not mine.

Pentheus

> You evade the question.

Dionysus

> Talk sense to a fool
> and he calls you foolish.

Pentheus

> Have you introduced your rites   480
> in other cities too? Or is Thebes the first?

Dionysus

> Foreigners everywhere now dance for Dionysus.

Pentheus

They are more ignorant than Greeks.

Dionysus

                  In this matter

they are not. Customs differ.

Pentheus

             Do you hold your rites

during the day or night?

Dionysus

          Mostly by night.   485

The darkness is well suited to devotion.

Pentheus

Better suited to lechery and seducing women.

Dionysus

You can find debauchery by daylight too.

Pentheus

You shall regret these clever answers.

Dionysus

            And you,

your stupid blasphemies.

Pentheus

         What a bold bacchant!   490

You wrestle well—when it comes to words.

Dionysus

                Tell me,

what punishment do you propose?

Pentheus

            First of all,

I shall cut off your girlish curls.

Dionysus

My hair is holy.

My curls belong to god.

(Pentheus shears away the god's curls.)

Pentheus

Second, you will surrender

your wand.

Dionysus

You take it. It belongs to Dionysus.   495

(Pentheus takes the thyrsus.)

Pentheus

Last, I shall place you under guard and confine you
in the palace.

Dionysus

The god himself will set me free
whenever I wish.

Pentheus

You will be with your women in prison
when you call on him for help.

Dionysus

He is here now
and sees what I endure from you.

Pentheus

Where is he?   500

I cannot see him.

Dionysus

With me. Your blasphemies
have made you blind.

Pentheus (to attendants)

Seize him. He is mocking me
and Thebes.

Dionysus

      I give you sober warning, fools:
place no chains on *me*.

Pentheus

       But *I* say: chain him.
And I am the stronger here.

Dionysus

        You do not know   505
the limits of your strength. You do not know
what you do. You do not know who you are.

Pentheus

I am Pentheus, the son of Echion and Agave.

Dionysus

Pentheus: you shall repent that name.

Pentheus

         Off with him.
Chain his hands; lock him in the stables by the palace.
Since he desires the darkness, give him what he wants. 510
Let him dance down there in the dark.

     (*As the attendants bind Dionysus' hands, the Chorus
       beats on its drums with increasing agitation
         as though to emphasize the sacrilege.*)

          As for these women,
your accomplices in making trouble here,
I shall have them sold as slaves or put to work
at my looms. That will silence their drums.

           (*Exit Pentheus.*)

Dionysus

         I go,   515
though not to suffer, since that cannot be.
But Dionysus whom you outrage by your acts,

who you deny is god, will call you to account.
When you set chains on me, you manacle the god.

(*Exeunt attendants with Dionysus captive.*)

Chorus

  —O Dirce, holy river,   520
    child of Achelöus' water,
    yours the springs that welcomed once
    divinity, the son of Zeus!
    For Zeus the father snatched his son
    from deathless flame, crying: 525
    Dithyrambus, come!
    Enter my male womb.
    I name you Bacchus and to Thebes
    proclaim you by that name.
    But now, O blessèd Dirce,   530
    you banish me when to your banks I come,
    crowned with ivy, bringing revels.
    O Dirce, why am I rejected?
    By the clustered grapes I swear,
    by Dionysus' wine,   535
    someday you shall come to know
      the name of *Bromius!*

  —With fury, with fury, he rages,
    Pentheus, son of Echion,   540
    born of the breed of Earth,
    spawned by the dragon, whelped by Earth!
    Inhuman, a rabid beast,
    a giant in wildness raging,
    storming, defying the children of heaven.
    He has threatened me with bonds   545
    though my body is bound to god.
    He cages my comrades with chains;
    he has cast them in prison darkness.
    O lord, son of Zeus, do you see?   550

O Dionysus, do you see
how in shackles we are held
unbreakably, in the bonds of oppressors?
Descend from Olympus, lord!
Come, whirl your wand of gold
and quell with death this beast of blood   555
whose violence abuses man and god
    outrageously.

—O lord, where do you wave your wand
among the running companies of god?
There on Nysa, mother of beasts?
There on the ridges of Corycia?
Or there among the forests of Olympus   560
where Orpheus fingered his lyre
and mustered with music the trees,
mustered the wilderness beasts?
O Pieria, you are blessed!   565
Evius honors you. He comes to dance,
bringing his Bacchae, fording the race
where Axios runs, bringing his Maenads   570
whirling over Lydias,
generous father of rivers
and famed for his lovely waters
that fatten a land of good horses.   575

        (Thunder and lightning. The earth trembles.
           The Chorus is crazed with fear.)

Dionysus (from within)

  Ho!
  Hear me! Ho, Bacchae!
  Ho, Bacchae! Hear my cry!

Chorus

  Who cries?
  Who calls me with that cry
  of Evius? Where are you, lord?

Dionysus

    Ho! Again I cry—   580
    the son of Zeus and Semele!

Chorus

    O lord, lord Bromius!
    Bromius, come to us now!

Dionysus

    Let the earthquake come! Shatter the floor of the world!   585

Chorus

    —Look there, how the palace of Pentheus totters.
    —Look, the palace is collapsing!
    —Dionysus is within. Adore him!
    —We adore him!   590
    —Look there!
                —Above the pillars, how the great stones
    gape and crack!
                —Listen. Bromius cries his victory!

Dionysus

Launch the blazing thunderbolt of god! O lightnings,
come! Consume with flame the palace of Pentheus!   595

          (*A burst of lightning flares across the façade of the palace*
                    and tongues of flame spurt up from the tomb of
                          Semele. Then a great crash of thunder.)

Chorus

    Ah,
    look how the fire leaps up
    on the holy tomb of Semele,
    the flame of Zeus of Thunders,
    his lightnings, still alive,
    blazing where they fell!
    Down, Maenads,   600
    fall to the ground in awe! He walks
    among the ruins he has made!

He has brought the high house low!
He comes, our god, the son of Zeus!

*(The Chorus falls to the ground in oriental fashion, bowing
their heads in the direction of the palace. A hush;
then Dionysus appears, lightly picking his way
among the rubble. Calm and smiling still,
he speaks to the Chorus with a solic-
itude approaching banter.)*

Dionysus

What, women of Asia? Were you so overcome with fright
you fell to the ground? I think then you must have seen   605
how Bacchus jostled the palace of Pentheus. But come, rise.
Do not be afraid.

Coryphaeus

O greatest light of our holy revels,
how glad I am to see your face! Without you I was lost.

Dionysus

Did you despair when they led me away to cast me down   610
in the darkness of Pentheus' prison?

Coryphaeus

What else could I do?
Where would I turn for help if something happened to you?
But how did you escape that godless man?

Dionysus

With ease.
No effort was required.

Coryphaeus

But the manacles on your wrists?   615

Dionysus

There I, in turn, humiliated him, outrage for outrage.
He seemed to think that he was chaining me but never once

so much as touched my hands. He fed on his desires.
Inside the stable he intended as my jail, instead of me,
he found a bull and tried to rope its knees and hooves.
He was panting desperately, biting his lips with his teeth,   620
his whole body drenched with sweat, while I sat nearby,
quietly watching. But at that moment Bacchus came,
shook the palace and touched his mother's grave with tongues
of fire. Imagining the palace was in flames,
Pentheus went rushing here and there, shouting to his slaves   625
to bring him water. Every hand was put to work: in vain.
Then, afraid I might escape, he suddenly stopped short,
drew his sword and rushed to the palace. There, it seems,
Bromius had made a shape, a phantom which resembled me,   630
within the court. Bursting in, Pentheus thrust and stabbed
at that thing of gleaming air as though he thought it me.
And then, once again, the god humiliated him.
He razed the palace to the ground where it lies, shattered
in utter ruin—his reward for my imprisonment.
At that bitter sight, Pentheus dropped his sword, exhausted   635
by the struggle. A man, a man, and nothing more,
yet he presumed to wage a war with god.

                          For my part,
I left the palace quietly and made my way outside.
For Pentheus I care nothing.

                     But judging from the sound
of tramping feet inside the court, I think our man
will soon be here. What, I wonder, will he have to say?   640
But let him bluster. I shall not be touched to rage.
Wise men know constraint: our passions are controlled.

      (*Enter Pentheus, stamping heavily, from the ruined palace.*)
Pentheus
    But this is mortifying. That stranger, that man
    I clapped in irons, has escaped.

                     (*He catches sight of Dionysus.*)

What! *You?*   645
Well, what do you have to say for yourself?
How did you escape? Answer me.

Dionysus
                        Your anger
walks too heavily. Tread lightly here.

Pentheus
   How did you escape?

Dionysus
                  Don't you remember?
Someone, I said, would set me free.

Pentheus
                        Someone?   650
But who? Who is this mysterious someone?

Dionysus
   [He who makes the grape grow its clusters
   for mankind.]

Pentheus
               A splendid contribution, that.

Dionysus
   You disparage the gift that is his chiefest glory.

Pentheus
   [If I catch him here, he will not escape my anger.]
   I shall order every gate in every tower
   to be bolted tight.

Dionysus
                  And so? Could not a god
   hurdle your city walls?

Pentheus
                  You are clever—very—   655
   but not where it counts.

Dionysus

Where it counts the most,

there I *am* clever.

(*Enter a messenger, a herdsman from Mount Cithaeron.*)

But hear this messenger
who brings you news from the mountain of Cithaeron.
We shall remain where we are. Do not fear:
we will not run away.

Messenger

Pentheus, king of Thebes,   660

I come from Cithaeron where the gleaming flakes of snow
fall on and on forever—

Pentheus

Get to the point.

What is your message, man?

Messenger

Sir, I have seen

the holy Maenads, the women who ran barefoot   665
and crazy from the city, and I wanted to report
to you and Thebes what weird fantastic things,
what miracles and more than miracles,
these women do. But may I speak freely
in my own way and words, or make it short?
I fear the harsh impatience of your nature, sire,   670
too kingly and too quick to anger.

Pentheus

Speak freely.

You have my promise: I shall not punish you.
Displeasure with a man who speaks the truth is wrong.
However, the more terrible this tale of yours,
that much more terrible will be the punishment   675
I impose upon that man who taught our womenfolk
this strange new magic.

Messenger
                    About that hour
when the sun lets loose its light to warm the earth,
our grazing herds of cows had just begun to climb
the path along the mountain ridge. Suddenly
I saw three companies of dancing women,   680
one led by Autonoë, the second captained
by your mother Agave, while Ino led the third.
There they lay in the deep sleep of exhaustion,
some resting on boughs of fir, others sleeping
where they fell, here and there among the oak leaves—   685
but all modestly and soberly, not, as you think,
drunk with wine, nor wandering, led astray
by the music of the flute, to hunt their Aphrodite
through the woods.
                    But your mother heard the lowing
of our hornèd herds, and springing to her feet,   690
gave a great cry to waken them from sleep.
And they too, rubbing the bloom of soft sleep
from their eyes, rose up lightly and straight—
a lovely sight to see: all as one,
the old women and the young and the unmarried girls.
First they let their hair fall loose, down   695
over their shoulders, and those whose straps had slipped
fastened their skins of fawn with writhing snakes
that licked their cheeks. Breasts swollen with milk,
new mothers who had left their babies behind at home
nestled gazelles and young wolves in their arms,   700
suckling them. Then they crowned their hair with leaves,
ivy and oak and flowering bryony. One woman
struck her thyrsus against a rock and a fountain
of cool water came bubbling up. Another drove
her fennel in the ground, and where it struck the earth,   705
at the touch of god, a spring of wine poured out.
Those who wanted milk scratched at the soil
with bare fingers and the white milk came welling up.   710

Pure honey spurted, streaming, from their wands.
If you had been there and seen these wonders for yourself,
you would have gone down on your knees and prayed
to the god you now deny.

      We cowherds and shepherds
gathered in small groups, wondering and arguing   715
among ourselves at these fantastic things,
the awful miracles those women did.
But then a city fellow with the knack of words
rose to his feet and said: "All you who live
upon the pastures of the mountain, what do you say?
Shall we earn a little favor with King Pentheus   720
by hunting his mother Agave out of the revels?"
Falling in with his suggestion, we withdrew
and set ourselves in ambush, hidden by the leaves
among the undergrowth. Then at a signal
all the Bacchae whirled their wands for the revels
to begin. With one voice they cried aloud:
"*O Iacchus! Son of Zeus!*" "*O Bromius!*" they cried   725
until the beasts and all the mountain seemed
wild with divinity. And when they ran,
everything ran with them.

      It happened, however,
that Agave ran near the ambush where I lay
concealed. Leaping up, I tried to seize her,   730
but she gave a cry: "Hounds who run with me,
men are hunting us down! Follow, follow me!
Use your wands for weapons."

      At this we fled
and barely missed being torn to pieces by the women.
Unarmed, they swooped down upon the herds of cattle   735
grazing there on the green of the meadow. And then
you could have seen a single woman with bare hands
tear a fat calf, still bellowing with fright,
in two, while others clawed the heifers to pieces.
There were ribs and cloven hooves scattered everywhere,   740

and scraps smeared with blood hung from the fir trees.
And bulls, their raging fury gathered in their horns,
lowered their heads to charge, then fell, stumbling
to the earth, pulled down by hordes of women   745
and stripped of flesh and skin more quickly, sire,
than you could blink your royal eyes. Then,
carried up by their own speed, they flew like birds
across the spreading fields along Asopus' stream
where most of all the ground is good for harvesting.   750
Like invaders they swooped on Hysiae
and on Erythrae in the foothills of Cithaeron.
Everything in sight they pillaged and destroyed.
They snatched the children from their homes. And when
they piled their plunder on their backs, it stayed in place,   755
untied. Nothing, neither bronze nor iron,
fell to the dark earth. Flames flickered
in their curls and did not burn them. Then the villagers,
furious at what the women did, took to arms.
And *there*, sire, was something terrible to see.   760
For the men's spears were pointed and sharp, and yet
drew no blood, whereas the wands the women threw
inflicted wounds. And then the men *ran*,
routed by women! Some god, I say, was with them.
The Bacchae then returned where they had started,   765
by the springs the god had made, and washed their hands
while the snakes licked away the drops of blood
that dabbled their cheeks.
                                  Whoever this god may be,
sire, welcome him to Thebes. For he is great
in many other ways as well. It was he,   770
or so they say, who gave to mortal men
the gift of lovely wine by which our suffering
is stopped. And if there is no god of wine,
there is no love, no Aphrodite either,
nor other pleasure left to men.

                                                    (*Exit messenger.*)

Coryphaeus
                    I tremble   775
to speak the words of freedom before the tyrant.
But let the truth be told: there is no god
greater than Dionysus.

Pentheus
                    Like a blazing fire
this Bacchic violence spreads. It comes too close.
We are disgraced, humiliated in the eyes
of Hellas. This is no time for hesitation.   780

                    (*He turns to an attendant.*)

You there. Go down quickly to the Electran gates
and order out all heavy-armored infantry;
call up the fastest troops among our cavalry,
the mobile squadrons and the archers. We march
against the Bacchae! Affairs are out of hand   785
when we tamely endure such conduct in our women.

                    (*Exit attendant.*)

Dionysus
Pentheus, you do not hear, or else you disregard
my words of warning. You have done me wrong,
and yet, in spite of that, I warn you once
again: do not take arms against a god.
Stay quiet here. Bromius will not let you   790
drive his women from their revels on the mountain.

Pentheus
Don't you lecture me. You escaped from prison.
Or shall I punish you again?

Dionysus
                    If I were you,
I would offer him a sacrifice, not rage
and kick against necessity, a man defying   795
god.

Pentheus

    I shall give your god the sacrifice
that he deserves. His victims will be his women.
I shall make a great slaughter in the woods of Cithaeron.

Dionysus

    You will all be routed, shamefully defeated,
when their wands of ivy turn back your shields
of bronze.

Pentheus

          It is hopeless to wrestle with this man.   800
Nothing on earth will make him hold his tongue.

Dionysus

                           Friend,
you can still save the situation.

Pentheus

              How?
By accepting orders from my own slaves?

Dionysus

                  No.
I undertake to lead the women back to Thebes.
Without bloodshed.

Pentheus

          This is some trap.

Dionysus

                 A trap?   805
How so, if I save you by my own devices?

Pentheus

                  I know.
You and they have conspired to establish your rites
forever.

Dionysus

    True, I *have* conspired—with god.

Pentheus

Bring my armor, someone. And *you* stop talking.   810

> (*Pentheus strides toward the left, but when he is almost
> offstage, Dionysus calls imperiously to him.*)

Dionysus

Wait!
Would you like to *see* their revels on the mountain?

Pentheus

I would pay a great sum to see that sight.

Dionysus

Why are you so passionately curious?

Pentheus

Of course
I'd be sorry to see them drunk—

Dionysus

But for all your sorrow,   815
you'd like very much to see them?

Pentheus

Yes, very much.
I could crouch beneath the fir trees, out of sight.

Dionysus

But if you try to hide, they may track you down.

Pentheus

Your point is well taken. I will go openly.

Dionysus

Shall I lead you there now? Are you ready to go?

Pentheus

The sooner the better. The loss of even a moment   820
would be disappointing now.

Dionysus

First, however,
you must dress yourself in women's clothes.

Pentheus

What?
You want *me*, a man, to wear a woman's dress. But why?

Dionysus

If they knew you were a man, they would kill you instantly.

Pentheus

True. You are an old hand at cunning, I see.

Dionysus

Dionysus taught me everything I know.   825

Pentheus

Your advice is to the point. What I fail to see
is what we do.

Dionysus

I shall go inside with you
and help you dress.

Pentheus

Dress? In a *woman's* dress,
you mean? I would die of shame.

Dionysus

Very well.
Then you no longer hanker to see the Maenads?

Pentheus

What is this costume I must wear?

Dionysus

On your head   830
I shall set a wig with long curls.

« 579 »

Pentheus

And then?

Dionysus

Next, robes to your feet and a net for your hair.

Pentheus

Yes? Go on.

Dionysus

Then a thyrsus for your hand
and a skin of dappled fawn.

Pentheus

I could not bear it.   835
I *cannot* bring myself to dress in women's clothes.

Dionysus

Then you must fight the Bacchae. That means bloodshed

Pentheus

Right. First we must go and reconnoiter.

Dionysus

Surely a wiser course than that of hunting bad
with worse.

Pentheus

But how can we pass through the city
without being seen?

Dionysus

We shall take deserted streets.   840
I will lead the way.

Pentheus

Any way you like,
provided those women of Bacchus don't jeer at me.
First, however, I shall ponder your advice,
whether to go or not.

Dionysus

Do as you please.
I am ready, whatever you decide.

Pentheus

Yes.
Either I shall march with my army to the mountain   845
or act on your advice.

(*Exit Pentheus into the palace.*)

Dionysus

Women, our prey now thrashes
in the net we threw. He shall see the Bacchae
and pay the price with death.

O Dionysus,
now action rests with you. And you are near.
Punish this man. But first distract his wits;   850
bewilder him with madness. For sane of mind
this man would never wear a woman's dress;
but obsess his soul and he will not refuse.
After those threats with which he was so fierce,
I want him made the laughingstock of Thebes,
paraded through the streets, a woman.

Now   855
I shall go and costume Pentheus in the clothes
which he must wear to Hades when he dies, butchered
by the hands of his mother. He shall come to know
Dionysus, son of Zeus, consummate god,   860
most terrible, and yet most gentle, to mankind.

(*Exit Dionysus into the palace.*)

Chorus

—When shall I dance once more
with bare feet the all-night dances,
tossing my head for joy
in the damp air, in the dew,   865
as a running fawn might frisk
for the green joy of the wide fields,

free from fear of the hunt,
free from the circling beaters   870
and the nets of woven mesh
and the hunters hallooing on
their yelping packs? And then, hard pressed,
she sprints with the quickness of wind,
bounding over the marsh, leaping
to frisk, leaping for joy,   875
gay with the green of the leaves,
to dance for joy in the forest,
to dance where the darkness is deepest,
    where no man is.

—What is wisdom? What gift of the gods
is held in honor like this:
to hold your hand victorious
over the heads of those you hate?   880
Honor is precious forever.

—Slow but unmistakable
the might of the gods moves on.
It punishes that man,
infatuate of soul
and hardened in his pride,   885
who disregards the gods.
The gods are crafty:
they lie in ambush
a long step of time
to hunt the unholy.   890
Beyond the old beliefs,
no thought, no act shall go.
Small, small is the cost
to believe in this:
whatever is god is strong;
whatever long time has sanctioned,
that is a law forever;
the law tradition makes   895
is the law of nature.

—What is wisdom? What gift of the gods
is held in honor like this:
to hold your hand victorious
over the heads of those you hate?   900
Honor is precious forever.

—Blessèd is he who escapes a storm at sea,
who comes home to his harbor.
—Blessèd is he who emerges from under affliction.
—In various ways one man outraces another in the
race for wealth and power.   905
—Ten thousand men possess ten thousand hopes.
—A few bear fruit in happiness; the others go awry.
—But he who garners day by day the good of life,   910
he is happiest. Blessèd is he.

> (Re-enter Dionysus from the palace. At the threshold
> he turns and calls back to Pentheus.)

Dionysus

Pentheus if you are still so curious to see
forbidden sights, so bent on evil still,
come out. Let us see you in your woman's dress,
disguised in Maenad clothes so you may go and spy   915
upon your mother and her company.

> (Enter Pentheus from the palace. He wears a long linen dress
> which partially conceals his fawn-skin. He carries a thyrsus
> in his hand; on his head he wears a wig with long blond
> curls bound by a snood. He is dazed and completely in
> the power of the god who has now possessed him.)

Why,
you look exactly like one of the daughters of Cadmus.

Pentheus

I seem to see two suns blazing in the heavens.
And now two Thebes, two cities, and each
with seven gates. And you—you are a bull   920

who walks before me there. Horns have sprouted
from your head. Have you always been a beast?
But now I see a bull.

Dionysus
                        It is the god you see.
Though hostile formerly, he now declares a truce
and goes with us. You see what you could not
when you were blind.

Pentheus (coyly primping)
                        Do I look like anyone?   925
Like Ino or my mother Agave?

Dionysus
                                So much alike
I almost might be seeing one of them. But look:
one of your curls has come loose from under the snood
where I tucked it.

Pentheus
                        It must have worked loose
when I was dancing for joy and shaking my head.   930

Dionysus
Then let me be your maid and tuck it back.
Hold still.

Pentheus
                Arrange it. I am in your hands
completely.
                        (*Dionysus tucks the curl back under the snood.*)

Dionysus
                        And now your strap has slipped. Yes,   935
and your robe hangs askew at the ankles.

Pentheus (bending backward to look)
                                    I think so.
At least on my right leg. But on the left the hem
lies straight.

Dionysus

        You will think me the best of friends
when you see to your surprise how chaste the Bacchae are.   940

Pentheus

  But to be a real Bacchante, should I hold
the wand in my right hand? Or this way?

Dionysus

                  No.
In your right hand. And raise it as you raise
your right foot. I commend your change of heart.

Pentheus

  Could I lift Cithaeron up, do you think?   945
Shoulder the cliffs, Bacchae and all?

Dionysus

                  If you wanted.
Your mind was once unsound, but now you think
as sane men do.

Pentheus

          Should we take crowbars with us?
Or should I put my shoulder to the cliffs   950
and heave them up?

Dionysus

            What? And destroy the haunts
of the nymphs, the holy groves where Pan plays
his woodland pipe?

Pentheus

          You are right. In any case,
women should not be mastered by brute strength.
I will hide myself beneath the firs instead.

Dionysus

  You will find all the ambush you deserve,   955
creeping up to spy on the Maenads.

Pentheus

Think.

I can see them already, there among the bushes,
mating like birds, caught in the toils of love.

Dionysus

Exactly. This is your mission: you go to watch.
You may surprise them—or they may surprise you.   960

Pentheus

Then lead me through the very heart of Thebes,
since I, alone of all this city, dare to go.

Dionysus

You and you alone will suffer for your city.
A great ordeal awaits you. But you are worthy
of your fate. I shall lead you safely there;   965
someone else shall bring you back.

Pentheus

Yes, my mother.

Dionysus

An example to all men.

Pentheus

It is for that I go.

Dionysus

You will be carried home—

Pentheus

O luxury!

Dionysus

cradled in your mother's arms.

Pentheus

You will spoil me.

Dionysus

I *mean* to spoil you.

Pentheus

I go to my reward. 970

Dionysus

You are an extraordinary young man, and you go
to an extraordinary experience. You shall win
a glory towering to heaven and usurping
god's.

(*Exit Pentheus.*)

Agave and you daughters of Cadmus,
reach out your hands! I bring this young man
to a great ordeal. The victor? Bromius. 975
Bromius—and I. The rest the event shall show.

(*Exit Dionysus.*)

Chorus

—Run to the mountain, fleet hounds of madness!
Run, run to the revels of Cadmus' daughters!
Sting them against the man in women's clothes, 980
the madman who spies on the Maenads, who peers
from behind the rocks, who spies from a vantage!
His mother shall see him first. She will cry 985
to the Maenads: "Who is this spy who has come
to the mountains to peer at the mountain-revels
of the women of Thebes? What bore him, Bacchae?
This man was born of no woman. Some lioness
gave him birth, some one of the Libyan gorgons!" 990

—O Justice, principle of order, spirit of custom,
come! Be manifest; reveal yourself with a sword!
Stab through the throat that godless man,
the mocker who goes, flouting custom and outraging god!
O Justice, stab the evil earth-born spawn of Echion! 995

—Uncontrollable, the unbeliever goes,
in spitting rage, rebellious and amok,
madly assaulting the mysteries of god,
profaning the rites of the mother of god.

Against the unassailable he runs, with rage   1000
obsessed. Headlong he runs to death.
For death the gods exact, curbing by that bit
the mouths of men. They humble us with death
that we remember what we are who are not god,
but men. We run to death. Wherefore, I say,
accept, accept:
humility is wise; humility is blest.
But what the world calls wise I do not want.   1005
Elsewhere the chase. I hunt another game,
those great, those manifest, those certain goals,
achieving which, our mortal lives are blest.
Let these things be the quarry of my chase:
purity; humility; an unrebellious soul,
accepting all. Let me go the customary way,
the timeless, honored, beaten path of those who walk
with reverence and awe beneath the sons of heaven.   1010

—O Justice, principle of order, spirit of custom,
come! Be manifest; reveal yourself with a sword!
Stab through the throat that godless man,
the mocker who goes, flouting custom and outraging god!
O Justice, destroy the evil earth-born sprawn of Echion!   1015

—O Dionysus, reveal yourself a bull! Be manifest,
a snake with darting heads, a lion breathing fire!
O Bacchus, come! Come with your smile!
Cast your noose about this man who hunts
your Bacchae! Bring him down, trampled   1020
underfoot by the murderous herd of your Maenads!

(*Enter a messenger from Cithaeron.*)

Messenger

How prosperous in Hellas these halls once were,
this house founded by Cadmus, the stranger from Sidon   1025
who sowed the dragon seed in the land of the snake!

I am a slave and nothing more, yet even so
I mourn the fortunes of this fallen house.

Coryphaeus

What is it?
Is there news of the Bacchae?

Messenger

This is my news:
Pentheus, the son of Echion, is dead.   1030

Coryphaeus

All hail to Bromius! Our god is a great god!

Messenger

What is this you say, women? You dare to rejoice
at these disasters which destroy this house?

Coryphaeus

I am no Greek. I hail my god
in my own way. No longer need I
shrink with fear of prison.   1035

Messenger

If you suppose this city is so short of men—

Coryphaeus

Dionysus, Dionysus, not Thebes,
has power over me.

Messenger

Your feelings might be forgiven, then. But this,
this exultation in disaster—it is not right.   1040

Coryphaeus

Tell us how the mocker died.
How was he killed?

Messenger
There were three of us in all: Pentheus and I,
attending my master, and that stranger who volunteered
his services as guide. Leaving behind us
the last outlying farms of Thebes, we forded
the Asopus and struck into the barren scrubland   1045
of Cithaeron.
                    There in a grassy glen we halted,
unmoving, silent, without a word,
so we might see but not be seen. From that vantage,   1050
in a hollow cut from the sheer rock of the cliffs,
a place where water ran and the pines grew dense
with shade, we saw the Maenads sitting, their hands
busily moving at their happy tasks. Some
wound the stalks of their tattered wands with tendrils   1055
of fresh ivy; others, frisking like fillies
newly freed from the painted bridles, chanted
in Bacchic songs, responsively.
                            But Pentheus—
unhappy man—could not quite see the companies
of women. "Stranger," he said, "from where I stand,
I cannot see these counterfeited Maenads.   1060
But if I climbed that towering fir that overhangs
the banks, then I could see their shameless orgies
better."
              And now the stranger worked a miracle.
Reaching for the highest branch of a great fir,
he bent it down, down, down to the dark earth,   1065
till it was curved the way a taut bow bends
or like a rim of wood when forced about the circle
of a wheel. Like that he forced that mountain fir
down to the ground. No mortal could have done it.
Then he seated Pentheus at the highest tip   1070
and with his hands let the trunk rise straightly up,
slowly and gently, lest it throw its rider.
And the tree rose, towering to heaven, with my master

huddled at the top. And now the Maenads saw him
more clearly than he saw them. But barely had they seen,   1075
when the stranger vanished and there came a great voice
out of heaven—Dionysus', it must have been—
crying: "Women, I bring you the man who has mocked
at you and me and at our holy mysteries.   1080
Take vengeance upon him." And as he spoke
a flash of awful fire bound earth and heaven.
The high air hushed, and along the forest glen
the leaves hung still; you could hear no cry of beasts.   1085
The Bacchae heard that voice but missed its words,
and leaping up, they stared, peering everywhere.
Again that voice. And now they knew his cry,
the clear command of god. And breaking loose
like startled doves, through grove and torrent,   1090
over jagged rocks, they flew, their feet maddened
by the breath of god. And when they saw my master
perching in his tree, they climbed a great stone   1095
that towered opposite his perch and showered him
with stones and javelins of fir, while the others
hurled their wands. And yet they missed their target,
poor Pentheus in his perch, barely out of reach   1100
of their eager hands, treed, unable to escape.
Finally they splintered branches from the oaks
and with those bars of wood tried to lever up the tree
by prying at the roots. But every effort failed.   1105
Then Agave cried out: "Maenads, make a circle
about the trunk and grip it with your hands.
Unless we take this climbing beast, he will reveal
the secrets of the god." With that, thousands of hands
tore the fir tree from the earth, and down, down   1110
from his high perch fell Pentheus, tumbling
to the ground, sobbing and screaming as he fell,
for he knew his end was near. His own mother,
like a priestess with her victim, fell upon him
first. But snatching off his wig and snood   1115

so she would recognize his face, he touched her cheeks,
screaming, "*No, no, Mother! I am Pentheus,*
your own son, the child you bore to Echion!
Pity me, spare me, Mother! I have done a wrong,   1120
but do not kill your own son for my offense."
But she was foaming at the mouth, and her crazed eyes
rolling with frenzy. She was mad, stark mad,
possessed by Bacchus. Ignoring his cries of pity,
she seized his left arm at the wrist; then, planting   1125
her foot upon his chest, she pulled, wrenching away
the arm at the shoulder—not by her own strength,
for the god had put inhuman power in her hands.
Ino, meanwhile, on the other side, was scratching off
his flesh. Then Autonoë and the whole horde   1130
of Bacchae swarmed upon him. Shouts everywhere,
he screaming with what little breath was left,
they shrieking in triumph. One tore off an arm,
another a foot still warm in its shoe. His ribs
were clawed clean of flesh and every hand   1135
was smeared with blood as they played ball with scraps
of Pentheus' body.
                    The pitiful remains lie scattered,
one piece among the sharp rocks, others
lying lost among the leaves in the depths
of the forest. His mother, picking up his head,   1140
impaled it on her wand. She seems to think it is
some mountain lion's head which she carries in triumph
through the thick of Cithaeron. Leaving her sisters
at the Maenad dances, she is coming here, gloating
over her grisly prize. She calls upon Bacchus: 1145
he is her "fellow-huntsman," "comrade of the chase,
crowned with victory." But all the victory
she carries home is her own grief.
                    Now,
before Agave returns, let me leave
this scene of sorrow. Humility,

a sense of reverence before the sons of heaven—   1150
of all the prizes that a mortal man might win,
these, I say, are wisest; these are best.

                                        (*Exit Messenger.*)

Chorus

—We dance to the glory of Bacchus!
   We dance to the death of Pentheus,
   the death of the spawn of the dragon!   1155
      He dressed in woman's dress;
      he took the lovely thyrsus;
      it waved him down to death,
         led by a bull to Hades.
   Hail, Bacchae! Hail, women of Thebes!   1160
   Your victory is fair, fair the prize,
      this famous prize of grief!
   Glorious the game! To fold your child
   in your arms, streaming with his blood!

Coryphaeus

But look: there comes Pentheus' mother, Agave,   1165
running wild-eyed toward the palace.
                                        —Welcome,
welcome to the reveling band of the god of joy!

         (*Enter Agave with other Bacchantes. She is covered with blood
            and carries the head of Pentheus impaled upon her thyrsus.*)

Agave
Bacchae of Asia—

Chorus
                    Speak, speak.

Agave
   We bring this branch to the palace,
   this fresh-cut spray from the mountains.   1170
   Happy was the hunting.

Chorus
>   I see.
> I welcome our fellow-reveler of god.

Agave
>   The whelp of a wild mountain lion,
>   and snared by me without a noose.
>   Look, look at the prize I bring.   1175

Chorus
>   Where was he caught?

Agave
>   On Cithaeron—

Chorus
>   On Cithaeron?

Agave
>   Our prize was killed.

Chorus
>   Who killed him?

Agave
>   I struck him first.
>   The Maenads call me "Agave the blest."   1180

Chorus
>   And then?

Agave
>   Cadmus'—

Chorus
>   Cadmus'?

Agave
>   Daughters.
>   After me, they reached the prey.
>   After me. Happy was the hunting.

Chorus

Happy indeed.

Agave

              Then share my glory,
share the feast.

Chorus

             Share, unhappy woman?

Agave

See, the whelp is young and tender.   1185
Beneath the soft mane of its hair,
the down is blooming on the cheeks.

Chorus

With that mane he *looks* a beast.

Agave

Our god is wise. Cunningly, cleverly,   1190
Bacchus the hunter lashed the Maenads
against his prey.

Chorus

           Our king is a hunter.

Agave

You praise me now?

Chorus

          I praise you.

Agave

The men of Thebes—

Chorus

            And Pentheus, your son?

Agave

Will praise his mother. She caught   1195
a great quarry, this lion's cub.

Chorus

    Extraordinary catch.

Agave

              Extraordinary skill.

Chorus

    You are proud?

Agave

           Proud and happy.
I have won the trophy of the chase,
a great prize, manifest to all.

Coryphaeus

    Then, poor woman, show the citizens of Thebes   1200
this great prize, this trophy you have won
in the hunt.

             *(Agave proudly exhibits her thyrsus with the head
                of Pentheus impaled upon the point.)*

Agave

          You citizens of this towered city,
men of Thebes, behold the trophy of your women's
hunting! *This* is the quarry of our chase, taken
not with nets nor spears of bronze but by the white   1205
and delicate hands of women. What are they worth,
your boastings now and all that uselessness
your armor is, since we, with our bare hands,
captured this quarry and tore its bleeding body
limb from limb?

            —But where is my father Cadmus?   1210
He should come. And my son. Where is Pentheus?
Fetch him. I will have him set his ladder up
against the wall and, there upon the beam,
nail the head of this wild lion I have killed
as a trophy of my hunt.

        *(Enter Cadmus, followed by attendants who bear upon
          a bier the dismembered body of Pentheus.)*

Cadmus
                              Follow me, attendants.   1215
Bear your dreadful burden in and set it down,
there before the palace.

                    (*The attendants set down the bier.*)

                    This was Pentheus
whose body, after long and weary searchings
I painfully assembled from Cithaeron's glens
where it lay, scattered in shreds, dismembered
throughout the forest, no two pieces   1220
in a single place.
                    Old Teiresias and I
had returned to Thebes from the orgies on the mountain
before I learned of this atrocious crime
my daughters did. And so I hurried back
to the mountain to recover the body of this boy   1225
murdered by the Maenads. There among the oaks
I found Aristaeus' wife, the mother of Actaeon,
Autonoë, and with her Ino, both
still stung with madness. But Agave, they said,
was on her way to Thebes, still possessed.   1230
And what they said was true, for there she is,
and not a happy sight.

Agave
                    Now, Father,
yours can be the proudest boast of living men.
For you are now the father of the bravest daughters
in the world. All of your daughters are brave,   1235
but I above the rest. I have left my shuttle
at the loom; I raised my sight to higher things—
to hunting animals with my bare hands.
                                        You see?
Here in my hands I hold the quarry of my chase,
a trophy for our house. Take it, Father, take it.   1240
Glory in my kill and invite your friends to share

the feast of triumph. For you are blest, Father,
by this great deed I have done.

Cadmus

This is a grief
so great it knows no size. I cannot look.
This is the awful murder your hands have done.   1245
This, this is the noble victim you have slaughtered
to the gods. And to share a feast like this
you now invite all Thebes and me?

O gods,
how terribly I pity you and then myself.
Justly—too, too justly—has lord Bromius,
this god of our own blood, destroyed us all,   1250
every one.

Agave

How scowling and crabbed is old age
in men. I hope my son takes after his mother
and wins, as she has done, the laurels of the chase
when he goes hunting with the younger men of Thebes.
But all my son can do is quarrel with god.   1255
He should be scolded, Father, and you are the one
who should scold him. Yes, someone call him out
so he can see his mother's triumph.

Cadmus

Enough. No more.
When you realize the horror you have done,
you shall suffer terribly. But if with luck   1260
your present madness lasts until you die,
you will seem to have, not having, happiness.

Agave

Why do you reproach me? Is there something wrong?

Cadmus

First raise your eyes to the heavens.

Agave

                        There.   1265

  But why?

Cadmus

               Does it look the same as it did before?

  Or has it changed?

Agave

                    It seems—somehow—clearer,

  brighter than it was before.

Cadmus

                       Do you still feel

  the same flurry inside you?

Agave

                  The same—flurry?

  No, I feel—somehow—calmer. I feel as though—   1270

  my mind were somehow—changing.

Cadmus

                         Can you still hear me?

  Can you answer clearly?

Agave

                   No. I have forgotten

  what we were saying, Father.

Cadmus

                    Who was your husband?

Agave

  Echion—a man, they said, born of the dragon seed.

Cadmus

  What was the name of the child you bore your husband?   1275

Agave

  Pentheus.

Cadmus
> And whose head do you hold in your hands?

Agave (averting her eyes)
> A lion's head—or so the hunters told me.

Cadmus
> Look directly at it. Just a quick glance.

Agave
> What is it? What am I holding in my hands?   1280

Cadmus
> Look more closely still. Study it carefully.

Agave
> *No!* O gods, I see the greatest grief there is.

Cadmus
> Does it look like a lion now?

Agave
>   No, no. It is—
> Pentheus' head—I hold—

Cadmus
>   And mourned by me   1285
> before you ever knew.

Agave
>   But *who* killed him?
> Why am *I* holding him?

Cadmus
>   O savage truth,
> what a time to come!

Agave
>   For god's sake, speak.
> My heart is beating with terror.

Cadmus
                              You killed him.
You and your sisters.

Agave
                    But where was he killed?   1290
Here at home? Where?

Cadmus
                    He was killed on Cithaeron,
there where the hounds tore Actaeon to pieces.

Agave
But why? Why had Pentheus gone to Cithaeron?

Cadmus
He went to your revels to mock the god.

Agave
                              But *we*—
what were we doing on the mountain?

Cadmus
                         You were mad.   1295
The whole city was possessed.

Agave
                    Now, now I see:
Dionysus has destroyed us all.

Cadmus
                    You outraged him.
You denied that he was truly god.

Agave
                         Father,
where is my poor boy's body now?

Cadmus
                         There it is.
I gathered the pieces with great difficulty.

Agave

Is his body entire? Has he been laid out well? 1300

Cadmus

[All but the head. The rest is mutilated
horribly.]

Agave

But why should Pentheus suffer for my crime?

Cadmus

He, like you, blasphemed the god. And so
the god has brought us all to ruin at one blow,
you, your sisters, and this boy. All our house
the god as utterly destroyed and, with it,
me. For I have no sons left, no male heir; 1305
and I have lived only to see this boy,
this branch of your own body, most horribly
and foully killed.

(*He turns and addresses the corpse.*)

—To you my house looked up.
Child, you were the stay of my house; you were
my daughter's son. Of you this city stood in awe. 1310
No one who once had seen your face dared outrage
the old man, or if he did, you punished him.
Now I must go, a banished and dishonored man—
I, Cadmus the great, who sowed the soldiery
of Thebes and harvested a great harvest. My son, 1315
dearest to me of all men—for even dead,
I count you still the man I love the most—
never again will your hand touch my chin;
no more, child, will you hug me and call me
"Grandfather" and say, "Who is wronging you? 1320
Does anyone trouble you or vex your heart, old man?
Tell me, Grandfather, and I will punish him."
No, now there is grief for me; the mourning

for you; pity for your mother; and for her sisters,
sorrow.

   If there is still any mortal man   1325
who despises or defies the gods, let him look
on this boy's death and believe in the gods.

Coryphaeus

 Cadmus, I pity you. Your daughter's son
has died as he deserved, and yet his death
bears hard on you.

[*At this point there is a break in the manuscript of nearly fifty lines.
The following speeches of Agave and Coryphaeus and the first part of
Dionysus' speech have been conjecturally reconstructed from fragments and
later material which made use of the Bacchae. Lines which can plausibly
be assigned to the lacuna are otherwise not indicated. My own inventions
are designed, not to complete the speeches, but to effect a transition between the fragments, and are bracketed. For fuller comment, see the Appendix.—*TRANS.]

Agave

       O Father, now you can see
how everything has changed. I am in anguish now,
tormented, who walked in triumph minutes past,
exulting in my kill. And that prize I carried home
with such pride was my own curse. Upon these hands
I bear the curse of my son's blood. How then
with these accursed hands may I touch his body?
How can I, accursed with such a curse, hold him
to my breast? O gods, what dirge can I sing
[that there might be] a dirge [for every]
broken limb?

. . . .

    Where is a shroud to cover up his corpse?
O my child, what hands will give you proper care
unless with my own hands I lift my curse?

(She lifts up one of Pentheus' limbs and asks the help of Cadmus in piecing the body together. She mourns each piece separately before replacing it on the bier. See Appendix.)

Come, Father. We must restore his head
to this unhappy boy. As best we can, we shall make
him whole again.
　　　　　　—O dearest, dearest face!
Pretty boyish mouth! Now with this veil
I shroud your head, gathering with loving care
these mangled bloody limbs, this flesh I brought
to birth

. . . .

Coryphaeus

Let this scene teach those [who see these things:
Dionysus is the son] of Zeus.

(Above the palace Dionysus appears in epiphany.)

Dionysus
　　　　　　　　[I am Dionysus,
the son of Zeus, returned to Thebes, revealed,
a god to men.] But the men [of Thebes] blasphemed me.
They slandered me; they said I came of mortal man,
and not content with speaking blasphemies,
[they dared to threaten my person with violence.]
These crimes this people whom I cherished well
did from malice to their benefactor. Therefore,
I now disclose the sufferings in store for them.
Like [enemies], they shall be driven from this city
to other lands; there, submitting to the yoke
of slavery, they shall wear out wretched lives,
captives of war, enduring much indignity.

(He turns to the corpse of Pentheus.)

This man has found the death which he deserved,
torn to pieces among the jagged rocks.
You are my witnesses: he came with outrage;

he attempted to chain my hands, abusing me
[and doing what he should least of all have done.]
And therefore he has rightly perished by the hands
of those who should the least of all have murdered him.
What he suffers, he suffers justly.

Upon you,
Agave, and on your sisters I pronounce this doom:
you shall leave this city in expiation
of the murder you have done. You are unclean,
and it would be a sacrilege that murderers
should remain at peace beside the graves [of those
whom they have killed].

(*He turns to Cadmus.*)

·   ·   ·   ·   ·   ·   ·   ·   ·   ·   ·   ·   ·   ·   ·   ·

Next I shall disclose the trials
which await this man. You, Cadmus, shall be changed   1330
to a serpent, and your wife, the child of Ares,
immortal Harmonia, shall undergo your doom,
a serpent too. With her, it is your fate
to go a journey in a car drawn on by oxen,
leading behind you a great barbarian host.
For thus decrees the oracle of Zeus.
With a host so huge its numbers cannot be counted,   1335
you shall ravage many cities; but when your army
plunders the shrine of Apollo, its homecoming
shall be perilous and hard. Yet in the end
the god Ares shall save Harmonia and you
and bring you both to live among the blest.
So say I, born of no mortal father,   1340
Dionysus, true son of Zeus. If then,
when you would not, you had muzzled your madness,
you should have an ally now in the son of Zeus.

Cadmus

We implore you, Dionysus. We have done wrong.

Dionysus

    Too late. When there was time, you did not know me.   1345

Cadmus

    We have learned. But your sentence is too harsh.

Dionysus

    I am a god. I was blasphemed by you.

Cadmus

    Gods should be exempt from human passions.

Dionysus

    Long ago my father Zeus ordained these things.

Agave

    It is fated, Father. We must go.

Dionysus

                   Why then delay?   1350
    For you must go.

Cadmus

            Child, to what a dreadful end
have we all come, you and your wretched sisters
and my unhappy self. An old man, I must go
to live a stranger among barbarian peoples, doomed   1355
to lead against Hellas a motley foreign army.
Transformed to serpents, I and my wife,
Harmonia, the child of Ares, we must captain
spearsmen against the tombs and shrines of Hellas.
Never shall my sufferings end; not even   1360
over Acheron shall I have peace.

Agave (embracing Cadmus)

                  O Father,
to be banished, to live without you!

Cadmus

                                        Poor child,
like a white swan warding its weak old father,   1365
why do you clasp those white arms about my neck?

Agave

But banished! Where shall I go?

Cadmus

                         I do not know,
my child. Your father can no longer help you.

Agave

Farewell, my home! City, farewell.
O bridal bed, banished I go,   1370
in misery, I leave you now.

Cadmus

Go, poor child, seek shelter in Aristaeus' house.

Agave

I pity you, Father.

Cadmus

                   And I pity you, my child,
and I grieve for your poor sisters. I pity them.

Agave

Terribly has Dionysus brought   1375
disaster down upon this house.

Dionysus

I was terribly blasphemed,
my name dishonored in Thebes.

Agave

Farewell, Father.

Cadmus
> Farewell to you, unhappy child.
> Fare well. But you shall find your faring hard.   1380
>
> > (*Exit Cadmus.*)

Agave
> Lead me, guides, where my sisters wait,
> poor sisters of my exile. Let me go
> where I shall never see Cithaeron more,   1385
> where that accursed hill may not see me,
> where I shall find no trace of thyrsus!
> > That I leave to other Bacchae.
>
> > (*Exit Agave with attendants.*)

Chorus
> The gods have many shapes.
> The gods bring many things
> to their accomplishment.
> And what was most expected   1390
> has not been accomplished.
> But god has found his way
> for what no man expected.
> > So ends the play.

APPENDIX TO *THE BACCHAE*

APPENDIX

Reconstruction of the long lacuna (l. 1329) can never be more than conjectural; but it can at least be that. I have attempted it in the conviction that its presence seriously hinders any possible production of the play.

The contents of the lacuna are, at least in outline, tolerably clear. A third-century rhetorician, Apsines, describes the speech of Agave, how she arouses pity by "picking up in her hands each one of her son's limbs and mourning it individually" (see Apsines *Rhet. Gr.* [ed.Walz], ix. 587). Then, according to the hypothesis of the play, Dionysus appears and addresses all, and foretells the future of each one in turn. The manuscript picks up the speech of Dionysus at line 1330 with an account, virtually complete, of the fate of Cadmus. Against this framework, scholars have been able to place a large number of Euripidean lines from the *Christus Patiens*, a twelfth-century cento, made up of lines from at least seven Euripidean plays. The bulk of the lines which fill the lacuna in my translation come from the *C.P.* Some of them are almost certain; others less so; but together they go a long way toward rounding out the gap. Thorough discussion of the lacuna problem may be found in the commentary on line 1329 in Dodds's edition of *The Bacchae*.

The order of my lines is as follows: beginning, *Bacchae*, l. 1329; *C.P.* ll. 1011, 1311, 1312, 1313, 1256, 1122, 1123; Schol. in Ar. Plut. l. 907; *C.P.* ll. 1466, 1467, 1468, 1469, 1470; Pap. Ant. 24 (*Antinoopolis Pap.* I, ed. C. H. Roberts, 1951) and *C.P.* l. 1472. The speech of Coryphaeus: pap. frag. (cf. Dodds, App. I). The speech of Dionysus: *C.P.* ll. 1360–62, 1665–66, 1668–69, 1678–80, 300; Lucian, *Pisc.* 2; *C.P.* ll. 1692, 1664, 1663, 1667, 1674–78, 1690.

CHRONOLOGICAL NOTE ON THE PLAYS OF EURIPIDES

By Richmond Lattimore

CHRONOLOGICAL NOTE ON THE
PLAYS OF EURIPIDES

THE chief data on the life of Euripides have been stated in the General Introduction to Euripides, Volume I in this series, but may be repeated here. They are:

485–480   Birth
455   First competition (including *The Daughters of Pelias*)
441   First victory (titles unknown)
408–407   Migration to Macedon
407–406   Death

Between 455 and 438, the date of *Alcestis*, we have only two performances for Euripides attested, and no extant play, except *Rhesus*, is likely to fall in that period. If these dates are really right, the blankness of the early years is rather surprising and can perhaps best be accounted for by assuming extensive military service.

I go on to give, as best I can, an outline of the extant plays in chronological order. Dates are derived as follows: (*a*) Recorded dates. These are found in ancient manuscripts, whether of Euripides or others. There is every probability that they are reliable, and they have not here been questioned. (*b*) Indications from style. These are chiefly metrical. It is well known that Euripides, as time went on, made freer use of resolution in iambic lines (see my Introduction to *Rhesus* in *Euripides IV*); was more likely to use trochees; and was more likely to use *antilabe*, the interruption of a line by a change of speakers. Such evidence will not date a play precisely, but it is reliable within limits; for instance, on metrical grounds alone, we could have stated that *Medea* (431) could not *possibly* have been written after 420. The implications of other stylistic variations have yet to be fully worked out. (*c*) Indications from content. Allusions to issues of the time are sometimes indicative, sometimes (if precise, as in *Electra*) even conclusive.

Question marks have been prefixed to those titles over which there could regularly be disagreement.

I have wished to keep discussion brief and have avoided the minutiae of scholarship which would be appropriate to a treatise dealing with Greek text.

?455–441 *Rhesus*

It has been doubted whether Euripides wrote this play at all, but if (as I think) he did, it fits best into the period before he achieved the general style familiar from his other preserved plays.

438 *Alcestis*

Date recorded in *Didascalia* (production notes on the manuscript).

431 *Medea*

Date recorded in *Didascalia*.

?429 *The Heracleidae*

The general period would be indicated by the metrical character; the conjectured year from the probable connection with the execution of the ambassadors during the course of the previous year, as explained in the Introduction to this play.

428 *Hippolytus*

Date recorded in *Didascalia*.

?426 *Andromache*

The *Didascalia* give no date. The *Scholia* (ancient notes on the manuscript) indicate that it was not performed at Athens, not at least under the name of Euripides; it may have been given under the name of Democrates. This curious fact prevents me from putting it in the same trilogy with *Hecuba* and *The Cyclops* (see below), as I should otherwise have been tempted to do. Mr. Nims suggests that the treatment of Andromache by the Spartans is based on the actions of the Spartans toward the Plataeans in 427, and I agree. The plausibility of this is perhaps helped a little (for me) by the similarity in situation with Sophocles' *The Women of Trachis*, which on other grounds I should like to place in 425. But all this is admittedly tenuous.

?425 Hecuba

There seems to be a reference to the Delian Festival, re-established in the winter of 426–425 (ll. 455 ff.); and Aristophanes parodies line 172 in his *Clouds* (423 B.C.). So too Mr. Arrowsmith dates it 425 or 424; see his Introduction to this play. There has been pretty general agreement about this, and, give or take a year, there is not really much doubt about the date of this play.

?425 The Cyclops

Mr. Arrowsmith would make this the satyr play for the set which contained *Hecuba*. I find this attractive, but there is nothing resembling certainty about the matter. Metrical tests are useless when it comes to satyr plays.

?423 The Suppliant Women

This is very much a matter of conjecture. The date I suggest is based on the idea that Euripides was thinking of the refusal by the Thebans to permit the Athenians, whom they had defeated at the Battle of Delium, to bury their dead (Thucydides iv. 97–101). This was in the summer of 424 B.C. Mr. Jones dates it 420–415, and he may well be right. The style supports the later date, but not decisively; the metrical habits of Euripides were changing between 425 and 415, but we cannot just fix the stages. I find the bitterly anti-Theban tone unlikely for the period of attempted reconciliation which came in after 423.

?420 Heracles

This could come at any time from 422 to 416. Mr. Arrowsmith would put it in 419 or 418. The play uses trochees, which are missing in the earlier complete plays. The lack of anti-Theban polemics is so striking as to make the tone seem (to me) positively conciliatory.

415 The Trojan Women

Date recorded by Aelian, *Varia historica* ii. 8.

?414 Iphigenia in Tauris

There is no external evidence, but style and structure support this date (see my Introduction to the play in *Euripides II*).

413 *Electra*

Lines 1347–48 are thought by almost everyone to refer to the relief expedition sent by the Athenians to Sicily in the early spring of 413 (Thucydides vii. 20. 2). The metrical character, particularly the absence of trochees, would otherwise have suggested a rather earlier date (see my Introduction to *Rhesus*). Mrs. Vermeule accepts the "traditional" date, and I follow, with only faint misgivings.

412 *Helen*

The date is secure from a combination of statements in the *Scholia* to Aristophanes' *Frogs* and *Thesmophoriazusae*.

?412 *Ion*

Mr. Willetts is content with the limits 420–410, and other good scholars have placed it before *The Trojan Women* and *Electra*, but I cannot believe that it is earlier than these plays. It has the late signs: a high rate of resolution (higher than *Electra*, though not so high as *Helen* or *The Phoenician Women*), abundant trochees and *antilabe*. The reference to Athens as a city where people are frightened (especially people who cannot demonstrate their right to citizenship?— see line 601) would *best* suit 410, after the reactionary revolution in Athens, but would do for any time just after the defeat in Sicily. The metrical style is better for 412.

One might add this consideration: For *Helen* and the lost, but parodied, *Andromeda* which was given along with it (*Scholia* on *Thesmophoriazusae*, l. 1021) Euripides obviously had the services of an actor who could do coloratura parts, and he obviously also had such an actor for *Ion*. We cannot say that 412 is a perfectly firm date for *Ion*, but I would feel pretty confident about narrowing the limits down to 413–410.

?410 *The Phoenician Women*

Presented after *Andromeda* (412), *Scholia* on Aristophanes, *Frogs*, l. 53. The lost *Antiope* and *Hypsipyle* are mentioned in the same connection, which may or may not mean they were given along with it. The particular date 410 has only the slight merit of spacing. It is plain that the "old swan" was immensely productive in the last decade of his life, but it might be better to leave whatever gap we can between the attested productions of 412 and 408.

408 *Orestes*
The date is from the *Scholia* to line 371.

406–405 *The Bacchae*
Posthumously presented along with *Iphigenia in Aulis* and *Alcmaeon in Corinth* (the latter lost); attested, *Scholia* to Aristophanes, *Frogs*, l. 67. The plays of course may well have been, and probably were, written in 407.

406–405 *Iphigenia in Aulis*
See under *The Bacchae*.

It will thus be seen that, except for the early period before 438 B.C., we have a reasonably good idea of the chronology for the plays of Euripides, which we owe to a combination of data. One could only wish that the objective evidence for Sophocles were half as good. I hope that students will also agree that, when it comes to Euripides' views about war, politics, women, domestics, and the gods, it is wiser to interpret him always within the limits of the particular piece which is being considered; for his opinions were not always the same from play to play.